Couple Therapy

This new edition of *Couple Therapy* reflects four challenges currently facing the field: (1) accountability and the increasing demands for demonstrating effectiveness as a condition for reimbursement, (2) the need for practitioners to reconfigure their practice patterns in an ever-involving health-care system, (3) training mental health practitioners who have not completed marital and family therapy (MFT) programs, and (4) integrating new couples approaches and interventions into everyday clinical practice.

The book offers a focused vision and successful strategies for working effectively with couples, both today and tomorrow. It incorporates the best insights from the neurosciences as well as new couples theories, research, and evidence-based interventions, introducing approaches including psychoanalytic, systemic, cognitive behavioral, Adlerian, constructivist, third wave, integrative, and mindfulness-based. Chapters also present practical applications and professional considerations, with a comprehensive look at how to work with diverse issues in couple therapy, such as substance abuse, domestic violence, sexual dysfunction, infidelity, aging, and much more.

This third edition of *Couple Therapy* is an essential resource for students as well as mental health practitioners, social workers, and family counselors who are keen to better meet the needs of couples and the demands of the changing health-care landscape.

Len Sperry, MD, PhD, is Professor at Florida Atlantic University, clinical fellow, American Association for Marriage and Family Therapy (AAMFT); editor-in-chief at *American Journal of Family Therapy*; and author of *Recovery of Intimacy in Love Relationships, Family Assessment, Family Therapy Techniques, The Intimate Couple*, and *The Disordered Couple.*

Paul R. Peluso, PhD, is Professor and Chair at Florida Atlantic University, Past-President of the International Association of Marriage and Family Counseling, author of *A Family Systems Guide to Infidelity*, coauthor of *Principles of Counseling and Psychotherapy*, and Series Editor of *Family Systems Counseling: Innovations Then and Now.*

Couple Therapy

Theory and Effective Practice

Len Sperry and Paul R. Peluso

3rd Edition

Routledge
Taylor & Francis Group
NEW YORK AND LONDON

Third edition published 2019
by Routledge
711 Third Avenue, New York, NY 10017

and by Routledge
2 Park Square, Milton Park, Abingdon, Oxon, OX14 4RN

Routledge is an imprint of the Taylor & Francis Group, an informa business

Library of Congress Cataloging-in-Publication Data
A catalog record for this title has been requested

[Second edition by Love Publishing Company 2006]

ISBN: 978-1-138-48464-1 (hbk)
ISBN: 978-1-138-48465-8 (pbk)
ISBN: 978-1-351-05158-3 (ebk)

Typeset in Galliard
by codeMantra

Contents

Introduction

The Present Practice of Couple Therapy

1 Psychological and Contextual Factors in Couples Relationships

LEARNING OBJECTIVES

In this chapter, the reader will learn the following:

1 The major societal shifts in the coupling process over the last 25 years.
2 The societal and personal factors that influence couples relationships.
3 An overview of the development of adult romantic relationships over the life span.
4 A brief overview of the history of marital or couple therapy.

When we think of relationships, couples, and marriage, we typically conjure up mental pictures of two people in love, soul mates embarking on a journey of blissful happiness together. When we embark on that journey ourselves, we usually do not consider the influence that our past relationships will have on our future together or how much the family we were raised in and our parents' marriages will shape the way we relate to each other. We think that our relationship is unique, that we have learned from past mistakes (in our own lives or those of others), and that our lives together will be perfect.

Though most people go into new relationships with virtually the same positive energy and hope, and the very best of intentions, the sad reality of our time is that 45% of first marriages result in divorce, and 60% of second marriages fail (Johnson & Lebow, 2000; Wallerstein, Lewis, & Blakeslee, 2000). Since the publication of the last edition of this book in 2006, there has been a slight overall decrease in the *rate* of marriages in the U.S. (CDC, 2016). Interestingly, this decline is in spite of the legalization of same-sex marriages, following the 2013 U.S. Supreme Court decision in the *United States v. Windsor*. This case struck down key elements of the Defense of Marriage Act (DOMA), which held that the legal definition of marriage was a union between a man and a woman. Over the same period of time, the rate of divorce has decreased at approximately the same rate (ranging from 3.7 to 3.1). In other words, the rates of marriage and divorce overall are keeping pace and still reflect an overall percentage of divorce between 40% and 50% annually (see Table 1.1).

Table 1.1 Rates of Marriages and Divorces from 2006 to 2016

Year	*Rate of Marriages (per 1,000 total pop.)*	*Rate of Divorces (per 1,000 total pop.)*
2016	6.9	3.2
2015	6.9	3.1
2014	6.9	3.2
2013	6.8	3.3
2012	6.8	3.4
2011	6.8	3.6
2010	6.8	3.6
2009	6.8	3.5
2008	7.1	3.5
2007	7.3	3.6
2006	7.5	3.7

Source: CDC (2016).

However, this is not the only way to consider divorce since the couples divorced in any given year are often not the same couples who married in that year. Looking at the average rate of marriage (7.0) and dividing it into the average divorce rate (3.42) gives the overall rate of nearly 50% (CDC, 2016).

For some researchers, this is statistically misleading. They prefer to look at surveys of actual couples and extrapolate a percentage of marriages ending in divorce. In analyzing historical records, approximately 45% of couples married in the 1970s and 1980s wound up divorced (and nearly 40% of couples married in the 1960s). By comparison, only 35% of couples married in the 1990s and only 15% of couples married in the 2000s have gotten divorced (Miller, 2014). These researchers conclude that the high levels of divorce have peaked. The question remains whether the *trajectory* of divorces for younger couples (married in the 1990s and 2000s) will match the levels of older couples (married in the 1970s and 1980s).

Perhaps this is having an effect on whether individuals are choosing to marry at all? According to the Pew Research Center (2014), in a survey across generations about marriage, the percent of Millennial adults who were married between the ages of 18 and 31 was 26%, compared to Generation X (36%), Baby Boomers (48%), and the Silent Generation (65%). Interestingly, most Millennials (approximately 69%) said that they would *like* to get married someday, but they cited economic and educational factors as impediments to committing to marry. Perhaps an even more serious issue is the large number of people who do not divorce but remain together and report deep levels of dissatisfaction (the impact of this type of couple arrangement on health is discussed in Chapter 2).

Distress in an intimate relationship continues to be the most common reason for the referral of clients to mental health professionals (Sholevar, 2003; Verkoff, Kulka, & Douvan, 1981). According to King (2016), marital satisfaction can be defined as the attitude individuals have toward their marital relationship. In fact, marital distress and marital dissolution account for many forms of psychopathology and dysfunction for individuals. Sholevar (2003) estimated that 75% of individuals entering psychotherapy do so because of relationship difficulties in addition to another presenting problem. In fact, using data from the General Social Survey, researchers found that of all of the sources of happiness (friends, work, etc.), marital happiness had the strongest impact on *overall* happiness, and people who stayed in unhappy marriages, in the long run, were less happy than people who got divorced or remarried (Hawkins & Booth, 2005). Couple therapy, once seen as a last resort for distressed couples, is now the preferred method of treatment for such couples in our culture.

Just as the field of couple therapy has become more sophisticated in the past two decades, so too has the understanding of the coupling process and its many varieties (Gottman & Gottman, 2017; Johnson, 2003; Sholevar, 2003). Previously, the term "marital therapy" suggested that only those couples who were legally married to each other would be eligible for treatment, which was considered exclusionary of gay and lesbian couples; couples who were considering marriage; and those who were in committed, but not legalized, partnerships. However, as mentioned, the U.S. Supreme Court decision (*United States v. Windsor*) to strike down components of DOMA allowed for the recognition of same-sex marriages and has created equality for the term "marriage." At the same time, given the fact that unmarried committed couples are often just as likely as married couples to come to therapy, the term couple therapy, which includes all those who are in committed, whether legalized or not, relationships, will be used in this text.

An examination of couple therapy best begins with a discussion of the larger contexts in which relationships exist and in which relational problems and issues arise. Specifically, this chapter provides an overview of the changing social and cultural trends that have influenced, and continue to influence, the institution of marriage. This chapter also provides a psychological perspective on the process of attraction and love, and the developmental phases of a committed, intimate relationship. Finally, we briefly describe the development of couple therapy as a professional discipline and profile the changing pattern of the clinical practice of couple therapy.

Social and Cultural Influences on Marriage

The Traditional Model of Marriage

During the last decade of the 20th century and the opening decades of the 21st century, the institution of marriage has undergone considerable change. For centuries, marriages were arranged. They had culturally defined, prescribed, and nonnegotiable rules and duties. The purpose of this type of marriage – known as a *traditional marriage* – was for each spouse to fulfill expected role obligations. There was common cultural agreement about what husbands and wives "should" do. Marital rules were closely associated with sex-role stereotypes, so men were reluctant to perform women's duties, and vice versa (Glick, Berman, Clarkin, & Rait, 2000; Gurman, 2015). The traditional male roles were husband, father, breadwinner, sexual initiator, financial planner, household mechanic, and so on. Traditional female roles were wife, mother, homemaker, sexual recipient, childcare provider, housemaid, and so on.

Two key concepts in the traditional marriage were *duty* and *responsibility*. Duty connoted a known set of role functions that each spouse accepted at marriage. If a person refused such role functions, he or she would not marry. Once married, each spouse was "responsible" for his or her role function. If love occurred at all in traditional marriages, it developed after the marriage was consummated. Basically, love was not a prerequisite in the decision to marry (Glick et al., 2000).

Traditionally, the marital agenda usually focused on the development of a family (i.e. children) and the acquisition of property (i.e. the home). Such an agenda insured a high degree of stability so that roots could be established. In the past, role conflict was less of a factor in marital strife than it is today because marital roles were relatively fixed by the state, religious teachings, and tradition. Also, there was little need to change role expectations because of the stability of the prevailing culture. Examples of the traditional marriage model can be seen today in the Old Order Amish and some of the conservative Mennonite sects. These groups follow the Bible literally and maintain stable relationships because of their fixed and socially supported devotion to biblical injunctions about the roles of husband and wife. When there is any doubt about what husband or wife should do, the family and group pressures combine to ensure that the couple capitulates to these roles. Traditional marriages are also prevalent in other cultures (Hardy & Laszloffy, 2002; McGoldrick & Carter, 2003; Ng, Peluso, & Smith, 2010; Peluso, Miranda, Firpo-Jimenez, & Pham, 2010; Sue & Sue, 1999), and couple therapists must be sensitive to cultural norms when working with immigrant couples.

Traditional marriages produced predictable marital problems. Because marital roles were prescribed and could not easily be changed, marital difficulty was usually related to role adaptation. Predictable patterns of role adaptation pathology could be identified, with the most common form being the *trapped wife syndrome*. Women were so constrained and bored by the repetitiveness and demands of child-rearing and household duties that they often became resentful, depressed, angry, and unfulfilled (Johnson, 2003). The most common clinical manifestation of this syndrome was depression, for which many sought the assistance of mental health professionals.

The Modern, or Companionate, Marriage Model

A perceptible shift away from the traditional model of marriage started with the Industrial Revolution in the of the 19th century but did not become obvious until after World War II. In the modern, or *companionate*, style of marriage, roles are not prescribed; they evolve through negotiation and can be variable and vague. Therefore, communication and negotiation skills are vital to the modern couple. The partners can no longer rely on society to establish marital roles but instead must decide for themselves what it means to be a husband or a wife. Each partner must also have attained sufficient maturity to know what he or she wants from the marriage (Glick et al., 2000; Gurman, 2015).

Key concepts in the companionate marriage are *love* and *choice*. In this type of marriage, the woman and man want to be together because they love each other and expect to obtain fulfillment from their intimate relationship. Relationships and marriage have evolved from functional roles, established for the purpose of reproducing and raising children, to an idealized and individualized version where partners seek fulfillment and self-actualization (Glick et al., 2000). The potential for attaining this romantic ideal is a relatively recent phenomenon that implies a level of prosperity sufficient to extricate persons from a survival mode of living. This model also requires a degree of equality between the spouses that was not possible in times when life expectancy was short, when there was a lack of economic opportunity and education for women, and when adequate birth control methods did not exist. The American family has undergone remarkable transformations since World War II, including changes in economic circumstances, gender roles, intimate relationships, and family structure. For example, in 1960 men were not present in the delivery room when their children were born; today greater than 90% of dads are a part of the birthing process (Leavitt, 2009). Dual-earner marriages are now a virtual necessity for most families to make ends meet. In fact, 69% of American children are currently living in two-parent families where both parents are in the labor force (CDC, 2016). Although the median family income was reported to have risen over the past two decades, this was found to be because men and women are working longer hours, leading to a decrease in the amount of time families can spend together (McGoldrick, Garcia-Preto, & Carter, 2015). Today, couples may enjoy more egalitarian relationships, with women in the workforce and men taking on more of the domestic and childcare responsibilities. The freedom of both spouses to choose marriage is a far cry from the arranged marriages of the past. This freedom appears to be an ongoing matter after marriage since there is increasing social acceptance of divorce as an option for marital conflict resolution. Also, divorce is relatively easy to obtain. Now that women have joined the workforce and are beginning to achieve financial independence, divorce is as much an option for them as it is for men (Glick et al., 2000; Gurman, 2015).

The increasing status and freedom of women are recent trends that derive largely from increased employment rates among women, increased educational achievement (of the high school graduates who enrolled in college in 2016, 71.9% were women), fewer children per woman, childbearing at a later age, and increased utilization of day care facilities (U.S. Department of

Labor, Bureau of Labor Statistics, 2017). In addition, there is a rise in the number of women who are now the primary wage earner and men who are raising children. According to the Bureau of Labor Statistics, in 2015, in approximately 29% of households, women earned more than their husbands. With this rise in status has come increased freedom of choice as well as increased marital stress, which has probably contributed to a higher divorce rate (Glick et al., 2000; Gurman, 2015).

In contrast to traditional marriages, companionate marriages lead to different kinds of marital issues and problems. Because companionate marriages focus on emotional fulfillment and personal happiness, role functions are not carefully considered during the courtship. Thus, marital difficulties manifest in terms of role definition and include role ambiguity, power struggles, communication problems, and unmet expectations (Glick et al., 2000; Gurman, 2015). Of these, communication difficulties are the most common manifestation, but they are usually the symptom, not the cause, of more basic problems. Not surprisingly, communication difficulties are unique to companionate marriage because communication is the sine qua non of love and is required for role negotiation. Yet these are techniques that have not traditionally been taught to children or adults (until recently), especially to men (Johnson, 2003).

The "All or Nothing" Marriage

Finkel (2017) described an additional change in marriages from the traditional model to the companionate model to include an expectation of the "all or nothing" model of marriage. In this approach, not only is your partner supposed to help create stability (as in the traditional model), and a loving connection (as in the companionate model), but there is also an added expectation that one's partner is supposed to facilitate one's self-actualization or self-fulfillment. Our partner is supposed to promote our personal growth and development, and if they cannot do that, then our marriage is considered to be stagnant or unfulfilling (which inevitably leads to divorce).

Leaning on the work of Abraham Maslow, and his hierarchy of needs, Finkel (2017) describes the attempt to meet the self-actualization needs (at the top of the hierarchy) as a mountain that couples try to climb. Achieving reasonable goals of safety and security is at the base (including financial), with the next level including love, passion, and friendship, which can be extremely satisfying. Summiting this mountain, however, is a thrill, and experiencing it together fosters growth and leads to new possibilities for one's life and deeper levels of intimacy with each other.

The problem, according to Finkel (2017), is that this kind of approach to marriage requires a considerable investment of time and emotional energy to meet this lofty expectation. However, a competing force against this is the amount of time and effort that *other* realities take up in people's lives, namely work and children. As a result, couples are often unable to meet the demands

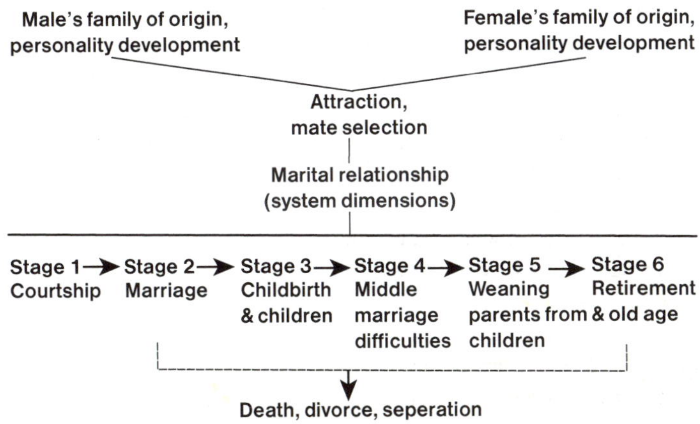

Figure 1.1 A developmental model of marriage.

of this expectation when they cannot or do not invest the time needed to truly know and understand their partner's needs and help them achieve their goals. Finkel suggests that one of two solutions is needed: (1) Find a way to go "all-in," and make the relationship (and one's partner) a priority, or (2) lower one's expectations for the relationship and realize that one's partner doesn't (or can't) fill all the emotional and growth needs that one might have.

So far, we have described a number of social, political, and economic influences that have radically changed marriage as an institution in our society. The discussion now shifts to the psychological processes of attraction and mate selection, and the developmental processes and phases of marriage. (Figure 1.1).

Family-of-Origin Influences

A basic tenet of marital and family theory is that an individual spouse's functioning in their marriage relationship is greatly influenced by his or her family of origin. The belief that a person can totally separate from the family of origin and become an autonomous individual is erroneous. The impact of a spouse's heritage and transgenerational background is strong. The influence is, however, not uniform from couple to couple. Some people do replicate dysfunctional, marital patterns from their families of origin, whereas others from disturbed and inadequate families of origin manage to achieve adequately functional marriages. Similarly, some individuals whose parents' marriages appear to be functional do not necessarily fare well in their own marriages.

A new marriage often becomes an extension of the larger, extended family context. The influence of relatives on a marriage can range from subtle to obvious, and varies from culture to culture. If parents are alive, they may be involved very clearly and specifically in a new or ongoing marriage. They may take sides, comment on child-rearing practices, or share housing with their adult child and his or her spouse. In healthy families, in-laws can provide a great deal of cohesion and emotional and financial support to make a new marriage function more efficiently. However, in-laws can also be a destructive force, often playing an active role in a couple's decision to divorce. Even as early as the 1940s, marital experts were observing this phenomenon (Dreikurs, 1946). Even when the extended family is not physically present, the patterns experienced by the spouses in their families of origin inevitably influence their current marital and family interactions.

Another basic tenet of marital and family theory is the *multigenerational-transmission hypothesis* (Berman, Lief, & Williams, 1981; Glick et al., 2000; McGoldrick et al., 2015; Roberto-Forman, 2002), which holds that values, beliefs, behaviors, and symptoms may be passed down from one generation to the next through a complex chain of relatedness. In a sense, this hypothesis is a restatement of the scripture maxim: The sins of one generation will be passed to the next (Exodus 20:5). Boszormenyi-Nagy and Spark (1976) noted that the major connecting tie between generations could be called "invisible loyalties." They believe that loyalty and justice play a major role in determining family relations. They view parenting and "childing" as relationships in which certain things, such as caretaking, are owed. According to Boszormenyi-Nagy and Spark, families keep account ledgers of balance and imbalance concerning what is owed: Indebtedness and reciprocity. An important task of adulthood is to balance loyalties to one's parents. Becoming a parent oneself most commonly does this. In short, invisible loyalties guide adults in relating to spouses and children.

Often, a person will attempt to live up to the normative value orientations of his or her family of origin and try to get their spouse to do likewise. Even if the couple is able to make a reasonable attempt to balance old loyalties with new ones, problems come up in a marriage because each family of origin has its own type of accounting system. For example, if the wife in a new marriage comes from a family in which affection is shown by the bestowing of large gifts, whereas the husband's family of origin does not use gifts as part of its accounting system but is affectionate and supportive. What does the couple owe to the latter family in response to affection and support? Boszormenyi-Nagy and Spark (1976) hypothesized that unconscious attempts to maintain invisible loyalty to the family of origin by rejecting a spouse may actually underlie sexual problems such as impotence, premature ejaculation, and anorgasmia. However, advances in the area of sex therapy and the treatment of these conditions suggests that the etiology is more complex and multi-determined (these topics will be covered in greater detail in Chapter 13).

Theories of Love, Attraction, and Mate Selection

We have already considered the questions of the impact of the family of origin and stage of personality development on couples and their relationships. We have also reviewed how both of these dimensions influence spousal expectations for the marriage relationship. However, according to Johnson (2003), the lack of a coherent theory of love is one of the major roadblocks to making well-informed interventions in couple therapy and one of the foremost challenges to the field in the 21st century. A related question is how do two individuals become attracted to one another and fall in love? Researchers have explored a number of evolving theories to explain this phenomenon, including similarity vs. complementary relationships; Sternberg's triangular theory of love; and the theory of "love as a story," Gottman's 3 Phases of Love. We will briefly explore these in the following.

Similarity vs. Complementary Relationships

Similarity, or "Birds of a Feather..."

Sternberg (1987) summarized research on the *similarities hypothesis* of interpersonal attraction. In essence, the similarities hypothesis states that the more similar two individuals are to one another, the more likely they are to be attracted to one another. Sternberg indicated that there are six components that affect the attraction of one person to another: Physical attractiveness, arousal, proximity, reciprocity, similarity, and barriers (see Table 1.2).

Table 1.2 Sternberg's Components for Attraction

Component	*Description*
Physical attractiveness	People look for partners whose level of physical attractiveness matches their own. In general, men tend to place more value on a woman's physical attractiveness than women do on men. However, one individual's perception of another's attractiveness increases to the extent that one likes the other and decreases to the extent that one does not.
Arousal	An individual is more likely to be attracted to another if he or she experiences some arousal. The arousal need not come from the other person; it may reflect the environment (e.g. taking a date to an exciting environment, such as a collegiate basketball game between two closely matched rivals).
Proximity	Proximity may be the most important factor in determining whom an individual will meet. Individuals are most likely to meet persons who are in close physical proximity to them. For the average person, mate selection occurs based on contact and experience with fewer than 12 potential mates.
Reciprocity	People tend to like those who think like them. They are more likely to be attracted to a person who is willing to self-disclose if they believe in self-disclosure and sharing.

(*Continued*)

Component	*Description*
Similarity	The more similar one person is to another, the more likely he or she is to be attracted to that person. Similarities typically involve background, education, life experiences, hobbies, religious affiliation, professional training and experience, and interests. People who are similar in a variety of ways tend to respond to situations in an emotionally congruent manner and become even more attractive to one another.
Barriers	These are defined as the "hard-to-get effect." In other words, individuals are more attracted to persons who seem to be a challenge than to people who are not. Difficulty getting to the other person not only intensifies passion but also renews the person's attempt to attain the goal.

Source: Adapted from Sternberg (1986, 1987).

Sternberg concluded that unless a number of these factors are operational, it is unlikely that the two individuals will reach the point of falling in love. Several researchers have provided additional empirical evidence for the validity of this hypothesis of attraction (Gottman, 1999; Napier, 2000). However, this "birds of a feather" perspective on interpersonal attraction has not received much empirical support. In fact, Wedekind et al. (1995) found (in the so-called "sweaty T-shirt" study) that women preferred the smell of men with genetic qualities on the major histocompatibility complex (MHC) that were *dissimilar* to their own. The MHC is related to immunofunction, suggesting that there may be some evolutionary basis behind this finding. Santos et al. (2005) found similar results in a sample of Brazilian students. Interestingly, this preference was not present if the women in the study were taking oral contraception.

Complementary Relationships, or "Opposites Attract"

Sperry (1978) contended that searching for similarities and commonalities is primarily a conscious process and follows the unconscious attraction of personalities. It is at this unconscious level that attraction of opposites or complementarity develops. From this perspective, there are three phases in the attraction process: *Love at first sight*, *checking each other out*, and *formalizing the private pact* (see Table 1.3).

This coupling does not mean a merging of the personality styles. On the contrary, opposites often attract because they complement one another. For example, an aggressive, determined person may want a spouse who is supportive and willing to be led just as a passive, submissive person may seek a mate on whose strength he or she can rely. Also, a person with a high need to please others and to be accepted may choose someone who demands admiration and submission, often in a selfish way. However, Napier (2000) cautions that, unlike similarity, the complementary relationship hypotheses in the coupling process has received little empirical validation and is not favored by couples researchers (J. Gottman, personal communication, July 2, 2018).

Table 1.3 Phases of "Opposites" Attraction

Phase	*Description*
Love at first sight	Within the first few moments of meeting – or even observing – another person, contact is made at a very deep, unconscious level. An individual somehow senses whether another person has the capability of fulfilling his or her deepest needs. This message is primarily unconscious and thus is largely transmitted nonverbally. It shows as much in how an individual speaks as in what he or she says. The love-at-first-sight feeling that poets and novelists have described is none other than an exuberant recognition that the other person has the capacity to offer fulfillment.
Checking each other out	Whether the relationship develops depends on Phases 2 and 3. In the second phase, prospective mates do what amounts to a credit check on each other that determines how closely the prospective mate resembles the consciously constructed picture of the ideal mate. This checking-out process, which also includes a scrutiny of the other person's background, interests, and values, may take ten minutes, ten months, or even longer.
Formalizing the private pact	In Phase 3, a mutual decision must be reached about the future of the relationship. The decision may be instant and idyllic or protracted and filled with turmoil. Relatives or friends may object. More often than not, the prospective mate will not match the culturally embodied stereotype of the ideal mate. Dissonance and confusion follow, often resulting in rationalization and unrealistic expectations for changing the prospective mate. This unconscious coupling of two personality styles ultimately can make or break a relationship.

Source: Adapted from Sperry (1978).

Triangular Theory of Love

Sternberg's (1986, 1987) original theory of love has provided some guidance for clinicians and is worth exploring. His triangular theory has three components: Intimacy, passion, and decision/commitment. Intimacy encompasses the feelings of closeness, connectedness, and bondedness. Passion encompasses the drive that leads to romance, physical attraction, and sexual consummation. Decision/commitment comprises a short-term decision to love one another and a long-term commitment to maintain that love (Sternberg, 2004, 2007).

Sternberg's research suggests that the amount of love one person experiences for another depends on the absolute strength of these three components. The kind of love an individual experiences depends on the strength of these components relative to one another. In their interactions, the three components give rise to a number of different kinds of loving experiences (Sternberg, 2004, 2007).

Sternberg (1986) and Goleman (1985) indicated that intimacy, passion, and commitment change in level or degree over the course of a long-term relationship. The reader should note that intimacy and passion develop rapidly in conjunction with one another, but at a certain point in the relationship, the level of commitment begins to rise and match the level of intimacy, while the level of passion greatly drops off. Couples often complain that their love has cooled when, in reality, they are speaking about a change in the level of passion. If commitment and intimacy continue to be adequate, the relationship is not in jeopardy (Sternberg, 2014).

Research into Sternberg's triangular theory has had some mixed results. Acker and Davis (1992) found that commitment was important for long-term relationships but that intimacy did not decline over time, as Sternberg predicted. Further, passion only declined for women and not for men. One of the recognized flaws of the study was the lack of psychometrically sound measures for Sternberg's constructs. Lomas (2018) conducted a cross-cultural lexical analysis of love defined in different cultures and found support for descriptions of love conforming to Sternberg's typology across the globe.

More recently, Sternberg has refocused his theory into a more narrative-based exploration of love. However, other researchers continue to validate and apply his triangular constructs (Lemieux & Hale, 1999, 2002). Conceptualization of love in terms of these three components and their changes remains useful for couple therapists until a more sophisticated theoretical explanation for love emerges (Johnson, 2003; Sternberg, 2014).

Love as a Story

Although Sternberg's triangular theory of love provided some systematization and description of the elements of different types of love relationships and was widely accepted by others, Sternberg himself felt that it did not fully explain the phenomenon of love. "It still did not explain why I, or anyone else, would fall in love or be able to maintain a loving relationship with one person but not another" (Sternberg, 1998, p. x). As a result, he began to conceptualize the theory of "love as a story." In this approach, an individual's personal attributes and environment interact in order to create a narrative or story about the love that the individual seeks to fulfill with another person (Sternberg, Hojjat, & Barnes, 2001). Sternberg (1998) believes that these stories are greatly influenced by the family of origin as well as cultural messages about love and relationships. Potential mates are selected according to the degree of congruity of the person to the story, and (presumably) vice versa (Sternberg, 2014).

Although there are potentially an infinite number of stories, Sternberg has proposed approximately 25 prototypical stories, which he has grouped a priori by their internal characteristics into five major themes: Asymmetrical, object, coordination, narrative, and genre (Sternberg, 1998). *Asymmetrical* stories are indicative of complementary relationships, where the concept of love is predicated on one person giving and the other person receiving something. Examples of this include "The Sacrifice Story" and "The Police Story." *Object* stories emphasize the role that the romantic partner plays rather than

Table 1.4 Types of Love Stories Grouped by Theme

Asymmetrical Stories	
Sacrifice	To love is to willingly give of oneself or for someone to give of him- or herself to you.
Government	(a) *Autocratic*: One partner holds power over the other. (b) *Democratic*: Partners share power equally.
Police	You have to keep a close watch on your partner to make sure she or he doesn't stray. Alternatively, this is the belief that someone has to be watched to make sure that she or he behaves.
Pornography	Love is dirty, and to love is to degrade or be degraded.
Horror	The relationship is only interesting if one person is the victim, and the other person is the tormentor.
Object Stories	
Science fiction	Feeling that your partner is an alien: Incomprehensible and strange. This weirdness is a force of attraction.
Collection	Partner seen as "fitting in" to some overall scheme; partner viewed in a detached way as part of a collection (like coins or stamps).
Art	Love of partner for physical attractiveness; important for partner to always look good.
House and home	The relationship is a means to get a beautiful house or home environment; its development and maintenance is the essence of stability.
Recovery	Survivor mentality; view that after past trauma, person can get through virtually anything.
Religion	Either views love as a religion, as a set of feelings and activities dictated by religious principles, or as a way to get close to God.
Game	Love is a game or a sport; being successful in the relationship is a "win."
Coordination Stories	
Travel	Love is a journey, and partners work together to arrive at a mutual destination.
Sewing	Love is whatever both people make it (i.e. knit together).
Gardening	Relationships need to be continually nurtured and tended.
Business	Relationships as business propositions; money is power; partners in close relationships are partners.
Addiction	Strong anxious attachment; clinging, codependent behavior; anxiety at any thought of losing partner.
Narrative Stories	
Fantasy	Relationship is lived as a fairy tale, with the partners' expectation of love either their being saved by a knight in shining armor or their marrying a princess and living happily ever after.

(*Continued*)

History	Past events of relationship form an indelible mark. Partners keep a record or "score" of the happenings in the relationship that dictates the present.
Asymmetrical Stories	
Science	Love can be understood, analyzed, and dissected, like any natural phenomenon. Love is formulaic.
Cookbook	Belief that doing things a certain way (like a recipe) will result in a relationship that works out. Fear that departing from the proven recipe will lead to disaster.
Genre Story	
War	Love is a battle, and waging war is more important than any goal.
Humor	Love is strange and funny. The relationship is lighthearted and never allowed to get too serious.
Mystery	Love is a mystery, and you shouldn't let too much of yourself be known. It is important for one partner to continually discover new information about the other.
Theatre	Love is scripted with predictable acts, lines, and scenes. Acting in the scripted role is most important and constantly acted.

Source: Adapted from Sternberg (1998) and Sternberg, Hojjat, and Barnes (2001).

the person him/herself, with the relationship being a means to an end. "The Game Story" and the "Science-Fiction Story" exemplify these stories. *Coordination* stories emphasize the idea of partners working together in the relationship to create or do something. "The Garden Story and "The Business Story" are examples of this theme. In *narrative* stories, the course of love and relationships are prescribed by some external text. Examples of this include "The Fantasy Story" and "The Cookbook Story." Lastly, *genre* stories place the general way of being or overall mode in the relationship over the principles or aims of the relationship. Genre stories are exemplified by "The War Story" and "The Theatre Story" (Sternberg, 1998, 2014). See Table 1.4 for a brief description of each story.

Sternberg has begun to empirically verify his love-as-a-story theory (Sternberg et al., 2001). In particular, he and his colleagues found that, as predicted by the theory, partners who have similar stories were more satisfied with their relationship, and couples with larger discrepancies were less satisfied. In addition, they found overall that maladaptive stories of love could predict dissatisfaction in relationships, but positive stories of love could not necessarily predict satisfaction (Sternberg, 2014). As Sternberg et al. concluded, "It appears then, that maladaptive stories are more likely to lead to dissatisfaction than adaptive stories are to lead to satisfaction, perhaps because certain stories can 'break' relationships but no particular story can 'make' relationships" (p. 214).

Sternberg's theory of love as a story may be useful for modern-day couple therapists because it is inclusive of a variety of conceptualizations of what love is (or could be) and is rooted in a holistic, narrative approach that is congruent with other theoretical systems that emphasize a schema approach to understanding behavior (attachment theory, emotionally focused couples theory, systems theory, and Adlerian theory, to name a few). Using this theory of love, couple therapists can ascertain the type of story that each person is operating from, the degree to which the stories are similar or dissimilar, and whether or not the stories are maladaptive as a starting point for understanding their presenting concerns (Sternberg, 2014). In addition, this theory incorporates and validates the ideas of complementarity and similarity in relationships as well as the triangular theory of love. Lastly, this theory begins to answer Johnson's (2002) call for a mature theory of love.

Phases of Love

Gottman and Gottman (2017) recently summarized their research and articulated a three-phase theory of the development of love in successful (and unsuccessful) relationships.

Phase 1: Falling in Love – Limerence

According to Gottman and Gottman (2017), limerence is characterized by "physical symptoms (e.g., flushing, trembling, palpitations), excitement, intrusive thinking, obsession, fantasy, sexual excitement, lust, hope, and fear of rejection. We now know a great deal about the first phase of love" (p. 21) due, in part, to advances in neuroscience. In this phase of love, the couple spends a lot of time with each other or thinking about each other. In addition, there are often feelings of unconditional acceptance and a sense of freedom and exhilaration that are often a result of bonding neurochemicals (particularly oxytocin and vasopressin – see Chapter 2 for details).

Phase 2: Building Trust

Phase 2 of love is predominantly occupied with the question of "Will you be there for me? Can I trust you?" If Phase 1 is characterized by being "swept away," in Phase 2, couples may be feeling a sense of "buyer's remorse" as they get to know each other. Personality dynamics (complementary and divergent) begin to emerge, and attachment needs getting met (or not) creates areas of conflict. Couples in this phase must learn to trust the other person and feel that they are going to be able to build a life together.

Phase 3: Building Commitment and Loyalty

According to Gottman and Gottman (2017), commitment and loyalty are built on trust, but they are not the same thing. After a couple establishes trust in one another to meet their emotional (and other) needs, a process must emerge in which they learn to "cherish" each other to the exclusion of anyone else. "This third phase of love is about a couple either cherishing each other and nurturing gratitude for what they have with their partner or nurturing resentment for what they think is missing" (p. 23). The work of Carol Rusbult (as cited in Gottman & Gottman) is central to understanding this important phase of relationship maintenance. If the couple does not feel that the other person is committed or loyal, they will begin to look for substitutes, or "a better deal" with someone elsewhere, and find ways to get their needs met outside of the marriage (see Chapter 13).

System Dimensions: Power, Intimacy, and Boundaries

Another convenient way of understanding marital relationships is through three system dimensions: Power, intimacy, and boundaries (Glick et al., 2000). The power dimension involves issues of competition and cooperation, and focuses on who is in charge of the relationship and who takes responsibility for specific aspects of the relationship. According to Gray-Little et al. (1996), power in relationships:

> has typically been conceptualized as the ability to influence or to control another's behavior, and investigators have measured power in one of three ways: (a) in terms of resources, such as education or income, that form the bases of power; (b) in terms of power processes, such as the amount of talking time; or (c) in terms of who has the final say, that is, who determines the outcome in problem solving or decision making. (p. 292)

Proceeding from this, rules governing intimacy and boundaries are set. The intimacy dimension involves the spouses' need for and fear of closeness and caring. The boundary dimension involves other influences that affect the marital system, such as relatives and friends, and time allocations for career, entertainment, and hobbies. (These dimensions are further elaborated in subsequent chapters.)

The way in which these dimensions are handled depends on each spouse's personality style, the marital pact, the relational style that has developed, and the stage or phase of the marriage itself at the time in question. Dysfunctional or negatively cooperative couples tend to be less flexible and more static and rigid; more functional couples can more easily adapt and change with new needs, demands, and circumstances (we will have more to say about this in Chapter 3).

Bound up in the issues of power, boundaries, and intimacy is the sexual relationship of the couple. Having a clear understanding of the interrelationship between sex, intimacy, power, and boundaries is crucial for couple therapists since approximately 75% of couples present with a combination of sexual and marital dysfunctions (Glick et al., 2000). Often, these dimensions are played out in the functioning or dysfunctioning of the sexual relationship. Questions of who has the power to initiate or deny sex, what constitutes too much or too little intimate contact, what the definition of intimacy is, and what is appropriate and acceptable sexual contact and what is not all reflect these underlying dimensions. Schnarch (1991, 1997) has developed a systemic approach of treating sexual problems by investigating the couple's attitudes about these dimensions as well as their own levels of differentiation (these issues will also be covered in Chapter 13).

Now that we have given an overview of the sociocultural basis of the institution of marriage, the psychological factors involved in the process of attraction, and the stages of the marriage relationship, we will turn our attention to other factors. The following section briefly describes the development of marital and couple therapy as a profession, current practices, and future trends.

What Successful Couples Do

In an article for *Business Insider*, Gillet (2017) looked at so-called "power couples" (couples where both partners are highly successful in their careers) that are successful in maintaining their relationships and the nine things that they seem to have in common. These power couples are frequently under considerable pressures (as many couples are) but have found strategies for making their relationships work in the face of modern challenges. We felt that it would be useful to consider what these couples do:

1 *They prioritize spending time together.* Time is the most precious resource that anyone has, and this is especially true in power couples. As a result, they have to be deliberate and mindful of their choices when they have free time. Their choices are a window into their priorities. Consider the example of Facebook founder Mark Zuckerberg and his wife Priscilla Chan. They drew up an agreement where he committed to take her on a date once a week and spend 100 minutes of alone time with her each week (outside of the office or apartment). While this might seem overly formulaic to some people, it is the *commitment* of the resource of time that matters. It is the vehicle for meaningful connection, regardless of the way in which it is arranged.
2 *They outsource tedious chores.* Again, because time is such a precious commodity, it can have a monetary value attached to it. It is the basis for everyone's salary ("time is money"), and it can be the basis for valuing the relationship too. Gillet (2017) looked at successful women's habits and found that they "outsource" many of the chores that they have to spend their off time doing so that they can spend time with families (and partners). While it might seem like an expensive and frivolous use of money, Gillet states the following, "If you make $45,000 annually and work 40 hours a week (that's 2,080 work hours a year), that means your time is potentially worth about $22 an hour ($45,000 divided by 2,080)." Therefore, anything that you can pay someone around $20 an hour is potentially worth the hour of your life that you can get back and spend with your partner.

3 *Their time is spent doing good.* Power couples like Zuckerberg and Chan or billionaires Bill and Melinda Gates have created entities whereby they can work together to do good in the community. For most couples, creating a charitable foundation is probably beyond their means, but the *idea* of working together to help out in the local community, or sometimes overseas, can build an intrinsic sense of positivity together.

4 *They listen and empathize.* The problem that highly successful people have is that they spend a lot of time during the day solving problems of their own (or are responsible for doing so). There are two pitfalls that they can fall into: (1) Rushing in to offer a solution (which is a problem because the other partner often feels like they aren't *able* to solve their own problem) or (2) being so overwhelmed with listening to and solving their own problems at work that when they come home, they don't have the mental and emotional capacity to listen to their partner's problems. Therefore, those power couples that are able to avoid the two pitfalls are the ones that have found ways to work together and understand each other's needs and communicate about them.

5 *They speak up about problems before it's too late.* Again, because these couples are aware of the value of time, they do not waste it on grudges or unspoken hurts. Instead, they make their concerns known at a very early stage. This may be borne out of their work experiences, where problem-solving is valued, and correcting errors is "good for business." As a result, these individuals tend not to be conflict-avoiders. Instead, they see conflict as an opportunity to make things better. Therefore, in their own relationships, they "cut to the chase" and make sure to air their grievances in a manner that is efficient but also sensitive to the needs of their partners.

6 *They express their appreciation.* This can be done with grand gestures (e.g. a giant bouquet of flowers sent to the office), but the most powerful expressions of appreciation are usually the small, timely ones. This can be in the form of text messages or conversations by phone in the middle of the day. While general expressions of appreciation are helpful, the most effective expressions are ones where one partner notices something small that the other person does that they like. It should be noted that appreciation does not have to be for things that a person's partner does for *them*; it can also be noticing and appreciating what the partner does for kids, family, community, etc.

7 *They agree upon important issues from the get-go.* Much like the shared and explicit wishes, and dreams that the couple creates for the relationship, so-called power couples are "up-front" about their needs and expectations from each other. Especially if two very successful people are each expecting the other person to submit to their needs or will, the *what* and *how* of that need to be explicit. And much like the issues of power sharing or power imbalances that have been discussed in this book, many expectations and agreements about issues like money and sex can stave

off misunderstandings and disappointments later. Again, coming from the world of business, these agreements may take the form of a negotiated contract that is written down, with periodic reviews for renegotiation as times and circumstances warrant.

8 *They commit to one another overall.* This may be easier said than done, but the idea of commitment is crucial. It is the sense that a person's partner "has their back." If the partners in a couple feel that this is the case, they will not feel anxious when distance or business keep them apart for a time. Of course, the other skills mentioned earlier are the building blocks for this implicit trust and commitment. It also provides the basis for the partners' supporting one another in a way that others cannot. For highly successful people, there will be a lot of people around them who will seem like they are trustworthy, committed, and supportive but who (in reality) will want something from them. By having a "safe harbor" with their partner, each person knows that they will have someone they can wholly rely on without having to question the validity of their support or commitment.

9 *They work somewhere that understands family come first.* This is easier for successful people who are the entrepreneurs and owners of their business than for people who work for firms or companies where they have high positions. However, many companies today are realizing the importance of having a corporate culture that supports their employees. This can include a "family friendly" environment which allows for a good work-life balance. Ultimately, this has a beneficial impact on the corporations' bottom line as an impaired worker (due to problems at home) can have a negative effect at work. This is especially true for people in upper management or who are very important to the company's mission.

Now that we have looked at various aspects of love and marriage/couples, before we end this introductory chapter, we will discuss the history of couples/marital therapy as a profession.

The History of Couples/Marital Therapy as a Profession

Marital therapy as a distinct mental health profession is only 80 years old. Initially, marriage counselors were physicians, lawyers, educators, and social workers who had little if any formal training but some degree of commitment to dealing with marital problems. Both clergy and physicians ordinarily had contact with family members at significant times in their life cycles: Birth, marriage, illness, and death. Therefore, it was not uncommon or unreasonable for people to turn to ministers or physicians for help with many personal and family problems.

Marital therapy as a specialized body of knowledge and techniques dates back to the 1920s and the 1930s (Sholevar, 2003). Abraham and Hannah Stone began offering professional marriage counseling at the Community

Church in New York City in 1929. Neither of the Stones was a member of the clergy, but the church sponsored their clinical work. Soon afterward, Paul Popenoe's American Institute of Family Relations in southern California and Emily Mudd's Marriage Counsel of Philadelphia were established. Both centers offered therapy specifically for marital issues. As such, these centers were different from other family agencies of that time. The 1930s saw the establishment of what became known as the Groves Conference on the Family and the National Council on Family Relations. Leaders from these two groups were among those who established the American Association of Marriage Counselors (AAMC) in New York City in 1942.

With the formation of the AAMC, marital therapy became a distinct professional field. In subsequent years, AAMC members began to conceptualize the marital relationship as an integral part of the family system. To reflect this trend, the AAMC changed its name and became the American Association of Marriage and Family Counselors (AAMFC). In 1963, the state of California became the first state to pass a licensure law for marriage and family counselors. With the enactment of this law, the profession of marital therapy came of age (Broderick & Schrader, 1981). In 1978, the AAMFC became the American Association for Marriage and Family Therapy (AAMFT), thereby dropping the word *counselor* in favor of the more accurate and contemporary term *therapy*. In the same year, the U.S. Commissioner of Education designated the AAMFT's Commission on Accreditation for Marriage and Family Education the task of accrediting training programs in marriage and family therapy. As of 2018, approximately 97 master's and 25 doctoral programs are accredited to specifically train marriage and family therapists. In addition, all states currently grant licenses and officially regulate the practice of marriage and family therapy, up from 11 states in 1986.

In addition, there have been several other movements within other organizations, or separate from professional organizations, which have greatly impacted the field of couple therapy. In 1985, the American Psychological Association created Division 43, Family Psychology, which focuses primarily on family issues but includes issues and research related to couple therapy as well. In 1989, the International Association of Marriage and Family Counselors (IAMFC) was chartered as a division of the American Counseling Association (ACA). It publishes *The Family Journal: Counseling and Therapy for Couples and Families* and has grown to become the largest division in ACA. In addition, in 1996, the Coalition for Marriage, Family and Couples Education was incorporated. This group was created by leaders who believed that most problems with contemporary couples and families are due to lack of skills. Since these skills can be taught, the primary mode of intervention and treatment is through education rather than therapy. The coalition sponsors an annual "Smart Marriages" convention that trains couple therapists to provide these educational components to clients. Each of these movements attests to the increasing scope and specialization of couple therapy in the last 30 years.

The Expanding Scope of Couple Therapy

According to Weeks, Fife, and Peterson (2016), working with couples can be challenging and requires specialized clinical knowledge and skills. The most comfortable, and certainly the easiest way, to practice couple therapy is to view many, if not all, couples and their problems as basically similar and then apply a standard therapy or mix of therapies to these couples. Many therapists do employ this strategy with some measure of success, particularly with a relatively young couple, married at least two but usually not more than seven years, with a fairly focused set of concerns (Berman et al., 1981). Such a strategy is misguided and deprives many couples of effective treatment. This is particularly apparent in the following types of couples, who are being referred with increasing frequency for couple therapy:

- One or both spouses are at or are past midlife.
- One spouse has a recurrent DSM-5 psychiatric disorder, such as panic attacks, agoraphobia, or depression.
- One spouse has an acute medical condition, such as recent recovery from a heart attack, and is fearful about returning to marital responsibilities.
- One spouse has a chronic health condition, such as hypertension or kidney dialysis, and this has become an issue in the marriage.
- One spouse has a mental illness and is noncompliant with sessions or medications.
- The progress of a client in a weight management or smoking cessation program appears to be impeded by his or her spouse.
- A couple presents with persistent sexual dysfunction that may or may not have a medical etiology.
- A couple in a gay or lesbian relationship (if the couple therapist is heterosexual).
- A couple who may be from a different culture of origin than the therapist or a couple in a bicultural relationship.
- An apparently motivated couple that has been in therapy for approximately six to ten sessions and is making little to no progress (this is the most common situation) (Gurman, 2015; Weeks et al., 2016).

Historically, the development of couple therapy can be divided into two periods. In the first period (1960s–1980s), the focus was on the therapist; developments in theory and technique emphasized the training of competent therapists to work with marital issues. The result was that couple therapy became therapist-centered. (This development was consistent with changes in other areas of the health and mental health fields.) During the second period (1980s–2000s), the focus shifted from the tailoring of treatment to the individual differences, needs, and styles of spouses, and the subsystem of marriage. In the last decade, especially, there has been a tremendous explosion of growth in the field of couple therapy. Johnson and Lebow (2000) distinguished several themes that emerged, including a focus on emotion as a force of change, an integration of different treatment models, and wider recognition of the diversity of clients. In short, couple therapy became more and more client-centered.

Gurman (2015) discussed four major shifts that have happened recently that "profoundly altered the field" of couple therapy (p. 7). They include:

1 A renewed interest in the psychology of the individual. While most of the field was dominated over the years with a virtually monolithic focus on the relationship system, new findings about the contribution of each individual (and his or her perspective) have introduced new elements for couple therapists. This includes things like findings from neuroscience, which "has helped couple therapy become more genuinely 'systemic'" (p. 7). We provide some discussion in Chapter 2 about these topics.
2 Traditionally, in couple therapy, psychological symptomatology was ascribed as an emergent property of the couple's systems dynamics, and treatment focused on changing the dynamic without considering the underlying psychopathology. There has been a greater embracing of the importance of psychiatric/psychological disorders and their influence on the ways in which partners interact with each other and formulate the patterns that make up their relationship. We cover these areas in Chapter 3.
3 Couple therapy as a field has been influenced by approaches and research findings that are outside of the more traditional domains of "marriage and family therapy." These include humanistic-experiential theory, social learning theory, and psychodynamic theory, among others. We review many of these in Chapters 4–8 and 10.
4 Finally, after years of being relegated to the sidelines of the family therapy movement, couple therapy is now one of the more dominant and vibrant domains of family therapy (and psychotherapy, in general). There are several reasons for this, including an increasing need for couple's issues to be addressed clinically and for more refined and subtle approaches to couples issues, and finally a robust research-base underlying many of the approaches and interventions in couple therapy (Gurman, 2015). This is reflected in multiple chapters of this book.

In addition, serious research, new theoretical conceptualizations, and a deeper understanding of the unique processes that shape the development and dysfunction of a couple relationship are elevating the field to newer heights (Johnson & Lebow, 2000; Sholevar, 2003). According to Blow and Karam (2017), "effective practice occurs through competent clinicians who draw from the best evidence available as well as lean on their clinical wisdom" (p. 716). Now, couple therapy in the 21st century has emerged as a field differentiated from family therapy, with demonstrated efficacy in treating both individual and relational issues. The bottom line is that this is a good time to be a couple therapist, and the need for well-trained clinicians has never been more necessary.

Concluding Note

We have now reviewed some of the major social and cultural changes and trends that impact the institution of marriage as well as the psychological factors involved in attraction, love, and the developmental phases of a marriage relationship. We have also reviewed the development of couple therapy as a profession. In the process, we have briefly introduced the reader to some of the principal concepts and constructs in couple therapy: Mate selection; marital pacts; cooperation and collusion; families of origin; and the system dimensions of boundaries, intimacy, and power. Finally, we have suggested that changes in the focus of treatment toward a more couple-centered marital therapy and the expanding varieties of couples as well as settings for marital therapy will all contribute to the further evolution of the profession.

References

Acker, M., & Davis, M. (1992). Intimacy, passion, and commitment in adult romantic relationships: A test of the triangular theory of love. *Journal of Social and Personal Relationships, 9*(1), 21–50. doi:10.1177/0265407592091002

Berman, E., Lief, H., & Williams, A. (1981). A model of marital interaction. In G. Sholevar (Ed.), *A handbook of marriage and marital therapy*. New York, NY: Spectrum Publications, Inc.

Blow, A. J., & Karam, E. A. (2017). The therapist's role in effective marriage and family therapy practice: The case for evidence based therapists. *Administrative Policy in Mental Health, 44*, 716–723. doi:10.1007/s10488-016-0768-8.

Boszormenyi-Nagy, I., & Spark, G. (1976). *Invisible loyalties*. New York, NY: Brunner/Mazel.

Broderick, C. B., & Schrader, S. S. (1981). The history of professional marriage and family therapy. In A. Gurman & D. Kniskern (Eds.), *Handbook of family therapy*. New York, NY: Brunner/Mazel.

Carter, E., & McGoldrick, M. (1999). *The expanded family life cycle: Individual, family and social perspectives* (3rd ed.). Boston, MA: Allyn & Bacon.

Centers for Disease Control and Prevention. (2016). *National marriage and divorce rate trends*. Retrieved from https://www.cdc.gov/nchs/fastats/marriage-divorce.htm

Dreikurs, R. (1946). *The challenge of marriage*. New York, NY: Duell, Sloan, and Pearce.

Finkel, E. (2017). *The all-or-nothing marriage: How the best marriages work*. New York, NY: Dutton.

Gillet, R. (2017, February 13). Power couples who stay together have 9 things in common. *Business insider*. Retrieved on December 18, 2017 from http://www.businessinsider.com/how-power-couples-stay-together-2017-2

Glick, I. D., Berman, E. M., Clarkin, J. F., & Rait, D. S. (2000). *Marital and family therapy* (4th ed.). Washington, DC: American Psychiatric Press.

Goleman, D. (1985, September 10). Patterns of love charted. *The New York Times*.

Gottman, J. M. (1999). *The marriage clinic*. New York, NY: W. W. Norton & Company, Inc.

Gottman, J., & Gottman, J. (2017). The natural principles of love. *Journal of Family Theory & Review, 9*, 7–26. doi:10.1111/jftr.12182

Gray-Little, B., Baucom, D. H., & Hamby, S. L. (1996). Marital power, marital adjustment, and therapy outcome. *Journal of Family Psychology, 10*(3), 292–303.

Gurman, A. S. (2015). The history and practice of couple therapy: History, contemporary models and a framework for comparative analysis. In A. S. Gurman, J. Lebow, & D. Snyder (Eds.), *Clinical handbook of couple therapy* (5th ed., pp. 1–22). New York, NY: Guilford.

Haley, J. (1973). *Uncommon therapy: The psychiatric techniques of Milton H. Erickson*. New York, NY: Norton.

Hardy, K. V., & Laszloffy, T. A. (2002). Couple therapy using a multicultural perspective. In A. S. Gurman & N. S. Jacobson (Eds.), Clinical *handbook of couple therapy* (3rd ed., pp. 569–596). New York, NY: Guilford.

Hawkins, D. N., & Booth, A. (2005). Unhappily ever after: Effects of long-term, low-quality marriages on well-being. *Social Forces, 84*, 451–471. doi:10.1353/sof.2005.0103

Johnson, S. M. (2003). Couple therapy research: Status and directions. In G. P. Sholevar (Ed.), *Textbook of family and couple therapy* (pp. 797–814). Alexandria, VA: American Psychiatric Publishing.

Johnson, S. M., & Lebow, J. (2000). The "coming of age" of couple therapy: A decade in review. *Journal of Marital and Family Therapy, 126*(1), 23–38.

King, M. E. (2016). Marital satisfaction. In C. L. Shehan (Ed.), *Encyclopedia of family studies*. doi:10.1002/9781119085621.wbefs054

Leavitt, J. W. (2009). *Make room for daddy: The journey from waiting room to birthing room*. Chapel Hill, NC: University of North Carolina Press.

Lemieux, R., & Hale, J. L. (1999). Intimacy, passion, and commitment in young romantic relationships: Cross-sectional analysis of intimacy, passion, and commitment: Testing the assumptions of the Triangular Theory of Love. *Psychological Reports, 90*(3), 1009–1014.

Lemieux, R., & Hale, J. L. (2002). Intimacy, passion, and commitment in young romantic relationships: Successfully measuring the triangular theory of love. *Psychological Reports, 85*(2), 497–503.

Lewis, J. M. (1998). For better or for worse: Interpersonal relationship and individual outcome. *American Journal of Psychiatry, 155*, 582–589.

Lomas T. (2018). The flavours of love: A cross-cultural lexical analysis. *Journal of Theory Social Behavior, 48*, 134–152. doi:10.1111/jtsb.12158

McGoldrick, M., & Carter, E. (2003). The family life cycle. In F. Walsh (Ed.), *Normal family processes* (3rd ed., pp. 375–398). New York, NY: Guilford Press.

McGoldrick, M., Garcia-Preto, N. A., & Carter, B. (2015). *The expanding family life cycle: Individual, family, and social perspectives* (5th ed.). New York, NY: Pearson.

McGoldrick, M., Giordano, J., & Pearce, J. K. (Eds.). (1996). *Ethnicity and family therapy* (2nd ed.). New York, NY: Guildford Press.

Miller, C. C. (2014, December 2). The divorce surge is over, but the myth lives on. *The New York Times*, pp. A3.

Napier, A. Y. (2000). Making a marriage. In W. C. Nichols, M. A. Pace-Nichols, D. S. Becvar, & A. Y. Napier (Eds.), *Handbook of family development and intervention* (pp. 145–170). New York, NY: John Wiley & Sons.

Ng, K., Peluso, P. R., & Smith, S. D. (2010). Marital satisfaction, intimacy, *enqing*, and relationship stressors among Asians. In J. Carlson & L. Sperry (Eds.), *Recovering intimacy in love relationships: A clinician's guide* (pp. 331–351). New York, NY: Routledge.

Nichols, W. (1988). *Marital therapy: An integrative approach*. New York, NY: Guilford Press.

Peluso, P. R., Miranda, A. O., Firpo-Jimenez, M., & Pham, M. (2010). Attachment dynamics and latin cultures: Areas of convergence and divergence. In P. Erdman, K. Ng, & Metzger (Eds.), *Cross-cultural perspectives of attachment: Theory, research, and clinical implications* (pp. 281–296). New York, NY: Routledge.

Pew Research Center. (2014, March). *Millennials in Adulthood: Detached from Institutions, Networked with Friends.*

Pinsof, W. M. (2002). The death of "till death us do part": The transformation of pair-bonding in the 21st century. *Family Process, 41*(2), 135–157.

Roberto-Forman, L. (2002). Transgenerational martial therapy. In A. S. Gurman & N. S. Jacobson (Eds.), *Clinical handbook of couple therapy* (3rd ed., pp. 118–150). New York, NY: Guilford.

Santos, P. S., Schindermann, J. A., Gabardo, J., & Bichalo Mda, G. (2005). New evidence that the MHC influences odor perception in humans: A study with 58 Brazilian students. *Hormonal Behavior, 47*(4), 384–388.

Schnarch, D. (1991). *Constructing the sexual crucible: An integration of sexual and marital therapy.* New York, NY: W. W. Norton.

Schnarch, D. (1997). *Passionate marriage: Love, sex, and intimacy in emotional committed relationships.* New York, NY: Henry Holt.

Sholevar, G. P. (2003). Couple therapy: An overview. In G. P. Sholevar (Ed.), *Textbook of family and couple therapy* (pp. 417–438). Alexandria, VA: American Psychiatric Publishing.

Sperry, L. (1978). *The together experience: Getting, growing and staying together in marriage.* San Diego, CA: Beta Books.

Sternberg, R. (1986). A triangular theory of love. *Psychological Reviews, 93*(2), 119–135.

Sternberg, R. (1987). *The triangle of love: Intimacy, passion, commitment.* New York, NY: Basic Books.

Sternberg, R. (1998). *Love as a story.* New York, NY: Oxford University Press.

Sternberg, R. (2014). *Love as a story* [Blog post]. Retrieved from https://www.huffingtonpost.com/robert-j-sternberg/love-is-a-story_b_5406203.html

Sternberg, R. J., Hojjat, M., & Barnes, M. L. (2001). Empirical test of aspect of a theory of love as a story. *European Journal of Personality, 15*, 199–218.

Sue, D. W., & Sue, D. (1999). *Counseling the culturally different: Theory and practice* (3rd ed.). New York, NY: John Wiley & Sons, Inc.

U.S. Department of Labor, Bureau of Labor Statistics. (2017, April). *College enrollment and work activity of 2016 high school graduates* [News release]. Retrieved from http://www.bls.gov/news.release/hsgec.nr0.htm

Verkoff, J., Kulka, R. A., & Douvan, E. (1981). *Mental health in America: Patterns of help seeking from 1957 to 1976.* New York, NY: Basic Books.

Waite, L. J., Browning, D., Doherty, W. J., Gallagher, M., Luo, Y., & Scott, S. M. (2000). *Does divorce make people happy? Findings from a study of unhappy marriages.* New York, NY: Institute for American Values.

Wallerstein, J. S., Lewis, J., & Blakeslee, S. (2000). *The unexpected legacy of divorce: A 25 year landmark study.* New York, NY: Hyperion.

Wedekind, C., Seebeck, T. Bettens, F., & Paepke, A. J. (1995). MHC-dependent mate preference in humans. *Processes in Biological Science, 260*(1359), 245–249.

Weeks, G. R., Fife, S. T., & Peterson, C. M. (2016). *Techniques for the couple therapist: Essential interventions from the experts.* New York, NY: Routledge.

Zilbach, J. (2003). The family life cycle: A framework for understanding family development. In G. P. Sholevar (Ed.), *Textbook of family and couple therapy* (pp. 303–316). Alexandria, VA: American Psychiatric Publishing.

Section 1

Science and Couples Relationships

2 Biology and Neuroscience in Couples Relationships

LEARNING OBJECTIVES

In this chapter, the reader will learn the following:

1 The regions of the brain and their functions.
2 The interplay of stress and physical and psychological functioning.
3 The impact of the various attachment styles on the coupling process.
4 How couple therapists can utilize this information in treating couples.

Historically, couple therapy has been practiced by nonmedical therapists with traditional married couples for a variety of emotional or communication problems. For the most part, these couples were seen conjointly in private practice settings or in the context of treatment for their children in community mental health clinics. Today, however, practitioners are increasingly confronted with clients who require both psychological and medical help with their presenting concerns. Often, these practitioners must make appropriate referrals with little formal training in medicine or neuroscience. Until recently, training in the behavioral sciences has been focused mostly on the psychosocial dimension of behavior. Within the past decade, however, training programs, particularly graduate programs in psychology, have included requirements for some training in the biological bases of behavior, namely, neuropsychology, cognitive neuroscience, and psychopharmacology. As a result of these new realities, the professional practice of psychology has shifted its identity from being a mental health specialty to a health care specialty (Sperry, 2002).

Because couple therapy is usually associated with the social and psychological sciences, the notion of associating biological factors with marital functioning may, at first, appear odd. In the past, influential writers in the field such as Haley (1980) repudiated biological influences on system functioning. However, as the field of couple therapy has matured, many, if not most, couple therapists have begun to conceptualize couples functioning in a more holistic and integrative fashion, where biological factors are as important as the psychological and social factors (Sperry & Carlson, 1999). Interestingly, conceptualizing biological as well as psychological and social factors reflects the biopsychosocial model, a model which has primarily been utilized by psychiatrists who practice couples and family therapy (Cozolino, 2002, 2016; Sperry, 2002).

The question that psychotherapists (including couple therapists) face is whether traditional psychotherapy will continue to have any relevance as neuroscience unlocks the secrets of the brain, its dysfunction, and how to repair it. Will the treatment of the future consist solely of genetic manipulation, microneurosurgery at the neuronal level, and psychopharmacology? Emerging research is beginning to attest to the fact that psychotherapy has demonstrable effects on the brain, its various structures, neurotransmitter systems, and even gene expression (Cozolino, 2016; Kandel, 1998; Sperry, 2002). In fact, the psychotherapeutic milieu may be uniquely suited to effect these changes, giving clinicians encouragement to cultivate a neurobiological dimension to their work (Cozolino, 2002, 2016; Wylie & Simon, 2003). The purpose of this chapter is to acquaint the reader with the basic and relevant aspects of the brain, attachment, and physical changes as it relates to relationships. It is *not* intended as an exhaustive review of the neuroanatomical structures of the brain, a detailed cellular account of neuronal functioning, or an in-depth treatise on physiological aspects of the endocrine system. We will present some of the latest thinking and research in the field of neuroscience related to couple therapy. It is our belief that understanding these elemental processes is not an adjunct to doing good couple therapy; they are becoming ever more essential to it.

The Contributions of Neurobiological Factors on Close Relationships

The human brain is arguably the most complex, dynamic, and mysterious organ system known to science. It is estimated that over half of the 40,000–50,000 genes in the human genome are expressed exclusively or indirectly in the brain (Cowan & Kandel, 2001; Naumova, Lee, Rychkov, Vlasova, & Grigorenko, 2013). Neuroscience is the branch of biology that has traditionally studied the brain and nervous system. However, recent developments in brain scanning techniques have created a radical transformation of present-day neuroscience as it intersects with (if not encompasses) psychiatry, psychology, and cognitive science. As a result, long-held ideas about the brain are being challenged as new findings of the plasticity of the brain and neural growth throughout the life span are transforming the field (Cowan & Kandel, 2001; Cozolino, 2002, 2006, 2016; Kandel, 1998; Naumova et al., 2013). In seeing the brain at work (or not working at all), scientists are better able to understand the organization, functioning, and healing of the brain and its systems. In this section, we will discuss briefly the physiological structures of the brain (lobes, hemispheres, limbic system) and their specific functioning in the creation of an integrated narrative of the self.

Overview of the Relevant Systems of the Brain

The organization of the brain is separated into three major areas of functioning: The cortex, the limbic system, and the brain stem (see Figure 2.1). The *brain stem* regulates automatic processes such as heart rate and respiration. Although it should be noted that studies of physiological responses (such as heart rate, blood pressure, and respiration) have been very useful in the study of couple interactions (Cozolino, 2006; Gottman, 2011), they are not as germane to our discussion of neuroscience and couple therapy as the cortex and the limbic system.

The Lobes and Structures of the Cortex

The *cortex* is comprised of the large outer layer of the brain and is responsible for many of the higher functions. It is divided into four lobes (temporal, parietal, occipital, and frontal), as well as divided laterally into right and left hemispheres (see Figure 2.1 and Table 2.1). The functions of the *temporal* lobe are primarily auditory processing, receptive language, and memory functions. The *parietal* lobe links sensory input from the outside world with motor functioning. It also is involved in orienting the body's spatial orientation in the world and coordinating movements. The *occipital* lobe is responsible primarily for visual processing (Cozolino, 2002, 2006, 2016). It is interesting to note that a large portion of our brain is dedicated to two of the five senses (vision and hearing), attesting to their relative importance.

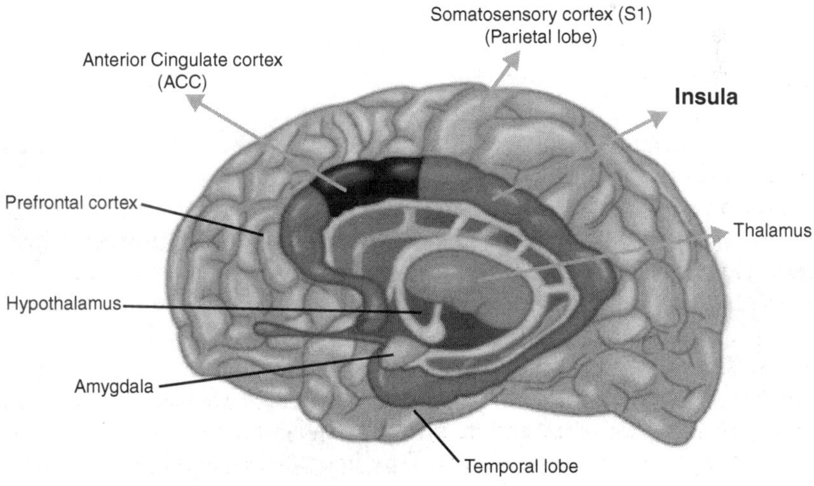

Figure 2.1 The lobes and areas of the human brain.

Table 2.1 Description of the Lobes and Hemispheres of the Brain

Lobe	*Primary Purposes*
Temporal	• Auditory processing • Receptive language • Memory functions
Parietal	• Links sensory input from the outside world with motor functioning • Orients the body's spatial orientation in the world • Coordinates movements
Occipital	• Responsible primarily for visual processing
Frontal	• Controls "executive" functions such as motor behavior, expressive language, and abstract reasoning • Allows individuals to respond to the needs of others, identifying the likes and dislikes, as well as plays an important role with motivational states for social functioning • The prefrontal cortex (the foremost portion of the frontal lobe) is an association area that mediates internal and external sensory information and is the connection point to the limbic system via the hypothalamus
Hemisphere	*Primary Purposes*
Left	• Responsible for the logical, linear, and sequential processing of Information • Involved with problem-solving and conscious coping, semantic aspects of language, and language comprehension • More closely identified with cortical functioning and the creation of a coherent narrative of the social self • Oriented toward (and responds best to) positive and prosocial emotions
Right	• Regulates the endocrine and autonomic nervous systems (often seen as more closely related to the unconscious mind) • Organizes sensory input from the body • Contains the centers for creative and nonlinear thinking, emotional and prosaic elements of speech, and musical ability • More highly connected with emotional and primitive functioning (limbic system and brain stem)

The *frontal* lobe has particular importance in the overall functioning of the brain. It controls "executive" functions such as motor behavior, expressive language, and abstract reasoning. In terms of the social functioning of the brain, the frontal cortex allows individuals to respond to the needs of others, identifying likes and dislikes, as well as playing an important role with motivational states. The *prefrontal cortex* (PFC), the area of the foremost portion of the frontal lobe, is an association area that mediates internal and external sensory information. It contains a large number of sensory neurons, and its connection to the hypothalamus is considered to be the zenith of the limbic system (Cowan, Harter, & Kandel, 2000; Cozolino, 2006, 2016; Wylie & Simon, 2003). In subsequent discussions of attachment, we will feature the role of the frontal and the orbital prefrontal cortexes in the formation and maintenance of relationships.

Lastly, there is the *insula* cortex and the *cingulate* cortex, which Cozolino (2006) argues "could, and perhaps should, be considered as the fifth and sixth cortical lobes" (p. 50). These areas are considered part of the "social brain network" which is a new area of discovery in neuroscience that includes the medial prefrontal cortex, posterior cingulate cortex (PCC), temporo-parietal junction (TPJ), and the insula cortex (Cozolino, 2016; Nohlen, van Harreveld, Rotteveel, Lelieveld, & Crone, 2013). These regions of the brain are associated with how individuals interact with others in a social context, take on multiple perspectives, and are influenced by other people. According to Cozolino (2016):

> The insula cortex and the anterior cingulate connect primitive bodily states with the experience and expression of emotion, behavior and cognition and are involved in mediating the gamut of emotion for disgust to love. The insula participates in the organization and experience of our core sense of self in space and our ability to distinguish between self and others. Interestingly, both the insula and the anterior cingulate become activated when subjects are asked to recall behavior for which they felt ashamed.
>
> (p. 234)

In particular, the insula cortex and the cingulate cortex are linked to experiences of empathy, pain, and ambivalence (Cozolino, 2016; Nohlen et al., 2013).

As mentioned earlier, the brain is also divided laterally. Each hemisphere has specific and specialized functioning, which has led some writers to talk about humans as having two brains. Some studies on patients who have had their corpus callosum (the bundle of tissues which connect the right and left hemispheres) surgically severed have found that there are often difficulties synthesizing information across the two hemispheres (Cozolino, 2006, 2016; Davidson, 2001). Specifically, the *left hemisphere* is responsible for the logical, linear, and sequential processing of information. It also is involved with problem-solving and conscious coping, semantic aspects of language, and language comprehension. The left hemisphere is more closely identified with cortical functioning than the right hemisphere and is necessary for creating a coherent narrative of the social self. In addition, it is more oriented toward (and responds best to) positive and prosocial emotions (Cozolino, 2006, 2016).

In comparison, the *right hemisphere* contains the centers for creative and nonlinear thinking, emotional and prosaic elements of speech, and musical ability. The right hemisphere regulates the endocrine and autonomic nervous systems (relative to the left hemispheres); hence, it is often seen as more closely related to the unconscious mind. Sensory input from the body is organized in the right hemisphere, as there is an entire representation contained within it. The right hemisphere is also more highly connected with emotional and primitive functioning (limbic system and brain stem) of the brain, as compared to the left hemisphere (Cozolino, 2002, 2016).

An example of how the different functions of the right and left hemispheres work together is in the area of being frightened or distressed. The right hemisphere is involved in comprehending emotional and nonverbal aspects of communication as well as in the appraisal of the safety and danger of others; whereas the functioning of the left hemisphere (i.e. language, logical thinking) is inhibited by strong affect. Thus, in times of stress, the experiences of stage fright and speechlessness, as well as social withdrawal, when under threat, can be demonstrated (Cozolino, 2002, 2016; Fuchs & Flügge, 2003).

One researcher who has recently explored this asymmetry of the brain between the right and the left PFC is Richard Davidson. He and his colleagues (Davidson, 2001; Davidson et al., 2003; Urry et al., 2004) have shown, through the use of magnetic resonance imaging (MRI) and positron emission tomography (PET) scans, how the left PFC is related to experiences of positive affect and overall experiences of well-being. At the same time, they have shown that the right hemisphere of the PFC is associated with fear-based, negative affect. In addition, they have shown how baseline levels of activity can affect a person's natural desire to either approach (greater left hemisphere activity) or withdraw (greater right hemisphere activity) from others (Lapate et al., 2014, 2017). More recently, Hostinar et al. (2017) reported that there is a link between early childhood maltreatment; right prefrontal activity; and a predisposition to chronic, low-grade inflammation (which can produce significant health risks). This has a significant impact on couples counselors, as it provides a biological explanation for some of the natural inclinations that a partner of a couple may display. A discussion of how amenable these tendencies are to change will be discussed later in this chapter (Davidson et al., 2003; Davidson & McEwen, 2012; Lapate et al., 2017; Urry et al., 2004).

The Structures of the Limbic System

The *limbic system* is a group of structures located at the base of the brain (see Figure 3.1), considered to be the intersection of the internal and external worlds, where the primal needs of the organism negotiate with the necessities of the outside world (Cozolino, 2006, 2016). The limbic system guides behavior that is required for self-preservation and preservation of the species (Ploog, 2003). In more specific terms, the limbic system is thought to be involved with attachment, emotion, and memory. The major structures of the limbic system (hippocampus, amygdala, and hypothalamus) will be discussed in the following section (see Table 2.2).

The *hippocampus* plays an important role in the control of autonomic circuits and emotional processing of events as well as learning and memory (Fuchs & Flügge, 2003). It works with the cerebral cortex to organize explicit memories as well (Cozolino, 2006, 2016). In its stress regulation function, it contains a high number of receptors for, and modulates the release of, glucocorticoids (stress hormones). Researchers believe that chronic exposure to stress hormones negatively affects the hippocampus, which seems to

Table 2.2 Major Structures of the Limbic System

Hippocampus	• Plays a role in the control of autonomic circuits, visual-spatial processing, emotional processing of events, and learning and memory • Works with the cerebral cortex to organize explicit memories • In its stress regulation function, it contains a high number of receptors for, and modulates the release of, glucocorticoids (stress hormones)
Amygdala	• Main function is the generation of fear in response to stress or danger • Facilitates immediate action via the fight-or-flight response • Plays an important role in the encoding of traumatic memories
Hypothalamus	• The convergence point for all the structures of the limbic system • Regulates body temperature, digestion, and hormones, and responds to sensory information being sent from within and outside the body • Mediates between the cortex and the rest of the limbic system • Acts as a control mechanism for the stress system (the hypothalamic-pituitary-adrenal cortex or HPAC) and for the pituitary gland

suffer shrinkage and possibly a loss of neurons. This may account for memory loss, difficulty learning new skills, and decrement in emotional processing of events (Cozolino, 2006, 2016; Fuchs & Flügge, 2003; Ploog, 2003).

The *hypothalamus* is the convergence point for all the structures of the limbic system. It regulates body temperature, digestion, and hormones, as well as responds to sensory information being sent from within and outside the body (Cozolino, 2006, 2016; Ploog, 2003). It also mediates between the cortex and the rest of the limbic system. As such, it acts as a control mechanism for the stress system (the hypothalamic-pituitary-adrenal cortex [HPAC]) and for the master hormonal gland in the brain, the *pituitary gland* (Cozolino, 2006; Fuchs & Flügge, 2003).

One of the *amygdala's* main functions is the generation of fear in response to stress or danger (Fuchs & Flügge, 2003). Its direct connection to the autonomous nervous system allows for quick appraisals of danger, which facilitates immediate action via the fight-or-flight response (Cozolino, 2006, 2016). The amygdala also plays an important role in the encoding of traumatic memories. It is a central component of the social brain for humans and is involved with fear, attachment, and early memories, as well as emotional experiences throughout life (Cozolino, 2006).

Another area that has recently gained the attention of affective neuroscientists is a cluster of neurons in the brain stem that is closely associated with the amygdala, called the *bed nucleus of the stria terminals* (BNST). The BNST is a subcortical structure that is involved in anticipatory and sustained reactivity to threat and is an important part of the anxiety and stress responses (Rabellino et al., 2018). According to Cozolino (2016), the BNST is unique because:

> Unlike the amygdala, the BNST is sensitive to abstract cues and is capable of long-term activation, suggesting both its later evolution and its role in anticipatory anxiety. It appears that the amygdala specializes in fear, while the BNST has evolved to deal with more complex anxiety triggers that emerges as our brains became more capable of future-oriented thinking, such as, "Will I have the money to pay my taxes next April?" The BNST in rats has been found to grow in response to maternal responsibilities. Perhaps this is why many parents mention constant worry as a primary emotion of having children, even before birth.
>
> (p. 191)

Hence, many of these newly discovered structures of the brain have a direct impact on romantic pair-bonding and are important for couple therapists to have, at least, a passing knowledge of.

Disintegration of Neural Networks and Problems

Healthy emotional, psychological, and neurological functioning is defined as the proper integration and balance between and among the lobes, left and right hemispheres, (pre)frontal cortex, and limbic system. This balance allows a person to experience a healthy mixture of negative and positive emotional experiences, as well as to regulate and manage anxiety. In addition to the absence of mental illness, a properly integrated neural structure is usually outwardly manifested by a coherent narrative, that is, no distortions or exclusions of memory that accompany such disorders. As Cozolino (2002) points out,

> [N]eural network integration corresponds to ego strength, the use of mature defenses, and mental health. If this is the case, dissociation or imbalance among networks should correlate with mental illness. Based on what we know about hemispheric specialization, we have to assume that integration between the right and left hemispheres is a vital element of healthy brain functioning. Anxiety and affective disorders, psychosis, alexithymia (inability to put thoughts into words), and psychosomatic conditions have all been hypothesized to be causally related to deficits in the regulation and integration of neural networks connecting the hemispheres.
>
> (p. 117, parenthesis added)

As mentioned earlier, the left hemisphere is geared toward positive affect and prosocial behavior, which aids in forming attachments with other people and deceasing anxiety. One of the main functions of the right hemisphere is to be suspicious, anxious, and alert to danger. When confronted with a threat, language and integrated information processing is curtailed (hence distorted or disintegrated narratives), regulation of these hemispheres is uncoordinated, and there is an imbalance in affect and mood states (Cowan et al., 2000; Cozolino, 2006, 2016; Wylie & Simon, 2003). Relational behaviors and the ability to soothe the self generally give way to feelings of anxiety and the desire for self-preservation. This disruption is useful for the diversion of cognitive resources to handle the threat; however, if individuals either are constantly in a stressful situation or feel that they are threatened, then they become vulnerable to longer-term psychological problems (Cozolino, 2016). As we will see, this problem of long-term stress has physical as well as psychological consequences, providing the most direct link between the mind and the body.

Psychoneuroimmunology

Can depression, anxiety, social support, or psychological stress positively or negatively alter one's ability to resist infection, disease, or cancer? Can immune function and disease susceptibility be altered through psychological intervention? What are the biological pathways by which psychological characteristics and states effect physical changes in the body? In the past decade, hundreds of studies have been published that address the relation of psychological characteristics and states to immune function and to health outcomes thought to be determined by immune alterations (Cohen & Herbert, 1996; Miller & Cohen, 2001; Miller, Cohen, & Ritchey, 2002). Psychoneuroimmunology (PNI) is the field of science that has emerged to study the interrelationship of four biological systems in humans that impact this process: The mind/brain, the nervous system, the endocrine system, and the immune system (Ray, 2004). Each of the systems (nervous, immune, endocrine) has receptors on certain key cells that can receive chemical information from each of the other systems, which allows for regulation and communication across the systems (Cohen & Herbert, 1996; Ray, 2004). In addition, the discovery of cytokines, chemical compounds produced by the immune system that cross the blood-brain barrier and alter the function of the central nervous system (CNS), has given further physiological evidence to the pathways of PNI (Cohen & Herbert, 1996; Miller et al., 2002). Nemeroff (2013) summed up over two decades of research into PNI thusly:

> Early-life trauma acts upon the developing CNS to produce structural alterations (hippocampus and cortical regions) associated with specific psychiatric symptoms (deficits in executive function, memory, and emotional and sensory processing), altered functional brain imaging responses to provocative emotional stimuli, as well as persistent alterations in a variety of brain neurotransmitter systems including the corticotropin releasing factor (CRF), serotonin, and dopamine circuits. Long-term

> effects of child maltreatment on immune mechanisms have been documented. One series of exciting findings has been the identification of specific genetic polymorphisms that mediate the depressogenic (e.g., CRF R1, Brain derived neurotropic factor (BDNF), and 5HT3) and anxiogenic (FKBP5 and PAC1) effects of early-life stress on psychiatric disease vulnerability, and more recently epigenetic mechanisms have been shown to play a seminal role in this process.
>
> (p. 286)

These findings are in addition to the myriad effects on cardiovascular disease, cancer, and other disease processes (Cozolino, 2016; Jaremka, 2017; Nemeroff, 2013); What a person thinks does make a difference as the body responds to the brain, regardless of whether the beliefs and ideas are imaginary or based in reality, or whether they are positive or negative (Ray, 2004). In this section, we will highlight what has been learned about the importance of stress on immunity and the physical mechanisms that link systems of the mind and the body (Jaremka, 2017).

Physical Pathways of PNI

Two physical systems working in parallel are the body's primary response to the demands and stressors of life (see Table 2.3). These structures of the nervous and endocrine systems function together to secrete stress hormones, which allows for survival in the face of threat (Cozolino, 2016; Jaremka, 2017). The first of the two systems is the HPAC. The hypothalamus receives sensory information via the limbic system and cortex and triggers the pituitary gland to secrete hormones, which travel throughout the body via the bloodstream and prepare for longer-term changes (growth, digestion, etc.). The endpoint of the HPAC system is in the adrenal cortex, which manufactures and releases *glucocorticoids* (i.e. cortisol) into the bloodstream in reaction to stress (Cozolino, 2016; Fuchs & Flügge, 2003). Glucocorticoids help to regulate metabolism, muscle tone, inflammation, and other bodily functions (Jaremka, 2017).

The second system for alerting the body to stress is a more active system involving the *sympathetic nervous system* (SNS) and the *adrenal medulla* (AM). The SNS is responsible for (among other things) increasing heart rate, blood pressure, and respiration in preparation for the fight-or-flight response to danger. Recall that the *amygdala* is a key component in the limbic system for fear, and when an individual perceives a threat, the SNS is activated by the amygdala, which releases norepinephrine stored at the nerve endings and activates the body's short-term stress response. The final part is the stimulation of the AM, which releases epinephrine (adrenalin) into the blood stream to keep the body in a heightened state of alertness or anxiety (Cohen & Herbert, 1996; Cozolino, 2016; Jaremka, 2017; Miller et al., 2002).

The short-term benefits of these hormone releases are to provide the body with the capability to take on a stressful situation for a brief period of time

Table 2.3 Two Physical Pathways for Responding to Stress

Hypothalamic-pituitary-adrenal cortex (HPAC)	The hypothalamus receives sensory information via the limbic system and cortex and triggers the pituitary gland to secrete hormones, which travel throughout the body via the bloodstream and prepare for longer-term changes (growth, digestion, etc.). The endpoint of the HPAC system is in the adrenal cortex, which manufactures and releases glucocorticoids (i.e. cortisol) into the bloodstream in reaction to stress. Glucocorticoids help to regulate metabolism, muscle tone, inflammation, and other bodily functions.
Sympathetic nervous system (SNS) and adrenal medulla (SAM)	The SNS is responsible for (among other things) increasing heart rate, blood pressure and respiration in preparation for the "fight or flight" response to danger. The amygdala is a key component in the limbic system for fear, and when an individual perceives a threat, the SNS is activated by the amygdala, which releases norepinephrine stored at the nerve endings and activates the body's short-term stress response. The final part is the stimulation of the adrenal medulla, which releases epinephrine (adrenalin) into the blood stream which continues to keep the body in a heightened state of alertness or anxiety.

(Kiecolt-Glaser, McGuire, Robles, & Glaser, 2002; Lekander, 2002). Theoretically, once the threat has been coped with, the HPAC and SAM systems, as well as their hormone secretions, should return to normal. However, if a person continues to perceive a threat or is in a chronically threatening situation, then the system will continue to be activated. Chronic activation of the SAM system is linked to cardiovascular disease and upper respiratory infections, whereas chronic exposure to glucocorticoids (due to chronic activation of the HPAC system) seems to be linked to diminished immune functioning and an increased vulnerability to a variety of autoimmune diseases and cancer (Jaremka, 2017; Jaremka, Lindgren, & Keicolt-Glaser, 2013; Lekander, 2002; Ray, 2004). In addition, researchers are beginning to relate the long-term effects of exposure to stress hormones to problems with cognitive functioning (processing of events), increased memory loss due to hippocampal damage, and depression (Cozolino, 2016; Jaremka, 2017; Jaremka et al., 2013; Kiecolt-Glaser et al., 2002).

Stress, Allostatic Load, and PNI

Stress is a major way of upsetting important health-related homeostatic balance in the various systems of the body (Lekander, 2002; Nemeroff, 2013). Both the endocrine system and SNS play central roles in the concept of ***allostatic load***, or the cumulative long-term effects of physiological responses to stress (Cozolino, 2016; Jaremka, 2017). As the primary mechanisms for conducting stress hormones in the body's adaptive processes, as well as being responsible for the deleterious physiological outcomes, the neuroendocrine system and SNS serve as the primary mediators of a person's allostatic load (Kiecolt-Glaser et al., 2002). There are two components that determine the development of allostatic load: (1) The demands of the individual's environment, *real or perceived*, and (2) the individual's appraisal of (or belief about) whether they have the necessary coping resources to deal with the demand. "It is important to note that it is not the coping skills that individuals have or do not have that are important. What counts are the coping skills that individuals believe they have or do not have" (Ray, 2004, p. 32). Thus, the experience of stress and/or allostatic load is an individual matter that is suffered when there is an inadequate match between coping skills and perceived demands, which, in turn, determines one's psychological and physical equilibrium or disequilibrium (Jaremka, 2017; Kiecolt-Glaser et al., 2002; Ray, 2004).

Many PNI theorists have argued that psychotherapy aimed at helping to improve a person's appraisal processes and increasing the awareness of coping resources could help restore equilibrium in the face of allostatic load. While there has been considerable study establishing the physiological and psychological link between allostatic load and immunity functioning (Cozolino, 2016; Jaremka, 2017; Kiecolt-Glaser et al., 2002; Lekander, 2002; Miller et al., 2002; Ray, 2004), empirically verifying the effectiveness of psychological interventions on immunity has had mixed results. Several researchers have been able to effect some change on biological functioning as a result of psychotherapeutic processes that focus on coping strategies (Kiecolt-Glaser, Bane, Glaser, & Malarkey, 2003; Robles & Kiecolt-Glaser, 2003).

Attachment Theory and Close Relationships

Up to now, we have discussed the systems of the brain and its interaction with the body related to the individual. We will now discuss how these processes function in order to relate to and fulfill the need to be with other people. This ultimately culminates in the formation of close relationships.

Description of Attachment

Attachment theory emphasizes the long-lasting effects of early close relationships to primary caregivers on individuals. Bowlby (1988) proposed that the maintenance of affectional bonds, especially between a mother and her young child, is essential to the survival of the human species. These bonds serve a protective and an instructive function (Bowlby, 1969). The protective function keeps the child close enough to the mother in times of potential danger. When there is no danger, the mother becomes a secure base from which the child can explore the environment (Bowlby, 1988; Krause & Haverkamp, 1996).

According to attachment theory, primary attachment relationships become internalized by the child, and the expectations of self and others become generalized to form the blueprint for future interactions with others outside the primary attachment relationship (Sroufe, 1988). Based on the type of primary attachment relationship experienced, the child begins to generate a framework of expectations concerning the availability and responsiveness of others, as well as a sense of his own worthiness of love and care (Verschueren, Marcoen, & Schoefs, 1996). These expectations provide a basic context for guiding behavior, interpreting experience, and negotiating subsequent interactions with the environment and other social relationships (Belsky & Nezworski, 1988; Hughes, 1997; Sroufe, 1988). About the age of four or five, these convictions about the world coalesce and the child develops a stable, internal working model of the self and others that shape the individual's behavior, affect, and ideas of the self, others, and relationships across the life span (Ainsworth, Blehar, Waters, & Wall, 1978; Bowlby, 1969; Hughes, 1997; Peluso, Peluso, Buckner, Kern & Curlette, 2009; Peluso, Peluso, White, & Kern, 2004; Verschueren et al., 1996).

Infant attachment relationships can be broadly classified as secure or insecure (Belsky & Nezworski, 1988). Ainsworth et al. (1978) experimentally defined three subgroupings of infant attachment relationships: Secure, anxious-avoidant, and anxious-resistant (or ambivalent). A secure attachment is characterized by intense feelings of intimacy, emotional security, and physical safety when the infant is in the presence of an attachment figure. Ainsworth et al. found that the securely attached children were more positive in their interactions with the primary caretaker, showing little anxiety when separated from their mothers. They surmised that this confidence frees the child from needing to always see the caretaker. This promotes an overall sense of self-worth and belongingness in the infant and serves to advance the emotional and social development of the child (Belsky & Nezworski, 1988; Lieberman & Pawl, 1988; Peluso et al., 2004; Sims, 2002).

However, when children experience an insecure attachment relationship (as the result of trauma or neglect, for example), significant deficits in their development of self occur, and their ability to relate to others suffers. These can have long-term negative psychological consequences for the individual (Hughes, 1997; Sims, 2002; Sroufe, 1988). Ainsworth et al. (1978) noted that the anxious-avoidant children were characterized by their low need to accept physical contact from the caretaker (parent) when reunited after a separation (Sagi, Donell, van Ijzendoorn, Mayseless, & Aviezer, 1994). In fact, the mothers of these children were observed to be rejecting and emotionally distant, and often displayed feelings of anger toward their children (Ainsworth et al., 1978). These children, who must live with parents that continually reject them, might utilize some form of disconnection or avoidance as a defense (Bowlby, 1980; Sroufe, 1988).

The third group identified by Ainsworth et al. (1978) was the anxious-ambivalent children, characterized by intense distress at their caretaker's departure and an inability to be soothed upon return of the caretaker (see also Sagi et al., 1994). Children with this type of attachment style seemed to show an unusual amount of internal conflict regarding the perceived physical and emotional availability of the attachment figure. This conflict indicates that parenting was inconsistent or unresponsive in meeting the child's needs (Ainsworth et al., 1978; Lieberman & Pawl, 1988). Research on the consequences of this attachment style indicates that children with an anxious-ambivalent attachment style show an inhibition of exploration tendencies, precociousness, and self-protection, along with an increase in recklessness and accident proneness (Lieberman & Pawl, 1988; Sroufe, 1988).

Recently, a fourth attachment classification was identified, which seems to be a mixture of the anxious-avoidant and anxious-ambivalent styles (Sagi et al., 1994). This is characterized by a disorganized or disoriented response of the child to the primary caretaker, which has led to the inclusion of the disorganized category in many new studies even though it has not been as thoroughly validated as the other three (Sagi et al., 1994).

The anxious-avoidant, anxious-ambivalent, and disorganized types of attachment support Bowlby's (1980) main thesis that a child must form some attachment regardless of the quality of the environment. That is, in order to survive, a child will mold her relationship to the primary caregiver(s), despite deprived emotional responsiveness from the caregiver. Furthermore, attachment relationships represent adaptive responses to the environment and/or caretakers that are useful for a period of time during childhood. However, since these attachment styles remain relatively fixed into adulthood (Sroufe, 1988), a relationship between the child and the caregiver that consists of not being attached at all, or being too closely attached to an unresponsive or rejecting caretaker, can become problematic as the child gets older and tries to form new relationships (Peluso et al., 2004, 2009). However, according to Johnson (2002):

> Insecure styles or strategies are not pathological; they are all adaptive at times. In certain situations, numbing ourselves and minimizing our attachment needs will maximize the responsiveness of a volatile and abusive attachment figure and protect us from the pain of frequent rejection. Such styles are best thought of as adaptive secondary strategies for maintaining proximity of less-than-responsive caregivers. They become risk factors, however, when they become rigid and closed and pull strongly for particular confirming responses from a partner.
>
> (p. 42)

We will discuss more about the practical applications of this approach for couple therapy later in the text.

Attachment and Emerging Neuroscience

The translation of attachment schemas into the neurobiological structure is primarily organized within the *orbital prefrontal cortex* (OPFC). This region of the cortex processes the contingencies (punishment and reward) of complex events, such as our relationship to our parents (Cozolino, 2006, 2016). As part of the mechanism that controls affect regulation, the orbitofrontal cortex mediates emotional and physiological responses (e.g. stress responses, SNS activation, parasympathetic inhibition). Secure attachments allow for a balance in the responses to complex stimuli (i.e. disappointment by an attachment figure) without eliciting a traumatic response. Imbalances in these reactions (either becoming too aroused and stressed in light of little threat, or not becoming aroused and stressed enough in light of significant threat) are the neurobiological hallmarks of insecure attachment styles (anxious-ambivalent and anxious-avoidant, respectively).

The various attachment styles have further neurobiological consequences to them. Positive experiences and social interactions stimulate the neurotransmitters (e.g. dopamine, serotonin, and norepinephrine) that power the frontal cortex (Cozolino, 2016), which further aids in forming attachments and making rational decisions. Likewise, individuals with secure attachments seem to have more coherent and balanced narratives about themselves. There is integration between the emotional and the cognitive aspects. However, these neurobiological correlates are greatly impacted by the quality of relationships the individual experiences in childhood. In contrast, for individuals who grew up in highly conflicted or dysfunctional families,

> the dysfunction becomes embedded in the personality and neural architecture of all the individuals; they collude to maintain the homeostasis because now they all require it in order to feel safe. These processes shape individuals to survive in the context of particular dysfunctions, and may also keep them from adapting to healthier relationships. As a result, many of us recreate the dysfunction from our family of origin in our choice of partners and in our shaping of relationships.
>
> (Cozolino, 2002, p. 58)

In addition to the social deficits, children who experience chronic stress due to insecure attachments may have some decrement in memory function or communication ability due to repeated exposure to stress hormones in childhood (Cozolino, 2016). Individuals with insecure attachments seem to either be excessively emotional and enmeshed with their childhood narratives, or overly cognitive and coldly detached emotionally from their experiences of childhood. In either case, the disintegration of autobiographical memory reflects disintegration of the neural networks as well, which impacts reactions to stress, arousal level, and predispositions to psychopathology (Cozolino, 2006, 2016; Sims, 2002; Wylie & Simon, 2003). In fact, these imbalances create the conditions for distorted self- or other-narratives (i.e. all or nothing thinking), which is characteristic of many psychopathologies and often the root cause of relationship problems.

Attachment and Coupling

There is a growing body of research that supports the view that adult romantic relationships seem to conform to earlier working models (see Peluso et al., 2004, 2009 for an overview), yet the systematic research into this process is relatively new (Sims, 2002). For example, studies on mate selection and attachment styles have supported Bowlby's prediction that, as anxious-avoidant children grow to adulthood, their intimate relationships are often characterized by such complications as withdrawal and emotional distance (Benoit & Parker, 1994). This can be explained from a neurobiological perspective: If an individual's brain is sculpted within the context of a dysfunctional family, then the functioning of that brain will reflect how it has been organized. In dysfunctional families, communication is usually dominated by the avoidance of thoughts and feelings; as a result, the neural systems of affect, cognition, sensation, and behavior for the family members are dissociated and disintegrated (Cozolino, 2006, 2016; Vangelisti & Maguire, 2002; Wylie & Simon, 2003).

In addition, two key chemical compounds that are only produced by mammals within the hypothalamus and are secreted through the pituitary gland (to the body), as well as through the limbic system and cortex (to the brain), are called *oxytocin and vasopressin*. Both chemicals are released by activities where there is touching, stimulation (affectionate, sexual, etc.) for the purpose of facilitating pair-bonding (Cozolino, 2016; Fishbane, 2015). "The large number of oxytocin and vasopressin binding sites in many areas of the amygdala plays a role in conditioned fear, autonomic regulation, HPA activation, and reproductive behavior" (Cozolino, 2016, pp. 118–119). According to Fishbane (2015),

> [Oxytocin] is released with gentle touch, massage, orgasm, childbirth, nursing and empathy. Oxytocin lowers cortisol, creating anxioltyic (anti-anxiety) effects. Present in both males and females, oxytocin, which has been called the "cuddle chemical"... facilitates bonding between mothers and babies; it bonds adult lovers as well.
>
> (p. 686)

Scientists can study the effects of oxytocin by spraying it in the nostril which bridges the blood-brain barrier. Subsequently, these couples showed greater feelings of empathy and trust, and reduction of conflicts in couples. Oxytocin elicits a "tend and befriend" response, which leads to greater connection with other people (Cozolino, 2016; Fishbane, 2015).

Vasopressin, for its part, also facilitates pair-bonding attachment by maintaining monogamy in mammals. It has an inverse relationship with testosterone, which can lead to a decrease in aggression for males in caregiving, intimate relationship. Vasopressin does this by targeting mate-guarding behavior and territoriality in males as well as in females (Cozolino, 2016;

Fishbane, 2015). Oxytocin and vasopressin are important for the synthesis of proteins that are involved in neoplastic processes in the brain that are associated with both in pair-bonding and (more broadly) learning social behaviors (Cozolino, 2006). In fact, Cozolino (2016) states that oxytocin and vasopressin release may also play a role in other social interactions, including success in psychotherapy. In particular, increases in oxytocin may create the opportunity for individuals to be more flexible and more open to change or being influenced.

The sum total of all of this neural shaping and imprinting is that the brain is conditioned to make immediate appraisals and place stimuli into categories according to patterns from the past. At the nucleus of the neural networks of our social brain, the amygdala organizes the appraisals of what we have learned from past interpersonal relationships and unconsciously appraises others in the context of these experiences. The OPFC houses the early social learning and attachments that shape our experiences and trigger past emotional memories, while the social brain (insula region and ACC) puts us in tune emotionally with the other person (Cozolino, 2006, 2016). Thus, when we meet new individuals, by the time we become conscious of them, our brain has already organized ways to think about them as friend or foe, as well as potential soul mate, depending on whether that individual fits a certain pattern (hence, love at first sight). This is a pattern that is generally passed down from generation to generation and influences the selection of a mate who conforms to, or is willing to cooperate with, the established pattern (Cozolino, 2006, 2016; Peluso et al., 2004; Sims, 2002; Vangelisti & Maguire, 2002).

However, the impact of these attachment styles and their impact on neurobiological structures don't end with merely being attracted to one another. In fact, it carries forward into the actual functioning (or lack of) within the relationship. One example of this is the reaction to emotional hurt and expression of conflict. People who have been hurt by a family member decrease their vulnerability to being repeatedly hurt by distancing themselves from individuals who hurt them as a way to avoid striking back (Vangelisti & Maguire, 2002). This behavior can be generalized in a person's approach to others, including their partners. In particular, issues relating to conflict avoidance and injury management become difficult to handle. However, according to Masuda and Duck (2002), arguments are just a matter of the ebb and flow of relationships and are necessary for maintenance and adaptation. So what happens when you have a person who is insecure and either chronically attacks or chronically avoids conflict? The relationship cannot progress, and it becomes stuck. Either one partner feels unresolved because the other won't engage in discussion and/or the other is in a constant state of terror because they believe that they are about to be hurt by their partner. According to Vangelisti and Maguire (2002), satisfaction within the relationship is the best predictor of persons able to overcome hurt and painful comments. Securely attached individuals have consistently been rated to have higher levels of relational satisfaction. The relationship described earlier, by comparison, becomes less and less satisfying. Thus, having secure attachments provides a mechanism for tolerating the inherent challenges in a relationship without being defeated by them.

Several longitudinal studies seem to attest to the long-term stability of and overall satisfaction within couples who have certain attachment style pairings. Kirkpatrick and Hazan (1994) found in a four-year study that participants who were rated as securely attached were most likely to be married and the least likely to be divorced or separated. Individuals who were anxious-ambivalent were most likely to be searching for a partner at both time intervals, while the avoidantly attached were most likely to be looking for a partner at all (Sims, 2002). In another study, Kirkpatrick and Davis (1994) looked at couple pairing with some interesting findings. First, they found no avoidant-avoidant pairings or anxious-anxious pairings, suggesting that the dynamics of two people with this type of insecure attachment style is probably too unstable to have any long-term viability. The researchers also found an interesting gender difference that moderated the long-term stability of relationships for certain pairings. It seemed that the relationships between anxious-ambivalent women and avoidant men were just as stable over a three-year period as securely attached couples, despite the fact that the anxious-avoidant pairing was rated most negatively in terms of satisfaction. Relationships between avoidant females and anxious-ambivalent males had the highest rates of endings (termination, separation, or divorce), but relationships with avoidant men (by either anxious or securely attached women) remained stable. This led the researchers to conclude that it was the women in these relationships who were chiefly responsible for the maintenance of the relationship. They have the power to end the relationship if they choose to, and yet, at the same time, these anxious-ambivalent women have the greatest fears of abandonment (Sims, 2002). This is a dynamic that many couple therapists encounter in pursuer-distancer couples.

This finding from this line of research (and others) raises the question: If you are a person with an insecure attachment, are you doomed to be chronically unhappy in relationships or alone? The short answer is unequivocally "no," but the process is not easy. We will discuss later in this chapter how individuals with insecure attachments can overcome and not create problems. Subsequent chapters in this book will specifically address issues related to the assessment and treatment of couples with insecure attachment.

Intersection between Physical Health and Research on Couples

We have reviewed the basic functioning and structures of the brain, the interrelationship of the brain and body, and the neurological basis for development of close relationships. In this section, we will attempt to show a link between close relationships and protection from stress-related illness. In addition, we will show how the biological correlates of stress (stress hormones) and attachment can have an effect on the long-term duration of close relationships. It should be noted that most of the research that will be presented is on married couples, as comprehensive studies on committed, long-term, unmarried relationships and health are relatively new and emerging.

Marriage, Health, and Longevity

Epidemiological data on physical and mental health show that marriage has a positive effect on individuals. But this relative health advantage appears to be more pronounced for men than for women. In the U.S., and with only a few exceptions, married men consistently have the lowest death rates for reported cases (Kiecolt-Glaser & Wilson, 2017; Robles & Kiecolt-Glaser, 2003). Among widowed and divorced white males, suicide rates are more than four and three times higher, respectively, than for married men, as are accident rates. For the most part, married women have the lowest reported death rates among the most common causes of death (Kiecolt-Glaser et al., 2002; Kiecolt-Glaser & Newton, 2001). We note from the outset that the majority of this research has been done using heterosexual married couples. What remains unknown, for the most part, is whether these findings are true in long-term, unmarried, committed partnerships, or in gay, lesbian, bisexual, or transgendered couples. It is an area where clearly more research is needed!

In terms of physical well-being, there are a number of interesting correlates of marital disruption. First, individuals who are married have the best overall health status. Married persons have substantially fewer physician visits per year than do never-married individuals. They have the fewest acute and chronic medical conditions as well as conditions that produce work disability. Routine habits, adequate nutrition, social support, intimacy, and possession of a reason for living are probable factors that confer this protection. Unmarried persons, by contrast, are likely to smoke more, drink more, and have more risk factors for illness or accidents (Kiecolt-Glaser & Wilson, 2017). For example, they are less likely to wear seat belts than their married counterparts. Single (never-married) persons report being ill more often than married individuals do. Those who are separated report being sick more often and having more physician visits than the married or the never-married. Similarly, the divorced and widowed are overrepresented among both inpatient and outpatient psychiatric populations. In addition, the relationship to health in women in long-term marriages was found to be stronger than that in men (Kiecolt-Glaser & Newton, 2001; Kiecolt-Glaser & Wilson, 2017).

In short, divorced and separated people have the worst health status of all marital groups. They have the highest rates of acute and chronic medical conditions, suffer the most partial work disability, take the most disability days per condition, and have the highest average physician utilization rate, and the longest hospital stays. Widowed persons rank second worst for overall health status. Research of recently separated or divorced men showed that both groups were less capable of fighting two common herpes virus infections, which suggested immuno-suppression difficulties, as predicted by the effects of stress hormones mentioned earlier (Glaser, Kiecolt-Glaser, Speicher, & Holliday, 1985). In fact, individuals who divorce and remarry successfully are less susceptible to health problems than are people who remain in an unhappy marriage. Remarriage appears to provide men, but not necessarily women, with increased resources for dealing with life stresses as well, with increased survival and mental health (Kiecolt-Glaser et al., 2002; Kiecolt-Glaser & Newton, 2001; Kiecolt-Glaser & Wilson, 2017). Lifestyle changes secondary to marital disruption also often result in psychosocial stresses that can have severe consequences. Some of these consequences are clinical depression, substance abuse, cardiovascular disease, and alterations in immune system functioning. Decreased immune functioning probably accounts for the known increases in the rates of death due to infections and cancers among the bereaved and divorced population (Kiecolt-Glaser & Newton, 2001). Finally, Robles, Slatcher, Trombello, and McGinn (2014) conducted a meta-analysis looking at the relationship between marital quality and health outcomes. Impressively, they found that the effect size was comparable to the effect sizes reported for exercise and diet on health outcomes, and that there was a lower risk for mortality in relationships with higher marital quality (Kiecolt-Glaser & Wilson, 2017; Robles et al., 2014).

Marital Discord and PNI

What impact can marital discord have on immunity? Researchers such as Kiecolt-Glaser et al. (2002) studied the impact of marital discord on immunity. Studying physiological samples from couples, they concluded that mental health affects physical health by altering the immune system, the body's defense against illness. Specifically, they found that women in unhappy marriages had suppressed immune functioning compared to women in more satisfying relationships. The most likely explanation for changes in physical well-being and longevity or life span of married persons is that marriage somehow protects spouses from stress. In a review of the literature, Kiecolt-Glaser and Wilson (2017) found that the quality of the marital relationship is significantly related to immunological, cardiovascular, and neurobiological wellness, and that a negative marital relationship correlated with symptom exacerbation in chronic, degenerative diseases. Marital harmony was associated with better sleep and fewer visits to a physician (Kiecolt-Glaser & Wilson, 2017). In addition, client's self-reported health was associated positively with measures of cohesion and marital quality, and negatively with spousal behaviors that are perceived as punishing and unsupportive. Thus, relationships characterized as unsupportive or punishing by partners resulted in poorer health. The researchers discovered that marital satisfaction seems to moderate the linkage between spouse responsiveness and pain outcomes by altering patients' appraisals and interpretations of their spouses' responses to communications of pain (Jaremka et al., 2013). Thus, it seems that if spouses are satisfied with their marriages as a whole, they will be more likely to view attempts to soothe as helpful. However, if the overall satisfaction with the relationship is low, then it will not be seen as beneficial. "A troubled marriage is itself a prime source of stress, while simultaneously limiting the partner's ability to seek support in other relationships" (Kiecolt-Glaser & Newton, 2001, p. 472).

Kiecolt-Glaser et al. (2003) conducted a ten-year longitudinal study in order to test the link between satisfaction, chronic stress, and marital status. They measured stress hormones in the blood of the participants, who were newlyweds, to ascertain if baseline differences could predict subsequent relationship status and satisfaction ten years later. The researchers found a robust relationship between stress hormones, marital satisfaction, and divorce. Specifically, the epinephrine levels of newlyweds who eventually got divorced were 34% higher at the beginning of the marriage than newlywed couples who stayed married ten years later. Even after a divorce, the epinephrine and norepinephrine levels of divorced couples were still 16% higher than married couples. In addition, stress hormones were related to marital satisfaction. In couples who were more dissatisfied, norepinephrine levels were 34% higher than for couples who had higher levels of marital satisfaction. Also, they found that negative reciprocity (the tendency to respond to negative behavior with negative behavior) was greater for newlyweds who eventually divorced than for couples who remained married. It would seem that individuals who are in stressful marriages go into the relationships with heightened levels of stress hormones. Although the researchers did not look at attachment styles, it is conceivable that individuals who are insecurely attached might be predisposed to have higher levels of stress hormones; may have disintegrated neural networks; may lack the ability to tolerate conflict in the relationship; and, as a result, may have a greater tendency to dissolve the relationship.

In short, being married offers a number of benefits to a person's health when compared to divorced, single, or separated individuals. It seems that the resulting stress of being divorced, single, or separated triggers the body's stress response. Given the destructive nature of chronic exposure to stress hormones, this can have long-term negative consequences for a person's health. However, being in a bad marriage can also be a significant and chronic source of stress, which would seem to negate the benefits or hasten the demise of the relationship (Jaremka et al., 2013). There is some hope, however. According to a study cited by Kiecolt-Glaser and Wilson (2017), when there was an improvement in marital quality, health symptoms also improved. In the next section, we will explore some of the ways that psychotherapy, and couples' therapy in particular, can have an impact on neurobiological, emotional, and physical health.

Psychotherapy, Neuroscience, Health, and Illness

A basic assumption of both neuroscience and psychotherapy is that optimal functioning and health are related to increasingly advanced levels of growth and integration (Wylie & Simon, 2003). On a psychological level, integration is the ability to experience the important aspects of life while employing a minimum of defenses. On a neurological level, this equates to the integration and communication of neural networks dedicated to emotion, sensation, and behavior (Cozolino, 2006, 2016). Growth and integration are optimized by a positive early environment; appropriate challenges; and parents who are supportive, capable, and willing to put feelings into words (Kandel, 1998). In fact, Cozolino (2002) proposes that neural growth and integration are uniquely enhanced by psychotherapy in the following ways:

1 The establishment of a safe and trusting environment.
2 Gaining new information and experiences across domains of cognitions, emotions, sensation, and behavior.
3 The simultaneous or altering activation of neural networks that are inadequately integrated or dissociated.
4 Moderate levels of stress or emotional arousal alternating with periods of calm and safety.
5 The integration of conceptual knowledge with emotional and bodily experience through narratives that are co-constructed with the therapist.
6 Developing a method of processing and organizing new experiences so as to continue ongoing growth and integration outside of therapy (see Table 2.4).

"These factors lead to positive affect regulation, biological homeostasis, and a quiet 'internal milieu' allowing for the consolidation of the experiences of subjectivity and a positive sense of self" (Cozolino, 2002, p. 27).

Table 2.4 Proposed Contribution of Psychotherapy to Neural Growth and Integration

1 The establishment of a safe and trusting environment;
2 Gaining new information and experiences across domains of cognitions, emotions, sensation, and behavior;
3 The simultaneous or altering activation of neural networks that are inadequately integrated or dissociated;
4 Moderate levels of stress or emotional arousal alternating with periods of calm and safety;
5 The integration of conceptual knowledge with emotional and bodily experience through narratives that are co-constructed with the therapist; and
6 Developing a method of processing and organizing new experiences so as to continue ongoing growth and integration outside of therapy.

Source: From *The Neuroscience of Psychotherapy: Rebuilding the Human Brain*, by L. J. Cozolino, 2002, New York, NY: W. W. Norton.

Brody et al. (2001) found some empirical support for the neural impact of psychotherapy. In a study investigating changes in brain structures in depressed patients taking paroxetine (Paxil) vs. depressed patients engaging in interpersonal therapy (IPT) for 12 weeks, using PET scans to measure metabolism of glucose (a sign of brain activity) in the PFC region of the brain (the area of the brain where higher executive functioning, as well as relationship and attachment capability, resides) and the temporal lobe of the brain (where speech processing commonly takes place), Brody and colleagues found that following treatment, depressed individuals in both groups showed relatively the same level of improvement over baseline readings. Specifically, metabolism in the PFC increased and metabolism in the temporal decreased toward normal levels. Brody et al. concluded that:

> it has been hypothesized that psychotherapy in general (as a learning experience) leads to changes in synaptic plasticity, through a retraining of implicit memory systems. Because a focus of IPT is improved socialization, areas of the brain associated with socialization may undergo an attenuation of neuronal connectivity during IPT.
>
> (2001, p. 638)

In a 2010 meta-analysis, Martire et al. looked at a limited number of studies of couples interventions for chronic illnesses. They found a small but significant effect size that showed the effectiveness in improved martial functioning, reduced levels of pain, and decreased depressive symptoms compared to either treatment as usual or individual patient-based interventions.

The process of psychotherapy encourages clients to behave in new ways, taking into account aspects of themselves of which they may be unaware; to take risks; and to consciously balance their focus between thoughts and feelings (Cozolino, 2016). At the same time, therapists become more attuned to the client's underlying issues and make certain interpretations of a client's behavior, or motive for behaving. Many times, these interpretations elicit often imperceptible changes in a client's affect or narrative, of which the client is unaware. These emotional and behavioral reactions to a particular interpretation may reflect the underlying neurobiological process of a defense mechanism. Through the course of therapy, however, as defenses are brought to conscious awareness, the subcortical networks that contain the negative memories and associated affect, as well as the cortical networks that organize the defense, become activated (Kandel, 1998). As the amygdala becomes reactivated and begins to alert the body to old dangers, the client becomes physiologically and emotionally aroused. This sequence could be the mechanism for regression as amygdaloidal systems are reactivated by old sensory-motor or affective memories, which are normally inhibited by the cortex as a defense but now can be dealt with in the safe environment of the therapeutic milieu (Cozolino, 2006, 2016; Wylie & Simon, 2003).

One of the more startling findings of the last few years demonstrating the impact of psychotherapeutic techniques on neuroanatomical structures was reported by Davidson and his colleagues (Davidson et al., 2003; Davidson & McEwen, 2012; Goldberg et al., 2018). They studied whether individuals who were trained in mindfulness meditative techniques could produce activity in the left PFC. Recall from the earlier discussion that activity in the left PFC is associated with positive affect, feelings of well-being, and approach-oriented behaviors. "The findings from this study are the first to suggest that meditation can produce increases in relative left-sided anterior activation that are associated with reductions in anxiety and negative affect and increases in positive affect" (Davidson et al., 2003, p. 569). In other words, this study provides some evidence that psychotherapy can be effective in creating positive changes in the brain. In addition, since the left PFC is associated with approach (vs. withdrawal) behaviors, couple therapists can use this technique to help couples who may be experiencing difficulty turning toward one another to use each other as a source of mutual support. This is also consistent with Story and Bradbury's (2004) finding that helping individuals to manage stress does not necessarily produce changes in their behavior toward their partner but that "*couples* who can learn to regulate affect under difficult circumstances while maintaining high levels of support should be less vulnerable" (p. 1151, *italics added*) to withdrawing from their partners. Finally, Davidson and McEwen (2012) noted that:

> There is a growing literature documenting functional and structural changes in the brain with specific interventions and training regimes. The behavioral evidence in support of such interventions and training provides a reasonable foundation for the exploration of neural changes that support these behavioral outcomes.
>
> (p. 692)

Taken together, this is good news for couples counselors. Several different types of social-emotional learning or stress management techniques, including a cognitive restructuring and relaxation (i.e. mindfulness) discipline, can have profound positive effects (Goldberg et al., 2018).

As mentioned earlier, the context in which an increased growth of neurons and neural network integration can successfully occur is one of increasing levels of affect tolerance and regulation, and the development of integrative narratives, which emerge out of the client-therapist relationship. In the context of empathic attunement, clients are encouraged to tolerate the anxiety of feared experiences, memories, and thoughts within a safe and structured environment in order for these elements to become included into conscious processing (Cozolino, 2006, 2016; Davidson & McEwen, 2012; Fishbane, 2015). In order for this conscious processing to take place, these interpretations, and the resulting neurological activation, need to undergo a process called working through. Working through refers to the fact that these experiences need to be stated, restated, and generalized to multiple situations and circumstances for the individual. This process connects new learning to multiple memory networks, reflects the expansion and stabilization of new associative matrices of memory, and allows for greater integration between the left and right hemispheres. In addition, the co-construction of a new, coherent narrative contains altered aspects of behavior, feelings, and self-identity. These altered aspects contain narrative pieces that were previously disintegrated within conscious awareness or autobiographical memory. When these aspects or issues are successfully worked through in therapy, the new self-narratives that are created serve as a way to retain new learning in consciousness, which continue to shape new, healthier ways of being (Cozolino, 2006, 2016; Wylie & Simon, 2003). With new discoveries in the realm of neuroscience and PNI, these processes are becoming clearer, and the reciprocal association to healthy relationships is illuminating the mechanisms and charting a roadmap for couple therapists to utilize in helping couples.

Therapy, Neuroscience, and Working with Couples

We have seen how all of Cozolino's six elements are successfully brought together within the framework of psychotherapy with individuals (Table 2.4). The same process is just as useful with couples, if not more so, since couple therapy, presumably, seeks to integrate both the individual's narrative and the couple's narrative. Secrets, collusion, and coalitions are all examples of destructive forces within a relationship and represent a type of disintegration of the couple's narrative. Couples who are able to provide coherent narratives that incorporate affect with events and who are able to give a balanced account of both their own and their partner's actions seem to fare better in solving problems and resolving differences. Whereas those couples who provide narratives that are characterized by all-or-nothing thinking and seek to blame the other person for their troubles are more destructive and less likely to solve problems cooperatively. Usually, the narratives of these couples are either disjointed and permeated with emotionality or are coldly logical, detached, and rigidly fixed. Both extremes are indicative of insecure attachment styles, as well as the lasting effects of these styles on individuals' particular brain functioning (Fishbane, 2015; Wylie & Simon, 2003). Again, the question arises: "Is there no hope?" Are partners who may have insecure attachment styles necessarily doomed to relate to others in a destructive fashion? It should be obvious that what is needed is that the individual must go through some process of working through (probably in therapy) in order to achieve better integration of the neural networks and (personal or couples) narrative. In fact, Cozolino (2002) reports that:

> Attachment research suggests that adults can create secure attachments for their children despite their own negative experiences as children. Earned autonomy, through enhanced integration of early experiences,

> results in the ability to serve as a safe haven for one's children. Thus, the powerful shaping experiences of childhood can be modified through subsequent personal relationships, psychotherapy, and self-awareness.
> (p. 210)

This is especially relevant for individuals who may have been the victims of abuse but have worked through the trauma and now have a sense of "perspective" or autonomy. This autonomy allows a person to mediate the effects of these early attachment models. In other words, for individuals who were insecurely attached, there are opportunities through supportive relationships and emotional effort to be able to modify the effects of early relationships. Again, it seems that for couples, couple therapy may hold a unique answer to these problems of communication, attachment, and satisfaction, provided that the therapist has a firm grounding in both the psychological and neurobiological aspects of dysfunction.

At the same time, couple therapists are becoming aware of the role of the autonomic nervous system in arousal, particularly when in conflict. Providing feedback to couples about the "fight or flight" response when heart rate reaches over 100 beats per minute, and/or when blood oxygen levels go below 95% is important in helping couples reduce the incidents of harsh and hurtful statements "in the heat of the moment." Gottman and Gottman (2017) routinely use finger-clip style pulse oximeters (which measures HR and O_2 saturation) with pre-set alarms to give couples immediate feedback on their level of arousal and ability to have constructive dialogue.

Psychotherapists are clinical neuroscientists who create individually tailored enriched environments to enhance brain development (Cowan & Kandel, 2001; Cozolino, 2016; Fishbane, 2015). Using a combination of language, empathy, emotion, and behavioral experiments, therapists attempt to promote neural integration. By reading, interpreting, and reflecting the nonverbal communication of the right hemisphere and exploring illusions, distortions, and defenses in the left hemisphere, therapists are skilled at teaching clients to become aware of their unconscious processing and guiding them in co-creating a coherent narrative. It is also possible that the therapist's encouragement, enthusiasm, and caring support and reinforce learning through the enhanced production of neurotransmitters such as dopamine, serotonin, and norepinephrine, which support neural plasticity and neural growth (Cozolino, 2006, 2016; Fishbane, 2015; Wylie & Simon, 2003).

Putting it All Together: Summary of Relevant Physical and Neurological Issues for Couple Therapists

We realize that a lot of complex information has been provided in this chapter. It might leave the reader saying, "Okay, what next? What do I do with this information when I am seeing a couple?" First, we think that this is only the beginning of knowledge that couple therapists should have, but we think that it is knowledge that *all couple therapists must have.* Second, we believe that this knowledge must be incorporated within a larger theoretical framework of how couples function and how to conduct couple therapy. Specifically, the key points of this chapter for couple therapists are:

1 The PFC and OPFC are critical for regulating personality, emotion, attachment, and relationship functioning. If a member of a couple has had any trauma to this area, there may be some physical explanation for behavioral deficits.
2 The left hemisphere of the PFC is associated with positive affect and relational connectedness. The right hemisphere of the PFC is associated with fear and suspicion and emotional withdrawal. Some individuals, by family or environmental conditioning, genetic predisposition, or some combination of the two, favor one or the other. This can explain differing emotional styles or reactions in two different partners, which may be complimentary or in conflict.
3 The social cortex of the brain (the cingulate cortex and insula cortex) is important for feeling empathy, taking another person's perspective, and understanding ambivalence. In addition, the neurochemicals oxytocin and vasopressin are the chemicals of bonding that are released with pleasurable touch and warmth.
4 There are ways to stimulate the left hemisphere in order to produce a decrease in tension and in emotional withdrawal. Several therapeutic techniques, such as mindfulness (meditation) and couple-based stress-coping techniques, have been demonstrated to help. Hence, couple therapy can have a positive effect on neuroanatomical functioning.
5 Chronic stress can have a serious impact on physical health and subsequently on the health of the relationship. There is significant evidence that suggests that a good marriage is good for a couple's physical health but that a dissatisfactory marriage can create either physical or psychological health problems for one or both partners. However, divorce has been shown to be even worse on the health of individuals.
6 Attachment theory provides a holistic way for understanding some of the patterns observed in relationships, which ties the family-of-origin dynamics of each individual and his or her unique view of the world to how each person behaves in an intimate relationship in order to meet his or her needs. This approach has gained acceptance in both the neurosciences and the couple therapy realms, and provides a critical linkage between the two. This will be demonstrated throughout the latter chapters of this book.
7 Couple therapists can have a demonstrable effect on multiple levels at the same time: The relationship level, the individual level, the strategic level, and the biological/neuronal level.

Perhaps it is all of these factors that make couple therapy such a unique and powerful milieu for effecting lasting change for couples, individuals, and families. We present the following case example to illustrate some of these elements.

Ellen (23) and Matt (22) have been dating for about three years. They met in college and have continued to see each other after graduation, despite the fact that they now live several states away from one another. While Ellen pursues a master's degree in Public Administration, Matt is beginning his career in an executive training program with a financial investment firm. This has led to some tension in the relationship as they have had to go for long periods of time apart from one another. They both express a desire to be with one another but acknowledge that this cannot happen right now. In terms of the future, both Ellen and Matt have said that they have talked about the prospect of marriage one day but have no real plans at this point.

Ellen and Matt have gotten into a pattern of arguing a lot whenever they get together. Both admit that they are not sure why it happens, but it usually lasts for an entire day (which wastes the little time that they have together). Ellen states that the argument usually starts over something small and escalates until they stop speaking to one another. Eventually, one person will apologize to the other, and they will see that their fight was silly and then enjoy their time together. Recently, however, their arguments have grown in frequency and intensity. For example, in the past, they would never argue over the phone, but now, they have begun to have arguments when they phone each other.

The final straw came several weeks ago when Matt was scheduled to visit Ellen's apartment. Upon his arrival, he found that she was not there to meet him. He waited for more than an hour and a half without hearing from her. He tried to reach her on her cell phone but could only get her voicemail. They had argued the night before about dinner plans over the weekend, and Matt thought that Ellen was doing this to spite him. Eventually, he got back in the car and drove home. Ellen, for her part, got called into an impromptu meeting with her professor in order to correct some last-minute information on an important grant. She attempted to reach Matt but could not get through to him. As he drove back home, he refused to take her calls until he arrived at his apartment. When he found out the miscommunication, he was embarrassed but still felt hurt and perseverated on the fact that Ellen didn't try hard enough to reach him. They went for several days without talking to one another, and when they did, they agreed that they needed couples counseling.

The couple therapist recognized that the majority of the issues that Ellen and Matt had were unsolvable at this time simply because neither one was in a position to make the kind of commitment decision to address the problem. In fact, the only thing that would solve some of their problems was time (i.e. if they stay together after they finish their entry-level training, then they could decide what to do next about their relationship). The therapist, following Gottman's (1999) work, suggested that Ellen and Matt try to solve only problems that they could solve now. This allowed the couple to bypass the tension that each felt about the uncertainties of the future.

Next, the therapist decided to address the conflict between Ellen and Matt. After taking a thorough history and deciding that there were no other psychiatric disorders, the therapist discussed the neurobiology of their conflict. After explaining how the different hemispheres of the PFC regulate positive and negative emotions, he told them that they had a choice about whether the left or right hemisphere of their brain would win. He explained that when they got together after long absences, their excitement about seeing each other also tended to activate the right hemisphere of the PFC. This would create an increased level of suspicion as well as a tendency toward withdrawing from one another, which fosters more suspicion and more withdrawal from the other person. A vicious cycle would ensue until either Mark's or Ellen's left hemisphere was activated, and one person would try to de-escalate the conflict by turning toward the other.

The therapist made some recommendations for Matt and Ellen to develop some agreed-upon procedures and/or rituals for helping them to overcome their anxieties about being together, not thinking about the future of their relationship, enjoying the moment, and activating each other's left hemisphere (i.e. positive affect, relational closeness) through a mindfulness exercise (e.g. deep-breathing mediation together, talking about three things that they are excited about doing during the time that they are going to spend together, etc.). In this way, Ellen and Matt can use their time together in a way that will be helpful and not hurtful to the relationship until they are in a position to make a decision on the deeper relationship issues.

Concluding Note: Into the Future … Genetics and Therapy

We have attempted to demonstrate how neuroscience, PNI, and advances in attachment theory have all impacted the field of couple therapy. In addition, it is increasingly clear that any practitioner in the future will have to have an understanding of the complex intertwining of these various biological facets in our clients. However, as we begin to peer into the not-too-distant future, we can speculate that neuroscience will continue to unlock the secrets of the brain. As researchers begin to take full advantage of the completed sequencing of the human genome, coupled with the finding of stem cells in the adult brain, the future might hold the promise of recreating the neurons of the cortex and perhaps effecting change on the cellular level (Cowan & Kandel, 2001; Cozolino, 2016; Fishbane, 2015; Jacobs, van Praag, & Gage, 2000; Nemeroff, 2013; Sapolsky, 2003). We have also shown how neurobiology affects the coupling process and vice versa. Perhaps the most tantalizing finding is the idea that couple therapy may be able to physically impact the very neural connections that make up our thought processes. The ultimate outcome of this scientific endeavor is not yet known, but we are confident that as these discoveries are made, psychotherapy as a whole, and couple therapy in particular, will have a place in understanding and remedying the various disorders of the human condition.

References

Ainsworth, M. D. S., Blehar, M. C., Waters, E., & Wall, S. (1978). *Patterns of attachment: A psychological study of the strange situation.* Hillsdale, NJ: Lawrence Erlbaum.

Belsky, J., & Nezworski, T. (1988). Clinical implications of attachment. In J. Belsky & T. Nezworski (Eds.), *Clinical implications of attachment* (pp. 3–17). Hillsdale, NJ: Lawrence Erlbaum.

Benoit, D., & Parker, K. C. H. (1994). Stability and transmission of attachment across three generations. *Child Development, 65*, 1444–1456.

Bowlby, J. (1969). *Attachment and loss: Vol. 1 attachment.* London, England: Hogarth Press.

Bowlby, J. (1980). *Attachment and loss: Vol. 3 loss, sadness and depression.* New York, NY: Basic Books.

Bowlby, J. (1988). *A secure base.* New York, NY: Basic Books.

Brody, A. L., Saxena, S., Stoessel, P., Gillies, L. A., Fairbanks, L. A., Alborzian, S., … Baxter, L. R., Jr. (2001). Regional brain metabolic changes in patients with major depression treated with either paroxetine or interpersonal therapy: Preliminary findings. *Archives of General Psychiatry, 58*(7), 631–640.

Cohen, S., & Herbert, T. B. (1996). Health psychology: Psychological factors and physical disease from the perspective of human psychoneuroimmunology. *Annual Review of Psychology, 47*, 113–142.

Cowan, W. M., Harter, D. H., & Kandel, E. R., (2000). The emergence of modern neuroscience: Some implication for neurology and psychiatry. *Annual Review Neuroscience, 23*, 343–391.

Cowan, W. M., & Kandel, E. R. (2001). Prospects for neurology and psychiatry: Research opportunities for specific diseases and disorders. *Journal of the American Medical Association, 285*(5), 594–600.

Cozolino, L. J. (2002). *The neuroscience of psychotherapy: Rebuilding the human brain.* New York, NY: W. W. Norton.

Cozolino, L. J. (2006). *The neuroscience of human relationships: Attachment and the developing social brain.* New York, NY: W. W. Norton & Company.

Cozolino, L. J. (2016). *Why therapy works: Using your mind to change your brain.* New York, NY: W. W. Norton & Company.

Davidson, R. J. (2001). Toward a biology of personality and emotion. *Annals of the New York academy of sciences, 935*, 191–207.

Davidson, R. J., Kabat-Zinn, J., Schumacher, J., Rosenkranz, J., Muller, D., Santorelli, S. F., … Sheridan, J. F. (2003). Alterations in brain and immune function produced by mindfulness meditation. *Psychosomatic Medicine, 65*, 564–570.

Davidson, R. J., & McEwen, B. S. (2012). Social influences on neuroplasticity: Stress and interventions to promote well-being. *Nature Neuroscience, 15*(5), 689–695.

Fishbane, M. D. (2015). Couple therapy and interpersonal neurobiology. In A. S. Gurman & N. S. Jacobson (Eds.) *Clinical handbook of couple therapy* (3rd ed., pp. 681–701). New York, NY: Guilford Press.

Fuchs, E., & Flügge, G. (2003). Chronic social stress: Effects on limbic brain structures. *Physiology and Behavior, 79*, 417–427.

Glaser, R., Kiecolt-Glaser, J., Speicher, C., & Holliday, J. E. (1985). Stress, loneliness, and changes in herpes virus latency. *Journal of Behavioral Medicine, 8*, 249–260.

Goldberg, S. B., Tucker, R. P., Green, P. A., Davidson, R. J., Wampold, B. E., Kearny, D. J., & Simpson, T. L. (2018). Mindfulness-based interventions for psychiatric disorders: A systematic review and meta-analysis. *Clinical Psychology Review, 59*, 52–60. doi:10.1016/j.cpr.2017.10.011

Gottman, J. M. (1999). *The marriage clinic*. New York, NY: W. W. Norton.

Gottman, J. M. (2011). *The science of trust: Emotional attunement for couples*. New York, NY: W. W. Norton.

Haley, J. (1980). *Leaving home: The therapy of disturbed young people*. New York, NY: McGraw-Hill.

Hostinar, C. E., Davidson, R. J., Graham, R. J., Graham, E. K., Mrocek, D. K., Lachman, M. E., ... Miller, G. E. (2017). Frontal brain asymmetry, childhood maltreatment, and low-grade inflammation at midlife. *Psychoneuroendocrinology, 75*, 152–163. doi:10.1016/j.psyneuen.2016.10.026.

Hughes, D. A. (1997). *Facilitating developmental attachment*. Northvale, NJ: Jason Aronson.

Jacobs, B. L., van Praag, H., & Gage, F. H. (2000). Depression and the birth and death of brain cells. *American Scientist, 88*, 340–345.

Jaremka, L. M. (2017). Close relationship, immune function, and health: Understanding the clinical importance of distressed relationships. In J. Fitzgerald (Ed.), *Foundations for couple therapy: Research for the real world* (pp. 197–205). New York, NY: Routledge.

Jaremka, L. M., Lindgren, M. E., & Keicolt-Glaser, J. E. (2013). Synergistic relationships among stress, depression, and troubled relationships: Insights from psychoneuroimmunology. *Depression and Anxiety, 30*, 288–296. doi:10.1002/da.22078

Johnson, S. M. (2002). *Emotionally focused couple therapy with trauma survivors: Strengthening attachment bonds*. New York, NY: Guilford Press.

Kandel, E. R. (1998). A new intellectual framework for psychiatry. *American Journal of Psychiatry, 155*(4), 457–469.

Kiecolt-Glaser, J. K., Bane, C., Glaser, R., & Malarkey, W. B. (2003). Love, marriage, and divorce: Newlyweds' stress hormones foreshadow relationship changes. *Journal of Consulting & Clinical Psychology, 71*(1), 176–188.

Kiecolt-Glaser, J. K., McGuire, L., Robles, T. F., & Glaser, R. (2002). Psychoneuroimmunology: Psychological influences on immune function and health. *Journal of Consulting and Clinical Psychology, 70*(3), 537–547.

Kiecolt-Glaser, J. K., & Newton, T. L. (2001). Marriage and health: His and hers. *Psychological Bulletin, 127*(4), 472–503.

Kiecolt-Glaser, J. K., & Wilson, S. J. (2017). Lovesick: How couples' relationships influence health. *Annual Review of Clinical Psychology, 13*, 421–443. doi:10.1146/annurev-clinpsy-032816-045111

Kirkpatrick, L. A., & Davis, K. E. (1994). Attachment style, gender, and relationship stability: A longitudinal analysis. *Journal of Personality and Social Psychology, 66*, 502–512.

Kirkpatrick, L. A., & Hazan, C. (1994). Attachment styles and close relationships: A four-year prospective study. *Personal Relationships, 1*, 123–142.

Krause, A. M., & Haverkamp, B. E. (1996). Attachment in adult child-older parent relationships: Research, theory, and practice. *Journal of Counseling & Development, 75*(2), 83–92.

Lapate, R. C., Samaha, J., Rokers, B., Hamzah, H, Postle, B. R., & Davidson, R. J. (2017). Inhibition of lateral prefrontal cortex produces emotionally biased first impressions: A transcranial magnetic stimulation and electroencephalography study. *Psychological Science, 28*(7), 942–953.

Lekander, M. (2002). Ecological immunology: The role of the immune system in psychology and neuroscience. *European Psychologist, 7*(2), 98–115.

Lieberman, A. F., & Pawl, J. H. (1988). Clinical applications of attachment theory. In J. Belsky & T. Nezworski (Eds.), *Clinical implications of attachment* (pp. 327–351). Hillsdale, NJ: Lawrence Erlbaum.

Martire, L. M., Schultz, R. Helgeson, V. S., Small, B. J., & Saghafi, E. M. (2010). Review and meta-analysis of couple-oriented interventions for chronic illness. *Annals of Behavioral Medicine, 40*(3), 325–342. doi:10.1007/s12160-010-9216-2

Masuda, M., & Duck, S. (2002). Issues in ebb and flow: Management and maintenance of relationships as a skilled activity. In J. H. Harvey & A. Wenzel (Eds.), *A clinicians guide to maintaining and enhancing close relationships* (pp. 13–42). Mahwah, NJ: Lawrence Erlbaum.

Miller, G. E., & Cohen, S. (2001). Psychological interventions and the immune system: A meta-analytic review and critique. *Health Psychology, 20*(1), 47–63.

Miller, G. E., Cohen, S., & Ritchey, A. K. (2002). Chronic psychological stress and the regulation of pro-inflammatory cytokines: A glucocorticoid-resistance model. *Health Psychology, 21*(6), 531–541.

Naumova, O. Y., Lee, M., Rychkov, S. Y., Vlasova, N. V., & Grigorenko, E. L. (2013). Gene expression in the human brain: The current state of the study of specificity and spatio-temporal Dynamics. *Child Development, 84*(1), 76–88. doi:10.1111/cdev.12014

Nemeroff, C. B. (2013). Psychoneuroimmunoendocrinology: The biological basis of mind–body physiology and pathophysiology. *Depression and Anxiety, 30*, 285–287. doi:10.1002/da.22110

Nohlen, H. U., van Harreveld, F., Rotteveel, M., Lelieveld, G. J., & Crone, E. A. (2013). Evaluating ambivalence: Social-cognitive and affective brain regions associated with ambivalent decision-making. *Social Cognitive Affective Neuroscience, 9*(7), 924–931. doi:10.1093/scan/nst074

Peluso, P. R., Peluso, J. P., Buckner, J. P., Kern, R. M., & Curlette, W. L. (2009). Measuring lifestyle and attachment: An empirical investigation linking individual psychology and attachment theory. *Journal of Counseling and Development, 87*, 394–403.

Peluso, P. R., Peluso, J. P., White, J. F., & Kern, R. M. (2004). A comparison of attachment theory and individual psychology: A review of the literature. *Journal of Counseling and Development, 82*(2), 139–145.

Ploog, D. W. (2003). The place of the triune brain in psychiatry. *Physiology and Behavior, 79*, 487–493.

Rabellino, D., Densmore, M., Harricharan, S., Jean, T., McKinnon, M. C., & Lanius, R. A. (2018). Resting-state functional connectivity of the bed nucleus of the stria terminalis in post-traumatic stress disorder and its dissociative subtype. *Human Brain Mapping, 39*, 1367–1379. doi:10.1002/hbm.23925

Ray, O. (2004). How the mind hurts the body. *American Psychologist, 59*(1), 29–40.

Robles, T. F., & Kiecolt-Glaser, J. K. (2003). The physiology of marriage: Pathways to health. *Physiology and Behavior, 79*, 409–416.

Robles, T. F., Slatcher, R. B., Trombello, J. M., & McGinn, M. M. (2014). Marital quality and health: A meta-analytic review. *Psychological Bulletin, 140*, 140–187.

Sagi, A., Donell, F., van Ijzendoorn, M. H., Mayseless, O., & Aviezer, O. (1994). Sleeping out of home in a kibbutz communal arrangement: It makes a difference for infant-mother attachment. *Child Development, 65*, 992–1004.

Sapolsky, R. M. (2003). Altering behavior with gene transfer in the limbic system. *Physiology and Behavior, 79*, 479–486.

Sims, L. J. (2002). The application of attachment theory to individual behavior and functioning in close relationships: Theory, research, and practical applications. In J. H. Harvey & A. Wenzel (Eds.), *A clinicians guide to maintaining and enhancing close relationships* (pp. 63–80). Mahwah, NJ: Lawrence Erlbaum.

Sperry, L. (2002). The relevance of the biological dimension and biopsychosocial therapy in maintaining and enhancing close relationships. In J. H. Harvey & A. Wenzel (Eds.), *A clinicians guide to maintaining and enhancing close relationships* (pp. 313–320). Mahwah, NJ: Lawrence Erlbaum.

Sperry, L., & Carlson, J. (1999). *The disordered couple*. Philadelphia, PA: Brunner/Mazel.

Sroufe, L. A. (1988). The role of infant-caregiver attachment in development. In J. Belsky & T. Nezworski (Eds.), *Clinical implications of attachment* (pp. 18–38). Hillsdale, NJ: Lawrence Erlbaum.

Story, L. B., & Bradbury, T. N. (2004). Understanding marriage and stress: Essential questions and challenges. *Clinical Psychology Review, 23*, 1139–1162.

Urry, H. L., Nitschke, J. B., Dolski, I., Jackson, D. C., Dalton, K. M., Mueller, C. J., … Davidson, R. J. (2004). Making a life worth living: Neural correlates of well-being. *Psychological Science, 15*(6), 367–372.

Vangelisti, A. L., & Maguire, K. (2002). Hurtful messages in family relationships: When the pain lingers. In J. H. Harvey & A. Wenzel (Eds.), *A clinicians guide to maintaining and enhancing close relationships* (pp. 43–62). Mahwah, NJ: Lawrence Erlbaum.

Verschueren, K., Marcoen, A., & Schoefs, V. (1996). The internal working model of the self, attachment, and competence in five-year-olds. *Child Development, 67*(5), 2493–2511.

Wylie, M. S., & Simon, R. (2003). Discoveries from the black box: How the neuroscience revolution can change your practice. *Psychotherapy Networker, 27*, 1–5. Need rest of this reference.

3 Functional and Dysfunctional Couples Relationships

LEARNING OBJECTIVES

In this chapter, the reader will learn the following:

1 The qualities of healthy, functioning relationships.
2 The skills and principles of healthy, functioning relationships.
3 Levels of happiness, life satisfaction, and relationship satisfaction over the time.
4 The impact of specific psychiatric disorders on relationship functioning.

In the previous chapter, we described the impact of biological and neuroscience influences on the health and relational functioning of couples. We continue the discussion in this chapter by describing the relational aspects present in healthy and unhealthy couples. Next, we survey the essential qualities and skills that effective couples exhibit and compare this to the way average functioning couples adapt to major life events. Then we look at specific DSM-5 disorders that impact relational functioning and consider some of the treatment options for these couples.

Healthy and Effective Relationships

What are the qualities that characterize health and high-functioning families and couples? This question is of considerable importance to both researchers and those practicing couple therapy. Families with healthy relationships have commitment, appreciation for one another, and good communication; spend time with one another; are spiritually well; and have good coping abilities (Stinnet & DeFrain, 1985). More recently, a national survey of participants that reflected the population of the U.S. (as measured by the 2000 census) described the communication style, conflict, and relational commitment of married, divorced, and cohabitating partners (Stanley, Markman, & Whitton, 2002). The survey found that partners who do not withdraw from conflict (solve problems constructively) and have positive interactions (communications) with one another tended to have better quality and more satisfying relationships. In addition, partners who report higher levels of commitment spend less time thinking about alternate partners or ending the relationship, did not feel trapped by their relationships, and reported greater satisfaction.

We believe that it is important for a therapist to know the factors involved in creating and keeping a good relationship going. Professionals are often trained to identify and treat pathology, rather than promote a successful and satisfying marriage. Couple therapists cannot articulate treatment goals that ensure a long-term relationship if they do not clearly understand the components of effective relationships. Therefore, we begin this chapter with an overview of the skills needed to make a relationship successful. Many of the problems that couples present occur when skills are absent. These presenting problems are resolved as skills are developed.

Qualities of the Healthy Couple

Couples who have been successful in maintaining satisfying relationships for many years possess certain characteristics. According to Beavers (1985), healthy couples have beliefs that include the following attributes: (1) Relative rather than absolute truth, (2) understanding of subjective reality, (3) the basic neutrality or benignity of people's motives, (4) human encounter as rewarding, (5) a system's point of view, and (6) value and meaning in the human enterprise. Table 3.1 summarizes each of these attributes.

Beavers (1985; Hampson & Beavers, 2012) also maintained that observable patterns differentiate healthy from unhealthy couples. These patterns include a modest, overt power difference; the capacity for establishing clear

Table 3.1 Attributes of Healthy Couples

1	*Relative rather than absolute truth.* Successful couples believe that people are limited and finite and therefore never possess the unchallengeable truth.
2	*An understanding of subjective reality.* These couples realize that individuals can see the same events differently.
3	*The basic neutrality or benignity of people's motives.* Successful couples have a fundamental belief that people close to them have decent and healthy motives.
4	*Human encounter as rewarding.* These couples believe that even miserable situations will get better.
5	*A systems point of view.* Successful couples assume that any individual needs a group, a human system, for individual definition, coherence, and satisfaction; causes and effects are interchangeable; any human behavior is the result of many variables; because humans are limited and finite, a social role of absolute power or helplessness prohibits many of the needed satisfactions to be found in human encounters.
6	*Value and meaning in the human enterprise.* Healthy couples have a belief in something that is larger than themselves. It may be provided by conventional religion or by a commitment to some passionate cause. The content seems unimportant; having a belief that directs energy and provides community with others outside the family is vital.

Source: Adapted from Beavers (1985).

boundaries; operation mainly in the present; respect for individual choice; skill in negotiating; and the sharing of positive feelings.

The work of John Gottman and his laboratory support many of Beavers's research and others' assertions about successful healthy marriages and unhealthy ones (Driver, Tabares, Shapiro, Nahm, & Gottman, 2003; Gottman, 2011; Gottman & Gottman, 2017; Gottman & Levenson, 2002). Gottman and his associates are singular in their empirical observation and verification of these relational qualities and in providing therapists with powerful information about relationships and their processes. We will provide an overview of his clinical findings here, and then, in Chapter 8, discuss his research and outcome findings in more detail. Simply put, they found that "success or failure of a marriage depends not on whether there is conflict, but rather how conflict is handled when it does occur" (Driver et al., 2003, p. 493). Couples who successfully handle conflicts can be grouped into one of three typical styles: Validators, volatiles, and avoiders.

As shown in Table 3.2, validator couples tend to be more supportive of each other and emphasize the couple ("we-ness") and resolve conflict through compromise. Volatile couples tend to have explosive conflicts with heated arguments. However, these arguments do not become ugly or personal but are energetic and passionate (as compared to unhealthy couples we will describe later). In addition, their interactions continue to be affectionate, warm, and often have constructive humor in them. The third category is the avoider couples, who ignore or downplay the negative interactions and choose to emphasize the positive qualities of the relationship. When they must acknowledge a difference between them, these couples will often "agree to disagree" and move forward (Driver et al., 2003; Gottman, 1994, 1999). An additional hallmark of these healthy relationship conflict styles is the ratio of five positive statements or behaviors to one negative statement or behavior. Even in the midst of a disagreement, these successful couples keep to this ratio, which communicates respect and affection for the other person (Gottman, 1994; Gottman & Gottman, 2017; Gottman & Levinson, 2002).

By comparison, Gottman and his colleagues have also observed the qualities and interactions of unhealthy couples (Driver et al., 2003). When these

Table 3.2 Description of Healthy Couples' Conflict Styles

1 *Validator couples*: Have a tendency to talk out problems; be supportive of each other; validate the other's position/feelings/opinions; have a strong sense of mutual respect; and resolve conflict through compromise.
2 *Volatile couples*: Have a tendency to have explosive conflicts with heated arguments; are high energy and passionate; express affection and warmth with equal passion; and view each other as equals and attempt to persuade by argument.
3 *Avoider couples*: Have a tendency to ignore or downplay the negative interactions; choose to emphasize the positive qualities of the relationship; will often "agree to disagree" and move forward.

Source: Adapted from Driver et al., (2002), Gottman (1994), Gottman (1999).

Table 3.3 Description of Gottman's "Four Horsemen of the Apocalypse"

1 *Criticism:* A broad and sweeping character attack that seems unfair to the other person and usually includes the words *always* and *never.*
2 *Contempt*: Characterized by corrosiveness, hostility, and disrespect. It can be conveyed with nonverbal behavior (i.e. eye rolls, scowls, looks of disgust) or directly by verbal behavior (i.e. mockery, insults, sarcasm). It usually provokes defensive responses or retaliation and cuts off any attempt for immediate reconciliation or de-escalation.
3 *Defensiveness:* The hallmark of a stalemate in the relationship, where each person is protecting themselves against the other's contemptuous attacks. Defensiveness always leads to more retaliation and escalation and can provide an excuse to place blame on the other person for the negative cycle (which provokes further attack).
4 *Stonewalling*: When one member simply withdraws completely for almost all interactions with the other partner. Usually a signal that one or both partners is feeling overwhelmed or emotionally flooded and must shut the other out (even if they are not being negative) for self-protection.

Source: Adapted from Driver et al., (2002), Gottman (1994), Gottman (1999).

couples get into conflict, they often exhibit one of the "Four Horsemen of the Apocalypse," which Gottman contends predicts relational difficulty (Gottman, 1999). The Four Horsemen are: Criticism, contempt, defensiveness, and stonewalling (see Table 3.3). *Criticism* is different from complaints, which exist in every relationship and are limited to a specific incident (e.g. "I'm upset that you forgot our anniversary") while respect for the other person is maintained. Criticism is a more broad and sweeping character attack, and usually includes the words *always* and *never* (e.g. "You are so selfish, you never think about anyone other than yourself").

Contempt is the next horseman and is even more corrosive since it adds a sense of hostility and disrespect to the criticism. It can be conveyed with nonverbal behavior (i.e. eye rolls, scowls, looks of disgust) or directly by verbal behavior (i.e. mockery, insults, sarcasm). An example of contempt might be "Oh, I can see that your diet is really melting the pounds off. How much have you lost, 2 maybe 3 pounds in the last four months?" Since these contemptuous behaviors usually provoke defensive responses or retaliation, it short-circuits any attempt by the other person to try to reconcile or scale back from the conflict (Driver et al., 2003; Gottman, 1999).

Defensiveness is the third of the horsemen and the hallmark of a stalemate in the relationship. Even though it may seem that each person is merely protecting themselves against the other's attack, defensiveness always leads to more retaliation and escalation. It gives one person a way to place blame on the other person for the negative cycle, which provokes further attack: "Congratulations, you've lost another job because of your drinking." "Oh yeah? Well if you weren't so lazy and spent so much money on crap, I wouldn't *have* to drink so much!"

The final horseman is *stonewalling*. This is when one member simply withdraws completely for almost all interactions with the other partner. This carries the message of "I don't want to have *anything* to do with you." This is usually a signal that one or both partners are feeling overwhelmed or emotionally flooded and increases the polarization between the two. There is no communication at any level and very little hope of the couple de-escalating without outside help (i.e. couple therapy). Gottman (2011) reports that when all the four horsemen are present, he can predict with over 90% accuracy which couples will get divorced (Carrere, Buehlman, Coan, Gottman, & Ruckstuhul, 2000; Gottman & Levinson, 2002). Other factors, such as the presence of emotional disengagement and negative reciprocity in the couple's interactions, also add to the negative atmosphere of relationships in trouble (Driver et al., 2003; Gottman, 1994).

Skills of Marriage

Paralleling Gottman's work, Carlson and Dinkmeyer (2003) also suggested that the success or failure of a relationship is due, in part, to the utilization of certain relational skills. A couple begins a relationship with an assortment of skills, some effective and some ineffective. The skills needed to enrich a relationship are listed in Table 3.4.

These skills are reflected in the healthy conflict styles, i.e. empathy, encouragement, acceptance (Table 3.2), and are the opposite of the "Four Horsemen" (Table 3.3). Many times, a couple's problems are a matter of deficits in these critical skills that require some remediation through therapy. While these problems do not rise to the level of a clinical diagnosis, they do require attention or else the relationship will suffer. However, before these skills can be enhanced, couples must have sufficient readiness for change. There are at least five principles of skill-building and change necessary for successful change in relationships. Briefly, these principles are (1) developing and maintaining a good relationship require a time commitment, (2) the specific skills that are essential to a healthy relationship can be learned, (3) each partner has a responsibility to change, (4) feelings of love and caring that had decreased

Table 3.4 Skills of Healthy Marriage

1	They individually accept responsibility for their behavior and self-esteem.
2	They identify and align their personal and marital goals.
3	They choose to encourage each other.
4	They communicate their feelings with honesty and openness.
5	They listen empathically when feelings are expressed.
6	They seek to understand the factors that influence their relationship.
7	They demonstrate that they accept and value each other.
8	They choose thoughts, words, and actions that support the positive goals of their marriage.
9	They solve marital conflicts together.
10	They commit themselves to the ongoing process of maintaining an equal marriage.

Source: Adapted from Carlson and Dinkmeyer (2003).

or disappeared often return once behavior changes, and (5) small changes are very important in bringing about big changes (Carlson & Dinkmeyer, 2003). See Table 3.5.

Unfortunately, many clients come to therapy believing that the opposite is true, due to either poor parental role models or bad experiences in relationships. These couples expect the other person to do the changing or think that once the feeling of love has subsided, the relationship is over. Couple therapists who are successful working with couples understand these principles and work to counteract these ideas in their work. In the following chapters, these skills will be elaborated on, in one way or another, in various approaches to couple therapy.

Table 3.5 Principles for Successful Change in Relationships

1 *Developing and maintaining a good relationship requires a time commitment.* For any relationship to succeed, it must be made an important priority. Each couple determines how that priority is defined and established. For some couples, priority means a large quantity of time spent together. In another relationship, a large portion of quality time is necessary. At different stages in the couple or marital relationship (early marriage, family, empty nest) more or less time is available.

2 *The specific skills essential for a healthy relationship can be learned.* Once a couple understands how to build a successful relationship, the partners can develop the skills that create a positive, rewarding relationship. The variable, as in most learning situations, is how long such skill acquisition takes, not if acquisition is possible. Some couples can acquire skills very quickly; others take a bit longer. Nevertheless, all couples can learn and grow.

3 *Each partner has a responsibility to change.* The first step in modifying a relationship involves creating a commitment to change. Each partner needs to understand what his or her role is in the marriage and what he or she needs to do to make it different. Patience and allowance for different rates of change are helpful. Each partner often has difficulty seeing just how he or she is involved in creating a less than satisfying relationship but often has no difficulty identifying what the other partner is or is not doing.

4 *Feelings of love and caring that had decreased or disappeared often return once behavior changes.* Romantic feelings, intimacy, and love often diminish in a relationship. When feelings change, many couples believe that the relationship is over. This need not be the case. A change in feelings usually means that the partners are not being reinforced and that the relationship deserves a higher priority. It is important at such time that they act as if all were well, and by acting as if their relationship is the intimate, satisfying relationship they desire, new behaviors and feelings can be established.

5 *Small changes are very important in bringing about big changes.* A happier relationship results from many small changes during a period of time. Often people attempt to bring about a change by focusing on a large task or a major accomplishment. Although this may help, it is often not necessary. Small changes will produce just as big a result. In any given day, there are hundreds of possible choices that can create small changes in a relationship.

Source: Adapted from Carlson and Dinkmeyer (2003).

Happiness, Life Satisfaction, and Relational Satisfaction over Time

What happens to a couple's happiness and life satisfaction in the years following major life events such as (1) getting married, (2) getting divorced, (3) having a child, or (4) becoming unemployed? Research is providing useful answers to this question, particularly a very large meta-analysis of 188 prospective studies (Luhmann, Hofmann, Eid, & Lucas, 2012). We review the findings of this major meta-analysis and suggest implications of it for couple therapy (Luhmann et al., 2012).

This mega study followed 65,911 individuals and assessed their adaption to these major life events, an average of five times over several years. In some studies, this spanned more than a decade. These were queried about well-being in terms of (a) happiness or affective well-being, that is, their level of happiness and unpleasant feelings, such as a depressed mood, but not clinical depression; (b) life satisfaction or cognitive well-being, that is, their satisfaction with their lives; and (c) relationship satisfaction, that is, satisfaction with their relationship with their partner.

The main finding was that average functioning individuals felt a little worse just after the event occurred but, over time, reported feeling better each time they were asked. Specifics varied somewhat on the type of the event. With regard to getting married and happiness, it was found that individuals became happier in anticipation of the wedding. Later, these married individuals reported lower satisfaction after the marriage than they did before, returned back to the level of satisfaction they felt before their wedding. Over time, on average, happiness did not change, meaning that these partners did not get either happier or less happy over the course of their marriage. With life satisfaction, there was an increase from just before the wedding to just after. But then life satisfaction decreased continually over time. With relationship satisfaction, it was also found to decrease from just before the wedding to just after. Over the course of the marital relationship, relationship satisfaction continued to decrease slightly at about the same rate as overall life satisfaction (Luhmann et al., 2012).

For the other events, such as divorce, childbirth, or job loss, individuals may have felt a bit better right after divorce or childbirth but not job loss. However, degree of happiness depended on the particular questions asked. Then, over time, individuals either felt no differently, or they reported feeling even worse (Luhmann et al., 2012).

Findings for divorce were somewhat different. It was found that levels of happiness were already decreasing for those who were moving toward divorce. Not surprisingly, getting divorced resulted in being happier relative to how increasingly miserable they had felt year after year when they were married (Luhmann et al., 2012).

So what are the implications of this meta-analysis for the couple therapist, particularly of the finding that marriage did not result in being happier or more satisfied over the long run? In fact, for life satisfaction and relationship satisfaction, the trajectories over time headed in the less satisfied direction. First, it should be noted that this is normative data, meaning that it reflects the functioning of average individuals and couples rather than healthy and highly functioning relationships. Second, it can be assumed that those without involvement in couples enrichment activities were not likely to experience the same happiness, life satisfaction, and relationship satisfaction trajectories as couples that with such involvement. Third, and most important, couples who have been involved in couple therapy and workshops or activities that foster couples enrichment – and continue to practice these skills – are more likely to experience increasing – rather than decreasing – trajectories of happiness, life satisfaction, and relationship satisfaction.

Impact of Mental Disorders on Relational Functioning

We turn our attention away from subclinical populations to couples who are experiencing dysfunction or discord in a relationship as a result of one partner having a serious disorder such as depression, mania, phobias, alcoholism, or schizophrenia. Having a partner with a serious DSM-5 symptom disorder (such as major depressive disorder, bipolar disorder, or a psychotic disorder) or a personality disorder (American Psychiatric Association, 2013) is likely to strain the couple's relationship. The relationship prior to, during, and following the onset of such disorders in the spouse is influenced by many factors and is quite variable across couples. To assume that the interaction between the partners brought on or caused the mental disorder and symptoms in the other spouse is often an unwarranted assumption.

In some cases, the couple's interaction neither caused nor precipitated the disorder in a spouse who was biologically predisposed to such symptoms. In other cases, the couple's interaction was a stressor that contributed to the onset of symptoms in a vulnerable partner. Occasionally, the couple's interaction does not initially stress the vulnerable partner, but as symptoms emerge, the relational interaction becomes dysfunctional, which results in further distress and more symptoms. Finally, in some relationships, psychiatric symptoms can be fully explained as a function of an interactional pattern between the partners. Whatever the case, the diagnostic and symptom picture of the psychiatrically disordered partner and characteristics of the other partner are related to the symptoms in the marital interaction and should influence treatment planning. As we move forward in this chapter, we will discuss the diagnostic system for individual pathology and some of the more common psychiatric disorders that couples present in therapy.

Relational Dysfunction – Individual Disorder Classification Model

Because of the mix of individual dynamics and relationship dynamics, the differences among couples presenting for therapy can be considerable. In addition to relational dysfunction, an increasing number of both partners presents with a DSM-5 diagnosis. DSM-5 has specific diagnostic labels and codes for both relationship dysfunction and symptom and personality disorders. Therapists do well to recognize these differences early, even in the first session. A useful way of understanding and classifying individual disorders and relationship dysfunction is the Relationship Dysfunction – Individual Disorder Classification Model (Sperry, in press). We have found it particularly in assisting trainees in understanding the interaction between individual and couples dynamics and psychopathology. Essentially, couples tend to fall in one of these four categories.

1. Relationship Dysfunction Only

In this instance, couples with no diagnosable DSM-5 symptom or personality disorder are classified here. Accordingly, the therapists may identify and code Relationship Distress with Spouse or Intimate Partner (V61.10) or Spouse or Partner Abuse (995.82) (APA, 2013). The focus of couple therapy is primarily on relational dysfunction.

2. Relationship Disorders Associated with Individual Disorders

In this instance, the relationship is still the primary focus of treatment. Part of the reason for treating the relational problem is that it is likely that this problem evokes or influences a more serious problem in one of the individual couple members. This level of analysis is used when both relationship and individual disorders are detected: For example, Relationship Distress with Spouse or Intimate Partner (V61.10) and Borderline Personality Disorder (BPD; 301.83) (APA, 2013).

3. Individual Disorders with Little or No Relational Impact

In this instance, an individual disorder is central in the presenting problem. For example, when there is another episode of Major Depressive Disorder (296.33) (APA, 2013) in a partner and it is effectively controlled with brief hospitalization or medication.

4. Individual Disorders Strongly Influenced by Relationship Factors

In this instance, the individual disorder is the primary focus and the continuing focus of attention, but additional treatment is needed for the couple in order to promote a rapid and full recovery. For example, the onset of the manic phase of Bipolar I Disorder (296.42) (APA, 2013) in one partner engenders considerable distress in the other partner for several days until the phase runs its course, and the distress resolves.

DSM-5 Diagnostic System

In the past, couple and family therapists have been disenchanted with diagnostic classification systems that focus on individual dynamics while overlooking the family and environmental dynamics. Today, couples and family therapists can no longer ignore diagnostic considerations. Diagnosis provides therapists critical information about client functioning and guides therapists in collaborating with other health professionals. In fact, diagnostic competence increases the likelihood that couple therapists will recognize and address the full range of couples issues, including individual dynamics and psychopathology (Sperry, in press).

In this section, we will present some of the more common diagnoses that couples present with symptom disorders and personality disorders. In some descriptions, only one spouse has a diagnosis, while other descriptions are for couples where both partners have a diagnosis. We do not present an exhaustive list of each diagnosis (or combination of diagnoses), nor a detailed treatment manual for these conditions in this short space. This requires much more in-depth discourse than can be afforded here. However, what we do offer is a cross section of the underlying dynamics in the relationships with more common diagnoses and some of the treatment considerations. These should be combined with the assessment and treatment methodologies presented in Chapters 9 and 10.

Couples with Symptom Disorders

Bipolar Disorder

Approximately 1%–2% of the population in the U.S. suffer from bipolar (or manic-depressive) disorder, which is characterized by cyclical periods of mania or elevated mood that can be marked by accelerated speech, grandiosity of thought, and decreased need for sleep (APA, 2013; Glick, Berman, Clarkin, & Rait, 2000). Normal periods of mania can last approximately a week or more, followed by periods of depression. The depressive mood is exemplified by a loss in pleasure for activities, decreased energy, feelings of worthlessness, and liability of mood. The period of time between cycles can vary widely from months and days to hours and moments. In terms of their personality structure, individuals suffering with bipolar disorder seem to tend toward expressions of strong emotion, a high need for achievement, and accentuating or sharpening their perception of experiences (Peven & Shulman, 1998).

Obviously, living with the highs and lows of a partner with bipolar disorder can have profound effects on the relationship (Milkowitz & George, 2002). The response of the partner depends on the severity of moods and the behavior of the affected partner, as well as the expression of the personality traits of the affected partner. If the symptoms are mild, then the pressure toward staying together is increased, but if the interpersonal dynamics of the couple place enough stress to trigger the mood swings, then the tendency for couples is toward ending the relationship. In the majority of cases, if the first episode occurs during the relationship, the partners stay together, "usually the nonbipolar (*sic.*) spouse learns to recognize the signs of a developing episode and quickly seeks help for the sick mate, who often does not recognize the need for intervention" (Peven & Shulman, 1998, p. 18).

In terms of treatment, pharmacological agents, such as mood stabilizers, are effective; however, given the particularly high noncompliance rate (over 50%), they may not be sufficient. Glick et al. (2000) suggest a psychoeducational couples intervention approach. This approach is based on four premises: (1) Medication compliance, (2) engagement in the psychoeducational couples intervention treatment, (3) change in partner's negative attitudes, and (4) an increase in problem-solving skills. Each of these variables seems to address factors that promote stabilization and mediate the onset of episodes within the relationship. Milkowitz and George (2002) reported the treatment gains that a course of psychoeducational treatment had on the functioning of a couple with bipolar disorder. They concluded that "educating a couple about what behaviors of the ill partner can and cannot be attributed to the bipolar disorder, and enhancing the couple's communication and problem-solving behavior in the aftermath of the episode have the potential to improve post-episode functioning of the couple" (Milkowitz & George, 2002, p. 681). In particular, this approach seems to work well with couples that have more severe illnesses to cope with or a concomitant personality disorder.

Anxiety Disorders

The DSM anxiety-related disorders include panic disorder, agoraphobia, other phobias, and generalized anxiety disorders (APA, 2013). Each of these disorders is characterized by hyperactivity of the nervous system and some form of psychomotor agitation. In many of these disorders, there is a particular trigger for the anxiety attack (fear of something). The triggering event may be real (e.g. seeing a spider) or imagined (e.g. imagining a spider), but the client nonetheless feels a terrorizing and overwhelming sense of being out of control. In some cases, the panic or anxiety attack can seem to come "out of the blue" with no discernable trigger. Most recently, neuroscientists have begun to show a strong familial link with some anxiety disorders which may suggest a biological or genetic component to the illness (Cozolino, 2002; Grisel, Rasmussen, & Sperry, 2006). For the most part, however, anxiety disorders can be successfully treated with medication (antianxiolytics). In addition, cognitive behavioral techniques have also been shown to be significantly additive in the treatment of anxiety disorders, particularly through thought-stopping techniques and systematic desensitization (Carter & Shultz, 1998).

As with the couples that deal with partner suffering from bipolar disorder, relationships that must cope with an anxiety disorder have considerable strains on them as well. In addition, patterns established in the relationship may actually reinforce some of the behaviors. For example,

> a mutually reinforcing system may exist in which the agoraphobic person is kept in a dependent state by a significant other, usually a spouse, to cover up the latter's anger and dependence. The symptom bearer finds a symbolic, dysfunctional way of communicating with and controlling the spouse (e.g., a wife who refuses to leave the house thus forces her husband to stay at home and take care of her).
>
> (Glick et al., 2000, p. 499)

Therefore, the therapist must make decisions about whether to refer the client for medication initially, begin individual therapy, initiate couples and family therapy, or come up with some combination of these. A thorough assessment of the couple early in treatment can determine which level is warranted. The decision whether and if couple therapy is warranted depends on the particular disorder, the severity of the symptoms, and the amount of disruption it is causing to the system. In terms of effectiveness with anxiety disorders, couple therapy in conjunction with medication can be more effective in modifying behavior than individual therapy because often the interaction between the illness and the partner is overlooked in treatment.

Couples treatment of an anxiety disorder can consist of psychoeducation of the partners to the nature and progression of the illness and of providing support as they deal with the symptom behaviors. Therapy may also include working through issues of communications and problematic interactions with the couple that may be involved in the maintenance of the anxiety disorder. A final indication for couples treatment is the impact that the positive progress of the partner can have on the non-disordered partner. Often, new patterns and behaviors can "change" the partner and the relationship, forcing the non-disordered partner to adjust to an unfamiliar way of dealing. Providing support can forestall any systemic resistance that may result from the progresses in treatment (Carter & Shultz, 1998).

Depressive Disorders

It is estimated that by 2020, major depression will emerge as the second leading cause of disability worldwide (Gollan, Friedman, & Miller, 2002). Up to 20% of adults will likely experience a major depressive disorder at least once in their lifetimes. Symptoms include depressed mood, anhedonia (the loss of pleasure), sleep disturbance (either too much or too little), and an inability to concentrate (APA, 2013). A major depressive disorder can develop either slowly or quickly, and a person who previously displayed good mood and social functioning may begin to develop personality changes and have difficulty with social situations. Once an individual has one depressive episode, the likelihood for experiencing another is significantly increased.

Episodes of major depressive disorder, if left untreated, can last between 6 and 12 months. However, "most depressed persons in the community remain untreated, or are treated in the primary care settings" (Coyne, Thompson, & Palmer, 2002, p. 27). For this reason, Palmer and Coyne (2003) advocate for the routine screening for depression by physicians using accurate screening and assessment tools.

Although it has been long acknowledged that depression tends to be related to relational distress, the exact nature of the relationship between the two is complex (Coyne et al., 2002). Much of the literature has been a "chicken or egg" debate with no real consensus. Do depressed partners cause the relationship to be distressed, or do dissatisfying relationships cause partners to become depressed? Coyne et al. (2002) also suggest that aspects of an individual's personality (i.e. a deficient interpersonal style) may not only cause relationship distress but may consequentially lead to the development of depression. In looking at the differences between couples with a depressed partner and couples without a depressed partner, Coyne et al. (2002) found that depressed couples had more relational distress and more destructive methods of coping with conflict. In addition, there seems to be fewer exchanges of affection, more sexual dissatisfaction, and a greater number of disagreements about finances as well as boredom with the relationship. Glick et al. (2000) and Gollan et al. (2002) also cite the role that contextual factors in the relationship (such as concomitant substance abuse or violence) play in the development and persistence of depression. Hence, involving the partner in therapy can make a significant difference in understanding and treating depression when the client is involved in a close relationship (Coyne et al., 2002; Gollan et al., 2002). We present the following case example to illustrate this further:

Janice is a 29-year-old woman who was diagnosed with (severe) depression. She currently lives with her 28-year-old partner of four years, Chris. Janice has been in individual therapy for the last two and a half years for depression after a suicide attempt and brief hospitalization following the death of her mother from an aggressive case of breast cancer only three months after her diagnosis. Recently, Janice has been relatively stable but has expressed concerns that Chris is spending more time at work and with friends, rather than spending time with her. Her individual therapist has suggested that couple therapy might be helpful in addressing Janice's concerns.

In therapy, Chris expressed feeling anxious about Janice's condition despite her improvement. Specifically, Chris related concerns that Janice would relapse soon into a bout of depression: "She never goes longer than this without a bad turn." Chris also expressed feelings of frustration about being Janice's primary caretaker when she was depressed and that the stress of Janice's condition was taking its toll on the relationship: "It wasn't like this in the beginning, but now it has all changed, I'm always worrying about what is coming next." In addition, Chris began to admit feeling ambivalence and guilt about the future of the relationship, stating, "I'm just not sure if this is the way I want to live the rest of my life. But if I leave now, I would be abandoning her and that would be devastating."

In this scenario, the depressive disorder occurred in conjunction with the relationship but not as a result of it. The main precipitating factor was the death of Janice's mother and her reaction to it. While Janice may have had some predisposing factors for depression, neither she nor Chris was cognizant of it. The couple therapist would need to address the ongoing management of Janice's condition, the impact of the changes to Janice on the relationship, and the level of commitment that Chris has to the relationship. Specifically, the issue of continuing the relationship (or not) and rebalancing the emotional needs of each partner would be processed in couples sessions.

Depression is one of the most commonly studied illnesses for the effectiveness of treatment. Antidepressants are one of the most common classes of drugs to be prescribed today, and have had moderate success treating major depression. However, in head-to-head comparisons between various schools of therapy, medication management, and a combination of the two, the results have consistently shown that there is no difference in improvement between therapy and medication but that the combination of the two modalities is generally more effective than the constituent models. Research conducted by the National Institute of Mental Health Treatment of Depression Collaborative Research Program that compared cognitive behavioral therapy (CBT), medication with clinical management (IMI-CM), and interpersonal therapy (IPT) did not find any differences in the degree of symptom reduction (Elkin et al., 1989). Additional analyses of the data suggest that clients rate greater satisfaction with IPT than clients who received medication, and that clients who received IPT and CBT were able to recognize and cope with the symptoms of depression as well as maintain interpersonal relationships better than with medication (Blatt, Shahar, & Zuroff, 2002). This is an intriguing finding, especially in light of Kirsch, Moore, Scoboria, and Nicolls's (2002) research reinvestigating the data from the original Food and Drug Administration (FDA) clinical trials for antidepressant medication and calling into question some of the treatment effectiveness of the medication compared to placebo.

Despite these insights into the treatment of depression, it can be a very difficult disorder to treat (Grisel et al., 2006). According to Gollan et al. (2002), approximately 30%–40% of clients do not fully respond to therapy. In addition, among successfully treated individuals, approximately half experience a recurrence of depressive symptoms within two years. Several practitioners have attempted to develop couples-based treatments to address depression. "Couple therapy for depression is based on the premise that maladaptive relationship processes contribute to depression and that depression alters relationship health. Because depression and relationship distress reciprocally and influence each other, the aim of treatment is to change relationship patterns to alleviate depression" (Gollan et al., 2002, p. 656). Research comparing couples-based treatments to individual-based treatment has found that when a combination of cognitive and behavioral techniques is used in couple therapy, the treatment gains are superior to individual CBT (Gollan et al., 2002). As a result, Coyne et al. (2002) suggest that couple therapy should be the primary mode of therapy when both partners are available.

Psychotic Disorders

The range of psychotic disorders in DSM-5 are grouped under "Schizophrenia Spectrum and Other Psychotic Disorders" and include schizophrenia, schizoaffective disorder, delusional disorder, catatonia, psychotic disorder due to a general medical condition, and other specified schizophrenia spectrum and psychotic disorders. All of these behaviors share common, psychotic elements including a tendency to hallucinate, have periods of gross impairment of functioning, show impairment of reality testing, evidence delusional thinking, and have difficulty managing relationships (Maniacci & Sperry, in press). These disorders are considered to be an organic brain disorder with strong familial (genetic) links and an environmental component that can potentiate the individual's vulnerability toward a psychotic episode.

The two most dysfunctional pairings are the psychotic-controlling couple and the psychotic-dependent couple where the dynamics of the relationship are as detrimental as the individual pathology (Maniacci & Sperry, in press). The dynamics of the psychotic-controlling relationship reflect a controlling individual who was most likely a parentified child and thus feels a sense of fulfillment taking care of the "sick" partner. However, there is also a lack of fulfillment as their needs cannot be met by their partner. The psychotic partner lives with a sense of "learned helplessness," as he or she cannot outperform the controlling partner in managing their lives. As a result, issues of power, achievement, and perceptions of responsibility become valid treatment concerns.

The dynamics of the psychotic-dependent relationship revolve around the dependent partner's need for a relationship with "someone special" and recognition of the specialness of the prepsychotic presentation of the other person. The dependent partner (like the controlling partner) takes good care of the needs of the psychotic partner but (unlike the controlling partner) is not apt to make very many demands of the psychotic partner. The conflicts that these couples present have more to do with issues of dependability, loyalty, and intimacy, as the dependent partner feels shortchanged by the increasing inability of the psychotic partner to meet her dependency needs for attention and affection. When both types of couples reach a certain threshold, the expression of emotion can become toxic and possibly trigger a major psychotic crisis.

Here is a five-step treatment process for the couples intervention when dealing with psychotic episodes (Maniacci & Sperry, in press). The treatment process includes managing the psychosis, engaging the nonpsychotic partner, exploring the relational dynamics, modifying the individual dynamics, and revisiting the management of the psychosis. As the treatment progresses, the acute issues give way to the deeper underlying couple and individual issues, particularly with psychotic-controlling and psychotic-dependent couples. Even in treating a psychotic-nonpsychotic couple, where the psychotic episodes are usually the primary focus of treatment, this process can also be useful.

Couples with Personality Disorder Diagnoses

Two common couple types presenting for couple therapy are the Histrionic-Obsessive couple and the Dependent-Narcissistic couple (Nurse & Sperry, 2012). Couples in which one partner presents with BPD are increasingly common (Sperry, 2011). We begin this section with a discussion of BPD.

Borderline Personality Disorder

According to the DSM-5, individuals with BPD are characterized by an instability of self-image, an inability to maintain interpersonal relationships, a self-damaging impulsivity (with sex, spending, substance abuse, etc.), intense and inappropriate displays of anger, and a chronic sense of emptiness (APA, 2013). The exact etiology of BPD is not known, though some researchers have indicated the possibility of a biological connection, particularly given that approximately 75% of patients with BPD are women (Lockhart, 1998). However, there is no definitive research to support this, to date. Family pathology seems to play a role in the development of BPD, particularly in families characterized by alcoholism, affective disorders, or other personality disorders, early loss of a parent (through separation or death), or sexual abuse (Sperry, 2011).

It is in close, romantic relationships that the full range of BPD behaviors is displayed. Partners with BPD are likely to be involved with intense, emotional, and unstable relationships. The consequences of poor reality testing are that clients with BPD tend to become very intimate, especially sexually, very quickly without being very discriminating in their choice of partners. Frequently, they will be attracted to partners who are emotionally unavailable due to circumstances (such as engaging in relationships with married men) or are constitutionally unable to reciprocate affection (individuals who have a narcissistic personality disorder) to them (Lockhart, 1998; Solomon, 1998).

As a result, the underlying feelings of abandonment, projective identification, and splitting that are hallmarks of individuals with BPD are allowed to continue (please see Chapter 4 for a full explanation of these terms in the context of object-relations theory). Behaviorally, these clients manifest their feelings with "all or nothing" sentiments (indicative of splitting) of either believing that the partner is supremely wonderful, and they are detestable and unworthy or, if the partner has disappointed them in some way, that they are being grossly mistreated, and the partner is horrible and cruel. This is usually accompanied with seemingly uncontrollable bouts of rage directed at the partner and often can be accompanied with suicidal gestures. Often, it is at this point that the couple is referred for couple therapy (Sperry, 2011).

Therapy with BPD individuals can be a challenge for many practitioners because of the mood lability, rejection sensitivity, and rageful reactions common in these individuals. In couples work, if the partner with BPD feels that the therapist is siding with the other partner in the slightest, she is likely to become enraged and threaten to end therapy. Individuals with BPD will not refrain from attacking the therapist in session and questioning their capability, which often creates overlapping (and sometimes overwhelming) transference and countertransference issues (Solomon, 1998).

Treatment suggestions for avoiding traps or triangles include: seeing the couple together and not promising confidentiality for individual disclosures, honoring each individual's struggle (addressing the unique individuality of the partners, understanding the unique expressions of anxiety), proceeding slowly with the therapeutic relationship, and working with the specific issues endemic to the disorder (confronting client's aggression, avoiding self-disclosure, being directive with the clients). Therapists working with these couples must be able to maintain clear boundaries and possess sufficient patience to weather the emotional storms that will be brought into session. Fortunately, establishing and maintaining a therapeutic relationship that fosters increasing levels of the couples' trust and problem-solving can greatly increase the prospect for long-term success (Solomon, 1998).

Histrionic-Obsessive and Dependent-Narcissistic Couples

The dynamics of both histrionic-obsessive and dependent-narcissistic couples are remarkably similar; the partners are "made for one another" and fit together "like puzzle pieces" (Nurse & Sperry, 2012; Sperry & Maniacci, in press). These styles represent the prototypical relationship dynamic that presents in couple therapy: One person is needy and employs a variety of elaborate behaviors to get their needs met by their partner, while the partner is distant and aloof, unable to meet the emotional demands of the other partner. There are, of course, important distinctions between the two couple patterns. The histrionic personality is self-focused and self-absorbed, whereas the dependent personality is other-focused and lacks self-confidence. In the other partner, the differences are also salient. The obsessive partner is rigid, inflexible, and preoccupied with control, while the narcissistic personality is characterized by grandiosity, being self-absorbed, arrogance, and lacking empathy (Nurse & Sperry, 2012; Sperry & Maniacci, in press). Yet, the similarities of these two relationship patterns seem to outweigh the differences, particularly in the beginning of the relationship, as the obsessive and narcissistic partner appears outwardly cool and confident, while the histrionic and dependent partner seems keenly attentive and overtly affectionate toward the other partner. Each person attracts the other with these traits, which, in time, have a dramatically negative impact on the relationship.

Over time, the destructive personality traits of manipulation and dishonesty (from both partners) build resentment and distance in the relationship. In the histrionic-obsessive couple, the histrionic partner feels anger and hurt at the obsessive partner's inability to be authentic and fill her needs for deeper connection. Meanwhile, the obsessive partner senses the other partner's desire and cannot fulfill it. The histrionic partner's constant demands for attention may cause the obsessive partner to withdraw further, or to devote time and attention to something else (Sperry & Carlson, 2000). The histrionic partner senses this withdrawal and usually reacts with rage or by escalating the demands for intimacy, which perpetuates the destructive cycle.

In the dependent-narcissistic couple, a similar dynamic emerges where the dependent person realizes that their bid for more affection and attention by the narcissistic partner will not be met; however, unlike the histrionic personality, the dependent partner will not usually resort to escalating behavior, choosing to remain calm instead. The narcissistic partner, if rebuffed by the dependent partner, simply shrugs off the attack knowing that the other person won't leave (Nurse & Sperry, 2012). However, the ultimate cost is a lack of intimacy for both couples and an unfulfilled, dissatisfying relationship. We present the following case example to illustrate this:

> Alan and Margaret had been married for 15 years when they came for couple therapy. Alan (43 years old) initiated therapy as a result of his suspicions because his wife (age 39) was spending an inordinate amount of time at their church assisting the recently widowed pastor. Alan complained that Margaret was "not spending any time with me" and that she was "ignoring her responsibilities" with their two children (ages 12 and 10). Margaret objected to Alan's accusations, saying that she had been complaining of Alan's aloofness throughout the marriage and that she had tried to get him to come to therapy several times, only to have him tell her that she was "the one with the problem" and not him. Margaret defended her activities by saying that Alan was jealous because she had found "a ministry" for herself, which meant that at least once a week Alan would have to be responsible for an evening with the kids (meal, bedtime, etc.).

Margaret denied any adulterous relationship with her pastor but did admit that she enjoyed the fact that he "treats me like a person and not a maid." Margaret elaborated that Alan recently got upset and verbally abusive because she did not have time to go to the dry cleaners and pick up his shirts, which led to a protracted fight and Alan accusing Margaret of having an affair.

In fact, Alan was attracted to Margaret because she was "hot," and they had "great sex." Margaret was very helpful and got Alan organized early in his career. Now Alan was very successful in his job, which allowed Margaret to stay at home and primarily raise the children. Alan had expectations that Margaret would always be at home taking care of the things that he didn't have the time or inclination to do, which allowed him to concentrate on his career. Whereas Margaret was initially attracted to Alan because he seemed so confident and self-assured, she was now resentful of his indifference to her concerns, his self-absorbed lifestyle, and his controlling behavior.

There was considerable tension between what each partner wanted from the other and what each partner had traditionally gotten. Alan needed Margaret to be his organizer, and when this was threatened by her getting involved in other activities, he felt "second class," which was horrifying to him. As a result, he attempted to use guilt to get her to return to her previous role. Margaret wanted Alan to be her "rock" and security, but rocks are seldom warm and attentive. As a result, he was unmoved by her complaints and need for attention from him and, later, freedom to grow and try new things. For the couple therapist, the challenge was to avoid the trap of siding with either partner. If the therapist were overly sympathetic with Margaret, Alan would likely discontinue therapy, and if the therapist appeared to take Alan's side, Margaret would likely feel devalued and unappreciated, and conclude that therapy could not help them.

Sperry and Maniacci (in press) recommend a type of couple therapy, for couples with personality disorders, particularly for histrionic-obsessive couples, that comprises three phases, each with specific treatment goals. They are (a) establishing a working therapeutic alliance, (b) rebalancing the couple relationship, and (c) modifying individual dynamics in the partners. In addition, a phase devoted to specific skill-building may be warranted following Phase Two if the couple presents with significant deficits in communication or other unhealthy relationship skills. The specific goal of the first treatment phase is to relate to the couple several key assumptions that are designed to short-circuit the more destructive concepts that the couple generally holds. These assumptions include that neither partner is crazy nor the sole cause of the problem. This allows the couple to engage the therapist and to refrain from using techniques to distance themselves from each other or the treatment. In the second phase, rebalancing the relationship, the treatment goal is focused on issues of boundaries, power, and intimacy. Techniques borrowed from structural and strategic therapies would be effective in creating the systemic changes necessary for long-term success. In the final phase, the shift is more toward psychodynamic issues with the goal of helping the couple to be more honest and direct in their communication with one another, without distortion, exaggeration, and attempts to manipulate or control one another (Sperry & Maniacci, in press). An Adlerian or cognitive behavioral approach may be used in order to achieve this goal with the couple (Sperry, 2011; Sperry & Carlson, 2000). This approach could work equally well with the dependent-narcissistic couple.

Considerations for Including the Family in Treatment

Often when an individual is diagnosed with a mental or medical illness, it is the family (or significant other) that becomes the primary caregiver. Until recently, these crucial support systems were not considered to be part of the treatment regimen or involved in the treatment planning. In addition, these individuals were not usually included for treatment or intervention. With the advent of the consumer movement in mental health treatment, this has begun to change, and families are targeted for intervention in order to help guide them through the process of dealing with and caring for a loved one. Glick et al. (2000) present common goals of treatment when a family is confronted with a member who is ill. These goals are:

1 Accept the reality of the illness and understand the current episode.
2 Identify the current episode stressors.
3 Identify potential future stressors within and outside the family.
4 Clarify stressful family interactions.
5 Plan strategies for managing or minimizing future stressors.
6 Accept the need for continued treatment.

It is believed that the family system can provide a healthy context where treatment gains from the medical establishments (hospitals, etc.) can be extended. In addition, by targeting the family system for treatment and support, any maladaptive patterns that could interfere with recovery can be addressed and remediated.

Concluding Note

The characteristics, skills, and roles of functional and dysfunctional relationships have been presented. Because partners develop medical and mental illnesses that have an effect on couples' functioning, a solid working knowledge of these disease processes is important. Unfortunately, medical providers tend to focus on pathology and thus have a limited understanding of the impact of illness on relationships. Furthermore, they have little awareness of what constitutes an effective marriage relationship. Fortunately, effective therapists recognize the determinants of a healthy relationship as well as factors that undermine it. Their expertise extends to healing dysfunctional relationships and fostering healthy ones. The process involves building on existing strengths and developing skills to produce functional relationships that embrace the mind and the body. We now turn to an examination of some of the behavioral and biological influences on functional and dysfunctional couples.

References

American Psychiatric Association. (2013). *Diagnostic and statistical manual of mental disorders* (4th ed.). Alexandria, VA: American Psychiatric Association.

Beavers, W. R. (1985). *Successful marriage: A family systems approach to couple therapy.* New York, NY: Norton.

Blatt, S. J., Shahar, G., & Zurhoff, D. C. (2002). Anaclitic/sociotropic and introjective/autonomous dimensions. In J. C. Norcross (Ed.), *Psychotherapy relationships that work* (pp. 315–334). New York, NY: Oxford University Press.

Carlson, J., & Dinkmeyer, D. (2003). *TIME for a better marriage.* Atascadero, CA: Impact Publishers.

Carrere, S., Buehlman, K. T., Coah, J., Gottman, J. M., & Ruckstuhl, L. (2000). Predicting marital stability and divorce in newlywed couples. *Journal of Family Psychology, 14*(1), 42–58.

Carter, M. M., & Schultz, K. M. (1998). Panic disorder with agoraphobia: Its impact on patients =and their significant others. In J. Carlson & L. Sperry (Eds.), *The Disordered Couple* (pp. 29–56). Bristol, PA: Brunner/Mazel.

Coyne, J. C., Thompson, R., & Palmer, S. C. (2002). Marital quality, coping with conflict, marital complaints, and affection in couples with a depressed wife. *Journal of Family Psychology, 16*(1), 26–37.

Cozolino, L. J. (2002). *The neuroscience of psychotherapy: Rebuilding the human brain.* New York, NY: W. W. Norton & Co.

Driver, J., Tabares, A., Shapiro, A., Nahm, E. Y., & Gottman, J. M. (2003). Interactional patterns in marital successes and failure: Gottman laboratory studies. In F. Walsh (Ed.), *Normal family processes* (3rd ed., pp. 493–513). New York, NY: Guilford Press.

Elkin, I., Shea, T., Watkins, J. T., Imber, S. D., Sotsky, S. M., Clooins, I. F., & Glass, D. R. (1989). National institute of mental health treatment of depression collaborative research program: General effectiveness of treatments. *Archives of General Psychiatry, 46*(11), 971–982.

Glick, I. D., Berman, E. M., Clarkin, J. F., & Rait, D. S. (2000). *Marital and family therapy* (4th ed.). Washington, DC: American Psychiatric Press.

Gollan, J. K., Friedman, M. A., & Miller, I. W. (2002). Couple therapy in the treatment of major depression. In A. S. Gurman & N. S. Jacobson (Eds.), *Clinical handbook of couple therapy* (3rd ed., pp. 653–674). New York, NY: Guilford.

Gottman J. M. (1994). *What predicts divorce? The relationship between marital processes and marital outcome.* Hillsdale, NJ: Lawrence Erlbaum.

Gottman, J. M. (1999). *The marriage clinic.* New York, NY: W. W. Norton & Company, Inc.

Gottman, J. M. (2011). *The science of trust.* New York, NY: Routledge.

Gottman, J. M., & Gottman, J. S. (2017). The natural principles of love. *Journal of Family Theory and Review, 9*, 7–26. doi:10.1111/jftr.12182

Gottman, J. M., & Levinson, R. W. (2002). A two-factor model for predicting when a couple will divorce: Exploratory analysis using 14-year longitudinal data. *Family Process, 41*(1), 83–96.

Grisel, J., Rasmussen, P., & Sperry, L. (2006). Anxiety and depression: Physiological and pharmacological considerations. *Journal of Individual Psychology, 62*, 397–416.

Hampson, R., & Beavers, W. R. (2012). Observational assessment. In L. Sperry (Ed.). *Family assessment: Contemporary and cutting-edge strategies* (2nd ed., pp. 83–114). New York, NY: Routledge.

Kirsch, I., Moore, T. J., Scoboria, A., & Nicholls, S. S. (2002). The emperor's new drugs: An analysis of antidepressant medication data submitted to the U.S. food and drug administration. *Prevention & Treatment, 5*(23). Retrieved from http://www.journals.apa.org/prevention/volume5/pre0050023a.html

Lockhart, J. (1998). Narcissistic/borderline couples: A psychodynamic approach to conjoint treatment. In J. Carlson & L. Sperry (Eds.), *The disordered couple* (pp. 259–284). Bristol, PA: Brunner/Mazel.

Luhmann, M., Hofmann, W., Eid, M., & Lucas, R. E. (2012). Subjective well-being and adaptation to life events: A meta-analysis on differences between cognitive and affective well-being. *Journal of Personality and Social Psychology, 102*(3), 592–615.

Maniacci, M., & Sperry, L. (in press). The psychotic couple. In L. Sperry, K. Helm, & J. Carlson (Eds.). *The disordered couple* (2nd ed.). New York, NY: Routledge.

Milkowitz, D. J., & George, E. L. (2002). Couple therapy with a biologically based psychiatric disorder. In A. S. Gurman & N. S. Jacobson (Eds.), *Clinical handbook of couple therapy* (3rd ed., pp. 677–698). New York, NY: Guilford.

Nurse, R., & Sperry, L. (2012). Standardized assessment. In L. Sperry (Ed.). *Family assessment: Contemporary and cutting-edge strategies* (2nd ed., pp. 53–82). New York, NY: Routledge.

Palmer, S. C., & Coyne, J. C. (2003). Screening for depression in medical care pitfalls, alternatives and revised priorities. *Journal of Psychosomatic Research, 54*(4), 279–287.

Peven, D. E., & Shulman, B. H. (1998). Bipolar disorder and the marriage relationship. In J. Carlson & L. Sperry (Eds.), *The disordered couple* (pp. 13–28). Bristol, PA: Brunner/Mazel.

Solomon, M. F. (1998). Treating narcissistic and borderline couples. In J. Carlson & L. Sperry (Eds.), *The disordered couple* (pp. 239–258). Bristol, PA: Brunner/Mazel.

Sperry, L. (2011). Family therapy with personality-disordered individuals and families: Understanding and treating borderline families. *Journal of Individual Psychology, 67*, 222–231.

Sperry, L. (in press). Assessment, diagnosis and case conceptualization with couples. In L. Sperry, K. Helm, & J. Carlson (Eds.). *The disordered couple* (2nd ed.). New York, NY: Routledge.

Sperry, L., & Carlson, J. (2000). Couple therapy with a personality-disordered couple. *Family Journal-Counseling & Therapy for Couples & Families, 8*(2), 118–123.

Sperry, L., & Maniacci, M. (in press). The histrionic-obsessive couple. In L. Sperry, K. Helm, & J. Carlson (Eds.). *The disordered couple* (2nd ed.). New York, NY: Routledge.

Stanley, S. M., Markman, H. J., & Whitton, S. W. (2002). Communication, conflict and commitment: Insights on the foundations of relationship success from a national survey. *Family Process, 41*(4), 659–675.

Stinnet, N., & DeFrain, J. (1985). *Secrets of strong families.* Boston, MA: Little, Brown.

Section 2

Theories of Couple Therapy

4 Psychoanalytic Approaches to Couple Therapy

LEARNING OBJECTIVES

In this chapter, the reader will learn the following:

1 The contribution of psychoanalytic thought to the development of couple therapy.
2 The practice of object-relations couple therapy.
3 The practice of Imago relationship therapy.
4 The practice of relational psychoanalytic couple therapy.

Although psychoanalysis is among the oldest psychotherapeutic systems, until recently, therapists have shown relatively little interest in using it for the treatment of marital discord. Yet, psychoanalysis is the only major orientation that stresses the impact of individual personality forces on marital dysfunction. It was noted that "Psychoanalytic couple therapy is often overlooked as a valuable application of psychoanalytic theory and technique" (Scharff, 2001, p. 350). However, teaching and learning about the psychoanalytic perspective are probably more difficult and challenging than for any other counseling or psychotherapy system. Thus, even though this chapter contains basic concepts and principles, mastery of this information requires considerable effort and study.

This chapter begins with a discussion of the evolution of psychoanalytic thought to the development of couple therapy. It then turns to a description of the current practice of object-relations couple therapy. Then it describes Imago relationship therapy (IRT), which reintroduced psychodynamic theory into couples practice. Finally, it describes the new and promising relational psychoanalytic approach to couple therapy.

Psychodynamic Perspectives and Couple Therapy

As early as 1931, some analysts began to consider the effects of a relationship on the neurosis of an individual along with the intrapsychic aspects (Gurman & Fraenkel, 2002). For traditional analysts, this is tantamount to heresy, but there was a small group of analysts who tried to marry (pun intended) the traditional techniques of analysis (internal dynamics as the sole cause of disorders) with a relational perspective (interactions with another person as a contributor to problems). Some intrepid analysts even dared to see a couple together (although usually as a last resort) at a time when such practice was forbidden by the canons of best practice. However, by the 1960s and 1970s, psychoanalysis could not overcome two important challenges and subsequently diminished as a major force in couple therapy: (1) A lack of effective interventions developed from the psychoanalytic perspective that focused on the relationship level (they continued to focus on transference) and (2) the attack from family therapists disparaging any psychoanalytic (or psychodynamic) approaches (Gurman & Fraenkel, 2002).

Yet, despite the antipathy between early psychoanalysts and family therapists, psychoanalytic and psychodynamic thought has played a critical role in the development of couple therapy and is reemerging as an influential force in couple therapy. Specifically, psychodynamically trained theorists (such as David and Jill Scharff, Stephen Mitchell, Nancy Chodorow, and others) have refined the theoretical shortfalls mentioned earlier and created methods to pay attention to both the internal dynamics of the individual and the external dynamics of the relationship simultaneously. Most notably is the writing of Stephen Mitchell. His relational psychoanalysis has opened new channels for psychoanalysts to relate the ideas of classical psychoanalysis to more postmodern, contextual, and interpersonal concepts (Mitchell, 1986, 1992, 1997). Another reason for the reemergence of psychodynamic thought is the move toward theoretical integration. The development of integrated theories created a need to understand the "unconscious communication and behavior maintaining processes that characterize all intimate relationships and which are maladaptively rigid in conflict ridden couples" (Gurman & Fraenkel, 2002, p. 226). Integrationists began to borrow from modern-day analysts and object-relations theorists to fill in these gaps, and thus a reawakening of (or reorienting to) a psychodynamic approach dawned.

The terms psychodynamic, psychoanalytic, and insight-oriented are often used synonymously, but not precisely, with one another and need clarifying. Psychodynamic refers to a broad range of theories of human behavior that commonly assume that a person's thoughts, feelings, and behaviors are a function of the complex interaction of mind, body, and external environment. In addition, psychodynamic theories contend that human behavior can best be understood and predicted with specific constructs, two of which are the unconscious motivation of behavior and the influence of early life experiences. Psychoanalytic refers to constructs and principles of psychic functioning derived from Freud and his followers and to a set of techniques for treatment and for scholarly investigation. Insight-oriented approaches investigate the internal dynamics of early relationships in a person's life as a basis for conflict in other relationships but also embrace interpersonal dynamics as an equal determinant of conflict (Gurman & Fraenkel, 2002). More specifically, psychoanalytic theories and approaches are a subset of psychodynamic thinking, while insight-oriented approaches may be seen as extensions of psychodynamic approaches that incorporate other approaches as well (Gurman & Fraenkel, 2002; Polonsky & Nadelson, 2003; Snyder, 1999).

The Evolution of Psychoanalytic Therapies

Psychoanalytic theory and therapy has evolved considerably since Sigmund Freud's. Five different phases of this evolution can be identified. These phases are summarized with the key terms: Drive, ego, object, self, and relationship (Sperry, 2010).

Classical Psychoanalysis

The initial approach called classical psychoanalysis was developed by Freud. It emphasizes unconscious drives which the analyst (therapist) identified from the analysand's (client's) verbalized thoughts, free associations, fantasies, and dreams. The analyst's interventions include confrontation, clarification, interpretation, and working through, the process by which a new awareness generalizes to other aspects of the client's life.

Psychoanalytic Psychotherapy

Another drive-based dynamic approach is psychoanalytic psychotherapy. It is a modified form of classical psychoanalysis that is more widely practiced than classical psychoanalysis today. It is less intense and less concerned with major changes in the client's personality structure and focuses on the client's current concerns and the way these concerns relate to early conflicts.

Ego Psychology

Ego Psychology evolved out of Freud's later thinking and was the dominant form of psychoanalysis practiced until the 1970s. Freud's daughter, Anna Freud, played a significant role in its development (Freud, 1936). It focused on the ego's normal and pathological development and its adaptation to reality. Unlike the focus on libidinal and aggressive impulses of classical psychoanalysis, ego psychology focuses directly on the ego and its defenses. Through clarifying, confronting, and interpreting the client's commonly used defense mechanisms, the goal is to assist the client in gaining control over these mechanisms.

Object Relations

Since the 1970s, major reformulations of psychoanalysis have emerged. Among these was object-relations theory, which emphasizes interpersonal relations, especially between mother and child. Object refers to a significant other who is the object of another's feelings or intentions. Relations refer to interpersonal relations and to the residues of past relationships that affect a person in the present. Object-relations theory focuses on internal images or representations of the self and other and their manifestation in interpersonal situations. This therapy focuses on the ways the client projects previous object relationships into the relationship with the therapist. The goal is to assist clients in resolving the pathological qualities of past relationships through the corrective emotional experience. While some interpretation and confrontation may be involved, the working through of the original pathological components of the patient's emotional world and the objects is the primary intervention strategy.

Self-Psychology

Another reformulation was self-psychology, which emphasizes the development of a stable and cohesive or integrated sense of self through empathic contacts with significant others i.e. self-objects (Kohut, 1977). Self-objects meet the developing self's needs for mirroring, idealization, and twinship, and serve to strengthen the developing self. Treatment proceeds through transmuting internalizations in which the client gradually internalizes the self-object functions provided by the therapist.

Relational

This is a reformulation based on relational themes. Interpersonal psychoanalysis emphasizes the nuances of interpersonal interactions, especially the way in which individuals protect themselves from anxiety by establishing collusive interactions with others. It combines interpersonal psychoanalysis, object-relations theory, and intersubjective theory, and emphasizes how the individual's personality is shaped by both real and imagined relationships with others, and how these relationship patterns are reenacted in the interactions between therapist and client.

The reader will note that of these six phases, there are no current couple therapy approaches based on ego psychology or psychoanalytic psychotherapy. The remainder of this chapter will describe three approaches for working with couples: Object-relations couple therapy, IRT, and relational psychoanalytic couple therapy. We begin with a discussion of the basic concepts and practices of classical psychoanalysis.

Classical Psychoanalysis and Couples

Key Concepts

As previously noted, this approach views marital or relationship difficulties as the result of psychopathology in one or both spouses. Relationship discord is considered an acting out of internal conflicts within an interpersonal context. These conflicts are the result of developmental events within the spouse's early childhood.

In analytic terms, conflict has three elements: The defense, the anxiety, and the hidden impulse (Malan, 1986). The aim of analytic treatment is to clarify each of these elements. The defense and the anxiety are interpreted first, which facilitates conscious recognition of the hidden and feared impulse. Because the conscious experience of impulses can be frightening or threatening, the individual employs defense mechanisms to avoid such an experience. Because they are socially unacceptable, anger and sexual impulses are highly defended (Mitchell, 1992).

These elements are recognizable in three types of interpersonal relationships: The marriage, the therapeutic context, and the distant past (the original relationship, usually between the individual and his or her parents, in which the conflict initially arose). Presumably, a sequence of behaviors recurs predictably, and the intrapsychic roots of these *repetition compulsions* (a sequence of problematic behaviors that occur predictably) can be analyzed. As a result, through analytic treatment the individual should be able to understand and experience these three relationships so that he or she can recognize and self-correct these forces after treatment is terminated (see Table 4.1). In short, analytic treatment enables the individual to consciously experience his or her conflicts.

Table 4.1 Definition of Key Psychoanalytic Terms

Repetition compulsions	A sequence of (problematic) behaviors recurs predictably, the intrapsychic roots of which can be analyzed. Through analytic treatment the individual should be able to understand, recognize, and self-correct these forces after treatment is terminated.
Therapeutic alliance	The working relationship between the individual, spouse, and the therapist. The purpose of the alliance is to aid the individual in allying himself or herself with the analyst so that the individual can better understand the conflicts that inevitably impact on the marriage relationship.
Interpretation	The form of communication the analyst uses to elucidate the unconscious meaning in dreams, resistances, transferences, and other intrapsychic phenomena. The purpose of interpretation is to make the unconscious conscious, which is called insight. Interpretation is the chief tool of the analyst and the primary activity in the course of treatment.
Manifest content	The dream as it appears to the individual (e.g., a black bear attacking the dreamer's wife).
Latent content	The disguised and symbolic aspect of the dream, which, because such content can be painful and threatening, is transformed into the more acceptable manifest content (e.g. the bear attacking the wife represents the patient's desire to control, punish, or destroy his wife). The analyst works to uncover the latent content by analyzing and interpreting the manifest content.

(*Continued*)

Transference	The individual's misperceptions of the therapist's motives and feelings in the treatment context. A core therapeutic element of psychoanalysis whereby the analyst gains information about the client's intrapsychic conflicts.
Transference neurosis	The clarification and understanding of the transference by both therapist and individual, which permits the individual to avoid the repetition compulsions manifested in the marital discord. A basic element in classical therapy is to allow the transference to the therapist to develop fully.
Countertransference	The analyst's unconscious response to the individual's transference.
Resistance	The individual's efforts to obstruct the aims and process of therapy. Resistance is not so much an obstacle to treatment as it is a way in which the individual reveals the nature of his or her difficulties and conflicts.

Treatment Process

For the classical analyst, the treatment unit involves only one of the spouses, and the two basic treatment strategies are the therapeutic alliance and the interpretation of transferences and resistances (Malan, 1986; Zeitner, 2003). The "therapeutic alliance" is the working relationship between the individual spouse and the therapist. The purpose of the alliance is to aid the individual in allying himself or herself with the analyst so that the individual can better understand the conflicts that inevitably impact on the marriage relationship. Treatment progress occurs only when the individual can identify with the logic of the analyst, which allows the individual's circumstances to be appropriately analyzed.

"Interpretation" is the form of communication the analyst uses to elucidate the unconscious meaning in dreams, resistances, transferences, and other intrapsychic phenomena. The purpose of interpretation is to make the unconscious conscious, which is called *insight.* Interpretation is the chief tool of the analyst and the primary activity in the course of treatment.

Dream work is an important means of interpreting unconscious material. Analysts describe dreams as having two levels of content and/or meaning: Manifest and latent. *Manifest content* is the dream as it appears to the individual. *Latent content* is the disguised and symbolic aspect of the dream, which, because such content can be painful and threatening, is transformed into the more acceptable manifest content. The analyst works to uncover the latent content by analyzing and interpreting the manifest content.

In the treatment context, "transference" refers to the individual's misperceptions of the therapist's motives and feelings (Zeitner, 2003). Similar misperceptions were previously attributed to parental figures and often are presently attributed to the other spouse. A basic element in classical therapy is to allow the transference to the therapist to develop fully. This is called the *transference neurosis.* The clarification and understanding of the transference by both therapist and individual permit the individual to avoid the repetition compulsions manifested in the marital discord. "Countertransference" is the analyst's unconscious response to the individual's transference. "Resistance" refers to the individual's efforts to obstruct the aims and process of therapy. Resistance is not so much an obstacle to treatment as it is a way in which the individual reveals the nature of his or her difficulties and conflicts (Mozdzierz, Peluso & Liseckei, 2014; Zeitner, 2003).

In addition to the philosophical shifts in psychoanalytic thinking mentioned earlier, perhaps the most obvious modification in the practice of psychoanalytic couple therapy has been a shift from individual treatment to conjoint sessions. Dare (1998) utilizes a number of interventions from other orientations (from communication training and problem-solving strategies to postmodern family therapy interventions). Couples are seen in a conjoint format in which interpretation is used to neutralize and integrate aggressive and libidinal needs so that behavior can be motivated. Through conjoint work, the transference occurs mainly between the spouses rather than between one spouse and the therapist. While later-day analysts like Zeitner (2003) do not call for all practitioners of psychoanalysis to become couple therapists, he does emphasize the importance of understanding couple dynamics: "A firm knowledge base and psychoanalytic understanding of couple interaction, the interdependency of couples, and the mutual shaping process that occurs in marriage and couple formation through the vicissitudes of projective identification are indispensable for all practicing psychoanalysts" (p. 361).

Object-Relations and Object-Relations Couple Therapy

Perhaps no one has advanced the development, training, and practice of object-relations couple therapy more than Jill and David Scharff. They have together (Scharff & Scharff, 1991) and separately (Scharff, 2001, 2003; Scharff & Bagnini, 2002; Sharff & deVarela, 2000) written extensively about object-relations couple therapy. Drawing on the work of Dicks (1967), they have adapted group models of object-relations theory to address couples issues and have provided a bridge for many analysts to cross over and work with couples in their practice. This has established psychodynamic and insight-oriented constructs and techniques firmly into modern-day couple therapy. Much of their work is detailed in this section of the chapter.

Key Concepts

Whereas in classical analysis, the basic motivation is drive reduction, the basic motivation in the object-relations perspective is object seeking. It may be helpful to review some basic terminology before we describe the object-relations approach (see Table 4.2). *Self* refers to the individual, and *object* refers to some aspect or quality of another person that has been *introjected* – that is, symbolically absorbed within the individual. Thus, *object relations*

Table 4.2 Basic Terminology of Object-Relations Couple Therapy

Self	The individual.
Object	Some aspect or quality of another person that has been introjected.
Introject	An object that has been symbolically absorbed within the individual.
Object relations	The introjected representation of a previous interpersonal relationship, which becomes incorporated as a part of the developing ego. This relation represents the emotional bonds between one individual and another. Each object relation has a *self-representation*, an *object representation*, and an *affective component*.
Projective identification	An interactional style between partners that represents a reenactment of earlier relationships, which is then projected onto the partner. The object (partner) must periodically behave in a similar way as the behavior that is projected on him or her by the subject (i.e. they accept and identify with the projective identification).
Collusion	The unspoken process by which such mate selection arrangements (i.e. projective identification) are upheld in a relationship.

Source: Summarized from Scharff and Bagnini (2002).

refers to the introjected representation of a previous interpersonal relationship. Object relations can be further described as the emotional bonds between one individual and another. As such, the term suggests the individual's capacity for loving and relating appropriately to others. Each object relation has a *self-representation,* an *object representation,* and an *affective component.* Furthermore, object relations become incorporated as a part of the developing ego (Kernberg, 1996; Scharff & Bagnini, 2002).

The first object relationship – between mother and child – shapes the pattern of later interpersonal relationships, including that with the spouse. Object-relations theory holds that the infant is primarily seeking a relationship with the mother rather than seeking only instinctual gratification (Fairbairn, 1952). This early bond is important because if "good enough mothering" (the mother adapting to the child's needs without smothering or withdrawing from the child) is lacking, subsequent personality development will be impaired (Winnicott, 1965).

The formation of original ties is marked by varying degrees of ambivalence as the mother attempts to provide for the child's needs for food, protection, emotional nurturance and love, and discipline. Initially, the child perceives all objects as either all good or all bad, as he or she cannot emotionally or conceptually experience them as some combination of good and bad. Normally, this evolves toward an integration of ambivalence, which allows the child to experience an object as having good and bad features. As this can be tolerated in the self and with others, the child can forgo the primitive splitting of object components into opposing parts or representations. When perceived negative experiences can be tolerated and mastered, the child is said to have developed internalized object consistency (Mahler, Pine, & Bergman, 1994; Scharff & Bagnini, 2002).

Based in object-relations theory, object-relations couple therapy understands personality as a system of parts of self and object in dynamic relation which are formed in the context of relationships in early life that are replayed in the couple's relationship. Through projective identification, a partner finds lost parts of the self in the other partner, where they can be reintegrated into the self or held hostage. The couple's relationship provides a context for reworking the dynamic relation of parts of the self as they are modified through mutual unconscious interaction in both partners. The goal of object-relations couple therapy is to offer a space that encourages the partners to provide a better holding environment for each other. Such therapy can improve the couple's capacity for containing each other's projections and enable the projective and introjective systems of the relationship to function with greater concern for the other and respect for the self (Siegel, 2013).

Marital Choice

The object-relations therapist understands interpersonal relations, including marriage, as efforts by the individual to seek out and become emotionally attached to people and things outside himself or herself. Basic to marital satisfaction is the spouse's acceptance of the needs of his or her partner because he or she can projectively identify or tolerate these needs as a good parent does. Mate selection theory – the reasons marital partners are chosen and the relationship of these reasons to marital discord – is perhaps the most important legacy from the psychoanalytic orientation.

According to classical psychoanalytic view, need represents a form of idealization wherein the object becomes a substitute for an unattained ego ideal (Scharff, 2001). So, for example, the spouse with strong needs to dominate would be expected to select a mate with strong needs to submit. Unfortunately, the classical view cannot adequately explain mate selection as a mutual exchange, whereas object-relations theory does.

The object-relations view of mate selection is based on the constructs of projective identification and collusion. *Projective identification* is an interactional style between the spouses that represents a reenactment of earlier relationships. A child handles conflicts with his or her parents by introjecting (symbolically absorbing) the parental relationship, including both sides of the conflict. In projective identifications, some introjected parts of the self are split off or disavowed and then projected onto the spouse, who complies with the split (Scharff, 2003). In other words, a deep unconscious "idea" is arranged in which the fixed view that each spouse has for the other is swapped. For example, "I will regard you as nonsexual as long as you see me as nondemanding." For projective identification to occur and continue, the object must periodically exhibit the behavior projected on him or her by the subject. In other words, the relationship cannot continue unless each spouse is willing at the unconscious level to accept and identify with the projective identification.

Collusion, according to Dicks (1967/1993), is the unspoken process by which such mate selection arrangements (i.e. projective identification) are upheld in a relationship. There is an interesting paradoxical element to this unconscious agreement: Each spouse holds out the promise that he or she will help the other work through early life conflicts and hurts while at the same time guaranteeing that such conflicts will not be worked through and that nothing will change (Dicks, 1967/1993).

Furthermore, this contract relieves both partners of the responsibility for growing up and facing the requisite anxiety and effort needed for change and development. In short, collusion is a collaboration in which spouses do not merely choose the other but enter into an implicit agreement that they will meet the unfulfilled needs of the other. Another feature of this agreement is that each spouse will support and maintain the other's self-perception, even in the face of conflict or contrary information. It has been said that choosing a spouse is more a matter of refinding an old love object than finding a new one (Friedman, 1980). So, from an objective-relations perspective, there is more than a kernel of truth to the lyric "I want to marry a man just like dear ol' dad."

Relational Discord

A rather high level of maturity is required to sustain a love relationship. According to Kernberg (1976), staying in love requires the spouses to establish a total object relation rather than a partial one. Marital/relational satisfaction results when both spouses have adequately differentiated object relations. This kind of maturity is a function of clear sex roles, effective communication, and responsible behavior when dealing with issues and the ability to work together with mutual satisfaction. For most couples, such maturity results from a considerable expenditure of time and effort, a large part of it involving a change in the original collusion. Discord and dissatisfaction in the relationship result when the projective identification system is unbalanced by distress. Scharff and Bagnini (2002) list several causes for this unbalancing:

> (1) projective and introjective processes are no longer mutually gratifying; (2) containment of the spouse's projections is not possible; (3) cementing of the object relations happen instead of their modification; (4) unarousing projective identification of the genital zone cannot be modified by sexual experiences; and/or (5) aspects of the love object have to be split off and experienced in a less threatening situation, leading to triangulation, involving a child, hobby, work, friend, parent, or lover.
>
> (p. 63)

As the projective identification system breaks down and the implicit collusion comes to an end, each spouse may begin to see glimpses of the other as he or she really is for the first time. Often, the partners do not like what they see. Hence, from an analytic perspective, marital discord results from inappropriate needs and unconscious expectations combined with an inability to cope with disappointment and disillusion.

Paradoxically, the very traits that initially attracted the partners to each other become the focus for their discord. For example, a wife may have been initially attracted to her husband because she perceived him as "having it all together and knowing where his life was going." She was in awe of these qualities as she did not possess them herself. So the relationship developed based on the somewhat irrational notion that she could somehow share those admired qualities just by being around him. But, as conflict and dissatisfaction mounted in the marriage, she began to perceive the negative aspects of those once-attractive qualities. Now she considers him overbearing, overcontrolling, and narrow-minded.

As long as the other spouse was unconsciously idealized, any ambivalent feelings for that spouse were repressed. But as the idealized image of the love object became tarnished, ambivalent feelings welled up, resulting not only in interpersonal conflict but also in intrapersonal conflict. In short, what became problematic was not the husband's inability to meet the wife's needs but the ambivalence and contradictions within the wife's intrapsychic structure. These contradictions rendered it impossible for the wife's needs to be met and marital dissatisfaction and discord grew (Scharff, 2003).

Assessment Strategy

There are many ways in which analytic marital therapists can gather and organize information on a couple (Siegel, 2013). While diagnosis of the problem takes place relatively early in treatment, assessment is an ongoing process through termination. Over the course of several interviews, detailed information about the couple's relationship is elicited while the therapist analyzes her transference and countertransference. Martin (1976) outlined a three-step procedure for doing so that consists of opening presentation, individual history of each spouse, and history of the marital relationship.

In the opening presentation, the therapist examines the major complaints of each spouse, which usually include children, finances, sex, and in-laws. The interrelated questions "What needs to be increased, and what needs to be decreased in your relationship?" become central themes. The couple therapist attempts to articulate the positive as well as the negative forces that were involved in mate selection and that still affect marital satisfaction and discord.

The couple therapist then begins the assessment of the individual life history of each spouse in five areas: Earliest memories, later childhood and adolescent memories, current and recurrent dreams, fantasies and daydreams, and medical history (which should differentiate psychological from physical problems that result in physical symptoms). Using the spouses' individual histories as a basis for understanding, the therapist begins the assessment of the couple's relationship. The specifics of the first encounter, the conscious and unconscious forces of attraction, and the marriage contract (the expressed and unexpressed expectations and beliefs about each spouse's obligations to and benefits from the relationship) are explored. Developmental factors relating to stages of the marriage (the marital life cycle) are investigated in relation to the marital discord. A detailed sexual history is also taken to clarify the extent to which sexual problems mask individual and relationship issues (Scharff & de Varla, 2000).

A discussion of the therapeutic contract concludes the assessment phase. Just as a marital contract has its conscious and unconscious aspects, so does the therapeutic contract the couple makes with the therapist. Therefore, the therapist needs to elicit both spouses' beliefs and expectations about treatment outcomes as well as their perceived role in the treatment process. The specifics of a treatment agreement can then be negotiated. Not only does this process of clarifying a treatment contract help the therapist in understanding the couple and in guiding treatment, it also serves as a role model for the couple to follow in developing a workable marital contract (Siegel, 2013).

Treatment Process

Because object-relations theory considers marital discord the result of a breakdown in the mutual gratification of conscious and unconscious needs, the major goal of object-relations couple therapy is the restructuring of the couple's perceptions and expectations so that they are more reality-based. An increase in intrapsychic awareness and growth on the part of each spouse is prerequisite to improved marital functioning (Siegel, 2013).

The couple is usually seen conjointly, although individual sessions may also be arranged, particularly during the assessment phase. The therapist's role is to clarify and interpret the dysfunctional nature of the spouse's object relations. This occurs through the therapist's function as a transference object in which conflicts are re-experienced, reenacted, and then resolved. The spouses also function as transference objects for each other, with the therapist supplying clarification and interpretation.

Treatment Stages

Eleven components that comprise the essence of object-relations couple therapy are specified (Scharff & Bagnini, 2002). Table 4.3 identifies them. In the first component, *setting the frame*, object-relations couple therapists manage the anxiety of the initial session, set the structure of therapy, and conduct the diagnostic interview. This includes communicating a clear understanding of what therapy will entail and eliciting cooperation from the clients. *Listening to the unconscious* refers to the therapist's listening to what is not being said

Table 4.3 Components of Object-Relations Couple Therapy

1	Setting the frame
2	Listening to the unconscious
3	Maintaining a neutral position of involved partiality
4	Creating a psychological space
5	Use of the therapists' self: Negative capability
6	Working with transference and countertransference
7	Interpretation of defense and anxiety about intimacy: The "because clause"
8	Working with fantasy and inner object relations
9	Working with dreams
10	Working through
11	Termination

Source: Adapted from Scharff and Bagnini (2002).

and paying attention to unconscious reactions to the client's responses and nonverbal behaviors. *Maintaining a neutral position of involved partiality* is the therapist's overarching attitude of not taking the side of either spouse. The *creation of a psychological space* relates to the safe environment, provided by the therapist, where the anxiety of the clients can be contained (i.e. psychological "holding") as they address their issues. *Use of the therapists' self: Negative capability* refers to the therapist introducing him- or herself into the client's story as a neutral observer. It is related to the psychological space, where "we are not bound by our memory of what has gone before or blinded by our desire for their (the clients') relationship ... to be a certain way" (Scharff & de Varela, 2000, p. 85). It also sets up the necessary transference and countertransference work.

As object-relations couple therapists *work with transference and countertransference*, there are multiple therapeutic dimensions in play. Specifically, therapists are aware of two levels of transference: Individual, focused transference, and transference stemming from the couple, or contextual transference (Siegel, 2013).

The contextual transference, or the couple's shared feelings about the therapist, keys into the therapist's countertransference, which is not seen as a manifestation of the therapist's pathology but as an important instrument for getting to the heart of the couple's emotional issues (Siegel, 2013).

From the analysis of the transference and countertransference, the *interpretation of defenses and anxiety about intimacy* becomes possible. Once the therapist has a good idea as to the couple's projective identification process (by working through the previous stages), he or she can identify what the "avoided relationship" is (e.g. "becoming as overbearing as my mother because of being repeatedly disappointed by you and thus destroying the relationship and losing my object") and how the behaviors being manifested (through anxiety and defenses) help to keep the couple "safe" from the avoided relationship (hence, the "because clause"). Ironically, however, in protecting the relationship from this happening, the defense itself wreaks havoc on the couple in a self-fulfilling, self-defeating prophecy. By moving into the next domain of treatment, ***working with fantasy and inner object relations***, the therapist is able to understand the origins of the original object relations within the family of origin and how it led to the development of the projective identification system and the fear of the avoided relationship (Scharff & Bagnini, 2002).

"Working with dreams" is an important aspect of the therapeutic process for the object-relations couple therapist. Here, the underlying psychic conflict, repressed emotions, and unconscious object relations of the couple are made available to the therapist for interpretation (Siegel, 2013). Often, the imagery or interpretation can be a powerful metaphor for the work that the couple has to do.

The "working through" phase means replicating the work of exploration and interpretation in the previous phases until the spouses' defenses are understood and resolved. This process continues until the couple has internalized the therapeutic space, can relate intimately, understand, and hold the other person psychologically (Scharff & de Varela, 2000). As a result of working through the defenses and anxiety, each person becomes aware of his or her own projective identification processes and must take responsibility for it (rather than expect the other to fulfill it). At this point, termination is appropriate. During ***termination***, object-relations couple therapists mourn with the couple the loss of the therapy relationship as acknowledgment of the work that has been done as well as any changes to the relationship – positive or negative (Scharff & Bagnini, 2002).

Intervention Strategies

Object-relations couple therapists employ the same psychoanalytic methods described in the previous section: Development of the therapeutic alliance, dream work, and the analysis/interpretation of resistances and transferences. In working with couples, application of some of these strategies does differ, particularly with the interpretation of resistances and transferences (Siegel, 2013).

Resistances represent the spouses' defense against anxiety in their daily lives. Resistances are also a maneuver that interferes with the spouses' ability to experience satisfaction in their marriage relationship. Resistance operates in marital therapy by preventing the couple and therapist from gaining access to painful and anxiety-provoking unconscious thoughts (Scharff, 2001). By interpreting and working through resistances, both spouses gain insight, alleviate the maladaptive behaviors, and increase marital satisfaction (Scharff & Bagnini, 2002).

Analyzing and interpreting transference are particularly important for the object-relations marital therapist. When negative images and thoughts are projected onto one spouse, that spouse is likely to respond in a distorted manner stemming from early internalized objects. This results in an unconscious collusion that can maintain dysfunctional marital discord indefinitely.

By understanding and interpreting this collusive process, the therapist aids the spouses in achieving insight into their own intrapsychic conflicts. In this process, the couple begins to understand how past internalized objects influence present functioning. Furthermore, these types of interpretation help the couple work through early life maladaptive patterns that prevent satisfaction in the marriage. Because of this, each spouse is often relieved of the guilt, confusion, or frustration that resulted from self-blame for the other's response (Siegel, 2013).

Adjunctive Techniques

Object-relations couple therapists also utilize methods from other therapeutic orientations. A perusal of the writings of object-relations couple therapists strongly suggests that these therapists are primarily analytic in their formulation of the nature of a couple's marital discord but often behavioral, strategic, and systemic in their descriptions of therapeutic interventions (Siegel, 2013).

Self-Psychology and Imago Relationship Therapy

"Imago" is the Latin word for "image" that Freud originally used to describe a person's unconscious idealized mental representation of a parent, which is formed early in life and is retained in adulthood (Love & Shulkin, 2001). Harville Hendrix extended Freud's idea of the Imago and made it a central feature of relationship function *and* dysfunction and, in 1988, published a best-selling book entitled *Getting the Love You Want: A Guide for Couples.* Calling his system IRT, he and several other writers have created a dynamic approach to couple therapy that has helped to reinvigorate interest in psychodynamic approaches (Hendrix, 1988, 1992; Love & Shulkin, 2001; Luquet, 1998). IRT is an extension of self-psychology, which itself is a relatively new perspective within the psychoanalytic tradition, heralded and pioneered by Heinz Kohut (Luquet, 1998). In many respects, self-psychology is actually a refinement of the object-relations perspective, but with some differences in emphasis and intervention. We will first present some of the important influences of self-psychology on IRT and then discuss treatment using Imago couple therapy.

Self-Psychology

The basic concept in self-psychology is the *self-object.* From his or her earliest moments, the child experiences certain individuals, particularly the mother, as part of the self. They are so intimately entwined in the child's mind that self and object are one, merged into a self-object. The child's experience during this early stage determines to a large extent whether the child's self will emerge as relatively healthy or dysfunctional (Livingston, 1998).

There are three functions and qualities of self-objects (Kohut, 1977). The first is the *mirroring self-object*. This is somewhat like the proud parent who builds up the child's sense of control, energy, and achievement (self-esteem) through encouragement and praise. The second is the *idealized parent imago*. This refers to the calm, self-assured presence the parent provides the child. The child's sense of the world as basically predictable and secure develops from this parental imago. The third is the *alter-ego/twinship* function, which is characterized by the statement, "Be just like me and let me be just like you in the sharing of our common skills and abilities." Persons, usually the parents, who perform these functions for the child are examples of self-objects. In adulthood, spouses or partners become self-objects (this is an important concept in IRT).

To the extent that the parents have firmly grounded and independent selves, they are able to provide the child with mirroring, empathic nurturance, and a cohesive environment in which to grow and develop. This type of experience allows the child to exhibit a pride and exhibitionism that the parents can accept. As a result, the child is able to develop a secure, vigorous, and cohesive sense of self. When the parents possess fragile or insecurely established selves, however, the self-object experience of the child tends to be distorted. Habitually ignoring or refusing to encourage the child's accomplishments may bolster the parents' flagging self-esteem, but it is at the expense of the child developing a healthy and coherent sense of self. Where there is a significant failure in achieving or maintaining cohesion, vigor, and harmony, emergence of *self-disorders*, particularly narcissistic or borderline personality disorders, is possible (Kohut, 1977). As a result of distorted experiences in early self-object relations, the developing self tends to be extremely susceptible to fragmentation (a loss of a sense of cohesion of the self) in the face of threats to self-esteem, called *narcissistic injury*.

Kohut (1971) described narcissistic needs in terms of the mirror and the idealizing transferences. In a *mirror transference*, the individual's sense of self is maintained by an idealized or grandiose self that requires another person to be consistently and totally admiring. In an *idealizing transference*, the individual's sense of self is maintained by means of an idealized image of the other (the idealized parent imago), with the idealized other being totally and consistently attentive. Kohut noted that the individual with mirroring expectations tends to be hypersensitive to actual or imagined instances of disapproval and criticism, whereas the individual with idealizing expectations tends to be hypersensitive to instances of inattention or neglect. In IRT, when there are problems within the relationship, both of these processes are taking place and become the focus of treatment (Love & Shulkin, 2001; Luquet, 1998).

Key Concepts of IRT

IRT posits that unconscious factors play a significant role in mate selection and in the development of conflict in intimate relationships. Unconscious partner selection creates an opportunity to heal a connection that was lost in childhood by increasing empathy, understanding, and communication with one's adult romantic partner. In healing childhood wounds, IRT emphasizes growth within a relational paradigm by focusing on the self-in-relation rather than the self-as-independent. Growth is viewed as occurring through relationships, in contrast to through individuation and separateness which some consider the goal of personality development (Gehlert, Schmidt, Giegerich, & Luquet, 2017).

The self-in-relation first occurs in infancy between child and caretaker. In this first intimate relationship, a child learns to define the self through actions and words that receive either validation or neglect from early caretakers. Subsequently, these interactions facilitate a growth process that either establishes connectedness and empathy or fosters defensive disconnectedness. If there are ongoing violations in close relationships, then self-protection is learned and implemented. IRT can correct such childhood adverse experiences by restoring the connection between partners.

Treatment Process

The IRT therapist assumes a coaching stance wherein skills are taught, risks are encouraged, and progress is monitored. The couple bears the burden of making the changes work through mutually agreed to homework exercises based on what is discovered during the therapeutic process (i.e. the Imago). The ultimate goal of IRT is to teach the couple the skills necessary to utilize the natural healing properties of the relationship and decrease the need for the therapist (Gehlert et al., 2017).

Assessment

The main assessment strategy in IRT is the uncovering of each partner's Imago (see Table 4.4). This is accomplished by answering a series of questions about a person's recollections of their experiences (positive and negative) in childhood. In addition, each partner discusses their particular frustrations and how they dealt with them. Then these are recapitulated into an integrated whole, which forms their Imago and contains the crucial elements of conflict with the partner or spouse.

Treatment Intervention

There are four strategies in IRT couples work: (1) Couples dialogue and the creation of emotional safety, (2) Imago psychoeducation, (3) restructuring frustrations, and (4) re-romancing the relationship. In the first strategy, couples dialogue and emotional safety, couples are taught how to decrease the tensions between them. It is assumed that at the outset of therapy, both partners are highly defensive and not very receptive to what the other has to

Table 4.4 Imago Exercise

Take a sheet of paper and divide it into five sections labeled A, B, C, D, and E. Answer the following questions in the designated area of the paper:

A Think about yourself as a young child (from birth to 18 years old), list at least three outstanding negative traits of the people who raised you or had an influence on your life (e.g. angry, mean, disinterested, sad, depressed, etc.).

B Now list three positive characteristics of these people (e.g. caring, giving, jovial, smart, funny, etc.).

C Thinking back to your family growing up, what did you need or want the most from the people around you – what was your heart's desire (e.g. I needed to feel safe, I needed to feel important, etc.)?

D Now, recall the happiest memories of childhood. These can be with your family, friends, in school, out of school, etc. Then list how you felt during these times (e.g. happy, secure, loved, etc.).

E Lastly, think back on the frustrations that you had as a child, not just with your family but with anybody (friends, etc.), and describe how you responded to these frustrations (e.g. getting angry, yelling, working harder, keeping to myself, blaming others, etc.).

Once these are all completed, go back and write in the following statements before each of the responses:

1 I am attracted to a person who is ..."
2 "and I expect him or her to be ..."
3 "so that I can get ..."
4 "and feel ..."
5 "but I stop myself from getting this by ..."

Once all of these are filled out, then you have a picture of each partner's Imago.

Source: Adapted from Hendrix (1988) and Luquet (1998).

say. The couples dialogue is a structured communication tool, whereby each person takes turns talking and then listening to the other person without judgment. Next, couples learn how to validate the other person's point of view (which is not the same as agreeing with the other person) in order to build trust and mutual respect. Lastly, in the couples dialogue, each partner is taught how to empathize with the other person. Once this is accomplished and a safe environment is created, then exploration of each person's Imago and psychoeducation about the impact of the Imago can take place (see Table 4.4 for details). Next, the couple looks at reviewing how they express and handle frustrations. Luquet (2000) illustrates this central tenet of IRT by saying, "frustrations possess the seeds of personal growth. Nature has set up the relationship to help individuals heal from wounds started by frustrations in childhood relationships and healed by positive interactions in adult relationships" (p. 119). Lastly, the couple begin to "romanticize the relationship," which is a type of starting over, and developing new, positive habits for the relationship. These include behavior change requests, which follow the respectful communications model of the couples dialogue and caring behaviors list, whereby each partner creates a list of things that the other partner can do to demonstrate affection and attention that the other partner will be able to recognize and respond to. This begins a positive cycle of mutually healing and beneficial interactions with the other partner, allowing for growth, rather than discord.

The couple therapist actively assists the couple in learning and applying connection-building skills though a number of specific interventions. These include couples dialogue, parent-child dialogue, behavior change request dialogue, and Imago workup [Imago Relationships International (2014)]. The following case example will demonstrate how these strategies are used together in a clinical setting.

The case of Alan and Margaret was introduced in Chapter 3. They had been married for 15 years when they came for couple therapy. Alan complained that Margaret was "not spending any time with me" and that she was "ignoring her responsibilities" with their two children, because she was spending time at their church assisting the pastor. Margaret's main complaint about Alan was that he was aloof and controlling. If they were being seen by an Imago relationship therapist, they might begin with some reconnection exercises in order to restore some level of safety and trust in the relationship. Next, they would probably work through the My Imago exercise (see Table 4.4), which might look like this:

Alan's Imago

- A *"I am attracted to a person who is …" smothering, overprotective, and needy.*
- B *"and I expect her to be …" capable, dedicated, and loving.*
- C *"so that I can get …" stability, comfort, and peace.*
- D *"and feel …" successful and powerful.*
- E *"but I stop myself from getting this by …" getting angry and being demanding.*

Margaret's Imago

- A *"I am attracted to a person who is …" cocky, cold, and controlling.*
- B *"and I expect him to be …" stable, exciting, and knowledgeable.*
- C *"so that I can get …" safety and to be cared for.*
- D *"and feel …" special and needed.*
- E *"but I stop myself from getting this by …" running away from conflict and pleasing others.*

At this point in their lives, we could see where each did fit the other's needs based on their Imago. However, this has also begun to break down and cause the conflict that is bringing them into therapy. Recall that Alan had expectations that Margaret would always be at home taking care of the things that he didn't have the time or inclination to do, which allowed Alan to concentrate on his career. He needs her to be his organizer, and his success is threatened by her getting involved in other activities. As a result, he throws temper tantrums to try to get her to conform to his needs, which usually works but not now. Margaret was initially attracted to Alan because he seemed so confident and self-assured, whereas now she is resentful of his indifference to her concerns, his self-absorbed lifestyle, and his controlling behavior. As a result, when he was unmoved by her complaints and need for attention from him, she would try harder to show him how helpful she could be and stop nagging.

Treatment for Alan and Margaret from an IRT approach would include taking the Imago information and building on the reconnection exercises. The emphasis would be on the frustrations that each person perceives in the relationship, and how they respond to that in a destructive way (i.e. temper tantrums, withdrawal from conflict, etc.). The couple would be taught strategies to understand their own needs and cues for frustration, as well as their partner's needs and expressions of frustrations. Then the couple would be taught ways that each person can help meet the other's needs and heal the frustrations of the past without negatively impacting the relationship. Lastly, from an IRT perspective, the couple would work on romanticizing the relationship, whereby positive interactions would take the place of negative ones. An exercise often used by IRT therapists is to help each partner create a list of caring behaviors that the other partner can do to demonstrate affection and respect that will be instantly recognizable. The Imago information helps the partners shape this list so that it is comfortable and doable, rather than a setup for failure. For many couples, these goals can generally be accomplished in 10–12 sessions with and IRT therapist (Luquet, 2000).

Research Support

Although anecdotal reports and case studies show that IRT improves couples relationships, experimental research is necessary to attest to an approach's effectiveness and efficacy. A number of quasi-experimental design studies suggest IRT's effectiveness. One of these studies found significant changes in marital satisfaction, including a pre-, post-, and three-month follow-up study of more than 200 Imago couples workshop participants. The two-day intensive training produced significant changes in marital satisfaction and communication from the beginning to the end of the workshop (Schmidt, Luquet, & Gehlert, 2016). Another workshop study of low-income Hispanic couples found similar changes (Muro & Holliman, 2014). A study of a short training of Imago Therapy showed a significant increase in empathic behavior between couples as noted by trained observers (Holliman, Muro, & Luquet, 2016).

The gold standard for attesting to an approach's efficacy is a randomized controlled trial study. Recently, the results of such a study were reported (Gehlert et al., 2017). It involved 14 distressed, treatment-seeking couples who completed 12 sessions of IRT and the impact their involvement had on their marital satisfaction after treatment and follow up for 12 weeks. The control group consisted of 16 distressed couples. Couples in the treatment condition experienced statistically significant increases in marital satisfaction, while couples in the control group did not. Even though levels of marital satisfaction decreased significantly from posttreatment to follow-up, they remained significantly higher than at pretreatment. Also noted was that although statistically significant, the improvements experienced by the treatment group were not clinically significant. The researchers concluded that limiting treatment to 12 sessions was not sufficient to produce meaningful change for most couples, although it was enough for one-third of the participants (Gehlert et al., 2017).

Relational Psychoanalysis and Relational Psychoanalytic Approach to Couple Therapy

For some time, contemporary psychoanalysis has been devoid of a comprehensively relational way to think about the practice of couples treatment. It is true that relational psychoanalysis provides an alternative stance to the earlier psychoanalytic views that psychic structures were innately organized by drives and that human development was based on these drives. Relational psychoanalysis effectively challenged early psychoanalytical practices which emphasized neutrality, abstinence, neutrality, and when rigidly employed, left clients feeling pathologized and misunderstood. Relational psychoanalysts, both in their clinical work and writing, were much more interactive, direct, disclosing about their personal experiences in the course of treatment. Clearly, relational psychoanalysis had produced a new and invigorating reinterpretation of some basic psychoanalytic theory which resulted in new ways of thinking, practicing, and training.

But until recently, contemporary psychoanalysis had not developed a relational approach to addressing the treatment issues of couples. Relational psychoanalysis was the most likely development in psychoanalysis since it explicitly focuses on an individual's relationships with others. Accordingly, relational psychoanalysis seemed best suited to the treatment of couples. However, this was not realized in a comprehensive and systematic approach for couple therapy. That has all changed with the publication of *A Relational Psychoanalytic Approach to Couples Psychotherapy* by Philip A. Ringstrom (Ringstrom, 2014).

This relational approach for working with couples is set out in six steps of treatment, which Ringstrom describes as nonlinear, nonhierarchical steps or stages. He emphasizes that the approach to treatment is not a therapeutic process that is rigidly followed. Rather, these six stages are recursive (i.e. they repeat and are circular). Instead of following a clear trajectory, therapy is a journey into the still-to-be-discovered world of the unconscious. In this regard, this approach differs from a more cognitive approach of moving from one step to another.

This approach is based on three therapeutic objectives which inform the treatment process (Ringstrom, 2014).

1 The actualization of the self in the context of an intimate relationship.
2 Each partner's capacity for mutual recognition instead of mutual negation.
3 That the relationship has a mind of its own.

Because problems of blame, failure of mutual recognition, and difficulties in achieving some level of self-actualization in an intimate relationship are so commonplace, this approach has been very well received by psychoanalytically oriented therapists who work with couples.

These three objectives are the foundation for the six steps of the treatment process. These states are delineated in terms of the therapist's six tasks. They also provide the therapeutic aim for the couple over the course of treatment. Table 4.5 lists these six stages.

These steps initially address the therapist's attunement to the partners' differing subjectivities including the critical importance of each one's perspective on the "reality" they co-habit. The couple's perspectives are fleshed out through the exploration of their developmental histories with a focus on gender, age, and culture. Out of this arises the examination of how each partner's conflictual past manifests in dissociated self-states. The result of this awareness is increased capacity for mutual recognition, more genuinely renegotiate their relationship, and further enrichment of self-actualization.

Table 4.5 Six-Step Therapy Process

1	Attune to each partner's subjectivity
2	Facilitate partners in asserting their own view of reality
3	Explore how the presenting problem is rooted in both partner's developmental histories
4	Focus on the transference and explore the meaning communicated by it
5	Enable partners to be reflective of the other in a manner that enriches instead of undermines
6	Enhance each partner's capacity to attune to the other and to overcome his or her struggles.

Concluding Note

This chapter has examined basic psychoanalytic concepts in the classical, object relations, self-psychology/IRT, and relational psychoanalytic approach to couple therapy approaches and described their corresponding treatment methods and processes. The object-relations approach was detailed because it has been more developed, disseminated, and better integrated with the systems perspective than either the classical approach has been. Imago couple therapy has also been detailed because it is the most commonly practiced psychoanalytic approach with couples. It also has considerable research support which will increase its chance of achieving evidence-based status. Finally, there has been considerable interest in psychoanalytically oriented therapists with relational psychoanalytic approach. Unfortunately, and like the classical and object-relations couples approaches, unless it develops research support and evidence-based status, its future is in question.

In Chapter 5, we will present theories that have been influenced by the behavioral and cognitive approaches to couple therapy.

References

Dare, C. (1998). Psychoanalysis and family therapy: The old, old story? *Journal of Family Therapy, 20*(2), 165–176.

Dicks, H. (1967/1993). *Marital tensions.* London, England: Routledge and Kegan Paul. (Reprinted 1993 by Karnac Books.).

Fairbairn, W. (1952). *An object-relations theory of personality.* New York, NY: Basic Books.

Framo, J. L. (1982). *Explorations in family therapy: Selected papers of James L. Framo.* New York, NY: Springer.

Framo, J. L. (1990). Integrating families-of-origin into couple therapy. In R. Chasin, H. Grunebaum, & M. Herzigs (Eds.), *One couple, four realities: Multiple perspectives on couple therapy.* New York, NY: The Guilford Press.

Framo, J. L. (1992). Integrating families of origin into couple therapy. In R. Chassin, H. Grunebaum, & M. Herzigs (Eds.), *One couple, four realities: Multiple perspectives on couple therapy* (pp. 49–57). New York, NY: Guilford Press.

Framo, J. L. (2013). *Family-of-origin therapy: An intergenerational approach.* New York, NY: Routledge.

Freud, A. (1936). *The ego and the mechanisms of defense.* New York, NY: International Universities Press.

Friedman, L. (1980). Integrating psychoanalytic object-relations understandings with family systems interventions in couple therapy. In J. Pearce & L. Friedman (Eds.), *Family therapy* (pp. 63–79). New York, NY: Grune and Stratton.

Gehlert, N., Schmidt, C., Giegerich, V., & Luquet, W. (2017) Randomized controlled trial of Imago relationship therapy: Exploring statistical and clinical significance, *Journal of Couple & Relationship Therapy, 16*(3), 188–209.

Gurman, A. S., & Fraenkel, P. (2002). The history of couple therapy: A millennial review. *Family Process, 41*(2), 199–260.

Hendrix, H. (1988). *Getting the love you want: A guide for couples.* New York, NY: Henry Holt.

Hendrix, H. (1992). *Keeping the love you find: A guide for singles.* New York, NY: Pocket Books.

Hendrix, H. (1996). The evolution of Imago relationship therapy: A personal and theoretical journey. *Journal of Imago Relationship, 1*(1), 1–17.

Imago Relationships International. (2014). *Clinical training in Imago relationship therapy: Training manual text.* Lexington, KY: Author.

Johnson, S. M. (2003). Couple therapy research: Status and directions. In G. P. Sholevar (Ed.), *Textbook of family and couple therapy* (pp. 797–814). Alexandria, VA: American Psychiatric Publishing.

Johnson, S. M., & Whiffen, V. E. (Eds.). (2003). *Attachment processes in couple and family therapy.* New York, NY: Guilford Press.

Kernberg, O. (1976). *Object-relations theory and clinical psychoanalysis.* New York, NY: Jason Aronson.

Kernberg, O. (1996). Object-relations, affects and drives: Toward a new synthesis. *Psychoanalytic Inquiry, 21*(5), 604–619.

Kohut, H. (1971). *The analysis of the self.* New York, NY: International Universities Press.

Kohut, H. (1977). *The restoration of the self.* New York, NY: International Universities Press.

Lanman, M., Grier, F., & Evans, C. (2003). Objectivity in psychoanalytic assessment of couples relationships. *British Journal of Psychiatry, 182*(3), 255–260.

Livingston, M. S. (1998). Conflict and aggression in couple therapy: A self-psychological vantage point. *Family Process, 37*(3), 311–321.

Love, P., & Shulkin, S. (2001). Imago theory and the psychology of attraction. *The Family Journal: Counseling and Psychotherapy for Couples and Families, 9*(3), 246–249.

Luquet, W. (1998). The relational paradigm. In W. Luquet & M. T. Hannah (Eds.), *Healing in the relational paradigm: The Imago relationship casebook* (pp. 1–18). New York, NY: Brunner/Mazel.

Luquet, W. (2000). Imago relationship therapy. In F. M. Dattilio & L. J. Bevilacqua (Eds.), *Comparative treatments for relationship dysfunction* (pp. 116–133). New York, NY: Springer.

Mahler, M., Pine, E., & Bergman, A. (1994). Stages in the infant's separation from the mother. In G. Handel & G. G. Whitechurch (Eds.), *The psychosocial interior of the family* (4th ed.). Hawthorne, NY: Aldine DeGruyter.

Malan, D. (1986). Beyond interpretation: Initial evaluation and technique in short-term psychotherapy. Part I. *International Journal of Intensive Short-Term Psychotherapy, 1*, 59–82.

Martin, P. (1976). *A marital therapy manual.* New York, NY: Brunner/Mazel.

Mitchell, S. A. (1986). The wings of Icarus: Illusion and the problems of narcissism. *Contemporary Psychoanalysis, 22*(1), 107–132.

Mitchell, S. A. (1992). True selves, false selves, and the ambiguity of authenticity. In N. J. Skolnick & S. C. Warshaw (Eds.), *Relational perspectives in psychoanalysis* (pp. 1–20). Hillsdale, NJ: Analytic Press, Inc.

Mitchell, S. A. (1997). *Influence and autonomy in psychoanalysis.* Hillsdale, NJ: The Analytic Press.

Muro, L., Holliman, R., & Luquet, W. (2016). Imago relationship therapy and accurate empathy development. *Journal of Couple & Relationship Therapy, 15*(3), 232–246.

Muro, L., & Holliman, R. (2014). Relationship workshop with high-risk, Hispanic couples. *North Carolina Perspectives, 9*, 51–62.

Offenkrantz, W., & Tobin, A. (1974). Psychoanalytic psychotherapy. *Archives of General Psychiatry, 30*(5), 593–606.

Polonsky, D. C., & Nadelson, C. C. (2003). Psychodynamic couple therapy. In G. P. Sholevar (Ed.), *Textbook of family and couple therapy* (pp. 439–460). Alexandria, VA: American Psychiatric Publishing.

Ringstrom, P. (2014). *A relational psychoanalytic approach to couples psychotherapy*. New York, NY: Routledge.

Scharff, D. E. (2001). Applying psychoanalysis to couple therapy: The treatment of a couple with sexualized persecutory internal objects resulting from trauma. *Journal of Applied Psychoanalytic Studies, 3*(4), 325–351.

Scharff, D. E. (2003). Psychoanalytic models of the mind for couple and family therapy. *Journal of Applied Psychoanalytic Studies, 5*(3), 257–267.

Scharff, D. E., & Scharff, J. S. (1991). *Object relations couple therapy*. Northvale, NJ: Jason Aronson.

Scharff, J. S., & Bagnini, C. (2002). Object-relations couple therapy. In A. S. Gurman & N. S. Jacobson (Eds.), *Clinical handbook of couple therapy* (3rd ed., pp. 59–85). New York, NY: Guilford.

Scharff, J. S., & deVarela, V. (2000). Object-relations therapy. In F. M. Dattilio & L. J. Bevilacqua (Eds.), *Comparative treatment for relationship dysfunction* (pp. 81–101). New York, NY: Springer.

Schmidt, C. D., Luquet, W., & Gehlert, N. C. (2016). Evaluating the impact of the "getting the love you want" couples workshop on relational satisfaction and communication patterns. *Journal of Couple & Relationship Therapy, 15*(1), 1–18.

Segraves, R. (1982). *Marital therapy*. New York, NY: Plenum.

Siegel, J. (2013). Object relations couple therapy. In A. Gurman, J. Lebow, & D. Snyder (Eds.), *Clinical handbook of couple therapy* (5th ed., pp. 224–245). New York, NY: Guilford Press.

Snyder, D. K. (1997). *Marital satisfaction inventory, revised* (MSI-R). Los Angeles, CA: Western Psychological Services.

Snyder, D. K. (1999) Affective reconstruction in the context of a pluralistic approach to couple therapy. *Clinical Psychology: Science and Practice, 6*(4), 348–365.

Snyder, D. K., & Schneider, W. J. (2002). Affective reconstruction: A pluralistic, developmental approach. In A. S. Gurman & N. S. Jacobson (Eds.), *Clinical handbook of couple therapy* (pp. 151–179). New York, NY: Guilford Press.

Snyder, D. K., & Wills, R. M. (1989). Behavioral versus insight-oriented marital therapy: Effects on individual and inter-spousal functioning. *Journal of Consulting and Clinical Psychology, 57*, 39–46.

Snyder, D. K., Wills, R. M., & Grady-Fletcher, A. (1991). Long-term effectiveness of behavioral versus insight-oriented marital therapy: A 4-year follow-up Study. *Journal of Consulting and Clinical Psychology, 59*(1), 138.

Sperry, L. (2010). *Core competencies in counseling and psychotherapy: Becoming a highly competent and effective therapist*. New York, NY: Routledge.

Winnicott, D. (1965). *The maturational processes and the facilitating environment.* New York, NY: International Universities Press.

Young, J. E. (1999). *Cognitive therapy for personality disorders: A schema-focused approach* (rev. ed.). Sarasota, FL: Professional Resource Press.

Zeitner, R. M. (2003). Obstacles for the psychoanalyst in the practice of couple therapy. *Psychoanalytic Psychology, 20*(2), 348–362.

5 Cognitive Behavioral Approaches to Couple Therapy

LEARNING OBJECTIVES

In this chapter, the reader will learn the following:

1 The role of cognitions and behaviors in relationship dysfunction.
2 The four major cognitive behavioral approaches with couples.
3 New advances in these approaches in terms of clinical applications and research support.
4 A promising online couple therapy program.

As noted in the previous chapter, the psychodynamic view of relationship interactions stressed the dysfunctional, intrapsychic processes that, when combined in a relationship, lead to dysfunction. Individuals frequently find themselves in relationships that recreate unresolved conflicts from earlier (family-of-origin) relationships. In this sense, each partner's historical material rather than current interaction is the primary focus of treatment. In contrast, the cognitive behavioral approach focuses more on the here-and-now elements of the couple. Historical (family-of-origin) material, experiences in past intimate relationships (friendships and romances), general thinking style, beliefs about relationships engendered by the culture as a whole, and the nature of the current interactions between the partners are all important targets of assessment and treatment but are only a part of the treatment (Baucom, Epstein, Kirby, & LaTaillade, 2015).

This chapter introduces the reader to the four major cognitive behavioral approaches with couples: Cognitive behavioral couple therapy (CBCT), traditional behavioral couple therapy (TBCT), integrated behavioral couple therapy (ICBT), and Dialectic couple behavior therapy.

It highlights several major advances in these approaches. First, an expanded range of new clinical applications of these approaches, particularly CBCT. Second, new research support for these approaches. Finally, it describes a promising online couple therapy program. This chapter begins with the basic premises and characteristics of cognitive behavioral approaches.

Premises and Characteristics of the Cognitive Behavioral Approaches

Cognitive behavioral therapy (CBT) is a category of psychotherapeutic approaches that emphasizes the role of cognitions in feelings and behavior. There are several approaches to CBT including Cognitive Therapy, Behavior Therapy, Schema Therapy, Dialectic Behavior Therapy (DBT), Cognitive-Behavior Analysis System of Psychotherapy (CBASP), and Mindfulness- Based Cognitive Therapy. Cognitive behavioral approaches to couple dysfunction use both behavioral interventions and cognitive interventions to change behaviors and cognitions.

A major premise of this approach is that partners' dysfunctional behavioral and emotional responses to events in the relationship are influenced by inappropriate or faulty information processing, in which cognitive appraisals of the events are either distorted, extreme, or are evaluated according to extreme or unreliable standards of what a relationship should be (Baucom et al., 2015). Changes in behavior are used to facilitate cognitive changes, and vice versa. In addition, it is presumed that once individuals understand and improve their information processing and cognitions, positive changes in behaviors and emotions will follow (Baucom et al., 2015).

While there are differences among the various cognitive behavioral approaches, they all share a number of common characteristics. Based on an empirical review of the literature, the following factors were found to characterize the commonalities shared by all cognitive behavioral therapies including couples approaches (Blagys & Hilsenroth, 2002) (Table 5.1, adapted from Blagy's and Hilsenroth, 2002).

Table 5.1 Common Characteristics of the Cognitive Behavioral Therapies

- **Cognitive and Behavioral Focus**. A basic assumption of these approaches is that clients' emotions and behaviors are influenced by their beliefs or thoughts. Since most emotional and behavioral reactions are learned, the goal of therapy is to help clients unlearn unwanted responses and to learn a new way of responding. Accordingly, therapy focuses on identifying these maladaptive beliefs and behaviors. By evaluating, challenging, and modifying them, clients are able to gains control over problems previously believed to be insurmountable.
- **Present and Future Emphasis.** CBT emphasizes the impact of present maladaptive thoughts on current and future functioning. This emphasis differentiates it from the psychodynamic and insight therapies that focus on the influences of past experiences on present functioning.
- **Directive.** CBT is a directive approach in which therapists structure session activity by setting an agenda, decide, plan what will be discussed prior to the session, and actively direct discussion of specific topics and tasks. They also endeavor to engage clients in the treatment process and these decisions. At the same time, these approaches are collaborative and encourage client input and involvement in the therapeutic process.

- **Skills.** Cognitive behavior therapists routinely teach clients skills to help them cope more effectively with problematic situations. Dealing directly with skill deficits and excesses is a central to clients achieving and maintaining treatment gains.
- **Psychoeducation.** Cognitive behavior therapists provide information and discuss the explicit rationale for their treatment and the specific techniques being used. Accordingly. They provide specific information (articles, books, or handouts) to clients to: (1) Orient them to the treatment process, (2) increase their confidence in treatment, and (3) enhance their ability to cope with problematic situations.
- **Homework.** Homework and between-session activities are another key feature of this approach. Such activities provide clients the opportunity to practice skills learned in sessions and transfer gains made in treatment to their everyday life. Such activities can also foster and maintain symptom reduction.

Cognitive Behavioral Couple Therapies Approaches

Currently, there are four recognized CBT-based couple therapies that have considerable empirical support. They are CBCT, TBCT, ICBT, and Dialectic couple behavior therapy.

Key figures in the CBT-based couples approaches are the founders and proponents of these major schools today. Andrew Christiansen, Norman B. Epstein, Neil Jacobson, Brian Doss, Donald Baucom, and Alan Fruzzetti are prominent figures in this rapidly growing field. It should be added that some consider John Gottman and his approach, Gottman method couple therapy, to be CBT-based. We agree that it is but have chosen to cover that approach in Chapter 8 entitled "Third Wave and Integrative Approaches to Couple Therapy."

The next four sections of this chapter describe and illustrate each.

Traditional Behavioral Couple Therapy

TBCT is also referred to as behavioral couple therapy.

It consists of a variety of learning-based procedures for building relationship skills and decreasing the rate of aversive exchanges between partners. The goals of TBCT are to change problematic behaviors by creating specific environmental conditions for new learning (Christensen et al., 2004). TBCT therapists identify both behavioral deficits and behavioral excesses that influence adjustment (Wheeler, Christensen, & Jacobson, 2001). Deficits in basic skills such as communication, problem-solving, assertiveness, and negotiation limit the extent to which partners can make their needs known to one another and resolve any conflicts that may develop between them. There is also substantial research evidence to support clinical observations that distressed couples use an inordinate amount of aversive stimulation such as criticism and threats in their attempts to influence each other and that such excesses are common targets for modification in therapy (Epstein, 2003).

Traditional behavioral couple therapists strive for precision in identifying a problem, employ quantification to measure change, and conduct further research to validate their results. They design programs that emphasize assessment (the behavioral analysis of the couple's difficulties) along with a number of direct and pragmatic treatment techniques to alleviate symptoms and teach couples to improve their skills in communication and self-management. The TBCT therapist is interested in increasing positive interaction between partners, altering the environmental conditions that oppose or impede such interaction, and training couples to maintain the improved behavior (Baucom et al., 2015). No effort is made to infer motives, uncover unconscious conflict, hypothesize needs and drives, or diagnose inter-pathological conditions producing the undesired behavior. The partners are not necessarily helped to gain insight into the origin of the current problems. Instead, emphasis is placed on the environmental, situational, and social determinants that influence behavior. Because almost all behavior is learned rather than innate, behavior can be altered by new learning. Thus, TBCT therapists attempt to train a person's behavior rather than probe those dimensions of personality that, according to other models, underlie behavior.

Since its initial development, TBCT became a widely studied treatment for distressed couples. "Currently, its documented success is unparalleled, with over 20 studies attesting to its efficacy" (Christensen, Dimijian, & Martell, 2015, p. 61). However, despite this impressive research record, clinicians and researchers became increasingly skeptical of its success. The reason was that many couples relapsed after completing therapy. A closer examination of research data found that TBCT worked particularly well for couples who were "less distressed, younger, not emotionally disengaged; were not experiencing concurrent individual problems (e.g. depression); and did not have a relationship based on rigidly structured, traditional gender roles" (Christensen et al., 2015, p. 62). On the other hand, TBCT was not effective with couples who struggled with issues of collaboration, compromise, or accommodation. Furthermore, problems that represented basic, irreconcilable difference between partners were less amenable to this approach. As a result, a new approach, ICBT, evolved.

The following case example illustrates the way in which TBCT is typically practiced.

Mark and Alex had been in a relationship for approximately six months when they entered couple therapy. They had moved in together about two months earlier and began to experience their first fights after four months of no disagreements. Both partners were very distressed that this was a bad omen for the relationship and feared that they had made a big mistake by moving in together. Each confessed to having deep feelings for the other and a real desire to make the relationship work, but each of the partners was having some serious doubts about the other's commitment to the relationship.

A traditional behavioral couple therapist would not be content with general statements of a problem but would pursue specific details of the behavioral sequence leading to the argument or problems. In Mark and Alex's case, the arguments come primarily in the evenings and weekends when they have unstructured time together. Mark is usually content with having "down time," which he defines as watching movies or sports on television for long periods of time. Alex prefers to go out and do outdoor activities or spend time with people. It became obvious to the therapist that when they were not living together, each could tolerate doing what the other wanted for short periods of time. Then each would have the ability to go to their respective homes and do what they needed to relax. Now that they live together, however, their ability to balance the demands of the other person with their own need to relax has been curtailed. This leads to periods of intense pressure to do what the other wants, and then arguments that would lead to either giving in and resentment or separation and guilt.

The treatment plan for Mark and Alex addressed deficits in appropriately communicating their needs for connection and independence and cooperatively solving their problems. Over the course of three sessions, they were able to practice being assertive and negotiating with each other, as well as putting into place a schedule of activities that they can do alone and together.

Integrative Behavioral Couple Therapy

Integrative Behavioral Couple Therapy (IBCT) was developed by Andrew Christensen and Neil Jacobson in the 1990s (Christensen et al., 2015). It is based on TBCT. IBCT extended the conceptualization of couple distress beyond TBCT's notions of positive to negative exchange ratios and extended the conceptualization of intervention beyond TBCT's focus on positive behavior change through communication and problem-solving skills. In this section, we briefly describe some of the theoretical basis of IBCT, how it assesses and conceptualizes couple distress, and specific interventions. We also review the empirical support of IBCT, and highlight some recent innovations in how this approach is delivered.

IBCT contends that couples often struggle with one or two broad themes in their relationship, such as a struggle over how interdependent or independent they should be. To understand this theme, IBCT borrows two central ideas from close relationship research: First, that the crux of relationships is the interaction between partners; second, the three broad factors that influence interaction. The three are the characteristics that each partner brings to the interaction and the context in which that interaction occurs.

IBCT conceptualizes these factors with a simple mnemonic: DEEP analysis or DEEP understanding of relationship problems (Christensen & Doss, 2017).

D = the differences between partners in personality, interests, goals, and others.

E = the emotional sensitivities or vulnerabilities that each partner brings to the relationship that may make the differences particularly problematic. For example, imagine that Jeff wants a closer, more interdependent relationship than Cindy who is more comfortable with greater independence than Jeff. This difference may become especially problematic as Jeff feels neglected when Cindy is not close and interconnected with him. Similarly, this difference may be especially problematic when Cindy feels controlled or guilty due to Jeff's efforts to have more connection with her.

E = external circumstances, particularly stressful circumstances, which may exacerbate the problems created by differences and emotional sensitivities. For example, if Cindy's job is very demanding, or if Jeff and Cindy live a distance from Jeff's circle of friends and family, contextual factors may make the differences between the partners more problematic.

P = patterns of interaction the couples experience in their attempt to navigate the problem created by the DEE. For instance, their interaction pattern involves Jeff complaining about how disconnected they are, while Cindy defends her need to work. Although meant to solve the problem, the pattern of interaction that couples unwittingly utilize often makes the problem worse. Cindy finds herself less interested in being with Jeff because of all his complaining while Jeff finds himself angry at her for her ongoing avoidance of contact with him. This is called the demand-withdraw interaction pattern which is described along with others, in Chapter 9.

Premises

The IBCT view of intervention is based on premise that all relationship problems result from the combination of a triggering action (or inaction) and a sensitive reaction. Accordingly, relationship problems can be resolved by altering the triggering action or by altering the vulnerable response. However, a combination of the two may be indicated. Whereas TBCT focuses on making change in the triggering action or inaction, IBCT puts equal or greater emphasis on changing the vulnerable response (i.e. emotional acceptance), given that most troublesome actions or inactions in relationships are not egregious acts such as violence or verbal abuse.

A second premise of IBCT is that altering both the triggering events and the emotional reactions is better achieved through "contingency shaped processes" than through "rule governed" processes. Whereas TBCT encourages couples to engage in more positive behaviors and teaches them communication and problem-solving strategies, contingency shaped change in IBCT comes about spontaneously as a result of a change in the context and the resultant emotional and cognitive reactions. For instance, a partner may become less blaming and more supportive when she sees that the other partner is in emotional pain or when she understands that both are trapped in a vicious cycle of interaction. Although IBCT employs both strategies, it focuses more on the latter and assumes that it will lead to more lasting change (Christensen & Doss, 2017).

This approach integrates acceptance with change strategies (Johnson, 2003). Change techniques are designed to remove a negative behavior or reduce the frequency of negative couple interactions, such as criticism, and increase emotional acceptance. According to Christensen et al. (2004), IBCT's focus on emotional acceptance is based on several assumptions: "all relationships are characterized by some genuine incompatibilities, the reactions to problem behavior are often as problematic as the behavior itself, and direct change efforts are often as much a problem for couples as they are a solution" (p. 180). Acceptance techniques are designed to change the way one experiences negative behaviors and emotions. This might involve teaching understanding and empathy. When spouses are more accepting, their partners are often more willing to change; when they change, their behavior becomes easier to accept. This is not the same as resignation or surrender. These strategies are designed to help both partners realize how they are caught in a mutual trap that is brought about by their interaction patterns and/or individual histories. IBCT theorists realize that many conflicts cannot be resolved and that the best that can be hoped for, by the couple, is a mutual acceptance of their differences (Dimidjian, Martell, & Christensen, 2002).

The IBCT approach is rooted in behavioral therapy but also contains some of the tolerance interventions of strategic therapy and the empathic joining of client-centered and emotionally focused therapies. This approach focuses as much upon the recipient of behavior as it does on the agent of behavior. The relationship context can change as a result of not only one partner's altering the frequency or intensity of the behavior but also from the other partner's receiving the behavior differently.

The treatment goals of IBCT are to help each partner better understand and accept each other as individuals and to develop a collaborative set where each partner is willing to make the changes necessary to improve the quality and satisfaction in the relationship. These treatment goals are guided by the formulation that occurs in the assessment phase.

Assessment

IBCT begins with a thorough assessment of the couple. This assessment consists of an initial conjoint session, one session with each partner individually, and specific questionnaires. This phase of therapy is designed to answer six questions:

1 How distressed is this couple?
2 How committed is this couple to continuing the relationship?

3 What are the divisive issues?
4 Why are these issues so sensitive for them?
5 What are the relationship's strengths that encourage them to keep trying?
6 What can treatment (couple therapy or other intervention) do to help them?

DEEP analysis is also included (Christensen & Doss, 2017). IBCT conceptualizes each problem in three parts: A theme, a polarization process, and a mutual trap. The *theme* is a brief summary of the main underlying issue in the couple relationship. This can take many forms such as closeness/distance, rigid/flexible, and saving/spending. Themes express the differences (not similarities) in the couple. The *polarization* process occurs as one partner repeatedly attempts to change the other. Couples feel hopeless and frustrated with this process, which is never resolved and leads to the *mutual trap.* Both feel stuck and unable to change (Dimidjian et al., 2002).

Once the assessment is completed, a feedback session occurs. The therapist describes the couple's level of satisfaction, the couple's formulation (their problematic issues, how they deal with those issues, and why those issues seem so difficult for them), strengths, and finally the process of therapy (Dimidjian et al., 2002).

Treatment

IBCT interventions fall into three categories: *Acceptance*, *tolerance*, and *change* techniques. There are two strategies for promoting acceptance: Namely, empathic joining and unified detachment. These strategies attempt to provide a couple with a new experience of the present problem, while the techniques aim to help the partners turn their problems into vehicles for greater intimacy. In contrast, tolerance interventions allow partners to let go of their efforts to change each other without aspiring to the somewhat greater goal of empathic joining and unified detachment. Tolerance is promoted through pointing out the positive features of negative behavior, practicing negative behavior in the therapy session, faking negative behavior between sessions, and self-care (Jacobson & Christensen, 1996). Finally, change techniques are used to directly promote change in partner's behavior and consist largely of behavior exchange and communication/problem-solving training. Therapy continues until the presenting concerns are resolved and when the treatment contract is completed. Typically, IBCT lasts 6–12 sessions (Dimidjian et al., 2002).

The IBCT therapist operates in different roles depending on the context of the therapy. Usually, however, the therapist is active and directive. Sometimes, the therapist may be a teacher or coach and help the couple learn or improve existing skills. At other times, the therapist may need to be a compassionate listener or the interpreter of the function the behavior is having on the relationship (Christensen et al., 2004). The highest priority is to maintain the focus on the couple's conceptualization.

We revisit the case of Mark and Alex, this time from an IBCT perspective. First, we look at how the assessment questions might be answered:

1. How distressed is this couple?
   - Mark and Alex are moderately distressed by their present conflict.
2. How committed is this couple to continuing the relationship?
   - They are very committed to each other and continuing the relationship.
3. What are the divisive issues?
   - As mentioned earlier, the issues are primarily about distance and togetherness, as well as allowing the other person to be independent without triggering the other person's anxiety.
4. Why are these issues so sensitive for them?
   - These issues are problematic because they raise fears in both Mark and Alex about the other person's level of commitment, abandonment, and making a mistake.
5. What are the relationship's strengths that encourage them to keep trying?
   - Their strengths are that they genuinely care about each other and are unwilling to give up on the relationship. As a result, they are motivated to work and try new behaviors.

IBCT can help Mark and Alex by introducing affective elements into the therapy, in addition to the behavioral and cognitive elements described previously. Specifically, an IBCT therapist would emphasize acceptance techniques ("I accept that Mark ..." "I accept that Alex ..."), increase empathy ("Because I love Mark, I can accept that ..." "Because I love Alex, I can accept that ..."), and increase tolerance for the problem behavior by focusing on the positive aspects of the negative behavior (i.e. "I see now that Mark's behavior means ..." "I see now that Alex's behavior means ..."). The underlying belief in IBCT is that without the emotional piece, the behavioral changes will not last.

As previously mentioned, IBCT represents an evolutionary leap forward from TBCT. Although TCBMT (traditional cognitive behavioral marital therapy) was found to be successful in helping couples with a variety of presenting concerns, in head-to-head comparisons of the two theories, IBCT is proving to be a superior improvement (Christensen et al., 2004; Johnson, 2003). Recent "efficacy research demonstrates that IBCT is comparable or superior to TBCT, particularly in the maintenance of treatment gains" (Christensen & Doss, 2017, p. 112).

Cognitive Behavioral Couple Therapy

While IBCT emphasizes the behavioral side of the CBT equation, CBCT emphasizes the cognitive side. It focuses on the interplay of cognitions, emotional responses, and behavioral interactions between partners. It involves cognitive therapy interventions for addressing partners' cognitions and emotional responses, along with behavioral interventions for improving a couple's communication, problem-solving, and exchanges of pleasing rather than distressing actions. CBCT is a systemic model of relationships in that it tracks interaction cycles in which partners continuously influence one another. For example, Partner A may fail to respond to Partner B's question. As a result, B interprets Partner A's behavior as uncaring and becomes verbally angry at Partner A. Then A perceives B's behavior as unjustified and walks away; B interprets A's walking away as disrespectful, and the cycle continues.

Initially, CBCT was developed to improve intimate relationships by reducing aversive behavioral interactions, increasing pleasing behavior, and reducing distorted or inappropriate cognitions contributing to conflict and dissatisfaction. It seeks to improve the couple's abilities to regulate negative emotions like anger. It also focuses on destructive behavior interaction patterns. For example, it seeks to identify and change relational patterns where one partner makes demands and the other withdraws, or where both partners escalate verbal or physical aggression. Furthermore, CBCT focuses on developing couples' skills for communication and problem-solving (Epstein & Zheng, 2017). Research continues to demonstrate its effectiveness in creating such positive behavior changes as well as improved relationship satisfaction (Belanger, Laporte, Sabourin & Wright, 2015).CBCT has identified five types of cognitions associated with relational distress (Simpson, Atkins, Gattis, & Christensen, 2008). The first three occur as "automatic thoughts" in stream of consciousness thinking, while the other two are relatively stable schemas or long-standing beliefs that individuals have developed over the course of their lives.

1 *Selective attention* involves noticing particular aspects of events in one's relationship while overlooking other aspects.
2 *Attributions* are inferences about factors that have influenced one's own or another's behavior. For example, one partner may conclude that the other partner's failure to respond to a question was due to her not being a caring person.
3 *Expectancies* are predictions about the likelihood or probability that a particular event will occur. For example, a partner who tries to engage one's partner in a discussion may come to expect that such an effort will lead the partner to withdraw.
4 *Assumptions* are beliefs about natural characteristics of people and relationships. For example, a male partner may assume that because his parents divorced when he was young, the institution of marriage is inherently unstable.

5 *Standards* involve beliefs about characteristics that individuals and relationships "should" possess. For example, a not uncommon standard among couples is that partners who really care should be able to sense the other partners' feelings without them needing to be expressed directly.

Assessment

In this approach, assessment is one of the most important aspects of treatment (Baucom et al., 2015). Accurate assessment and diagnosis of the couple's problem is conducted systematically and includes the couple's attributions, expectancies, selective perceptions, and standards concerning their perceptions. The methods traditionally utilized are clinical interview procedures, observation of the couple's spontaneous interactions and underlying cognitions, probing for specific emotional and behavioral responses, and assessment questionnaires (Baucom, Epstein, & LaTaillade, 2002; Epstein, 2003).

Clinical interviews are another source of information about partners' beliefs, expectations, and attributions. In this approach, therapists rely heavily on clinical interviews to collect detailed reports about relational interactions. The goal of these interviews is to create a functional analysis in which both the antecedent stimuli and the consequences of any problematic behavior are identified. The result of this analysis reveals how each person's behaviors stimulate and reinforce or punish the other's behaviors and how this pattern involves circular causality. It is crucial, however, that this analysis be restricted to concrete, observable behaviors.

This interview is used to probe for the automatic thoughts that occur when one partner becomes upset with the other (Beck, Freeman, & Davis, 2004). These are reactive thoughts that come up based on little or no information and are founded on experiences that may or may not fit the present situation. As a result, these automatic thoughts can often get a person in trouble when they make important relationship decisions based on them. By conducting an interview, a therapist can assess couples' selective perceptions of each partners' behavior by asking them questions about their observations of their partner, what circumstances, how often, and when they occur. Interviews can also elicit the underlying beliefs and expectancies by asking questions like "How does (what your partner does) compare with how you want it to be?" According to Epstein (2003), when interviewing couples about their cognitions and expectancies, it is important to be able to identify the partners' short-term and long-term expectations of what the partner will do since the expectancies may be different as time passes. An example of this is when a person attempts to communicate her needs, and her partner listens attentively but later (in a day or week) uses it against her. The task of the clinician is to observe changes in the partner's emotions and behaviors and then inquire about the thoughts that were occurring when those shifts took place. Some clients initially will not be skilled at monitoring their cognitions, but with practice, most can report relevant thoughts linked to dysfunctional relational interactions.

For the skilled cognitive behavioral couple therapist, spontaneous outbursts or "accidental" expressions can contain critical information about partners' beliefs or underlying cognitions. Such patterns as selective perception, misattributions, predictions, assumptions, and extreme standards for the relationship can be readily identified by the type of language that the partners use. For example, partners may make comments such as "You always/never ...," "A good [partner] should ...," "You always have the last word ...," in unguarded casual conversation that they may not say in a more formal setting (Epstein, 2003).

They may also directly manipulate the assessment in order to elicit these expressions. Often, this is done by asking the couple to engage in a discussion about an area of concern in the relationship, or share some thoughts or feelings about the partner or the relationship. Usually, the couple will engage in a more usual pattern of communication about each other, which allows the therapist to assess their specific communication skills, whether they can complete the task, and what the degree of damage the communication style inflicts. In addition, the therapist can ascertain (a) the clients' ability to interact with one another and (b) what specific underlying beliefs the couple may be operating under that is contributing to the dysfunction in the relationship (Baucom et al., 2002).

If, during the course of an assessment, the therapist notices beliefs or cognitions being demonstrated or if there is a reaction to what one of the partners is saying, the therapist will usually probe for more information about that particular subject. The couple's nonverbal behavior can also provide an opportunity to interrupt the conversation and ask questions about specific reactions. For example, if one partner reacts to the other with eye-rolls, negative facial expressions, or turning away, the therapist might say, "Just a moment ago, Joe said ________ and a look came across your face which showed (*a feeling*). Can you talk about what you were thinking and feeling at that moment?" When therapists seize the opportunity to respond to the couple's statements and nonverbal reactions, critical information that is needed for the next phases of goal-setting and treatment is gained.

Treatment

In a cognitive behavioral approach to couple therapy, the focus of treatment is on those faulty cognitions and behaviors impeding the couple's relationship and focuses primarily on the present and assumes that insight and reality testing are necessary for effective change. The therapist, serving as a consultant as the couple generates and either accepts or rejects new cognitions and behaviors based upon a rational evaluation of the evidence, completes an accurate and thorough assessment and then applies the appropriate intervention strategies in both cognitive and behavioral domains.

Following the assessment, the therapist will negotiate and set specific goals for treatment. A mutually agreed-upon treatment contract is set with the couple, laying out the length and scope of therapy. In addition to acting as a guide and educator, the therapist also monitors progress toward the therapeutic goals. The basic treatment interventions are discrimination training, homework, communication and assertiveness training, problem-solving training, cognitive restructuring, and Socratic questioning (Baucom et al., 2002). They are not mutually exclusive, and couples treatment usually involves combining these into a treatment regimen.

Discrimination Training – a technique used to help couples monitor their behavior, both positive and negative, and objective and subjective observations of each other in order to evaluate the accuracy of the appraisals made regarding each other's behaviors.

Homework Assignments – the typical form for practicing new strategies devised in therapy and monitoring the adherence to the agreed changes.

Communication Training – techniques that help couples develop expressive and listening skills (such as turn taking, structured listening exercises, etc.).

Assertiveness Training – techniques that teach couples to speak directly to each other in a brief and direct manner without being aggressive or passive.

Problem-Solving Training – a step-by-step technique that helps couples negotiate a solution that is acceptable to both parties and likely to be implemented successfully. The typical steps in a problem-solving technique are: (1) Get a clear definition of the problem, (2) brainstorm solutions to the problem, (3) evaluate each alternative, and (4) choose a solution.

Cognitive Restructuring – techniques designed to help partners increase their awareness of the thoughts that are contributing to their distress and conflict and to test the validity or appropriateness of them against reality or other alternative explanations in order to broaden their way of thinking about close relationships.

Socratic Questioning – a technique used by cognitive behavioral couple therapists to help couples probe and evaluate their logic for certain beliefs or viewpoints.

As mentioned earlier, treatment is goal-based, including length of treatment. Likewise, termination occurs when the agreed-upon goals are met and the set number of sessions has elapsed. If the initial assessment was thorough and accurate, and treatment proceeded smoothly, termination is appropriate with some follow-up. However, if in the course of treatment new issues emerge or additional issues outside of the original contract arise, then an additional treatment contract may be negotiated for couples or individual therapy.

We return to the case of Mark and Alex presented earlier in this chapter and examine their dynamics from a more cognitively oriented perspective. Such a therapist would probably do the same level of detailed assessment on the couple (and reach many of the same behavioral conclusions) but would also include a focus on Mark and Alex's beliefs, attributions, and expectations of each other and how that specifically affects their behavior toward each other. There is the belief on the part of both partners that "When I am in love, I should always want to be with (the other person) if we are truly made for each other." This belief feeds into the expectation that the partner would likewise want to spend time with the person, which leads to resentment when the partner wants to spend time alone, with others, or doing something that the other person doesn't care to do. In the same way, these beliefs and expectations color both Mark and Alex's perception of the other person's behavior. Instead of viewing the other person's actions as a need for downtime or alone time, it is misattributed to a lack of desire or interest in the relationship. In addition, instead of seeing the lack of a schedule as the cause for confusion, each person blames the other for not caring or begins to look for flaws in the relationship.

Treatment for Mark and Alex, from a cognitive perspective, would include the behavioral interventions described earlier but would also likely include discrimination training and cognitive restructuring. With discrimination training, Mark and Alex would be taught how to properly categorize their observations of the other's behavior without blaming or jumping to conclusions about the motives behind it (e.g. "He just doesn't want to be with me, he just wants to be with his friends."). In addition, cognitive restructuring would teach Mark and Alex how to reality test or challenge their initial thoughts and impressions about each other's behavior (based on their beliefs and expectations) and then replace them with new, nontoxic thoughts (e.g. "He is not rejecting me; he just needs time by himself to recharge his batteries. I love him enough to do that.").

New Applications

The application of this approach to various partner and couple concerns is quite remarkable. Ten concerns are described in this section, along with supporting research. The concerns are depression, post-traumatic stress disorder (PTSD), obsessive-compulsive disorder (OCD), substance use disorder, cancer, cardiac disease, financial strain, partner aggression, infidelity, and sexual dysfunction.

Depression

Relationship distress is a risk factor for the development of depression which is likewise a stressor on a relationship. CBCT-based interventions have been developed to decrease negative relational interactions and increase emotional support among partners (Whisman & Beach, 2012). It provides psychoeducation about risk factors for depression and interventions to reduce depression and improve relational functioning. Research has found that such couple therapy reduced both depression and relationship problems, in contrast with individual cognitive therapy which did not reduce relationship distress (Beach & O'Leary, 1992).

Post-Traumatic Stress Disorder

Partners who experience PTSD exhibit chronic symptoms in themselves and in their relationships. These include restricted communication, aggression, avoidance, anxiety, anger, depression, emotional numbing, and trauma-related beliefs and guilt. A CBCT-based approach was developed that helps to increase partners' expectancies that they can overcome the problem. It focuses on improving positive interactions, communication, and problem-solving skills, as well as reducing emotional numbing and avoidance. Cognitive restructuring is used to reduce the beliefs that maintain PTSD symptoms and relationship distress. Research has found improvements in PTSD symptoms, trauma-related beliefs, and relationship distress (Macdonald, Pukay-Martin, Wagner, Fredman, & Monson, 2016).

Obsessive-Compulsive Disorder

The symptoms of OCD commonly involve recurrent intrusive thoughts, anxiety, and compulsive rituals such as checking. Besides interfering with a partner's own functioning; they can be significant stressors in a couple's relationships. In turn, conflict between partners can exacerbate the OCD symptoms. A couple-based approach to exposure and response prevention procedures for OCD that emphasizes CBCT principles has been developed. It addresses partners' cognitions and anxiety with psychoeducation and cognitive restructuring of beliefs associated with obsessive thinking and ritualistic behavior, as well as behaviors through partner-assisted response prevention. Research found that OCD symptoms were reduced and maintained at 6-month and 12-month follow-ups (Abramowitz et al., 2013).

Substance Abuse

Substance abuse creates persistent distress for both partner and the relationship. These include denial that substance use is a problem, unregulated anger, and aggressiveness, social withdrawal, or failure to carry out family roles. Not uncommonly, the non-using partner can unintentionally "enable" or maintain substance use. A CBCT-based intervention has been developed to increase positive interactions, promote readiness for change, and resolve conflicts. It fosters constructive couple interactions, with couple practice during sessions and homework focused on increasing exchanges of caring behavior, increasing shared rewarding activities, and improving partners' communication and problem-solving skill (Birchler, Fals-Stewart, & O'Farrell, 2008). A meta-analysis of randomized controlled outcome studies for couples with a member diagnosed with a substance use disorder indicated that such couple therapy was more effective than individual therapy in reducing both substance use and relationship distress (Powers, Vedel, & Emmelkamp, 2008). We will cover the topic of substance abuse and its treatment in Chapter 12.

Cancer

A CBCT-based intervention has been developed for women treated for breast cancer and their male partners. It includes psychoeducation on the effects of cancer treatments on partners' sexual functioning, training in communication skills, and problem-solving skills. The intervention fosters mutual emotional support and effective decision-making (Baucom et al., 2009). Another CBCT-based intervention is used with colorectal cancer patients and their partners. It also uses cognitive behavioral sex therapy with sensate focus exercises, sexual communication training, challenging of negative sexually related cognitions, and problem-solving skills. The treatment produced improved sexual function but not for sexual distress, intimacy, or sexual communication for the patients. However, there was improvement in all factors for the patients' partners (Reese et al. 2014).

Cardiac Disease

A CBCT intervention has been developed for patients with heart conditions. It assists partners in coping with stresses associated with these conditions and developing risk-reducing health behaviors such as exercise and activity level, nutrition, and medication management. The treatment harnesses resources of partners' mutual emotional support and dyadic coping. This couples intervention was found to be more effective than individual treatment in improving exercise and activity level, although both treatments had limited effect on weight loss and nutrition (Sher et al., 2014).

Financial Strain

Financial strain is the subjective negative appraisal and associated emotional distress associated with job loss or debt (Gale, Goetz & Bermudez, 2009). It is more intense when partners believe that they lack sufficient financial resources to meet demands. This strain decreases couples' relationship satisfaction, especially when they express verbal hostility or engage in the demand-withdraw relational pattern (Falconier & Epstein, 2011). Because financial strain and couple relationship dynamics are intertwined, there is an emerging trend toward couple therapy and other professional services to integrate financial counseling and couple therapy, particularly CBCT (Gale et al., 2009).

Partner Aggression

Two types of such aggression are recognized: Severe physical violence and common couple violence. The severe form is perpetrated by one partner against the other for the purpose of control. The common form is bilateral and consists of psychological aggression and mild to moderate physical aggression (Epstein, Werlinich, & LaTaillade, 2015). Empirical evidence of the common form shows that it can be treated safely and effectively with CBCT which is the most commonly used therapy. It includes psychoeducation about partner aggression, anger management training, and interventions to modify cognitions that justify or elicit aggression. Also included is training in communication skills and problem-solving skills (Epstein et al., 2015). This topic will be discussed in depth in Chapter 12.

Infidelity

Infidelity is a major stressor for many couples. It often elicits trauma symptoms in the betrayed partner (Peluso, 2018). A CBCT-based program (Baucom, Snyder, & Gordon, 2009) helps partners cope with the trauma symptoms and understand the factors that led to a betrayal. It focuses on constructive communication and develops strategies for reducing risk factors for further infidelity as well as making informed decisions about the future of the relationship. Preliminary research found that the program improved relationship satisfaction of betrayed partners (Baucom, Gordon, Snyder, & Atkins, 2006). This topic will be covered in detail in Chapter 13.

Sexual Dysfunctions

CBCT has also been used to treat sexual dysfunctions, which are significant stressors in many couples' relationships. A clinical trial, compared the combination of Levitra (Vardenafil HCL) and cognitive behavioral sex therapy with the medication alone in treating a sample of men with erectile dysfunction and their female partners. The sex therapy included psychoeducation about the sexual disorder and training in communication and sexual skills, sensate focus exercise, and reframing negative cognitions about sexual function. They found that both treatments improved erectile function but that only the combined treatment involving cognitive behavioral interventions improved both partners' sexual satisfaction and females' sexual function (Boddi et al., 2015). This topic will also be covered in Chapter 13.

Dialectic Behavior Couple Therapy

Some couples experience high levels of conflicts due to a highly reactive relational style in which they are easily triggered to negative thoughts, words, or behaviors. In time, out-of-control emotions begin to dominate their relationship. While they may greatly desire to move out of these painful cycles, they are unable to do so. Their high reactivity makes them difficult to treat, and most therapy approaches don't seem to work with them (Fruzzetti & Fruzzetti, 2009).

Unlike other couples who seek couple therapy for help with communication and intimacy-building, high conflict couples need to get control of emotions first and then learn strategies for dealing with painful and unproductive conflict before working on enhancing their relationship. Effective work with such couples requires a keen understanding of emotions and emotional dysregulation. When a partner's emotional system becomes dysregulated, it is impossible to respond effectively to the situation. The reason is that parts of the brain are activated which interfere with logical thinking as well as effective problem-solving and conflict resolution efforts. It becomes increasingly difficult to see things from the partner's point of view. In this state of emotional arousal, validating one's partner, which is essential to communicating effectively, becomes impossible (Fruzzetti & Worrall, 2010). Fortunately, there is hope for such couples.

DBT which was originally developed by Marsha Linehan for working with para-suicidal substance abusing females with borderline personality disorder has been modified for use with couples. Linehan conceptualized this personality disorder in terms of the biosocial model wherein the biological component is emotional reactivity and the social component was parental invalidation (Linehan, 2015).

Treatment Process

It is preferable to infuse DBT with the nonjudgmental attitude that the therapist continually models. It promotes acceptance and validation of each partner such that they develop a mindful awareness of their own experiences moment to moment. DBT also focuses on needed change. This means shifting from negative and invalidating responses and judgments of one's partner as well as increasing emotional self-regulation and distress tolerance. Central to DBT is developing the requisite skills to shift from emotional dysregulation to increased regulation and effective communication.

So what do couple therapy sessions that incorporate DBT look like? First and foremost, they are skill-focused. Skills are taught in sessions which usually are between 60 and 90 minutes. Homework is an essential component of this therapeutic approach. Typically, it might include practicing newly learned skills, some reading, and keeping a log. Couples learn to develop skills in emotional self-regulation, mindfulness, and distress tolerance. They also learn self-expression of their needs, thoughts, concerns, and desires as well as effective problem-solving skills. A useful book for couples that describes the therapy process is *The High Conflict Couple: A Dialectical Behavior Therapy Guide to Finding Peace, Intimacy and Validation* (Fruzzetti, 2006). There is increasing research support for the effectiveness of this approach with high conflict couples (Fruzzetti & Payne, 2015). More details on the use of DBT with couples are presented in Chapter 8.

> We return again to the case of Mark and Alex. While disagreements are distressing to this couple, they would not be considered a high conflict couple. If they were, couples-focused DBT would likely be the treatment of choice. Nevertheless, it might still be a treatment option if the other approaches, CBCT and IBCT, were only partially effective. Given that their relational style is reactive, they might be good candidates for learning the skills of emotional self-regulation, mindfulness, and distress tolerance. One or more of these skills could be incorporated in the treatment process. These skills could be taught and practiced in session and then practiced between sessions.

Online Cognitive Behavioral Couple Intervention

One final area that we will focus on in this chapter is to briefly describe an online cognitive behavioral intervention for couples: Our Relationship Program (Doss et al., 2016). In this eight-hour self-help program, couples complete online activities consisting of text, audio, animations, graphics, and videos. They complete the majority of this three-phase program on their own. They come together at the end of the program for a focused conversation with their partner. "Observe" is the first phase of the program. Here, they complete relational assessments and mutually decide on one or two core issues or problems to focus on during the rest of the program. In the "Understand" phase, each partner goes through a DEEP analysis of the problem. These separate analyses are shared during subsequent structured conversations. Finally, during the "Respond" phase, they develop a plan for improving the issue or problem by viewing information about acceptance and self-change, communication tips, and tailored suggestions. During these conversations, partners share strategies to improve communications and engage in problem-solving exercises specific to their core concerns. Besides these online activities, couples participate in up to four 15-minute phone- or videoconferences with a program coach. These calls answer general questions about the program, tailor it to the couple's needs, and keep couples progressing through the program. To avoid these calls becoming a therapy session, they are limiting to specific topics.

Initial research on this program is quite encouraging. A sample of 300 distressed couples was randomly assigned to the online program or to a wait-list control. Remarkably, 86% completed the program, and 97% indicated that they would recommend it to a friend. Compared to the control condition, couples experienced significant improvements in relationship satisfaction

(d = 0.69) as well as significant effects on depressive (d = 0.50) and anxiety (d = 0.21) symptoms. Furthermore, these couples were only slightly less satisfied (d = 0.18) with the program than couples who engaged in regular IBCT or TBCT couple therapy (Christensen & Doss, 2017).

Concluding Note

Except for the cognitive behavioral couple therapy approaches described in this chapter, most other couples approaches described in Section 2 of this book have little or no empirical support. Two exceptions are emotionally focused couple therapy and Gottman couple therapy described in Chapter 8. Why is this research support important? Because of the increasing demand for accountability, and because only approaches that have achieved evidence-based status are likely to be reimbursed in the near future. Not surprisingly, the only two couple therapy approaches in the American Psychological Association's list of evidence-based psychological treatments are CBT couples approaches. Also, not surprising, is that students and those just starting to practice couple therapy are gravitating toward the evidence-based approaches.

Furthermore, most approaches have had limited theoretical developments since the second edition of this book was published in 2006, nor have they extended their applicability to the increasing types of psychological disorders, physical health problems, and severe relational problems that couples present with in seeking therapy. In contrast, the cognitive behavioral couple therapy approaches described in this chapter have distinguished themselves by increases in theoretical development significantly increased applicability, as well as research support. In short, cognitive behavioral couple therapy approaches have proven to be a versatile and effective modality of couple therapy and appear to be thriving while other approaches appear to be struggling to survive.

In the next chapter, we will explore the various systemic approaches to couple therapy.

References

Abramowitz, J. S., Baucom, D. H., Wheaton, M. G., Boeding, S., Fabricant, L. E., Paprocki, C., & Fischer, M. (2013). Enhancing exposure and response prevention for OCD: A couple-based approach. *Behavior Modification, 37*, 189–210.

Baucom, D. H., Epstein, N. B., Kirby, J. S., & LaTaillade, J. J. (2015). Cognitive behavioral couple therapy. In A. Gurman, J., Lebow, & D. Snyder (Eds.). *Clinical handbook of couple therapy* (5th ed., pp. 23–60). New York, NY: Guilford Press.

Baucom, D. H., Epstein, N., & LaTaillade, J. J. (2002). Cognitive–behavioral couple therapy. In A. S. Gurman & N. S. Jacobson (Eds.), *Clinical handbook of couple therapy* (3rd ed., pp. 26–58). New York, NY: Guilford.

Baucom, D. H., Gordon, K. C., Snyder, D. K., Atkins, D. C., & Christensen, A. (2006). Treating affair couples: Clinical considerations and initial findings. *Journal of Cognitive Psychotherapy, 20*, 375–392.

Baucom, D. H., Porter, L. S., Kirby, J. S., Gremore, T. M., Wiesenthal, N., Aldridge, W., … Keefe, F. J. (2009). A couple-based intervention for female breast cancer. *Psychooncology, 8*, 276–283.

Baucom, D. H., Snyder, D. K., & Gordon, K. C. (2009). *Helping couples get past the affair: A clinician's guide*. New York, NY: Guilford.

Beach, S. R., & O'Leary, K. D. (1992). Treating depression in the context of marital discord: Outcome and predictors of response for marital therapy vs. cognitive therapy. *Behavior Therapy, 23*, 507–528.

Beck, A. T., Freeman, A., & Davis, D. D. (2004). *Cognitive therapy of personality disorders*. New York, NY: Guilford Press.

Belanger, C., Laporte, L., Sabourin, S., & Wright, J. (2015). The effect of cognitive-behavioral group marital therapy on marital happiness and problem solving self-appraisal. *American Journal of Family Therapy, 43*, 103–118.

Birchler, G. R., Fals-Stewart, W., & O'Farrell, T. (2008). Couple therapy for alcoholism and drug abuse. In A. Gurman (Ed.). *Clinical handbook of couple therapy* (4th ed., pp. 523–544). New York, NY: Guilford.

Blagys, M., & Hilsenroth, M. (2002). Distinctive activities of cognitive-behavioral therapy: A review of the comparative psychotherapy process literature. *Clinical Psychology Review, 22*, 671–706.

Boddi, V., Castellini, G., Casale, H., Rastrelli, G., Boni, L., Corona, G., & Maggi, M. (2015). An integrated approach with vardenafil orodispersible tablet and cognitive behavioral sex therapy for treatment of erectile dysfunction: A randomized controlled pilot study. *Andrology, 3*, 909–918.

Christensen, A., Atkins, D. C., Berns, S., Wheeler, J., Baucom, D. H., & Simpson, L. E. (2004). Traditional versus integrative behavioral couple therapy for significantly and chronically distressed married couples. *Journal of Consulting and Clinical Psychology, 72*, 176–191.

Christensen, A., Dimidjian, S., & Martell, C. (2015). Integrative behavioral couple therapy. In A. Gurman, J., Lebow, & D. Snyder (Eds.). *Clinical handbook of couple therapy* (5th ed., pp. 61–96). New York, NY: Guilford Press.

Christensen, A., & Doss, D. (2017). Integrative behavioral couple therapy. *Current Opinion in Psychology, 13*, 111–114.

Dimidjian, S., Martell, C. R., & Christensen, A. (2002). Integrative behavioral couple therapy. In A. S. Gurman & N. S. Jacobson (Eds.), *Clinical handbook of couple therapy* (3rd ed., pp. 251–277). New York, NY: Guilford.

Doss, B. D., Cicila, L. N., Georgia, E. J., Roddy, M. K., Nowlan, K. M., Benson, L. A., & Christensen, A. (2016). A randomized controlled trial of the web-based our relationship program: Effects on relationship and individual functioning. *Journal of Consulting and Clinical Psychology, 84*, 285–296.

Epstein, N. (2003). Cognitive–behavioral therapies for couples and families. In L. L. Hecker & J. L. Wetcher (Eds.), *Introduction to marriage and family therapy* (pp. 203–254). New York, NY: Hawthorne Clinical Practice Press.

Epstein, N. B., & Zheng, L. (2017). Cognitive-behavioral couple therapy. *Current Opinion in Psychology, 13*, 142–147.

Epstein, N. B., Werlinich, C. A., & LaTaillade, J. J. (2015). Couple therapy for partner aggression. In A. Gurman, J. Lebow, & D. Snyder (Eds.). *Clinical handbook of couple therapy* (5th ed., pp. 389–411). New York, NY: Guilford Press.

Falconier, M. K., & Epstein, N. B. (2011). Couples undergoing financial strain: What we know and we can do. *Family Relations, 60*, 303–317.

Fruzzetti, A., & Payne, L. (2015). Couple therapy and borderline personality disorder. In A. Gurman, J. Lebow, & D. Snyder (Eds.). *Clinical handbook of couple therapy* (5th ed., pp. 606–634). New York, NY: Guilford Press.

Fruzzetti, A. E. (2006). *The high conflict couple: A dialectical behavior therapy guide to finding peace, intimacy and validation.* Oakland, CA: New Harbinger.

Fruzzetti, A. E., & Worrall, J. M. (2010). Accurate expression and validation: A transactional model for understanding individual and relationship distress. In K. Sullivan & J. Davila (Eds.), *Support processes in intimate relationships* (pp. 121–150). New York, NY: Oxford University Press.

Fruzzetti, A. R., & Fruzzetti, A. E. (2009). Dialectics in cognitive and behavior therapy. In W. T. O'Donohue & J. E. Fisher (Eds.), *General principles and empirically supported techniques of cognitive behavior therapy* (pp. 230–239). Hoboken, NJ: Wiley.

Gale, J., Goetz, J., & Bermudez, M. (2009). Relational financial therapy. *Family Therapy Magazine, 8*, 25–29.

Jacobson, N. S., & Christensen, A. (1996). *Integrative couple therapy: Promoting acceptance and change.* New York, NY: Norton.

Johnson, S. M. (2003). Couple therapy research: Status and directions. In G. P. Sholevar (Ed.), *Textbook of family and couple therapy* (pp. 797–814). Alexandria, VA: American Psychiatric Publishing.

Linehan, M. (2015). *DBT skills training manual* (2nd ed.). New York, NY: Guilford.

Macdonald, A., Pukay-Martin, N. D., Wagner, A. C., Fredman, S. J., & Monson, C. M. (2016). Cognitive-behavioral conjoint therapy improves various PTSD symptoms and trauma- related cognitions: Results from a randomized controlled trial. *Journal of Family Psychology, 30*, 157–162.

Peluso, P. R. (2018). *A family systems guide to infidelity: Helping couples understand, recover from, and avoid future affairs.* New York, NY: Routledge.

Powers, M. B., Vedel, E., & Emmelkamp, P. M. (2008). Behavioral couple therapy (BCT) for alcohol and drug use disorders: A meta-analysis. *Clinical Psychology Review, 28*, 952–962.

Reese, J. B., Porter, L. S., Regan, K. R., Keefe, F. J., Azad, N. S., Diaz, L. A., … Haythornwaite, J. A. (2014). A randomized pilot trial of a telephone-based couples intervention for physical intimacy and sexual concerns in colorectal cancer. *Psychooncology, 23*, 1005–1013.

Reese, J. B., Porter, L. S., Regan, K. R., Keefe, F. J., Azad, N. S., Diaz Jr, L. A., … & Haythornthwaite, J. A. (2014). A randomized pilot trial of a telephone-based couples intervention for physical intimacy and sexual concerns in colorectal cancer. *Psycho-Oncology, 23*(9), 1005–1013.

Sher, T. G., Braun, L., Domas, A., Bellg, A., Baucom, D. H., & Houle, T. T. (2014). The partners for life program: A couples approach to cardiac risk reduction. *Family Process, 53*, 131–149.

Simpson, L. E., Atkins, D. C., Gattis, K. S., & Christensen, A. (2008). Low-level relationship aggression and couple therapy outcomes. *Journal of Family Psychology, 22*, 102–111.

Wheeler, J. G., Christensen, A., & Jacobson, N. S. (2001). Couple distress. In D. H. Barlow (Ed.), *Clinical handbook of psychological disorders: A step-by-step treatment manual* (3rd ed., pp. 609–630). New York, NY: Guilford Press.

Whisman, M. A., & Beach, S. R. (2012). Couple therapy for depression. *Journal of Clinical Psychology, 68*, 526–535.

6 Structural and Strategic Approaches to Couple Therapy

LEARNING OBJECTIVES

In this chapter, the reader will learn the following:

1. A historical perspective and systems concepts common to systems-oriented couples work.
2. The structural approach to couple therapy.
3. The brief strategic approach to couple therapy.
4. The systemic approaches to couple therapy.
5. Common interventions shared by systems-oriented couple therapists.

Systems theory represents a significant element in the history of couple therapy, and many consider that systems thinking is basic to the practice of couple therapy. Accordingly, this chapter presents the systems-oriented approaches to couple therapy. It begins with a brief historical perspective on couple therapy. This is followed by an overview of basic systems concepts applicable to couples. Then, the major systems-based approaches are described. These include Structural Couple Therapy, Brief Strategic Couple Therapy, and some common systemic approaches to couple therapy. Next is a discussion of several common clinical interventions shared by many systems-oriented couple therapists. Finally, a case example illustrates many of these points.

Historical Perspective on Couple Therapy

Traditionally, couple therapy was viewed as an outgrowth of the family therapy revolution beginning in the 1950s and 1960s and coming into its own in the 1980s and 1990s. As a result, family systems theory was usually given primacy when discussing couple therapy. However, a critical historical review shows that this is not an accurate reflection of either the development of couple therapy or its practice (Gurman & Fraenkel, 2002). In fact, the caseload of most family therapists is predominantly couples rather than families (Gurman, 2015). In addition, most family systems therapy writers have focused as much attention on couples issues as on family issues (Dattilio & Bevilacqua, 2000).

Nevertheless, the similarities of couple therapy and family therapy cannot be overlooked or dismissed, particularly the contributions of the systems-oriented family therapies. These approaches have provided a solid grounding in working with multiple clients at the same time even as the field of couple therapy continues to sharpen the distinctions between itself and family therapy (Gurman, 2015).

It is useful to note that four recent developments have profoundly altered the field of couple therapy (Gurman, 2015). The first has been the re-inclusion of individual partner dynamics that complements couples dynamics. The second is the acknowledgment of psychiatric disorders and their impact of relational functioning. The third is that most of the growth in the field has come from breakthroughs in the psychological sciences rather than from family therapy theory and research. Fourth, couple therapy has emerged as a vibrant force within the psychotherapeutic realm. Accordingly, "(t)hese developments help to explain the penetration of couple therapy into the overall practice of psychotherapy" (Gurman, 2015, p. 8).

Basic Systems Concepts Applicable to Couples

Strategic, structural, and systemic approaches to couple therapy are concerned with how couples organize and communicate. Despite some differences among these approaches, they have several commonalities. Each systems-based approach contends that individuals can best be understood within the systemic context in which they live. This system generates the rules that the members of the system operate under. The presenting problem is viewed in terms of the function it serves within the relationship, relative to the rules, which can best be understood by examining the couple's interactions. All of these approaches employ general systems concepts such as homeostasis and positive feedback in understanding how a dyad functions. All are similar in practice. They observe the results of the therapeutic interventions in order to assess and plan future interventions. Practitioners of systems-based therapies maintain that they use whatever techniques work. There are many techniques common to these schools, including joining, reframing, and therapeutic paradox. All emphasize process over content and present behavior over past behavior (Gurman, 2015). All use both in-session and homework assignments to produce change. The therapist takes a directive role, and all approaches are basically brief (between 10 and 20 sessions).

These approaches are concerned with how people organize and communicate. The focus of the intervention is on current behaviors, communication, and roles. The fundamental belief of systemic approaches is that whatever affects one part of a system affects all parts. Table 6.1 provides a summary of each of the concepts and interventions, which will be described in detail as they relate to this basic premise.

Table 6.1 Basic Concepts Shared by Systems-Oriented Couple Therapists

Organization of Relationships: Relationships in systemic therapies are organized and conceptualized according to the concepts of *wholeness*, *boundaries*, and *hierarchy*.

- *Wholeness* refers to the understanding of patterns, rather than to an analysis of elements. Rather than looking at a couple's interaction, the therapist sees the larger pattern of interaction (e.g. withdrawal → nagging → passive-aggressive behavioral outburst → withdrawal → attacking → passive-aggressive behavioral outburst, etc.).
- *Boundaries* are invisible lines of demarcation in a relationship that may be defined, strengthened, loosened, or changed as a result of therapy. Boundaries range from rigid (extreme separateness) to diffuse (extreme togetherness). Ideally, boundaries are clear and help the couple's relationship to function effectively.
- *Hierarchy* refers to the fact that systems have several different levels. Hierarchies can refer to neutral structures for how information flows or upon which actions are decided. Hierarchies can also be indicators of how power is distributed in relationships and may be oppressive and dominating if it is unbalanced.

Homeostasis: Homeostasis is the tendency within a system to seek equilibrium or balance through maintenance of the status quo and resistance to change. Couples use various mechanisms, both positive and negative, to maintain balance and stability when there is disequilibrium.

Triangles/Coalitions: When a couple gets into conflict, there is no majority rule, which can lead to a stalemate or instability in the relationship. Triangulation, which is defined as a situation where a third party is brought into the conflict and sides with one of the partners, allows for the tension to be diffused and a stalemate to be broken. This triangle (or coalition) ultimately leads to resentment and dissatisfaction in the relationship as one person perceives him-/herself as the loser.

Enmeshment: Enmeshment is a state of the relationship characterized by intense dependence on the partner for emotional stability to the point where independence and autonomy are perceived threats to the homeostasis of the couple. Individual needs and outside influences are degraded or avoided (possibly including other family members), and change is actively resisted.

Communication: For systems therapists, both verbal and nonverbal communication, are important. Patterns of communication not only help to shape the behavior and functioning of family members; they also provide clues to the relative openness/closeness of the system and its interaction with other parts of the environment. Communication and feedback processes help to maintain a steady-state condition, in which the disequilibrium that produces growth and development and the continuity of the system are adequately balanced. It is a primary mode of change for couples.

Equifinality: This concept indicates that there are many different paths or procedures that will yield the same results. It is not necessary to begin at the same place or in the same way. This allows for a maximum level of flexibility on the therapist's part to meet the clients' needs, while at the same time maintaining a therapeutic focus on the underlying issues or concerns.

Circular Causality: This concept purports that both parties are involved in any problem. Frequently this will elicit resistance from the clients as it implicates both parties. The benefit for the couple is that each person can be empowered to make a change to the pattern. For the clinician, there is no need to search for a cause, as he or she can intervene from any one of several starting points and be successful. Any change in one aspect in one partner will affect the other.

(*Continued*)

Nonsummativity: This is the systemic belief that the relationship, as a whole, is different from the sum of its parts. In couple therapy, it is necessary to look at the parts and sum them up *and* to pay attention to the pattern that connects them in order to appreciate the structure.

First-Order Change: First-order change pertains to those alterations in a system that leave the fundamental organization of that system unchanged. It is superficial in nature, so while the change may reduce a symptom or resolve surface issue, it will not substantially affect the relationship.

Second-Order Change: Second-order change refers to alterations in a system that changes the fundamental organization of the system. Often this is a change in the way a couple operates or interacts with one another via attitudinal changes, which usually result in new behaviors and a reordering of the relational dynamics. This level of change is generally considered better than first-order change because it is structural and more permanent.

Organization of Relationships

According to system theorists, key concepts for organization are wholeness, boundaries, and hierarchies (Keim & Lappin, 2002). *Wholeness* refers to the understanding of patterns as opposed to an analysis of elements. Rather than looking at a couples interaction and seeing only that Bob is a bore or that Sally is wild, the therapist sees the larger pattern of interaction:

Withdrawal → nagging → passive-aggressive behavioral outburst → withdrawal → attacking → passive-aggressive behavioral outburst → and so on

The concept of *boundaries* refers to "the degree of emotional connection, dependence, support, and influence between different subsystems within the family, and between these subsystems and other social systems" (Keim & Lappin, 2002, p. 93). Boundaries are invisible lines of demarcation in a relationship that may be defined, strengthened, loosened, or changed as a result of therapy. Boundaries range from rigid (extreme separateness) to diffuse (extreme togetherness). Ideally, boundaries are clear and help the couple's relationship to function effectively.

The term *hierarchy* refers to the fact that systems have several different levels. Hierarchies can refer to neutral structures for how information flows or actions are decided upon. However, a hierarchy can also be oppressive and dominating if it is unbalanced. Healthy couple relationships require the perception of a hierarchical balance (Minuchin, Reiter, & Borda, 2013).

Homeostasis

Homeostasis is the tendency within a system to seek equilibrium or balance through maintenance of the status quo and resistance to change. Increases in tension or anxiety within the relationship cause disequilibrium. Couples use various mechanisms, both positive and negative, to maintain balance and stability. In addition, partners may use extreme behavior in order to bring a relationship back into balance, such as having an affair if the partner is a workaholic and doesn't spend time with them (Roberto-Forman, 2002).

Triangles/Coalitions

Bowen (1978) defined a triangle as the unit whereby emotionality could be most easily balanced and contained. When a couple gets into conflict, there is no majority rule, which can lead to a stalemate. There is tension between the desire to be close and the desire to be separate that cannot be negotiated in the conflict. Couples who are frequently in conflict usually develop instability in the relationship. Triangulation, which is defined as a situation where a third party is brought into the conflict and sides with one of the partners, allows for the tension to be diffused and a stalemate to be broken. One partner may feel justified and vindicated, and the other may feel unfairly ganged up on by the third party, but both can now avoid having to deal with one another solely. Inevitably, this leads to resentment and creates a pattern of disengagement from one another, particularly when problems need to be solved (Keim & Lappin, 2002).

Another variation of this, the coalition, takes place in the context of couple therapy when a partner tries to change the dynamics of a marriage by actively involving another generation of the family, such as a child or in-law. For example, a spouse enters a coalition with a member of another generation of the family to deal with responsibilities that were previously the responsibilities of the other spouse. The left-out partner is free to under-function, and the partner in the coalition is empowered to over-function by the other generation. Like any triangle/coalition, this ultimately leads to resentment and dissatisfaction in the relationship. These cross-generational coalitions can be a destructive force in the relationship that must be addressed (Minuchin et al., 2013; Roberto-Forman, 2002).

Enmeshment

Enmeshment is a state of the relationship characterized by intense dependence on the partner for emotional stability to the point where independence and autonomy are perceived as threats to the homeostasis of the couple. Individual needs and outside influences are degraded or avoided (possibly including other family members). Change is actively resisted by the partner or the couple, and the relationship can become stifling or constricting. This is frequently the relationship pattern in volatile relationships (Minuchin et al., 2013).

Communication

Within a systems perspective, all behavior is considered to be communication. Verbal communication and nonverbal communication are both viewed as very important. It is impossible, according to systems theorists, for an individual *not* to communicate. Patterns of communication not only help to shape the behavior and functioning of family members; they also provide clues to the relative openness/closeness of the system and its interaction with other parts of the environment (Keim & Lappin, 2002). Systems cannot be either too closed or too open and still function in a healthy manner.

Communication and feedback processes help to maintain a steady-state condition in which the disequilibrium that produces growth and development and the continuity of the system are adequately balanced. Negative feedback is a communication process used to correct system deviations by reestablishing a previous state of equilibrium. This process is usually at work in families where a child acts out in order to bring quarreling parents back together again. Positive feedback is a change-activating process within systems. Any tactic, whether from a therapist or a family member, that challenges the family homeostasis and changes the family's way of behaving is an example of positive feedback.

Systems theorists are also concerned with a process known as metacommunication, which is communication about communication. This term usually refers to the covert, nonverbal message (tone of voice, inflection, body language) that gives additional meaning to an overt, verbal message. Often, this level of communication reveals more about the real state of affairs in a relationship than the verbal communication.

Another systems concept is "double bind" which is a form of communication that leaves a responder unable to answer in a way that is likely to have a positive outcome. It includes a double message (e.g. "I'm glad to see you" while looking away) within an emotionally important relationship where the receiver of the message is unable to comment on the message. An example of a double bind would be one partner saying to the other, "No, go ahead, have a good time playing golf. I'll just stay here and clean the *whole house* because we've made so much of a mess this week." Here, there is a double message (play golf/I want you to help me), in an emotionally important relationship, with the partner unable to respond to the message without "losing" (if he goes, he'll be a jerk for leaving; if he tries to stay, he'll be told to go). In other words, there is no winning here (Keim, 2000).

Equifinality

This concept indicates that there are many different paths or procedures that will yield the same results. It is not necessary to begin at the same place or in the same way. Systemic theory indicates that a therapist can work with couples individually or conjointly and on any of their problems and make a significant intervention. This allows for a maximum level of flexibility on the therapist's part to meet the clients' needs, while at the same time maintaining a therapeutic focus on the underlying issues or concerns (Minuchin et al., 2013).

Circular Causality

This concept purports that both parties are involved in any problem. Partner A influences Partner B and vice versa. Does Jim leave and go out drinking with the boys because Jane nags him, or does Jane nag him because Jim goes out drinking with the boys? The answer is, of course, both. Frequently, this will elicit resistance from the clients as it implicates both parties, especially when one partner has taken on the role of victim in the relationship. Couple therapists must have a solid grounding in systems theory and have a good understanding of the underlying dynamics of the couple to be able to win the couple over to this way of conceptualizing their particular issue. The benefit for the couple is that each person can be empowered to make a change to the pattern. For the clinician, the implication associated with the concept of circular causality is that the therapist does not need to search for a cause but can intervene from any one of several starting points and be successful. Any change in one aspect in one partner will affect the other.

Nonsummativity

The marriage as a whole is different from the sum of its parts. Marriage is not understandable merely through a summarizing of the attributes or characteristics of the individual partners. To describe Judy as an individual and Tom as an individual is not the same as describing the pair in a relationship. Summing up of the parts does not provide the whole picture. That can be done only by looking at the picture as a whole.

It is also fair to say that the whole is different than the sum of the parts. According to Bateson (1980, p. 3), to use an analogy, a house is made of nails, lumber, electrical wiring, and other materials, but to say that a house is composed of so many nails, so much lumber, and so on does not describe the house. Rather, it is necessary to look at the parts and sum them up *and* to pay attention to the pattern that connects them in order to appreciate the structure. The clinician must similarly look not merely at the bits and pieces of behavior that form a couple's relationship but for the larger pattern that encompasses the couple.

First- and Second-Order Change

According to Watzlawick, Weakland, and Fisch (1974), change can be either first-order or second-order. First-order change pertains to those alterations in a system that leave the fundamental organization of that system unchanged. It is superficial in nature, and the change may reduce a symptom or resolve surface issues. If the relationship is otherwise stable and healthy, then a simple problem-solving approach will be sufficient to put an end to the problem. However, if the relationship has deeper, underlying issues, then merely addressing the first-order change may arrest a destructive behavior pattern, but it will not substantially affect the relationship.

Second-order change refers to alterations that change the fundamental organization of the system. Often, this is a change in the way a couple operates or interacts with one another. There may be attitudinal changes, which usually result in new behaviors and a reordering of the relational dynamics. It requires a good-faith commitment from both partners to change, and mutual respect in order for change to take hold. Second-order change is generally considered better than first-order change because it is structural and more permanent (Keim, 2000; Mozdzierz, Peluso, & Lisecki, 2014).

Structural Couple Therapy

The Basics of Structural Therapy

Structural therapy emerged from Salvador Minuchin's work with low socioeconomic status families (Minuchin et al., 2013). Minuchin used an active problem-solving approach. He has extended his work to include psychosomatic families (as well as patients of varying socioeconomic classes). In structural therapy, the focus is less on theory of change than on theory of family (Minuchin, Lee, & Simon, 2006).

The primary concept is that of proximity and distance, which are defined through the boundaries or rules (i.e. structures) that specify who participates and in what way (Minuchin et al., 2013). Proximity/distance may be determined by examining the spouses' respective turfs, such as where one member has primary influence concerning budgets and children compared to the other member. Boundaries can also connote coalitions, such as when one or all children are united with one parent against the other or when one or more of a spouse's parents are involved in a coalition against the other spouse (Minuchin, Nichols, & Lee, 2007).

A central concept in structural therapy is the continuum of enmeshment-disengagement. These are the extremes of proximity/distance or boundary functioning. An enmeshed subsystem is overly tight, and members are allowed little or no autonomy. If the integrity or closeness of the system is threatened, the enmeshed couple often responds rapidly and defensively without thoughtful consideration of all options. Furthermore, behavior change or reaction to stress in one spouse greatly affects the other and may reverberate throughout the system. The heightened sense of belonging in enmeshed systems or subsystems comes at the expense of individual independence (Minuchin et al., 2013).

In disengaged couples, members may function autonomously, but there is little loyalty and a distorted sense of independence. They cannot request support when needed and lack a capacity for interdependence. In such marriages, individuals tend to operate within their own separate little domains relative to their partners. Stresses in one member do not readily affect the other (Minuchin et al., 2013). In general, then, the thrust of structural therapy is toward differentiating enmeshed members and increasing the involvement of disengaged couples (Minuchin et al., 2006).

Minuchin's approach to therapy is characterized by an emphasis on hierarchical issues. Therapy usually involves changing the structure by modifying the way people relate to each other. The therapist is an active participant in the therapy, hence Minuchin's use of the word "joining" (or mimesis) to describe the therapist's early tasks in relating to the family in treatment. The focus is on the present, and the therapist uses direct, indirect, and paradoxical procedures. In addition, the therapist may draw a structural map (similar to a genogram) in order to graphically represent their boundaries and level of functioning, as well as any coalitions in the family (Aponte & DiCesare, 2000). Therapy is terminated once the structure is positively altered and able to maintain itself without the use of the presenting problem (Minuchin et al., 2013).

The Practice of Structural Couple Therapy

In this approach, assessment primarily focuses on the structure of the couple subsystem. It includes assessing the permeability of the boundary surrounding the subsystem, as well as assessing differentiation within the subsystem. Typically, couples present for treatment with an external boundary that is either overly diffuse or overly rigid. Likewise, most of these couples will either avoid differentiation between the partners, or they will exaggerate differentiation to the extent of being in a state of perpetual conflict, or they will avoid meaningful interaction entirely (Simon, 2015).

Regarding the goals of therapy, the structural couple therapist's main aim is to change how partners experience each other. The mechanism of change of this approach involves producing new relational experiences for the couple. In addition, the therapist accepts the couple's goal of alleviating their presenting problem and considers therapy successful only if this goal is achieved.

This type of therapy can be thought of as a play wherein the therapist functions as director and supporting actor and the play has two acts. The first act involves destabilizing the old relational structure, while the second act involves nurturing a new structure, i.e. new relational experiences (Simon, 2015). Several interventions are utilized in both acts. Chief of these is enactment. Because it is assumed that a couple carries its structure with them into the therapy process, enactment becomes the primary medium for changing the couple subsystem's structure.

Again, the therapist is the play's director who perturbs the system because the structure is too rigid or closed, or because it is too diffuse. The therapist facilitates the restructuring of the system, and gives homework to solidify changes. In short, this is clearly a directive approach (Simon, 2015).

Research Support

The main limitation of Structural Family Therapy is its empirical support (Simon, 2015). There are no reported outcome studies of this approach with couples. In contrast, there are a few studies on the effectiveness of Structural Couple Therapy. These studies mostly involve two-parent families, wherein the therapist attempts to restructure the parental subsystem in ways that are similar to the ways in which Structural Couple Therapy endeavors to restructure the couple subsystem. While it may seem reasonable to conclude that these studies provide indirect evidence of the efficacy of Structural Couple Therapy interventions across a broad range of presenting problems and client populations, "indirect evidence is hardly sufficient in the face of the current quest for empirically supported psychotherapeutic practice" (Simon, 2015, p. 377).

Brief Strategic Couple Therapy

Brief Strategic Couple Therapy has its roots in the Palo Alto Research Group, which was founded in the early 1950s and was led by Gregory Bateson, Jay Haley, John Weakland, Don D. Jackson, and Virginia Satir, who ushered in what has come to be known as the *family systems theory* revolution (Gurman & Fraenkel, 2002). Many articles and books were published by this group describing communication strategies for changing couples and family relationships. More recently, Brief Strategic Couple Therapy has become more focused on research and theory development with couples wherein one partner experiences health problems, most notably at the University of Miami Medical School (Rohrbaugh & Shoham, 2015).

Background of Strategic Therapy

Strategic therapy evolved from this work at the Mental Research Institute (MRI) in Palo Alto and was further influenced by the work of Milton Erickson and his use of hypnosis and paradoxical strategies (Keim, 2000). One of the more influential members of this early group was Don Jackson, who pioneered the communication concepts of the double bind, family homeostasis, and the marital quid pro quo. Jackson stressed that the role of the couples counselor was to expose the unconscious rules by which they were living (and subsequently causing problems) and help them develop new, more workable guidelines (Lederer & Jackson, 1968). Jackson was responsible for coining the term conjoint therapy, which would revolutionize the field in the years following his sudden death in 1968 (Gurman & Fraenkel, 2002).

At MRI, others such as Watzlawick, Weakland, and Fisch (1974) focused on the process rather than on the organization of the relationship. Interventions are made that change the interaction between the spouses. Issues of hierarchy and power are not viewed as important. How a couple resolves a conflict or attempts to solve a life cycle challenge is assumed to be maintaining the presenting problem (Watzlawick, Weakland, & Fisch, 1974). The therapist identifies a pattern of spousal behavior by asking questions and observing, and then prescribes a specific homework assignment for the couple.

The homework assignment may be done directly or in a paradoxical fashion with the end goal to disrupt the existing sequence of couple behavior.

This model is designated as "strategic" because the therapist intervenes to interrupt ironic processes. However, calling it "strategic therapy" alone risks confusing it with the considerably different approach developed by Jay Haley (1976, 1980). Although Haley was an early member of the MRI Brief Therapy Center, he posits assumptions about the structure of the relationship and the adaptive function of symptoms that the MRI group has deemphasized (Rohrbaugh & Shoham, 2015).

Jay Haley and Cloe Madanes spearheaded the development of a form of strategic therapy with the belief that problems are maintained by a faulty hierarchy within the couple's relationship. The goal of therapy is to alter the interactions and change the structure of the relationship. Haley and Madanes believed that the presenting problem is actually a metaphor for the real problem or issue the couple is experiencing (Haley, 1984; Madanes, 1981, 1984).

Brief Strategic Couple Therapy

Brief Strategic Couple Therapy is based on the premise that resolving a couple's problematic interaction pattern will result in improved functioning. More specially, this approach focuses on identifying and interrupting "ironic" relational processes which are defined as repetitive attempts to solve a problem or concern but result in a worsening of the problem. Instead of providing a solution to the problem, they create a loop or cycle that reinforces the problem. The process of conceptualizing these "ironic problem-solution loops" provides a map for both assessment and strategic intervention. The map specifies how to understand what keeps a problem going, i.e. "more of the same" solution, and what needs to happen for the complaint to be resolved, i.e. "less of the same" solution. This approach appears to be well suited for change-resistant couples.

The basic structure for doing Brief Strategic Couple Therapy is captured in the following eight-step therapeutic process (Rohrbaugh & Shoham, 2015). First, define the couple's complaint in specific behavioral terms. Second, establish one or two specific goals for change. Third, investigate specific solutions to the complaint. Fourth, conceptualize ironic problem-solution loops and indicate how "more of the same" solution leads to more of the presenting problem or concerns. Fifth, specify what "less of the same" will look like. Sixth, understand each partner's preferred views of themselves, their problem, and of the other partner. Seventh, use the partners' views to frame suggestions for "less of the same" solutions. Finally, nurture and solidify the change that is occurring.

The key element in planning an intervention is to stop the partner's performance of the attempted solution. This usually means asking the partner to say or do something incompatible with their typical solution. This approach also uses other strategic *interventions.* These include suggesting that partners go slow, cautioning the couple about dangers of improvement, and making a therapeutic U-turn. Of these, the most common intervention is the injunction to "go slow", which is given to prepare couples for change, and to communicate acceptance of their reluctance to change.

FAMCON

FAMCON is an acronym for family consultation, which is a promising approach for helping couples cope with addictions and difficult health problems using Brief Strategic Couple Therapy (Rohrbaugh et al., 2001). The approach consists of up to ten sessions, which are scheduled over a three- to six-month period. It begins with a semi-structured preparation and assessment phase which is followed by a focused feedback session. Then the follow-up phase involves couples sessions to initiate, solidify, and amplify relational changes. Strategic interventions are utilized to interrupt ironic interaction sequences that maintain the complaint or targeted symptom. Interventions are also employed to add or reinforce effective coping behaviors. This approach has been used with health compromised couples, for example, where one partner continues to smoke compulsively, despite physician warnings that smoking will further exacerbate their heart disease (Robbins et al., 2011).

Research Support

Initial research suggests that it effectively interrupts well-intentioned "solutions" that previosuly reinforced smoking behavior and to help clients realign their couples relationships in ways that are no longer organized around smoking. Smoking cessation outcomes for couples completing this approach are noteworthy. There is a 50% rate of stable abstinence in these health compromised couples at six months, which is twice that found in a meta-analysis of other intensive interventions (Rohrbaugh & Shoham, 2015).

The research support for the Brief Strategic Therapy model is growing. However, it is primarily directed at adolescents and family issues (Robbins et al., 2011), rather than issues involving couples. Hopefully, additional research will be undertaken to gain empirical support for Brief Strategic Couple Therapy.

Systemic Therapies

Systemic therapy has its roots in the work of Gregory Bateson and contends that problems are maintained by behavioral sequences (Selvini-Palazzoli, Boscolo, Cecchin, & Prata, 1978, 1980). The therapist takes responsibility for observing the patterns of behavior and changing the interaction through either direct or indirect interventions. The couple is viewed as a constantly changing and evolving system. Problems arise when the old procedures for handling issues do not fit current situations. The therapist's role is to help the couple develop a new way for handling the problem by creating an environment in which new information is introduced and change occurs spontaneously. In the next section, we will look at four approaches that are generally grouped under systemic therapy; however, each has very distinctive elements to them.

Bowen Systems Theory (Murray Bowen)

Bowen systems theory, as applied to couples, is an outgrowth of the family systems theory approach as developed by Murray Bowen. One of the main elements of this approach is the idea of differentiation of the self vs. fusion. Differentiation of the self refers to an individual's ability to remain nonreactive in the face of their own anxieties or someone else's (Bowen, 1978; Papero, 2000). Individuals who are well differentiated are not as likely to get overwhelmed cognitively or emotionally when under stress. Bowen believed that this was a natural, developmental force, which exerts pressure on each person. At the same time, another force, fusion or the togetherness force, pressures individuals to be connected to another person or (family) group. A proper balance between the two is the mark of good health in a relationship. However, there is always tension between these two (seemingly) opposite forces, which must be negotiated by each partner in the couple. If there is too much togetherness without sufficient differentiation, the relationship will become fused or enmeshed. Each person in a fused relationship becomes highly reactive, emotionally, to the other person. The intensity of emotion is experienced initially as love and strong attraction, but the relationship very quickly becomes characterized by dependence and anxiety. On the other hand, too little togetherness and an insufficient degree of differentiation lead to disengaged relationships whereby the partners distance or "cutoff" themselves from each other. Both styles are destructive to relationships over time.

Relationship difficulties, from a Bowen systems perspective, result from a mixture of the level of differentiation of self plus the level of anxiety within the relationship. As anxiety increases in the relationship, pressure is exerted on the couple to conform to the expectations of the other (related to togetherness or separateness). This process does not occur in a vacuum, as models of negotiation and dealing with tension are derived from each partner's family of origin and help shape the set points of how much togetherness is tolerable. The level of differentiation of each individual can either mediate or amplify the pressure on the relationship. As anxiety mounts in current relationships, each person brings the basic sensitivities and reactivity from his or her own family systems and other intense relationship experiences and displays them (Kerr & Bowen, 1988). A pattern of couples behavior begins to emerge and takes on one of four qualities: Distance, conflict, reciprocal shifts in functioning (via negotiation), or projection of tension on a third party (triangulating). The present relationship develops over time its own reactive patterns based on past and present experiences (Papero, 2000). If the tension is not resolved satisfactorily and a destructive pattern is established, eventually resentment builds and instability can result.

In terms of assessment and treatment, Bowen was the first therapist to use the genogram. Genograms provide information on multiple generations and the relationships among the family members and reflect intergenerational patterns of interaction. A dysfunctional pattern that gets in the way of couple functioning is what Bowen referred to as triangles. Triangles are a mechanism for a couple to decrease anxiety and tension by projecting their attention away from each other and onto a third person (often a child), who becomes emotionally entangled. This temporarily stabilizes the couple but does not resolve the underlying issues (Kerr & Bowen, 1988; Papero, 2000; Roberto-Forman, 2002).

Clinically, Bowen made the important observation that tension between two people could be resolved if there was a third person who remained emotionally neutral and would refuse to take sides, thus allowing the couple to balance their reactivity to one another as the systemic anxiety decreases. Thus, for a couple therapist operating from a Bowen systems perspective, in addition to remaining neutral in the therapy, there are two main tasks to accomplish: (1) Increase the differentiation of each partner in order to decrease reactivity to one another, and (2) decrease the level of anxiety within the relationship (Papero, 2000). If these tasks can be accomplished, according to Bowen (1978), the couple should negotiate a balanced, reciprocal shift in functioning on their own without resorting to triangles or other dysfunctional patterns of interaction (Roberto-Forman, 2002).

Symbolic-Experiential Relationship Therapy

Napier (1999) admits that the symbolic-experiential approach is very difficult to describe definitively as a result of the power of the character and personality of its progenitor, Carl Whitaker. In addition, symbolic-experiential family (or couple) therapy is difficult to describe because it borrows or shares many different elements with other theories (Keith, 1998). As Whitaker (2000) put it, "I'm a lumper, not a shredder" (p. 7). However, as a systemic approach, it has provided one of the closest linkages between the systems therapy and the psychodynamic approach as well as many of the latter-day contextual and emotion-focused approaches. As a result, it is an approach that deserves some discussion here.

When couples get together, it is often with the unexpressed desire for a *reparenting* process whereby the other partner completes them in the ways that they feel inadequate or deficient. When the partner either fails to do this or refuses to continue acting in this role (as with some long-term relationships), the partners feel as if they are reliving their experiences from their families of origin (in a symbolic way). This produces feelings of dependence, isolation, and defensiveness and can provoke childish acting-out behaviors (e.g. affairs, withholding affection, excessive arguments, etc.) as a type of self-protection (Napier, 1999).

For Whitaker (2000), success in therapy results from "increasing the power of the family and then its generosity in the use and distribution of its power to the individuals and to the subgroups. With the increasing individuation thus created, there comes increasing homeostasis that is the family's increased freedom to expand its boundaries and contract them" (p. 12). Treatment often lasts over six months to a year and may include a series of breaks before a couple is ready to pay attention to the next set of relationship struggles.

However, the time for treatment is not as much of a concern for these therapists, as they endorse a more long-term approach to relational and individual functioning (though it can take less time to have a positive impact).

Virginia Satir's Communications/Systems/ Experiential Approach

According to Gurman and Fraenkel (2002), Virginia Satir was one of the most visible and influential marketers of couples and family therapy to both professionals and lay audiences alike from the1960s until her death in 1988. Her trainings and video demonstrations have inspired thousands of couple therapists. Again, like many other systems-oriented therapists, although most of her work referred to family therapy, she focused on the dyadic and relational level, making her work applicable to couple therapy (Banmen, 2002).

Satir (1964) believed that when individuals form couples, they form a couple system that is composed of three parts: (1) Each person's perceptions of themselves and the other, (2) how each person thinks and feels, and (3) each person's reaction to the other. Psychological health, for the individual and the couple, would be the result of several factors, including:

- Acceptance of oneself and others.
- Comfort in acknowledging such acceptance.
- Awareness of one's own needs and feelings.
- The ability to communicate clearly.
- The ability to accept disagreements and others' points of view (Gurman & Fraenkel, 2002; Haber, 2002).

Thus, for Satir, the overarching goal of couple therapy was to foster greater self-actualization and self-esteem, which, in turn, would make each partner more congruent in his or her communication with the other person. Of course, these goals were geared more toward growth than stability. According to Satir (1964), her goal was "not to maintain the relationship nor to separate the pair but to help each other to take charge of himself [*sic*]" (p. 125).

In terms of her work with couples in therapy, Satir often worked with the body and affect. She believed that these nonrational, i.e. noncognitive, pathways were a more direct path to reach an individual's core issue. Satir believed that these nonrational methods were natural survival mechanisms for handling emotional threats when individuals have no other method for coping. As a result, her famous sculpturing technique would open up opportunities for couples to explore these long-held (mistaken) beliefs and feelings that had shaped their views of each other and the relationship. As dysfunctional and warped as these may seem, Satir was respectful of these coping responses, since they represented the individual's best attempt to cope with a threat (which would then became generalized to similar perils). This is why Satir is often quoted as saying, "The problem is not the problem, coping is the problem"

(Haber, 2002). In many ways, Satir was ahead of her time, and her influence is still felt in such modern-day approaches as emotionally focused couple therapy and solution-focused couple therapy (Gurman & Fraenkel, 2002).

Milan Associates

Mara Selvini-Palazzoli, Luigi Boscolo, Gianfranco Cecchin, and Guiliana Prata worked collaboratively in Milan, Italy, and developed an innovative method for helping families with severe emotional problems (Boscolo, Cecchin, Hoffman, & Penn, 1987). The Milan associates explain their in-session behavior in terms of three themes: Hypothesizing, circularity, and neutrality (Selvini-Palazzoli et al., 1980). The therapist is constantly generating hypotheses about why the couple acts as it does. These hypotheses create a map by which questions can be asked of the couple, and interventions can be made. All hypotheses, including those developed by the couple, are seen as equally valid. Circularity exists in the ways in which the therapist conducts the session. Partners are often asked to comment on what is going on between them. The therapist is also involved in the same process. In this way, new information is introduced that allows partners to experience themselves in new contexts. According to Selvini-Palazzoli et al. (1980), simply conducting a session this way may introduce enough new information to produce change. The therapist remains neutral throughout the session. He or she avoids issues of hierarchy, power, and side-taking and is therefore free to experience the system in its entirety. Within this sense of neutrality, the couple is free to decide whether it wishes to change.

One of the interesting features of this Italian intervention team is the scheduling of appointments. Often, sessions are spread a month or two apart, and each session may last several hours. Interventions are given implicitly using a ritual or explicitly with paradoxical prescriptions that may ask the couple not to change. The interventions are different from those used in strategic approaches in that their aim is to put new information into the system, not necessarily to alter patterns of interactions. Whether the couple does a task or accepts the hypothesis is not important. The important aspect is that the partners are exposed to a different way of viewing their problems.

Treatment Process: Commonalities in the Systemic Approaches

Working with couples from a systems perspective allows the therapist to operate in myriad ways. Therapists can make changes anywhere within the couple's system and expect changes to occur within the relationship. Interventions can be made directly with the couple, with the partners individually, or with the larger family. Boundaries can be strengthened and clarified, communication improved, and the relationship enriched. This flexibility affords many available techniques to change the system. Table 6.2 outlines some of the clinical skills utilized by systemic therapies and they are explained in the following sections.

Table 6.2 Common Interventions Shared by Systems-Oriented Couple Therapists

Boundary Marking: These are the nonverbal elements that are used to set the stage for systemic interventions. By modifying or changing the physical boundaries and positions of the family, the therapist reinforces appropriate boundaries and defuses inappropriate boundaries.

Circular Questioning: These are interview questions used to learn more about changes and differences in relationships as well as old behavioral patterns. Circular questions are useful in generating systemic hypotheses and interventions. These questions cut into escalations and fights and address a difference or define a relationship as they force people to stop and think rather than react in a stereotypical way.

Family Ritual: This is an individualized prescription of an action or a series of actions designed to change family members' roles. Often these rituals are meant to dramatize (paradoxically) the underlying "positive" purpose of the problematic behavior by making the family members artificially vocalize or act out the reasons for their behavior each day at mealtime or bedtime. This clarifies for each person the reason for the behavior and potentially changes the need to engage in the behavior in the future.

Joining: This is the process whereby the therapist establishes rapport with family members and temporarily becomes a part of the family system. Structural therapists use either *tracking* or *mimesis* to accomplish this. Tracking is a nondirective, open-ended method for gathering information by asking clarification questions. Mimesis is a process whereby the therapist adopts the particular communication styles or colloquial phrases used by the family. Since one of the most common reasons for failure in therapy is a failure in the relationship, this phase must not be overlooked.

Therapeutic Paradox: This is a strategic intervention designed to move the clients away from entrenched, problematic positions very quickly. Major classes of therapeutic paradox are prescribing, restraining, and positioning.

- *Prescribing* is a strategy in which the therapist encourages or instructs the client to engage in or practice his or her symptom. The client either rebels against the directive and gives up the symptom or obeys the therapist and continues the symptom, thus putting the maintenance of the symptom under his or her conscious, voluntary control.
- *Restraining* is a strategy in which the therapist discourages change, usually by outlining the dangers implicit in improving. Often, restraining is called the "go slow" approach, as in "Go slow, or else you might get what you are asking for."
- *Positioning* is a strategy in which the therapist accepts and exaggerates what the client is saying. This often has the effect of underlining the absurdity in the situation and forces the client to take a different position.

Restructuring: A therapeutic intervention that facilitates structural changes and reduces dysfunctional patterns. Examples of restructuring maneuvers include assigning tasks, shifting power systems, escalating stress, and marking boundaries.

Relabeling/Reframing: This is the purposeful use of language by the therapist to give new meaning to a situation. This new interpretation invites the possibility of change for the clients by viewing the situation from a different point of view or context.

Unbalancing: This occurs when a therapist allies him-/herself with one member against other members of the family in order to change the patterns of interaction. It is frequently used to either support or disrupt a dysfunctional hierarchy.

Boundary Marking

By marking boundaries, the therapist reinforces appropriate boundaries and defuses inappropriate boundaries by modifying clients' transactional patterns. For example, the therapist may sit next to one partner to strengthen that person's position and weaken the other's. The therapist may also break up coalitions or triangles by asking people to move their seats or reinforce a parental system by having the parents sit separately from the children. All of this operates on the nonverbal level to set the stage for systemic interventions by changing the physical boundaries and positions of the family.

Circular Questioning

Introduced by Selvini-Palazzoli and her associates (Selvini-Palazzoli et al., 1978), *circular* questions are interview questions used to learn more about changes and differences in relationships that might provide clues to recursive family patterns. The questions force people to stop and think rather than react in a stereotypical way. The person who is not talking also listens attentively. These questions cut into escalations and fights and address a difference or define a relationship. Examples are questions that ask a client to comment on his parents' marriage, to rank family members on the basis of who has suffered the most from someone's death, or to rate on a scale from 1 to 10 his mother's and then his father's anger when the client came home late at night. Even hypothetical questions are used: "If you'd not been born, what do you think your parents' marriage would be like now?" or "If you would not have married each other, how would your life be today?" Circular questions are useful in generating systemic hypotheses and interventions and in allowing a couple to begin viewing itself systemically.

Family Ritual

Used extensively by the Milan Group (Selvini-Palazzoli et al., 1978), this is an individualized prescription of an action or a series of actions designed to change family members' roles. Often, these rituals are meant to dramatize (paradoxically) the underlying "positive" purpose of the problematic behavior by making the family members artificially vocalize or act out the reasons for their behavior each day at mealtime or bedtime. For example, a ritual for a couple that argues over money may be to require them to say to one another, "I argue with you over the finances because money makes me feel more secure than you do." This clarifies for each person the reason for the behavior and potentially changes the need to have to engage in the behavior in the future.

Joining

Described earlier in this chapter, joining is an accommodating maneuver in which the therapist establishes rapport with family members and temporarily becomes a part of the family system. Often, this appears to be a social time for more casual conversation, but it is considered to be a vital step in allowing the therapist to be accepted openly by the family and have permission to bring about change. For Minuchin and colleagues (Minuchin et al., 2013), this is done through tracking or mimesis. *Tracking* is a nondirective, open-ended method for gathering information by asking clarification questions. *Mimesis* is a process whereby the therapist adopts the particular communication styles or colloquial phrases used by the family. One of the most common reasons for failure in therapy is failure in the relationship (Keim & Lappin, 2002); thus, the joining phase must not be overlooked.

Therapeutic Paradox

This is a strategic intervention that has been defined and implemented in many ways (Keim, 2000; Keim & Lappin, 2002). Generally, it entails maneuvers that are in apparent contradiction to the goals of therapy yet are actually designed to achieve them (Haley, 1976). Although these interventions can be controversial, they can also be very powerful because they can move the clients away from entrenched, problematic positions very quickly (Mozdzierz et al., 2014). Major classes of therapeutic paradox are *prescribing, restraining,* and *positioning.*

Prescribing

This is a strategy in which the therapist encourages or instructs the client to engage in or practice his or her symptom. For example, a depressed spouse may be asked to stay depressed on a particular day and keep notes on his or her depression, ostensibly so that the therapist can learn more about the depression. The client either rebels against the directive and gives up the symptom or obeys the therapist and continues the symptom, thus putting the maintenance of the symptom under his or her conscious, voluntary control (Mozdzierz et al., 2014).

Restraining

Restraining is a strategy in which the therapist discourages change, usually by outlining the dangers implicit in improving. Often, restraining is called the "go slow" approach, as in "Go slow, or else you might get what you are asking for." For example, the therapist might say, "If your son got better, you and your husband might not have anything to talk about." Frequently, this procedure will outline the secondary gains or the real purpose of the problem behavior (Mozdzierz et al., 2014).

Positioning

Positioning is a strategy in which the therapist accepts and exaggerates what the client is saying. This often has the effect of underlining the absurdity in the situation and forces the client to take a different position (Mozdzierz et al., 2014). For example, when the couple complains about how awful their marriage is, the therapist could say, "Why not get a divorce?" and thereby move the couple to take a position defending rather than attacking the relationship.

Restructuring

Any therapeutic intervention that confronts and challenges the family and facilitates structural changes is a restructuring. The goal is to reduce dysfunctional patterns by reordering the hierarchy along more healthy lines so that the problem behavior is not maintained. Examples of restructuring maneuvers include assigning tasks, shifting power systems, escalating stress, and marking boundaries (Keim & Lappin, 2002).

Relabeling/Reframing

This is the use of language by the therapist to give new meaning to a situation. This new interpretation invites the possibility of change for the clients by viewing the situation from a different point of view or context. For example, relabeling a wife's depression as caring in order to keep her husband home and from working so much may change the partner's response to that behavior. This type of intervention usually requires the clients to rethink their explanation or conceptualization of certain behaviors or patterns and can frequently give clients an alternative perspective that creates the motivation to change.

Unbalancing

This occurs when a therapist allies him-/herself with one member (or members) of the family against other members of the family for the purpose of changing the fundamental dynamics or unsettling patterns of interaction. In this way, the therapist (temporarily) takes the side of an individual in order to introduce another perspective, reframe a certain viewpoint, or force the other family members to look at a situation in a new way. It is frequently used to either support a hierarchy or disrupt a dysfunctional one (Keim & Lappin, 2002).

The following case example illustrates several of these key concepts and strategies.

Jerry and Anna had been married for seven years prior to entering couple therapy. Anna initiated the therapy after her discovery of a recent affair between Jerry and a coworker. The couple have a five-year-old daughter and a three-year-old son, and both state that they want to stay together, primarily for the children, if possible. Anna stated that she had been at her mother's summer house on an extended trip with the children when Jerry engaged in the affair. She learned about the affair when she arrived home earlier than expected and discovered Jerry's coworker in a bathrobe. Jerry defended himself by saying that he and Anna had not had sex in more than a year and that they had been growing apart since the birth of their son three years earlier. Jerry stated that the problems between them actually started at the beginning of their marriage because Anna was "attached at the hip" to her mother.

Exploration of the couple's families of origin produced a genogram (see Figure 6.1), which revealed that Anna was estranged from her father from her late teens to his sudden death from a heart attack ten years ago. Anna described him as aloof and "clueless" about the family's day-to-day functioning. Anna is also enmeshed with her mother and reported that she usually calls her mother several times a day and

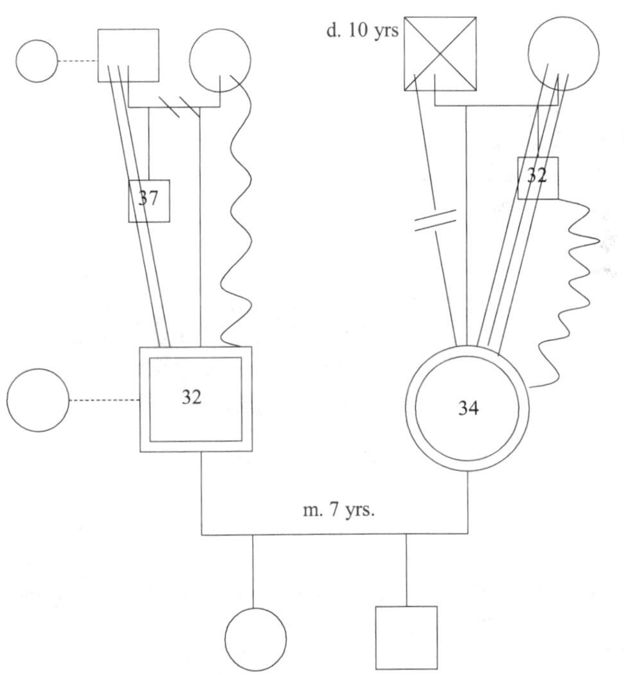

Figure 6.1 Genogram for Anna and Jerry.

at least every night (usually when Jerry was home), at which time they would talk at length. Jerry complained that Anna "would always make time for her mother but never put in that type of effort with me." Anna indignantly retorted that her mother needs her, "and besides, I like her. Is there anything wrong with being friends with your mother?"

Jerry's family of origin revealed that his mother and father divorced following an affair that his father had with a neighbor, which he described as devastating to his mother, who was anxious before the divorce and became clinically depressed following it. Jerry recalled that he was 13 years old at the time of the divorce and that he was close to his father, whom he admired as strong and decisive compared to his mother's apparent weakness. Jerry also revealed that he resented his mother and blamed her controlling behavior for driving his father away from the family (and him).

The couple therapy focused in on both the relationship dynamics and the communication patterns of the couple. In focusing on the patterns in the relationship dynamics from the family of origin, it was obvious that, like his father, when Jerry no longer felt like he was a contributing member of the family (as evidenced by his wife's over-functioning at home following the birth of their son), he began to withdraw and invest his time and energy at work, which led to a relationship (and subsequent affair) with a coworker. In addition, his disdain for anxious and controlling women like his mother made it difficult to hear Anna's pleas for connections with him as anything but demands on him. This was intolerable, since it would be akin to his father's relationship with his mother (a pattern he swore that he would not repeat). In addition, the growing influence of Anna's mother on her strengthened his desire to withdraw from her.

In Anna's family of origin, the relationship dynamics were that of a powerful, dominant mother and an aloof father who seemed indifferent to his wife. Anna interpreted her father's behavior as cold and selfish, while she saw her mother as caring, self-sacrificing, and effective at managing her family. Anna looked for a husband who would be attentive and supportive and thought that Jerry would be able to provide that. However, when Jerry began to disappoint her, she felt the need to take charge "because no one else was going to."

In terms of the relationship patterns, a systems-based couple therapist would work with Jerry and Anna so that they could see that their reactions to the other's behaviors were (in part) driven by these early family-of-origin dynamics. In their present marriage, each person has turned to someone outside the marriage (Anna to her mother, Jerry to his mistress) in order to get their needs met. This is because each perceived some hurt or disappointment from the other, which caused them to withdraw (in a similar fashion to their parents). These coalitions have hurt the relationship and must be dealt with in order for the relationship to be successful. This is an issue of boundaries, whereby both partners must make a good faith effort to resist using these surrogates and turn their attention to their marriage.

One of the underlying issues for this couple is how their communication patterns get in the way of meeting their emotional needs (or allowing the other person to do so). However, if they could relate to one another in terms of the present moment, rather than reliving the past hurts, then they would have a better chance of getting their emotional needs met from each other. In other words, each person has to learn how their particular needs evolved from these family-of-origin dynamics (e.g. Anna really needs a caring father figure who respects her intelligence without disrespecting her; Jerry needs a spouse who fully engages him and values him as a partner, rather than denigrates his efforts at contributing to the family). Unfortunately, neither one of the two can do this effectively. To correct this, each person is taught the basics of how to communicate his or her needs explicitly and congruently, as well as see and hear the other person's bid for being taken care of emotionally.

For couple therapy to work, from a systemic perspective, at least one of the partners has to buy into the characterization of the relationship patterns. It is not necessary (though it is preferable) to have both partners agree or change their behavior in order to have an impact. Instead, if one person can make substantive changes in their choices, behaviors, or reactions, then the other partner is forced to either try to change the person back to the way things were or adapt to the new person, situation, or relationship. In Anna and Jerry's case, if one of the partners makes a concerted, positive effort, then the other person must reevaluate their position. If they cannot, then the relationship may not be salvageable. However, for systems-based couple therapists (and indeed for others), this is not always a treatment failure.

Concluding Note

This chapter discussed structural, strategic, and systemic approaches. The key concepts common to all these system-oriented approaches and the common treatment interventions shared by these approaches were highlighted. These approaches represent a significant chapter in the history of couple therapy. Unfortunately, the future of some of these approaches is far from certain.

Unlike the increasing research literature that supports the effectiveness of cognitive behavioral approaches to couple therapy, there is little or no research support for the systems-oriented approaches. The exceptions are Structural Couple Therapy and Brief Strategic Couple Therapy where there is some recently reported research. Given the temper of the time wherein reimbursement for therapy services is increasing contingent on utilizing evidence-based approaches, survival may be a problem for a number of the approaches described in this chapter.

References

Aponte, H. J., & DiCesare, E. J. (2000). Structural theory. In F. M. Dattilio & L. J. Bevilacqua (Eds.), *Comparative treatment for relationship dysfunction* (pp. 45–58). New York, NY: Springer.

Banmen, J. (2002). The Satir model: Yesterday and today. *Contemporary Family Therapy, 24*(1), 7–22.

Bateson, G. (1980). *Mind and nature*. New York, NY: Bantam Books.

Boscolo, L., Cecchin, G., Hoffman, L., & Penn, P. (1987). *Milan systemic family therapy*. New York, NY: Basic Books.

Bowen, M. (1978). *Family therapy in clinical practice*. New York, NY: Jason Aaronson.

Dattilio, F. M., & Bevilacqua, L. J. (2000). A cognitive-behavioral approach. In F. M. Dattilio & L. J. Bevilacqua (Eds.), *Comparative treatments for relationship dysfunction* (pp. 137–159). New York, NY: Springer.

Gurman, A. (2015). Theory and practice of couple therapy: History, cotemporary models, and a framework for comparative analysis. In A. Gurman, J. Lebow, & D. Snyder (Eds.). *Clinical handbook of couple therapy* (5th ed., pp. 1–22). New York, NY: Guilford Press.

Gurman, A. S., & Fraenkel, P. (2002). The history of couple therapy: A millennial review. *Family Process, 41*(2), 199–260.

Haber, R. (2002). Virginia Satir: An integrated, humanistic approach. *Contemporary Family Therapy, 24*(1), 23–34.

Haley, J. (1976). *Problem-solving therapy*. San Francisco, CA: Jossey-Bass.

Haley, J. (1980). *Leaving home: The therapy of disturbed young people*. New York, NY: McGraw-Hill.

Haley, J. (1984). *Ordeal therapy: Unusual ways to change behavior*. San Francisco, CA: Jossey-Bass.

Keim, J. (2000). Strategic therapy. In F. M. Dattilio & L. J. Bevilacqua (Eds.), *Comparative treatment for relationship dysfunction* (pp. 58–78). New York, NY: Springer.

Keim, J., & Lappin, J. (2002). Structural-strategic marital therapy. In A. S. Gurman & N. S. Jacobson (Eds.), *Clinical handbook of couple therapy* (3rd ed., pp. 86–117). New York, NY: Guilford.

Keith, D. V. (1998). Symbolic-experiential family therapy for chemical imbalance. In F. M. Dattilio (Ed.), *Case studies in couples and family therapy* (pp. 179–202). New York, NY: Guilford Press.

Kerr, M. E., & Bowen, M. (1988). *Family evaluation: An approach based on Bowen theory*. New York, NY: Norton.

Lederer, W., & Jackson, D. (1968). *The mirages of marriage*. New York, NY: Norton.

Madanes, C. (1981). *Strategic family therapy*. San Francisco, CA: Jossey-Bass.

Madanes, C. (1984). *Behind the one-way mirror: Advances in the practice of strategic therapy*. San Francisco, CA: Jossey-Bass.

Minuchin, S., Lee, W.-Y., & Simon, G. M. (2006). *Mastering family therapy: Journeys of growth and transformation* (2nd ed.). Hoboken, NJ: Wiley.

Minuchin, S., Nichols, M. P., & Lee, W. Y. (2007). *Assessing families and couples: From symptom to system*. Boston, MA: Allyn and Bacon.

Minuchin, S., Reiter, M., & Borda, C. (2013). *The craft of family therapy: Challenging certainties*. New York, NY: Routledge.

Mozdzierz, G., Peluso, P. R., & Lisiecki, J. (2014). *Advanced principles of counseling and psychotherapy: Learning, integrating, and consolidating the nonlinear thinking of master practitioners*. New York, NY: Routledge.

Napier, A. Y. (1999). Experiential approaches to creating the intimate marriage. In J. Carlson & L. Sperry (Eds.), *The intimate couple* (pp. 298–327). Philadelphia, PA: Brunner/Mazel.

Papero, D. V. (2000). Bowen systems theory. In F. M. Dattilio & L. J. Bevilacqua (Eds.), *Comparative treatment for relationship dysfunction* (pp. 58–78). New York, NY: Springer.

Robbins, M., Feaster, D., Horigian, V., Rohrbaugh, M., Shoham, V., Bachrach, K., ... Szapocznik, J. (2011). Brief strategic family therapy versus treatment as usual: Results of a multisite randomized trial for substance using adolescents. *Journal of Consulting and Clinical Psychology, 79*(6), 713–727.

Roberto-Forman, L. (2002). Transgenerational marital therapy. In A. S. Gurman & N. S. Jacobson (Eds.), *Clinical handbook of couple therapy* (3rd ed., pp. 118–150). New York, NY: Guilford.

Rohrbaugh M., & Shoham, V. (2015). Brief strategic couple therapy. In A. Gurman, J., Lebow, & D. Snyder (Eds.). *Clinical handbook of couple therapy* (5th ed., pp. 335–357). York, NY: Guilford Press.

Rohrbaugh, M. J., Shoham, V., Trost, S., Muramoto, M., Cate, R. M., & Leischow, S. (2001). Couple dynamics of change-resistant smoking: Toward a family consultation model. *Family Process, 40*(1), 15–31.

Satir, V. (1964). *Conjoint family therapy*. Palo Alto, CA: Science and Behavior Books.

Selvini-Palazzoli, M., Boscolo, L., Cecchin, G., & Prata, G. (1978). *Paradox and counter-paradox: A new model in the therapy of the family in schizophrenic transaction*. New York, NY: Jason Aronson.

Selvini-Palazzoli, M., Boscolo, L., Cecchin, G., & Prata, G. (1980). Hypothesizing circularity-neutrality: Three guidelines for the conductor of the session. *Family Process, 19*, 3–12.

Simon, G. (2015). Structural couple therapy. In A. Gurman, J., Lebow, & D. Snyder (Eds.). *Clinical handbook of couple therapy* (5th ed., pp. 358–384). New York, NY: Guilford Press.

Watzlawick, P., Weakland, J. H., & Fisch, R. (1974). *Change: Principles of problem formation and problem resolution*. New York, NY: Norton.

Whitaker, C. A. (2000). Hypnosis and family depth therapy. *The Family Journal: Counseling and Therapy for Couples and Families, 8*(1), 7–13.

7 Adlerian and Constructivist Approaches to Couple Therapy

LEARNING OBJECTIVES

In this chapter, the reader will learn the following:

1 The basic principles of constructivism.
2 How Adlerian couple therapy shares many of the philosophical and treatment strategies with constructivist approaches and is practiced.
3 How solution-focused couple therapists utilize client's resources to solve problems.
4 How narrative couple therapists create new meaning for couples.

Adlerian therapy was developed in the first half of the 20th century as a reaction to psychoanalysis and reflected a revolutionary approach to human development where individual's perceptions of reality were more important than the therapist's view. This came to be understood as the constructivist perspective (Neimeyer, 2009). It also contained controversial notions, such as working with multiple clients at once (such as couples), viewing clients as equal to the therapist, and having an active role in the treatment process. Essentially, the Adlerian approach predated and foretold the major shift to constructivism in therapy, particularly family and couple therapy.

This chapter continues the discussion of the emergence of constructivist perspective. Then it describes the Adlerian approach to couple therapy. Next, it describes the couple's approach to solution-focused therapy. Finally, it discusses the narrative therapy approach with couples.

Emergence of the Constructivist Approaches to Couple Therapy

Epistemology is the branch of philosophy that studies knowledge. The prevailing epistemology of most current therapy approaches has been *logical positivism*, which assumes that truth (knowledge) is primarily a neutral value with observable referents (Neimeyer, 2009). When truth is discovered in the (scientific) process of treatment and is properly revealed, it should be undeniable and obvious, and the outcome should be increased psychological health.

Therapists were often the referees of truth, making judgments about illness and health and right and wrong behavior based on a series of given laws of behavior (Bevcar, 2003). By the 1980s, the dominant paradigm in couples and family therapy had shifted from logical positivism toward general systems theory. The pioneering work of Gregory Bateson, Salvador Minuchin, Jay Haley, and others had taken root as therapists began to look at how the system maintained homeostasis and the importance of boundary structures, and as the consideration of first- and second-order changes became more common. However, even larger questions of epistemology were forcefully entering the consciousness of rank-and-file couple and family therapists (Bevcar, 2003).

As general systems theory was becoming the dominant paradigm and metaphor for family therapy, new philosophies also began to emerge (Neimeyer, 2009). These philosophies sprung from sociopolitical movements such as feminism and multiculturalism and have been labeled as postmodernism or constructivist approaches. Such approaches to therapy maintain that objective reality does not exist apart from the perceiver's construction of it. Everything derives its meaning from its context. Removing something from its context changes or even nullifies its meaning, whereas placing something in a new context gives it new meaning. Constructivism holds that all human undertakings are value laden. The heart of this viewpoint is the recognition that a person's hypotheses about the world cannot be directly proved or disproved.

This does not mean that there is no place for science or that there is no scientific basis for couple therapy. Rather, the constructivist holds that scientific hypotheses exist for two reasons: First, because they are useful in clinical work and, second, because they have yet to be disproved or replaced by an alternative hypothesis. Scientific hypotheses are constructions that have utility in that they help portray reality. Psychological problems and couples issues are not merely symptomatic expressions or actions occurring in isolation. They are attributions of meanings that have arisen within a particular context. More specifically, therapists can never be objective observers because they cannot be disentangled from the observations they make (Bevcar, 2003; Watts & Shulman, 2003). As a result, constructivists place certain restrictions on how therapy is to be conceived. In particular, issues of power and authority are important for therapists to monitor, as they have the power to either support or remove the client's concern from its proper context (Watts, 2003). According to Friedman (1996), the following describes the essential qualities of the constructive therapist:

- Believes in a socially constructed reality.
- Emphasizes the reflexive nature of the therapeutic relationship in which client and therapist co-construct meanings in dialogue or conversation.
- Moves away from hierarchical distinctions toward a more egalitarian offering of ideas and respect for differences.

- Maintains empathy and respect for the client's predicament and a belief in the power of the therapeutic conversation to liberate suppressed, ignored, or previously unacknowledged voices or stories.
- Co-constructs goals and negotiates direction in therapy, placing the client back in the driver's seat as an expert on his or her own predicaments and dilemmas.
- Searches for and amplifies client competencies, strengths, and resources, and avoids being a detective of pathology or reifying rigid diagnostic distinction.
- Avoids a vocabulary of deficit and dysfunction, replacing the jargon of pathology (and distance) with the language of the every day.
- Is oriented toward the future and optimistic about change.
- Is sensitive to the methods and processes used in the therapeutic conversation.

In short, a constructivist therapist does not embrace "the objectivist notion that it is the therapist who knows what is 'right' and will thus 'intervene' or 'treat' the 'patient' (or client) to bring about what is 'best' (and thus 'fix' the 'problem')" (Hoyt, 1998, p. 2), although he or she does bring certain skills and expertise to the clinical interaction. Instead, the therapist and client cocreate the therapeutic intervention in a collaborative spirit in which each person is an equal partner (though each may have different functions and information).

> More specifically, the constructivist therapist conceptualizes and responds to a wife's complaint that her husband is no longer romantic in a very different fashion than does an objective therapist.
>
> Constructive therapies are approaches that begin with the recognition that humans are meaning-makers who construct, not simply uncover, their psychological realities. They are based on … (the premise) that we are actively building a worldview that influences our actions. … The goal of constructive therapies is to bring about positive consequences in clients' lives via attention to the social construction of preferred ("clinical" or "therapeutic") realities.
>
> (Hoyt, 1998, p. 1)

Accordingly, indirect methods and techniques such as reframing and paradox are more consistent with constructivist thinking. In contrast, active and directive techniques are more compatible with predictive, objective, epistemological perspectives such as the cognitive behavioral approach. However, this historically has not been the case in the realm of couples and family therapy, where the dominant epistemology is systems theory (Hoyt, 2015).

Adlerian Couple Therapy

At the same time, some Adlerian theorists have argued that Adler's ideas reflect just as much a systemic, cognitive, affective, or even psychodynamic ideology as a constructivist ideology as does the constructivist ideology. Accordingly they characterize the Adlerian approach as a constructivist approach (Sperry, 2003; Watts & Shulman, 2003). The Adlerian approach predates the formal development of marriage and family therapy (and, in fact, was a forerunner to the field). It has a long tradition of successfully working with couples and a rich, practical philosophy that spans many theoretical realms within the field of couple therapy. However, "many constructivists credit Adler as a forerunner to constructivism … and an increasing number now contend that Adlerian psychotherapy is a full-fledged constructivist psychotherapy" (Carlson & Sperry, 1998, p. 69). It should be noted that narrative therapy and solution-focused therapy have been formally integrated with Adlerian couple therapy (Robideau, 2008).

Perhaps the best advocate for the placement of Adlerian couple therapy with other constructivist approaches is Adler himself. In his book, *What Life Should Mean to You*, Adler (1958) wrote,

> Human beings live in the realm of meanings. We do not experience pure circumstances; we always experience circumstance in their significance for men. Even at its source, our experience is qualified by our human purposes … We experience reality always through the meanings we give it; not in itself, but as something interpreted. It will be natural to suppose, therefore that this meaning is always more or less unfinished, incomplete; and even that it is never altogether right. The realm of meaning is the realm of mistakes.
>
> (p. 4)

This understanding that individuals are intimately involved in the creation of their realities (which is at the same time part of the problem and the solution for couples) is the crux of the constructivist approach, and it is also at the heart of Adlerian couple therapy (Carlson & Sperry, 2011; Jones & Lyddon, 2003; Robey & Carson, 2011). For this and other reasons, we believe that this is the best place to showcase this vibrant, dynamic approach.

Key Concepts

Adlerian and constructivist approaches share a similar philosophical heritage. Both espouse *phenomenological, holistic, teleological*, and *socially embedded* principles in the creation of a person's understanding of reality and the way that he or she relates to others. This has wide-ranging implications for couples, relationship dysfunctions, and couple therapy (Carlson & Sperry, 2011; Jones & Lyddon, 2003; Watts & Shulman, 2003).

Adlerian counselors also believe that behavior is driven by a set of beliefs that are based on subjective perceptions of the world (Carlson & Sperry, 2000). As such, these subjective perceptions are susceptible to distortions, exaggerations, mistakes, and preconceptions (referred to as the client's private logic). In addition to the perceptions, Adler believed that individuals formulate a coherent set of rules by which their lives are governed. These rules are based on past experiences and family-of-origin dynamics and called the lifestyle (or often referred to as the "style of life"). The lifestyle represents the individual's creative attempt at making sense of life and getting his or her needs met (emotional, physical, etc.). Constructivist therapists also share this phenomenological approach to understanding how individuals construct their reality, according to their perceptions of the world around them (Jones & Lyddon, 2003). As a result, the behavior that is exhibited by a couple, even if it is prima facie destructive, may actually represent a creative attempt at negotiating a balance between each partner's needs (much like the previous discussion of self-object transference and projective identification) (Robey & Carson, 2011).

Thus, the Adlerian therapist looks for the creativity in the solution and attempts to marshal the same resources toward a more equitable and constructive solution (Carlson & Sperry, 2000).

Constructivist and Adlerian therapists both share the idea that each individual operates with a specific goal or set of goals in mind, which drives behavioral strivings. These are based on their subjective perceptions (or private logic), which color their construction of reality. This *teleological* or goal-directed approach allows therapists to look for the personal meaning to a person's (or a couple's) behavioral interaction. As a result, Adlerian counselors adhere to the motto of "trust only movement." That is, the behavior (interactions, verbal and nonverbal communications, and movement) between partners is important in determining the intent, or goal, of the particular behavior. Adler believed that all behavior has a goal, which may be facilitative or destructive to the relationship. Thus, understanding of the client's goal via movement is a key to unlocking the couple's conflict (Carlson & Sperry, 2000).

Another important aspect of Adler's theory for couple therapists is the concept that people are social beings, and thus any problems are created socially (with other people). The main construct is called "social interest" or "community feeling." "Social interest, for Adlerians, is the gauge by which an individual's lifestyle is assessed as either useful or useless" (Jones & Lyddon, 2003, p. 46). Many constructivists also share this belief that a person's *social embeddedness* is a central aspect in the construction of a person's knowledge base, personality, and methods of self-expression. Hence, the couple relationship is a social system that is either positively or negatively impacted by input from either member. When it is an equal and balanced relationship, the couple dyad allows for the creation of a healing and fulfilling forum for each partner. Likewise, when it is not a collaborative relationship, the partners in a couple end up hurt and dissatisfied (Carlson, Johnson-Migalski, & Spriggs, 2017).

When Adlerian couples counselors look at treating a couple, they reflect these philosophical underpinnings and then look to intervene. In addition, they work on developing a strong, collaborative therapeutic alliance with the couple by focusing on their strengths and resources. Again, this is very similar to the constructivist approach (Watts & Shulman, 2003). We present the treatment process that utilizes these elements next.

Treatment Process

As mentioned earlier, the relational dyad forms a system that is influenced by each partner (and vice versa). The individual choices of each partner have a unique bearing on the functioning of the system. Thoughts, feelings, and attitudes all influence the behavior of either person as well as the direction of the couple system. This is why, according to Adlerian theorists, the choices that a couple makes are not accidental and are directed toward the goal of communication and respect as equals (Carlson et al., 2017). However, this does not always materialize as individual private logic, goals, and lifestyle dynamics can uniquely guide the system into function or dysfunction.

Goals and Roles

Adlerian theory is neither deterministic nor fatalistic. Instead, at any time, either partner can effect change by making different choices and thus impacting the system. The ability to make changes within a system, however, requires insight, courage, and a sense of humor about one's self and life. Couples harmony is a function of such factors as individual self-esteem, social interest (ability to give and take), and a sense of humor about life (Carlson & Carlson, 2012). It is the therapist's role to act as detective, encourager, and (where appropriate) humorist as the couple is guided through the therapeutic process toward a more equal and just solution to their problem (Carlson & Sperry, 2000).

Treatment Stages

As previously noted, almost all Adlerian therapy uses some variation of the four-stage model of relationship building, investigation, interpretation, and reorientation outlined by Dreikurs (1967). In the first stage of relationship building, it is incumbent upon the therapist to create a solid therapeutic alliance with the couple, demonstrate fairness in dealing with both partners, and provide a secure base from which to work. In the next phase, assessment, lifestyle analyses of each person are conducted and include an examination of family-of-origin dynamics (psychological birth order, family atmosphere, etc.) and early recollections. From this analysis, the couple's private logic and goals can be determined. Interpretation allows the therapist to juxtapose the lifestyles of both partners and reflect how the dynamics and behavioral choices of each partner are contributing to the disruption in the marital system. The insight into the couple's relationship allows the therapist to begin interventions and help the couple to make some different choices in relating to one another. The reorientation phase is the aspect of therapy where the couple, under the guidance and encouragement of the therapist, creates an action plan based on the result of the lifestyle assessment and in light of the presenting problem (Robey & Carson, 2011). The couple makes specific changes in their interactions with each other and evaluates the effect on the relationship. Termination is usually based upon mutual agreement between client and therapist once the main goals of therapy have been accomplished (Carlson & Sperry, 2000).

Assessment

Assessment is not only an important stage in the treatment of couples, but it is an ongoing process as well (Carlson & Sperry, 2000). Lifestyle assessments conducted today by Adlerians are not too different from what Adler did 70 years ago (see Table 7.1). These assessments can be in-depth or modified to fit a shorter time span but essentially help the therapist to gather important data about how each partner found a way to belong in the family of origin and get his or her emotional needs met, discover what struggles (real or perceived) with which each had to contend, and assess the overall level

Table 7.1 Sample Lifestyle Assessment Questions

1	Who is in your family (siblings, etc.)?
2	Describe the nature of your parents' relationship.
3	Choose five words that describe your relationship with your mother as a child?
4	Choose five words that describe your relationship with your father as a child?
5	Which of your parents was your personal favorite? Who were you most like? Mother or father?
6	Which child was your mother's or father's favorite?
7	Did you ever feel rejected as a child? How old were you when you first felt this way?
8	When you misbehaved, who disciplined you?
9	To what extent did you accept, reject, or modify the family motto and other family values?
10	Why do you think that your parents behaved as they did during your childhood?
11	Were there any other significant people in your childhood?
12	Did you experience the loss of a parent or close loved one as a child?
13	What were some of your childhood fears or traumas?
14	Were there any changes in your relationship with your parents after childhood?
15	What were your parents' ambitions for the children?
16	What is your relationship with your parent(s) now as an adult?
17	How do you respond now, in terms of feelings, to separations with your children?
18	If you had three wishes for your child for 20 years from now what would they be?
19	What would you hope your children might learn from their experiences of being parented by you?

Source: Adapted from Kern (1988).

of discouragement. In addition, lifestyle analyses can provide clinicians with important diagnostic, relational, and sexual information, along with social development and current functioning (Carlson et al., 2017). Early recollections are another diagnostic tool that helps the Adlerian therapist to understand the private logic and lifestyle dynamics of the client. In addition, some Adlerian therapists use structured marital inventories that look at specific relationship domains (Sperry, 2019).

Intervention Strategies

Partners are chosen based on the compatibility of lifestyles, goals, and belief systems. Dreikurs (1946) believed that when there is stress or discord, those elements in one's partner that attracted us become the same behaviors that create problems. In Adlerian therapy, each member of the couple must take responsibility for his or her own behavior. Once he or she knows how mistaken goals or lifestyle dynamics create problems in the relationship, then that person must take the initiative and make the effort to change his or her responses. Adlerian therapists use several interventions in order to help uncover these underlying goals and ultimately give the clients the courage to be able to change their behavior on their own (Carlson & Carlson, 2012). Several of these interventions include "the question," paradoxical intention, "spitting in the client's soup," catching one's self, and assigning homework.

"The question" is a technique that many Adlerians use to understand how the particular problem or symptom is being used to avoid the responsibilities of life (hence, the purpose or goal of the behavior). The client is prompted to imagine that they no longer suffered with the particular symptom or problem and then asked what they could do that they are not able to at present. It should be mentioned that solution-focused therapists utilize a form of this called the "miracle question" (Ratner, George, & Iveson, 2012).

In a similar fashion, paradoxical intention is a nonlinear method for symptom alleviation that requires the client to purposely engage the symptom to see what can be learned about it. The belief behind this technique is that in order to maintain a symptom, one has to fight it. If it is not fought, it is not maintained but seen as ridiculous. Once the paradox exposes the symptom as illogical, its purpose is revealed. If a more socially useful alternative is suggested and adopted by the individual, the symptom can frequently be dismissed by the client (Carlson et al., 2017).

Another way of exposing the discontinuity of a particular behavior set is "spitting in the client's soup." In this technique, the therapist deduces the goal of the behavior set and reveals it to the couple. The couple may choose to continue the behavior, but it no longer achieves the same emotional payoff when the goal is uncovered (Carlson & Sperry, 2000).

As clients understand their own selves and goals, they will have a greater capacity to be able to critically evaluate their own behavior, as well as develop more confidence in their ability to make cooperative choices. This even includes being able to laugh at their mistakes or develop the courage to be imperfect. Catching one's self is a behavior-monitoring ritual where the therapist helps the couple put their insights into action by stopping themselves from falling into old traps that are destructive to the relationship. Lastly, homework is a series of assignments tailored to the clients that will bring about desired change (Carlson & Sperry, 2000).

Because Adlerian theory relates to many different systems of psychotherapy, Adlerian psychotherapists are able to utilize new techniques without necessarily abandoning their own theoretical framework (Carlson & Carlson, 2012). Many times, the technique that is "borrowed" is actually a repackaging of an Adlerian technique (e.g. the miracle question, the push-button technique, etc.). However, several Adlerian theorists have begun to incorporate new modalities of treatment and integrate them well within an Adlerian context. Recently, the theoretical links between attachment style, working models of self and others, and the Adlerian construct of lifestyle have been delineated (Peluso, Peluso, White, & Kern, 2004). In addition, Watts and Shulman (2003) have described how many constructivist therapies are turning to attachment theory to provide a theoretical grounding for their systems. These linkages provide a bridge for Adlerian couple therapists and other attachment-theory-based approaches (such as emotion-focused couple therapy) to share resources, techniques, and research methodologies, and provide avenues of mutual growth and development. We present a case example to demonstrate some of these treatment considerations.

Paula (38) and Gene (39) came to couple therapy having been married for 12 years. They have two daughters, ages 7 and 4, and a one-year-old son. Their presenting problem areas are work conflict and intimacy. Specifically, Gene is constantly traveling for his work (at least ten days out of the month). In addition, Paula recently lost her younger sister to breast cancer and has sunk into a depression. As a result of this and other issues, they have grown apart and "just don't feel it" anymore. An Adlerian couple therapist would first start out by doing an in-depth lifestyle assessment of each partner, generally with that person present. A lifestyle analysis includes an analysis of early recollections, family constellation (family of origin), and other information, which is summarized to determine the person's view of him- or herself, others, and the world. We present an abbreviated lifestyle analysis of both Gene and Paula.

Lifestyle Assessment: Paula

Early Recollection 1: I remember being at the beach; I was about five years old. I was standing on the shoreline, while my mom had my younger brother and sister in the water. A giant wave came up, knocked my mother down, and swept my brother and sister out of my mother's arms, and they started to drown. I was so scared, but there wasn't anything that I could do. I just remember the panicked look in all of their faces. Eventually, Mom grabbed them, but it really frightened me.

Early Recollection 2: I remember that my father was leaving for work, and my brother was about four years old. For some reason, he got upset that day and started to cry as my dad walked out of the door. He was pounding on the door saying, "Don't go, Daddy, please don't go!" And for a long time after Dad left, he kept screaming, "I want my Daddy! I want my Daddy!" There was nothing that my mother could do to soothe him. I remember thinking, "Why are you so upset? He's just going to work; he'll be back." I was confused; I just didn't get what was wrong.

Family Constellation (Family-of-Origin) Dynamics: Paula is the eldest of four children. Her mother and father are still married, though frequently in conflict. She described their marriage as companionate though devoid of passion.

Lifestyle Assessment: Gene

Early Recollection 1: I remember being in a car late at night with my family. I think I was about two or three years old. Someone was going to the hospital, and we were driving fast. I was going to be dropped off at my grandparents' house while my parents at the hospital. They seemed nervous, but I was excited. I felt grown-up.

Early Recollection 2: I was five years old and in first grade. We had to do worksheets in class, and I could never finish them in time. When we had to hand them in, my teacher would mark mine as "Incomplete." I felt bad, embarrassed. I was supposed to have brought those worksheets home, but I didn't. I was just too ashamed, so I stuffed them in my desk. One day after school, my mom came to pick me up, and she met with the teacher to see how I was doing. The teacher asked her if she had seen my work. My mother said that she hadn't, and they went to my desk and discovered all of the worksheets. My mom was shocked, and I was humiliated. From then on, I had to show my mom all of my papers, she had to sign them to say that she had seen them, and then I had to deliver them to my teacher. It was awful.

Family Constellation (Family-of-Origin) Dynamics:

Gene is the eldest of two children. His mother and father are still married, and he described their relationship as close and affectionate. In addition, he claimed that he frequently had conflicts with his younger sister growing up and that she was more outgoing and assertive, while he was more bookish and studious.

Lifestyle Summary: For Gene, his lifestyle can be best conceptualized by the following: "Life is best when I am a part of things and feel involved. I don't like to be left out." However, he cannot bear people finding out that he cannot do what he says that he will do. His perfectionist tendencies keep him involved but only if he performs to his impossibly high standards. He frequently overcommits himself and sometimes has to let some things slip, which is embarrassing to him when he lets others down or they perceive him as being incapable.

Treatment

An Adlerian therapist would begin to work with this couple by going over the lifestyle assessments and sharing the dominant themes and goals under which each individual operates, as well as how these impact their relationship. Looking at the interaction of the lifestyles for Paula and Gene, they work together well when tension is low because Paula craves control and Gene craves involvement. Therefore, when Paula feels that Gene is attentive to her needs and wishes or agrees with her plans, she is satisfied. Additionally, she values Gene's participation in her life, which increases her level of warmth and care toward him. For his part, Gene craves the attention and the feeling that he belongs with Paula. Therefore, he works hard to please her and to be seen in a positive light by her. He doesn't like for her image of him to be tarnished in any way. However, when he cannot meet her needs, or if she becomes tense and overbearing, he may try to hide his irritation with her. Often, this can work for a while, but when he disappoints her or feels that she is displeased with him, he becomes very moody and anxious, and may try to overcorrect to make up for his shortcomings. Paula generally sees this as Gene trying to take over the situation, which gets her upset because she feels that her point of view is not being validated. Therefore, she will either try to reassert control over the situation or withdraw and give Gene the cold shoulder. Likewise, Gene may begin to withdraw or invest his attention elsewhere, such as work.

Frequently, problems arise over the work issue. Gene over-performs at work, which gets him the praise and attention he craves, but the price is that he shortchanges his family. As a result, his wife complains, which makes him feel inadequate and uninvolved with the family. She pleads with him, sometimes pushing him to a point where he lashes out in anger, which creates an overwhelming sense of guilt that he will be cast out and rejected. Or she will give him the cold shoulder, which creates real tension within him. At this point, he does whatever Paula wants in order to be back in her good graces, which ameliorates the situation but leaves neither person satisfied.

These dynamics are translated back to the client, and if the couple feels that this conceptualization is on target, some goals would be agreed upon. The overall goals for Paula and Gene might be to decrease their tension, increase positive communication, increase their level of social interest, and alter their perceptions of the other person's motives from a win/lose perspective to a win/win mentality. Some strategies for moving toward these goals might come in the form of homework (such as "catching one's self" during one of these cycles). In addition, the couple would be taught encouragement techniques to help them communicate genuine respect for the other and facilitate emotional closeness.

The couple is expected to work on the relationship issues outside of therapy and check in on their progress in therapy. Progress is checked by the degree of behavioral commitment and success in changing the old patterns or understanding of the other person. If the couple is able to make the alterations to their interactions and the goals are met, then treatment will end. If one or both partners are not progressing, then reviewing the instances of success and failure since the past meeting will reveal the areas that may need further attention, or some reorientation vis-à-vis the lifestyle might be recommended.

Solution-Focused Couple Therapy

The solution-focused approach was developed by Steve de Shazer and Insoo Kim Berg in the 1970s and 1980s, and came to prominence in the field of couples and family therapy in the 1990s (Hoyt, 2015). de Shazer was greatly influenced by the strategic family therapy work of the Mental Research Institute in Palo Alto, California, whose work was described in Chapter 6. As the name implies, the focus of therapy is on solutions rather than problems. Solution-focused therapists rely on the power of the subjective perspective of the couple and operate with the assumption that clients have the competency and creative capacity to be open to new options for experience and interaction. According to Hoyt (2002), "Solution-focused therapy respects clients' own resources and is directed toward ***building solutions*** rather than increasing insight into punitive maladaptive psychological mechanisms. It is optimistic, collaborative, future-oriented, versatile, user-friendly, and often effective" (p. 335.). There are several philosophical principles about solution-focused couple therapy that are important to highlight (Hoyt & Berg, 1998):

1 Solution-focused therapists draw attention toward what the clients will be doing differently in the future when they have achieved a desired outcome or solution. This way of "language-ing" presumes, predicts, and presupposes that change will happen. As a result, questions are

designed to evoke a vision of the future, not uncover the past. "The purpose is therapy, not archeology; blame-talk and escalation of negative affect are avoided in favor of eliciting movement in helpful directions" (p. 316).

2 Clients are viewed to be the experts on their own lives, rather than the therapist telling the clients what is really wrong and how to fix it. Instead, the therapist assumes a posture of not knowing and seeks to understand the client's perspective and worldview. The therapist does not abandon his or her role as a skillful facilitator but does imply that the clients' language and ideas will be more important than the therapists ideas and views.

3 The therapist-client relationship is always evolving and dynamic. This means that there is a cooperative spirit that shows appreciation for the clients' sense of their situation and allows for flexibility to renegotiate goals. In addition, "focusing on strengths, exceptions, and solutions, and a more favorable future inspires clients (and therapists) and promotes empowerment" (p. 316).

4 Lastly, solution-focused goals are carefully constructed and generally "are small rather than large; salient to clients; articulated in specific, concrete behavioral terms; achievable within the practical contexts of client' lives; perceived by clients as involving their own hard work; seen as the 'start of something' and not as the 'end of something'; and treated as involving new behavior rather than the absence or cessation of existing behavior" (p. 316).

Assessment and Treatment

Assessment in solution-focused couple therapy is idiomorphic or nonnormative (Hoyt, 2015). That means meeting couples where they are rather than imposing an a priori idea of where they should be. "Although general guidelines can be described, every case is considered to be unique" (Hoyt, 2015, p. 301). Assessment is also ongoing in treatment. Each session has its own assessment relative to the goals that are set, what solutions have been employed, and which ones have worked (Trepper et al., 2012).

Goal setting is a critical part of assessment. The therapist helps establish the climate for goal setting by asking simply, "what brings you here today; how can I be helpful to you?" This gives the therapist some initial information about the couple and their presenting problem. Follow-up questions to further clarify goals and help the couple to imagine a time without the problem include the use of scaling questions to assess the impact of the problem on the couple (e.g. "on a scale of one to ten..."), asking when is the problem not a problem (finding exceptions to the problem sequence), and ultimately the "miracle question" ("Suppose a miracle occurred overnight, and the problem goes away, how would you know the difference?") (Connie, 2013; deShazer 1991; Hoyt, 2015).

O'Hanlon (1999) listed eight solution-focused methods for resolving relationship crises (see Table 7.2). The focus of these interventions is obvious: Don't focus on the past, don't focus on the other person, and don't focus on

Table 7.2 Eight Solution-Focused Methods for Resolving Relationship Crises

1	Change your usual conflict patterns. i.e. demand-withdraw pattern.
2	"Catch" your partner doing something right.
3	Use action talk instead of blaming and loaded words.
4	Shift your complaints to "action requests."
5	Develop a specific plan for change.
6	Focus on how you (not your partner) can change and take responsibility for making that change.
7	Modify your partner's stereotype of you.
8	Listen with compassion.

Source: Adapted from O'Hanlon (1999).

problems; rather, focus on the present and future, yourself, and solutions. These action-oriented, rather than insight-oriented, guidelines have resulted in several basic rules of treatment for solution-focused couple therapy (Ratner et al., 2012). These include:

- If it isn't broken, don't try to fix it.
- Once you know what works, do more of it.
- If it doesn't work, don't do it again; and do something different.

In other words, don't complicate matters more by searching for problems, bogeymen, pathology, or grand theories of interaction. Do things that work, and the rest will follow.

Once the goals have been set and strategies are put into place, they are monitored from session to session. Treatment lasts anywhere from one to ten sessions, with an average length of three to four sessions. There are no preset session limits, and solution-focused couple therapists work one session at a time. Termination occurs when the client believes that their problem is adequately resolved (Trepper et al., 2012). We present a case example to illustrate this approach.

Recall from Chapter 5 the case of Mark and Alex. When they entered couple therapy, they had been in a relationship for approximately six months and had moved in together about two months earlier. They soon began to experience their first fights, after four months of no disagreements and were very distressed. The arguments were primarily in the evenings and weekends when they had unstructured time together. Mark was usually content with having down time, which he defined as watching movies or sports on television for long periods of time. Alex preferred to go out and do outdoor activities or spend time with people. Each wanted to make the relationship work, but both were afraid that the other person was not committed to the relationship.

Like the behavioral approaches, a solution-focused therapist would not be content with general statements and would get specific details. However, unlike the behavioral therapists, a solution-focused therapist would concentrate on the solutions that the couple has attempted to see if any interventions were needed. Next, it would be important to look at each of the client's individual strengths along with the couple's strengths. In Mark and Alex's case, they said that they were most successful when they were not living together (i.e. the exception question). During this time, each partner could tolerate doing what the other wanted for short periods of time since afterward, each was free to go to his respective home and do what he needed to relax. Now that they were living together, however, they were not able to do this, but they attempted to continue their former solution of the problem. This solution led to periods of intense pressure to do what the other wanted and then arguments that would lead to either giving in and resentment or separation and guilt. Therefore, the "solution" was not working.

The couple and the therapist worked together to define goals for therapy. Specifically, Alex and Mark were asked the "miracle question" in order to develop some common goals (e.g. "If overnight a miracle occurred and the problem that you came in here with was solved, but you didn't know it, when you awoke how would you know it had occurred? What would be the first clue to you when you awoke?"). Both responded similarly. Mark replied that, "I would know what Alex and I were going to do that day." Alex stated that, "He would let me know what he wanted to do, and we would be on the same page." It was clear that both of them wanted some form of order and planning in their lives when they have free time together. The couple was asked to try to think of ways that they could schedule their time better. In addition, they were asked how they might be able to reinstitute some of the same principles that they lived by when they were not living together.

These suggestions would be offered to the couple to see if it would solve the problem. If they agreed to try to do this, the couple would implement the plan and then return to couple therapy and determine if the solution actually solved the problem. If it had and there were no additional problems, then therapy would be terminated.

Narrative Therapy

The final theoretical approach we will present here is an extension of the constructivist approaches. Considered to be one of the postmodern theories, *narrative therapy* was first described by Michael White and David Epson (Freedman & Combs, 2015). It represented a radical departure from most schools of therapy for its emphasis on the client's perspective and active participation in determining treatment outcome. Drawing on the philosophy and writing of Michael Foucault and his critical analysis of the interplay of language, knowledge, and power on society's marginalized individuals (i.e. the others, sick, insane, or criminal), narrative therapy sought to elevate the client's story to become the primary medium of change in therapy, rather than a method of information transmission (White, 1995). Carr (1998) describes the narrative approach in this way:

> Within a narrative frame, human problems are viewed as arising from and being maintained by oppressive stories which dominate the person's life. Human problems occur when the way in which peoples' lives are storied by themselves and others does not significantly fit with their lived experience. Indeed significant aspects of their lived experience may contradict the dominant narrative in their lives. Developing therapeutic solutions to problems within the narrative frame involves opening space for the authoring of alternative stories, the possibility of which have [*sic*] previously been marginalized by the dominant oppressive narrative which maintains the problem. These alternative stories typically are preferred by clients, fit with, and do not contradict significant aspects of lived experience and open up more possibilities for clients controlling their own lives. The narrative approach rests on the assumption that narratives are not representations of reflections of identities, lives and problems. Rather narratives constitute identities, lives and problems.
>
> (p. 486)

Although White's use of the term *narrative* was based on the work of Gregory Bateson, who was an early developer of family systems theory, the focus is clearly on a constructivist theoretical framework of prizing the client's perspective (Freedman & Coombs, 2015). Valuing the client's perspective, seeing them as full participants in the treatment process, and paying close attention to the language of treatment are all critical elements of constructivist approaches that narrative therapists strongly emphasize (Scherrer, Ingersoll-Dayton, & Spencer, 2014). In fact, the narrative therapy approach has become a powerful technique for refocusing many of the more radical traditions of family systems theory, as well as embracing the modern strengths-based psychotherapy (Sween, 2003).

Assessment

Therapists operating from a narrative approach view assessment differently than many couple therapists (Dickerson, 2013). Instead of gathering information as traditional couple therapists do, narrative therapists generate information about the client along with the client. There are no assumptions about a couple's particular relationship or interactional style, nor are there a priori ideas about what constitutes healthy relationships (Scherrer et al., 2014).

Instead of assessment, narrative therapists are interested in hearing detailed, context-specific narratives about the couple's experiences. To facilitate this conversation, questions are asked about the couple's current situation, how the couple sees the problem and their relationship to the problem, what particular stand they've taken to the problems, and what more satisfying stories about the relationship they can tell. In this way, a collaborative understanding of the couples is constructed and the therapist works, in concert with the couple, to discover their alternative narratives, which contain the information necessary to make alterations to the problem. Narrative therapists also eschew traditional DSM diagnoses, as they are representations of societal characteristics that are oppressive, reductionistic, and categorical (Freedman & Combs, 2015; Hyejin, Prouty, & Roberson, 2012).

Treatment

The overarching goal of narrative therapy is to help the couple to see that their lives are a matter of active (over which they have a great deal of control) rather than passive construction and to begin to re-author the story of their lives to incorporate better outcomes (Freedman & Combs, 2015; White & Epston, 1990). In treating clients, narrative therapists look for "an opening that will allow the person to select to construct the story of their lives in terms other than those dictated by the dominant narrative which feeds the problem" (Carr, 1998, p. 491).

There are several practices that narrative therapists employ to meet these goals, including positioning collaboratively, externalizing the problem, naming the problem and the project, excavating unique outcomes, thickening the new plot, and linking to the past and extending into the future (Freedman & Combs, 2015). Table 7.3 summarizes these practices. Like many other constructivist approaches, narrative therapists adopt a "not knowing" stance, which places them in an equal (or even inferior) position to the client and allows the therapist to privilege listening over questioning. Another similar approach to the solution-focused approach is the utilization of unique outcomes when the problem behavior did not exist. This points to the direction of possible solutions and empowers clients (Freedman & Coombs, 2015; White & Epston, 1990).

Two of the more unique and revolutionary elements of narrative therapy are *externalizing the problem* and the focus on *nondominant vs. dominant* stories or narratives (White & Epston 1990).

When narrative therapists place the problem outside of the individual or couple, this frees the couple to stop fighting with each other (which creates a useless cycle of shame, blame, and denial) and join together to fight against the problem. The couple gains a greater sense of control, and by labeling what the problem is (an extension of externalizing), the couple begins to exert some power over it by setting some boundaries on the problem's influence. In addition, by defining the project, the solution is given priority and progress can be

Table 7.3 Therapeutic Practices of Narrative Therapy

Practice	*Description*
Position Collaboratively	Therapist adopts coauthoring stance, privilege listening over questioning, question about multiple viewpoints rather than objective facts.
Externalize the Problem	Place problem outside of the individual or couple, use therapy to join with couple to fight against the problem.
Name the Problem and the Project	By labeling what the problem is (an extension of externalizing), the couple begins to exert some power over it by setting some boundaries on the problem's influence. In addition, by defining the project, the solution is given priority and progress can be easily assessed.
Look for Unique Outcomes	Find out "when the problem is not the problem" for the couple, look for the exceptions when problem doesn't arise, and discover the reason (i.e. solution) for it.
Thicken the New Plot	Take unique outcomes and nondominant narratives in the couple's life, expand their scope, and bring them into the forefront.
Link the Past and Extend into the Future	Incorporate the unique outcome more fully into the context of past events, extend it into the future, and create a new story where the couple is more important than the problem.

Source: Summarized from Freedman and Coombs (2015).

easily assessed. The next element, focusing on the nondominant narratives of the couple's lives, takes the unique outcome information; elevates it into the forefront of the couple's consciousness; and allows the couple to rewrite, or "re-story," their narrative from one of weakness to one of strength. In essence, the clients create a new story where the couple is more important than the problem (Carr, 1998; Freedman & Coombs, 2015; White & Epston 1990).

In order to be able to utilize these narrative practices, the therapist is required to prize listening and understanding first and questioning second. Questions should only be used to help couples to see that the narratives of their lives and relationship are actively constructed rather than passively recounted and given. Therapists who begin to use the narrative approach are "interested in collaborating with people to change their lives through enriching the narratives they and others tell concerning their lives … It seems that through these alternative stories, people can live out new identities, new possibilities for relationships, and new futures" (Freedman & Combs, 2002, p. 308). Treatment continues until the clients are ready to stop. The couple is the authority on when the issues have been fully addressed, and when they are finished.

Research Support for Constructivist Approaches

Research support for constructivist therapies is growing. However, since constructivist theorists and therapists are generally unsympathetic to positivist approaches to research, carefully constructed research studies with experimental controls are very limited. Instead, empirical support for constructivist therapies comes largely from case studies (Bonjean, Ronch, & Goldfield, 2003; Hurn, 2006) and anecdotal reports (Bliss, 2005; Selekman, 2003). Unfortunately, very little of this research has been reported on working with couples. In contrast, solution-focused brief therapies have been more widely researched than any other constructivist approach. It was demonstrated to be effective in working with at-risk junior high school students (Newsome, 2005), older adults (Dahl, Bathel, & Carreon, 2000), and domestic violence (Lee, Uken, & Sebold, 2004). Research also supports these approaches in working with couples in which one partner has a chronic illness (Johnson & Webster, 2002; Costantino, Malgady, & Cardalda, 2005).

Narrative therapy approaches also have some empirical support. Narrative therapy has been reported to be successful in treating abuse (Draucker, 2003) and Hispanic children and adolescents (Costantino, Malgady, & Cardalda, 2005).

Concluding Note

The practitioners of approaches presented here share some common elements with which most modern-day practitioners agree. They each view the clients as equals and therapy as a collaborative experience whereby couples can discover the courage or nurturance they need to solve the challenges of their relationships. These principles are the hallmarks of the best practices in the field today. In addition, they each draw heavily on other theories (e.g. family systems theory) while challenging the field to continue to value each partner's point of view over that of the experts. In the following chapters, many of the elements of the theories presented here will be elaborated on (affective approaches) or incorporated into other approaches (integrative approaches), which attests to the strength of the constructivist point of view. Unfortunately, in the current era, in which reimbursement for therapy services is becoming dependent on achieving evidence-based status, these approaches may be short-lived.

References

Adler, A. (1958). *What life should mean to you.* New York, NY: Capricorn Books. [Original work published 1931.]

Bevcar, D. S. (2003). Eras of epistemology: A survey of family therapy thinking and theorizing. In T. L. Sexton, G. R. Weeks, & M. S. Robbins (Eds.), *Handbook of family therapy: The science and practice of working with families and couples* (pp. 3–20). New York, NY: Brunner-Routledge.

Bliss, E. V. (2005). Common factors, a solution focus and Sarah. *Journal of Systemic Therapies, 24*(4), 16–31.

Bonjean, M. J., Ronch, J. L., & Goldfield, J. A. (2003). Solution-focused therapy: Elders enhancing exceptions. In J. L. Ronch & J. A. Goldfield (Eds.), *Mental wellness in aging: Strengths-based approaches* (pp. 201–235). Baltimore, MD: Health Professions Press.

Carlson, J., & Sperry, L. (1998). Adlerian psychotherapy as a constructivist psychotherapy. In M. Hoyt (Ed.), *The handbook of constructivist therapies: Innovative approaches from leading practitioners* (pp. 62–82). San Francisco, CA: Josey-Bass.

Carlson, J., & Sperry, L. (2000). Adlerian therapy. In F. M. Dattilio & L. J. Bevilacqua (Eds.), *Comparative treatment for relationship dysfunction* (pp. 102–115). New York, NY: Springer.

Carlson, J., & Sperry, L. (Eds.). (2011). *Recovering intimacy in love relationships: A clinician's guide*. New York, NY: Routledge.

Carlson, M., & Carlson, J., (2012). Adlerian couple therapy. In D. Shepard & M. Harway (Eds.), *Engaging men in couple therapy* (pp. 81–104). New York, NY: Routledge.

Carlson, J., Johnson-Migalski, L., & Spriggs, E. (2017). Adlerian couple therapy. In M. Reiter & R. Chenail (Eds.), *Behavioral, humanistic-existential, and psychodynamic approaches to couples counseling* (pp. 51–84). New York, NY: Routledge.

Carr, A. (1998). Michael White's narrative therapy. *Contemporary Family Therapy, 20*(4), 485–503.

Connie, E. (2013). *Solution building in couple therapy*. New York, NY: Springer.

Costantino, G., Malgady, R. G., & Cardalda, E. (2005). TEMAS narrative assessment: A multicultural therapy modality. In P. Jensen & E. Hibbs (Eds.), *Psychosocial intervention research of child and adolescent disorders. Part II empirically based strategies for clinical practice*. Washington, DC: American Psychological Association.

Dahl, R., Bathel, D., & Carreon, C. (2000). The use of solution-focused therapy with an elderly population. *Journal of Systemic Therapies, 19*(4), 45–55.

deShazer, S. (1991). *Putting differences to work*. New York, NY: Norton.

Dickerson, V. (2013). Patriarchy, power, and privilege: A narrative/poststructural view of work with couples. *Family Process, 52*(1), 102–114.

Draucker, C. B. (2003). Unique outcomes of women and men who were abused. *Perspectives in Psychiatric Care, 39*(1), 7–16.

Driekurs, R. (1946). *The challenge of marriage*. New York, NY: Hawthorne.

Driekurs, R. (1967). *Psychodynamic psychotherapy and counseling*. Chicago, IL: Alfred Adler Institute.

Freedman, J. H., & Combs, G. (2002). Narrative couple therapy. In A. S. Gurman & N. S. Jacobson (Eds.), *Clinical handbook of couple therapy* (3rd ed., pp. 308–334). New York, NY: Guilford.

Freedman, J. H., & Combs, G. (2015). Narrative couple therapy. In A. Gurman, J. Lebow, & D. Snyder (Eds.), *Clinical handbook of couple therapy* (5th ed., pp. 271–299). York, NY: Guilford Press.

Friedman, S. (1996). Couple therapy: Changing conversations. In H. Rosen & K. T. Kuehlwein (Eds.), *Constructing realities: Meaning-making perspectives for psychotherapists* (pp. 413–453). San Francisco, CA: Josey-Bass.

Hoyt, M. (1998). Introduction. In M. Hoyt (Ed.), *The handbook of constructivist therapies: Innovative approaches from leading practitioners* (pp. 1–30). San Francisco, CA: Josey-Bass.

Hoyt, M. (2002). Solution-focused couple therapy. In A. S. Gurman & N. S. Jacobson (Eds.), *Clinical handbook of couple therapy* (3rd ed., pp. 335–369). New York, NY: Guilford.

Hoyt, M. (2015). Solution focused couple therapy. In A. Gurman, J. Lebow, & D. Snyder (Eds.), *Clinical handbook of couple therapy* (5th ed., pp. 300–332). New York, NY: Guilford Press.

Hoyt, M., & Berg, I. (1998). Solution-focused couple therapy: Helping clients construct self-fulfilling realities. In M. Hoyt (Ed.), *The handbook of constructivist therapies; Innovative approaches from leading practitioners* (pp. 314–340). San Francisco, CA: Josey-Bass.

Hurn, R. (2006). Snakes and solutions: An example of using a traditional board game to exemplify the techniques of Solution-focused therapy. *Counselling Psychology Review, 21*(2), 12–18.

Hyejin, K., Prouty, A., & Roberson, P. (2012) Narrative therapy with intercultural couples: A case study. *Journal of Family Psychotherapy, 23*(4), 273–286.

Johnson, C., & Webster, D. (2002). *Recrafting a life: Solutions for chronic pain and illness.* New York, NY: Brunner-Routledge.

Jones, J. V., & Lyddon, W. L. (2003). Adlerian and constructivist psychotherapies: A constructivist perspective. In R. E. Watts (Ed.), *Adlerian, cognitive and constructivist therapies: An integrative dialogue* (pp. 38–58). New York, NY: Springer.

Kern, R. M. (1988). *The lifestyle questionnaire inventory (LSQI).* Unpublished manuscript, Atlanta, GA: Georgia State University.

Lee, M. Y., Uken, A., & Sebold, J. (2004). Accountability for change: Solution-focused treatment with domestic violence offenders. *Families in Society, 85*(4), 463–476.

Neimeyer, R. (2009). *Constructivist psychotherapy.* New York, NY: Routledge.

Newsome, W. S. (2005). The Impact of solution-focused brief therapy with at-risk junior high school students. *Children & Schools, 27*(2), 83–90.

O'Hanlon, W. H. (1999). *Do one thing different: And other uncommonly sensible solutions to life's persistent problems.* New York, NY: Morrow.

Peluso, P. R., Peluso, J. P., White, J. F., & Kern, R. M. (2004). A comparison of attachment theory and individual psychology: A review of the literature. *Journal of Counseling and Development, 82*(2), 139–145.

Ratner, H., George, E., & Iveson, C. (2012). *Solution focused brief therapy: 100 key points and techniques.* New York, NY: Routledge.

Robey, P., & Carson, J. (2011). Adlerian therapy with couples. In. D. Carson & M. Casado-Kehoe (Eds.), *Case studies in couple therapy: Theory-based approaches* (pp. 41–51). New York, NY: Routledge.

Robideau, A. (2008). *An integration of Adlerian theory with marriage and family therapy in a postmodern world* (Master's thesis). Adler Graduate School of Minnesota. Retrieved from http://alfredadler.edu/library/masters/2008/andrea-lynn-robideau

Scherrer, K. S., Ingersoll-Dayton, B., & Spencer, B. (2014). Constructing couples' stories: Narrative practice insights from a dyadic dementia intervention. *Clinical Social Work Journal, 42*(1), 99–100.

Selekman, M. (2003). Living on the razor's edge: Solution-oriented brief family therapy with self-harming adolescents. *Family Therapy, 30*(2), 122–123.

Sperry, L. (2003). Commonalities between Adlerian psychotherapy and cognitive therapies: A cognitive therapy perspective. In R. Watts (Ed.), *Adlerian, cognitive, and constructive therapies: An integrative dialogue* (pp. 59–70). New York, NY: Springer.

Sperry, L. (2019). Assessment, instrument selection, and case conceptualization with families and couples. In L. Sperry (Ed.), *Family assessment: Contemporary and cutting-edge strategies* (3rd ed.). New York, NY: Routledge.

Sperry, L., Helm, K., & Carlson, J. (Eds.). (2019). *The disordered couple* (2nd ed.). New York, NY: Routledge.

Sween, E. (2003). Accepting the rest-of-the-story in couple therapy. *The Family Journal: Counseling and Therapy for Couples and Families, 11*(1), 61–67.

Trepper, T. S., McCollum, E. E., De Jong, P., Korman, H., Gingerich, W. J., & Franklin, C. (2012). Solution-focused brief therapy treatment manual. In C. Franklin, T. Trepper, W. Gingerich, & E. McCollum (Eds.), *Solution-focused brief therapy: A handbook of evidence-based practice* (pp. 20–36). New York, NY: Oxford Press.

Watts, R. E. (2003). An introduction to the dialogue. In R. E. Watts (Ed.), *Adlerian, cognitive and constructivist therapies: An integrative dialogue* (pp. 1–8). New York, NY: Springer.

Watts, R. E., & Shulman, B. H. (2003). Integrating Adlerian and constructivist therapies: An Adlerian perspective. In R. E. Watts (Ed.), *Adlerian, cognitive and constructivist therapies: An integrative dialogue* (pp. 9–37). New York, NY: Springer.

White, M. (1995). *Re-authoring lives: Interviews and essays.* Adelaide, Australia: Dulwich Centre.

White, M., & Epston, D. (1990). *Narrative means to therapeutic ends.* New York, NY: Norton.

8 Third Wave and Integrative Approaches to Couple Therapy

LEARNING OBJECTIVES

In this chapter, the reader will learn the following:

1 How the subject of emotion has been treated by traditional couple therapy.
2 The principles and techniques of Emotionally Focused Couple Therapy.
3 The principles and techniques of Gottman Couple Therapy.
4 The principles and techniques of Acceptance and Commitment Therapy.
5 The principles and techniques of Dialectical Behavioral Therapy.

The central question of "Does the heart rule the mind, or does the mind govern the heart" is one that philosophers and poets have wrestled with since the dawn of civilization. Indeed, the issue of the role of emotion has been a debate within schools of therapy from the time of Freud, Charcot, and Janet. The central problems have been how to understand it and what to do with it? Initially, it was thought that catharsis and abreaction (venting of repressed feelings) were the key, and various versions of that (most notably primal-scream therapy from the 1960s and 1970s and its heir, rebirthing techniques) have endured but have never proven to be effective. In fact, some researchers have found that merely venting or ruminating over negative affect without placing it in some meaningful framework can in fact be damaging to a client (Lewis & Bucher, 1982; Nolen-Hoeksema, McBride, & Larson, 1997). This has bolstered the argument of theorists from behaviorally and cognitively oriented schools of therapy that emotion is a quagmire that can only suck in a therapist and for which no therapeutically meaningful work can be done (Schwartz & Johnson, 2000). However, it isn't necessarily so.

In a *Family Process* article entitled "Does Couple and Family Therapy Have Emotional Intelligence?" Schwartz and Johnson (2000) challenged some of the theories of couple therapy presented in previous chapters in this book (most notably solution-focused couple therapy) as being indifferent to emotions. They said,

> Family therapy has never been terribly comfortable with emotions. The models that dominated its early development (structural and strategic)

> were primarily aimed at changing behavior patterns, and, through reframing, the cognitions that maintained them. Virginia Satir's empathic style and focus on getting family members to express their emotions clearly to one another was disdained as "touchy/feely" by the systemic thinkers of the day who, over the years, have introduced a variety of intellectual philosophers to buttress their nonemotional preferences (from Bateson to Maturana to Foucault); and de Shazer's version of solution-focused therapy continues that legacy of marginalizing emotion within the field.
>
> (p. 29)

In fact, while one of the great strengths of the cognitive behavioral movement has been its drive for empirical validation of its effectiveness, it has exposed the crucial weakness of the theories. While they achieve great successes with clients in treatment, they do not seem to be able to maintain treatment effectiveness over time (once the therapy has ended). Yet according to Gurman (2015), "couple therapy has also been influenced by a growing research base...never dreamed of in its formative years" (p. 6). For example, Gottman's approach has been shaped by studying the emotional influence of one person on another. This research has led one school of couple therapy, integrated behavioral couple therapy (IBCT), to integrate emotion into its approach. Not surprisingly, this has created an approach that is more effective than traditional behavioral couples counseling (see Chapter 5, Christensen et al., 2004; Schwartz & Johnson, 2000).

At the same time, approaches that use a mindfulness-based approach as a way to understand and embrace the experience of emotion have also come into the fore. These approaches also have an empirical base to them, suggesting that the field of couple therapy may "have developed approaches that center on inner and outer conversations about vulnerable emotions ... It seems that the field is slowly catching up with that 'touchy/feely' visionary Virginia Satir, and shaking off its no-emotion legacy" (Schwartz & Johnson 2000, p. 29). In this chapter, we will present several approaches that integrate emotion into the heart of their approaches: namely, Susan Johnson's *Emotionally Focused Couple Therapy*, John and Julie Gottman's *Gottman Method Couple Therapy*, Steven Hayes's *Acceptance and Commitment Therapy*, and Marsha Linehan's *Dialectical Behavioral Therapy.*

Emotionally Focused Couple Therapy (EFCT)

The EFCT approach was developed by Leslie Greenberg and Susan Johnson (1988). "The name, emotionally focused, was given to this model of intervention to stress the primary significance of emotion and emotional communication in the organization of the reciprocally determining system of responses that constitute an attachment relationship" (Johnson & Best, 2003, p. 165). EFCT is an integration of an experiential/gestalt approach with an interactional/family systems approach. It is also a constructivist approach in that it focuses on the ongoing construction of present experience, as well as its focus on the impact of attachment models on relationships (Johnson, 2015; Wiebe & Johnson, 2017).

Attachment theory, as originally developed by Bowlby (1969), was described in detail in Chapter 3. For EFCT, attachment theory provides the underlying structure of the relationship dynamics that create difficulties for couples, as well as define the course of recovery from relational problems.

> The key elements in marital distress are absorbing states of negative affect and the rigid negative interaction sequences that reflect and create these states ... The EF[C]T model assumes that the negative emotions and interactional cycles typical of distressed couples represent above all a struggle for attachment security.
>
> (Johnson & Whiffen, 1999, p. 369)

EFCT also echoes and reinforces Gottman's research (noted in Chapter 2) on negative affect and how it impacts couples (Johnson, 2015). In fact, according to Johnson and Best (2003):

> Negative attachment-related events, particularly abandonments [*sic*] and betrayals, often then cause seemingly irreparable damage to close relationships ... These incidents, usually occurring in the context of life transitions, loss, physical danger, or uncertainty, can be considered relationship traumas and, if unresolved, tend to block the creation of trust and undermine relationship repair ... When the other partner then fails to respond in reparative, reassuring manner or when the injured spouse cannot accept such reassurance, the injury is aggravated.
>
> (p. 177)

EFCT focuses on reshaping a distressed couples structured, repetitive interactional patterns, and "the emotional responses that evoke these patterns, and fostering the development of a secure emotional bond" (Johnson & Whiffen, 1999, p. 366). EFCT provides couples with a safe corrective experience of trying out new responses, in highly emotionally charged attachment situations, when old default attachment models automatically arise. However, attachment models that are closely guarded, defensive, rigid, or undifferentiated are difficult to access and revise. As a result, these couples are more likely to be reactive and distressed. Therapy can be slower with these couples, but it is not hopeless, though it will require more traditional family systems work (Johnson, 2015).

According to Johnson and Best (2003), there are four important links between attachment theory and family systems theory that relate to EFCT (see Table 8.1). First, both theories embrace the concept of circular causality to explain how couples interact and create stable patterns using feedback

Table 8.1 Four Links between Systems Theory and Attachment Theory

1	Both theories *use the concept of circular causality* to understand couples interactions and stable patterns where one person's behavior triggers the other's behavior.
2	Both theories view of dysfunction as rigidity, and unable to adapt to changes.
3	Both theories are nonpathologizing.
4	Both theories take a holistic approach to the couple.

Source: Adapted from Johnson and Best (2003).

loops. This same process allows therapists to access these patterns and either disrupt or change them altogether. Second, both theories have a similar view of dysfunction. Healthy interactions are those that are flexible and responsive to the needs of others. Unhealthy (or problematic) interactions are those that are characterized by rigidity and a constricted range of responses. Third, both theories adopt a non-pathologizing stance toward the couple. Negative working models make perfect sense in some circumstances, but they become unproductive when there is no threat. As in family systems theory, there is no attempt to assign blame, just to find new ways to interact. Fourth, both theories are holistic in nature, in that they are able to "integrate inner and outer, intrapsychic and interpersonal into a whole" (Johnson & Best, 2003, p. 167).

However, while EFCT is compatible with family systems theory, it also represents an extension of it. Systems theory therapies have the tendency to focus on the development and maintenance of a couple's patterns of interaction, whereas attachment theory (and EFCT, in particular) focuses on the couple's experience of the emotions of security, separation, and loss in the relationship. In general, systems theory offers basic principles for understanding any system, while attachment theory gives more information about the intimate relationship (Johnson, 2015; Johnson & Best, 2003; Wiebe & Johnson, 2017). EFCT has taken these elements of systems theory and attachment theory and uniquely synthesized them into several key guiding principles (see Table 8.2).

Principle 1: The therapist focuses on the process of deescalating negative cycles of separation distress rather than on general skill building or finding solutions to pragmatic content issues. A collaborative alliance offers the members of a couple the security that is needed to explore their relationship. The therapist also validates attachment needs and processes, and frames such needs as adaptive (Johnson, 2015; Johnson & Best, 2003; Wiebe & Johnson, 2017).

Principle 2: Emotion is primary in organizing attachment behaviors and determining how self and other are experienced in intimate relationships. "Emotion guides and gives meaning to perception, motivates and cues behavior, and when expressed, communicates to others. It is a powerful link between intrapsychic and social realities" (Johnson & Whiffen, 1999, p. 367). As a result, EFCT therapists must privilege emotional communication and

Table 8.2 The Key Principles of Emotionally Focused Couple Therapy

1	A collaborative alliance offers the members of a couple the security needed to explore their relationship. The therapist serves as process consultant to the relationship.
2	Emotion is primary in organizing attachment behaviors and determining how self and other are experienced in intimate relationships.
3	The attachment needs and desires of partners are essentially healthy and adaptive. It is the way such needs are enacted in a context or perceived insecurity that creates problems.
4	Problems are maintained by the ways in which interactions are organized and by the dominant emotional experience of each partner in the relationship.
5	Change occurs not through insight into the past, catharsis, or negotiation but through new emotional experience in the present context of emotional-salient interactions.
6	In couple therapy, the actual client is the relationship between partners.

Source: Adapted from Greenberg and Johnson (1988), Johnson (1996), Johnson and Best (2003), Johnson and Denton (2002), and Johnson and Whiffen (1999).

pay particular attention to the cycles of escalation and soothing of fear (Johnson, 2015; Wiebe & Johnson, 2017).

Principle 3: The attachment needs and desires of partners are essentially healthy and adaptive. It is the way such needs are enacted in a context or perceived insecurity that creates problems (Johnson, 2015; Wiebe & Johnson, 2017).

Principle 4: Problems are maintained by the ways in which interactions are organized and by the dominant emotional experience of each partner in the relationship. Affect and interaction form a reciprocally determining feedback loop (Johnson, 2015; Wiebe & Johnson, 2017).

Principle 5: As a result, change occurs not through insight into the past, catharsis, or negotiation but through new emotional experience in the present context of emotionally salient interactions. Therefore, EFCT therapists encourage couples to create new bonding cycles and experience new, more positive attachment events. This creates both first- and second-order changes and allows the positive experience (and associated positive emotions) to feedback onto the relationship, creating a new pattern of interaction (Johnson, 2015; Wiebe & Johnson, 2017).

Principle 6: In EFCT, the actual client is the relationship between partners. Problems are viewed in terms of adult insecurity and separation distress (Johnson, 2015).

Now, with an understanding of the underlying theoretical dynamics of EFCT, we present the actual treatment model of EFCT.

Assessment and Treatment

The process of change in EFCT is grouped into three stages – *cycle de-escalation*, *changing interactional positions*, and *consolidation and integration* – and further

Table 8.3 The Stages of Therapeutic Change of Emotion Focused Couple Therapy

Stage One: Cycle De-Escalation
Step 1: Identify the relational conflict issues between the partners.
Step 2: Identify the negative interaction cycle where these issues are expressed.
Step 3: Access the unacknowledged emotions underlying the interactional position each partner takes in this cycle.
Step 4: Reframe the problem in terms of the cycle, accompanying underlying emotions, and attachment needs.

Stage Two: Changing Interactional Positions
Step 5: Promote each partner's identification with disowned attachment needs and aspects of self. Such attachment needs may include the need for reassurance and comfort. Aspects of self that are not identified may include a sense of shame or unworthiness.
Step 6: Promote acceptance by each partner of the other partner's experience.
Step 7: Facilitate the expression of needs and wants to restructure the interaction based on new understandings, and create bonding events.

Stage Three: Consolidation and Integration
Step 8: Facilitate the emergence of new solutions to old problems.
Step 9: Consolidate new positions and cycles of attachment behavior.

Source: Adapted from Johnson and Denton (2002).

organized into nine treatment steps (see Table 8.3). The process of therapy evolves with the couple and the therapist attuning to each other and the therapist matching interventions to each partner's style. The timing and delivery of the interventions are as important as the interventions themselves. The therapist guides the couple through each of the steps in a spiral fashion, meaning that each step incorporates and leads into the next (Johnson, 2015; Wiebe & Johnson, 2017). We present a discussion of each of them in the following.

Stage One: Cycle De-Escalation

The first task of EFCT therapists is to structure the therapy as a secure base for the couple. The quality and timing of the therapist's empathic responsiveness in the therapy can reassure anxious clients. In addition, in the early stages, the therapist must validate each client's experience and relate it to the negative cycles of interaction (i.e. presenting problems) as well as access the underlying feelings that each person has and place them within the context of the negative interactional cycle in a way that expands their awareness beyond merely blaming the other person (Wiebe & Johnson, 2017). "Assessment particularly focuses on how partners have experienced and understood their relationship and their emotional responses, and how they deal with conflict, distress, and attachment needs" (Johnson & Whiffen, 1999, p. 375). This is done in the first four steps, which involve assessment and the de-escalation of problematic interactional cycles.

In the first step, the couple is assessed, and the relational conflict issues between the partners are identified. The basic techniques of creating a therapeutic alliance are important at this phase. In the second step, the elements that maintain the couple's problem (negative interaction cycle) are identified and explored. In the third step, the underlying emotions that keep the cycle going (but which are not openly acknowledged) are accessed. Then, in the fourth step, these feelings and the entire problem cycle are reframed in terms of each partner's attachment needs (Johnson, 2015; Wiebe & Johnson, 2017).

> The goal by the end of Step 4 is for the couple to have a meta-perspective on their interactions. They are framed as unwittingly creating, but also being victimized by, the narrow patterns of interactions that characterize their relationship. This is first-order change.
>
> (Johnson & Whiffen, 1999, p. 368)

The clients are still emotionally reactive, but their intensity is decreased as each person begins to risk trusting the other. In addition, at this point, couples are at risk for prematurely terminating therapy with the belief that their problem is "solved" or that they are "cured." This is a false assumption since what they have undergone is change without creating lasting, structural reorganization, which, in EFCT, occurs primarily in Stage Two.

Stage Two: Changing Interactional Positions

In the second stage of EFCT, "the therapist's goal is to reprocess emotional experience and to set interactional tasks based on that experience, in order to shape emotionally engaged interactions the disconfirm negative working models [of the self and other]" (Johnson & Whiffen, 1999, p. 376, [phrase] added). Clients may feel (or witness their partner's feeling) new emotions at this point, such as grief that was never allowed to surface before or attachment longings that have always been hidden. Most importantly, in this middle stage of therapy (Steps 5–7), withdrawn partners begin to reengage their partners emotionally, and blaming clients soften their stance toward their partner and allow themselves to be vulnerable and ask for their needs to be met (Johnson, 2015; Johnson & Best, 2003; Wiebe & Johnson, 2017). Thus, the interactional positions of the couple shift, and the relationship is reorganized to foster supportive and reassuring bonding interactions.

In Step 5, the therapist works to promote each partner's identification with his or her own disowned attachment needs, such as the need for reassurance and comfort. In addition, aspects of self, such as a sense of shame or unworthiness (related to attachment needs) which was suppressed, are integrated into the relationship. In Step 6, the partners are encouraged to accept these elements in the other partner along with their reactions to the other person's needs. Lastly, in Step 7, a new form of emotional engagement is possible, and bonding events can occur. The couple is coached to create bonding events by experiencing a new understanding of their needs being accepted by their partner (Johnson, 2015; Wiebe & Johnson, 2017).

In addition, when both partners complete this stage, a prototypical bonding event is able to occur, where the previously unresponsive partner will reach out and offer comfort and reassurance, while the other, more critical spouse will ask for their attachment needs to be met from a position of vulnerability. This is referred to as a "softening" event, which is associated with clinically significant (i.e. second-order) change in EFCT (Johnson, 2015; Wiebe & Johnson, 2017).

Stage Three: Consolidation and Integration

In the last stage of EFCT, the couple shares in the consolidation of their new responses, interactional cycles, and working models. They make a shared, coherent story of their attachment history and how this influences the relationship, positively and negatively. The last two steps of therapy address the consolidation of change and the integration of these changes into the everyday life of the couple. They learn how to create a more secure bond and tolerate the individual differences and needs without feeling that the relationship is threatened or jeopardized (Johnson, 2015; Wiebe & Johnson, 2017). According to Johnson and Whiffen (1999), at this point, "a specific form of trust, faith in each other's caring, is the variable most associated with success in EFT … This kind of trust offers an antidote to the attachment fears that arise when a close relationship becomes distressed" (p. 378).

Overall, treatment with EFCT is relatively brief and generally has been employed in 8–12 sessions; however, Johnson (2015) concedes that the number of sessions may increase depending on the severity of the couple's distress. In addition, she recommends that one partner may go through some of the steps more quickly than the other if he or she requires more attention to attachment issues. This allows the partner to learn more about becoming more securely attached and to act as a secure base for the other partner (Wiebe & Johnson, 2017). We present the following case to illustrate this treatment model.

Donna and Phil were in their mid-20s when they came for couple therapy. They initially met at a bar about three years ago and "took it slowly" at first. Donna stated that at the time they met, she had just gotten out of an abusive relationship and was not looking for another one. In fact, she states that in the beginning, she was in the power position as Phil pursued her. They dated for about two years before moving in together nine months ago. Recently, they were engaged but have not yet set a date for the wedding, which does not seem to be acceptable to Donna. A few months back, during a time when they were arguing about getting married, Donna found Tina's (Phil's ex-girlfriend) phone number on the recent caller list on his cell phone. Phil noted, "This drove her crazy. She hounded me day and night about why she called and what we talked about." In fact, Donna also accused Phil of restarting his relationship with her. Phil maintained that Tina had accidentally called his cell phone, and they exchanged pleasantries and hung up. This was not satisfactory to Donna, however, and she demanded that he call Tina while she listened in to prove that nothing had happened or was happening. For her part, Donna said that she was now feeling insecure and blamed Phil for "making me feel that way."

In their respective families of origin, Phil was an only child, while Donna was the youngest child and only daughter of three siblings. Phil's parents are still married, whereas Donna's parents got divorced when she was 15 years old. While she had been estranged from her mother in her teens, Donna's mother has been giving her advice, telling her "Men can't be trusted." Donna used to attribute her mother's attitude to her bad experience with her father and dismissed it. However, recently she has been consulting her mother for advice about how to handle Phil.

Meanwhile, Phil complied with her wishes initially, hoping that it would satisfy her curiosity. It did not stop her obsessing with what he does with his time away from her or the ex-girlfriend. Donna would occasionally spot Tina near Phil's office or hear from friends that Tina was talking about her and Phil. All of these instances escalated her feelings of insecurity and inspired her to "play detective" (as Phil termed it).

The final straw came when Donna and Phil went to a nightclub and ran into Tina there. Phil tried to keep Donna away from her, "because I knew nothing good was going to come from it." He was right. At the end of the evening, as the nightclub closed, Donna confronted Tina and "got up in her face," according to Phil, saying, "leave my man alone; why don't you get a guy of your own." She also called Tina a "home-wrecker" and accused her of sabotaging their relationship. As other people got involved, there was some pushing and shoving, which prompted Tina to file a restraining order against Donna. Phil stated that he felt exasperated and embarrassed by Donna's behavior.

In terms of EFCT, Donna's attachment style is quintessentially anxious-ambivalent, or preoccupied (to use the adult classification). When her primary attachment relationship (with Phil) is threatened, she feels anxious to the point of panic and attempts to control the situation (and Phil) in order to reduce her anxiety. However, she is unable to convince herself that the threat is gone (or nonexistent). Because you can't disprove a negative (i.e. Phil telling her, "I'm not seeing Tina"), the scenario becomes a setup for the relationship to fail under the pressure. Without intervention, Donna will continue to pursue the issue until Phil either leaves (thus proving her fear that her attachment relationship was in jeopardy) or, out of frustration, confesses that he did see Tina (which confirms her suspicion and reinforces that her attachment relationship was in jeopardy).

Overall, Phil seems to have a secure attachment style. This is a positive indicator for the relationship in terms of the potential for a successful treatment. However, it is easy to see that he has begun to pull away from Donna as her negative interactions toward him escalate. One potentially fatal trap for the couple therapist is that it would be easy to feel sympathy for Phil and take his side. EFCT therapists typically avoid this mistake by concentrating on the patterns of interaction as elements of the couple's overall attachment styles, which are healthy and adaptive but become problematic at times.

EFCT treatment would, of course, take Phil and Donna through each of the nine steps of EFCT. Depending on how the couples work is going, it might be fruitful to have Phil complete the steps sooner so as to continue to encourage Donna and provide a secure base for her. Recall from the previous discussion of Stage One that the steps are designed to identify and dismantle the negative interaction cycle around Tina. The couple may negotiate and contract around ways to help Donna feel more secure, while respecting Phil's need to be accepted as is. Once each understands the other's attachment needs and keeps the conflict around Tina in check, then first-order change will have been achieved, though not all treatment goals will have been met.

Stage Two will require more substantial issues to arise, and one could speculate that Phil's potential ambivalence about committing may arise here. It will be important for Donna to soften her stance toward Phil and provide some understanding and reassurance. This would be a demonstrable second-order change, as Donna would be taking care of Phil (rather than the other way around). Lastly, through the steps of Stage Three, the couple's newly learned ways of interacting and expressing their emotional needs to one another will be crystallized and refined.

In terms of the outcome of treatment, several observations might be made: Donna might learn to organize her emotional experience differently, in terms of vulnerability and fear rather than in terms of anger. This opens up new ways for her to regulate her emotion within the safety of the relationship, which pulls Phil toward her, not against her. Eventually, this affects the way both of them think about their interactions as they move from a negative ("He doesn't care for me; he is leaving me") to a more positive style ("He has told me the truth all along; I may just need reassurance from him"). This will allow Phil to turn toward Donna and provide the reassurance that she needs and even to ask for her to meet his needs as well. As Johnson (2003) indicates, this is consistent with the research of Gottman and others regarding long-term relationship success.

Research

One of the major strengths of the theory is the strong base of research that was conducted to validate the efficacy of the theory (Greenberg & Johnson, 1988; Johnson, 1996, 2003, 2015; Johnson & Denton, 2002; Wiebe & Johnson,

2017). Perhaps no other theory of couple therapy has received more empirical attention recently than EFCT. EFCT has been found to be effective with couples relative to other treatment approaches. EFCT has been subjected to validation, with randomized trials on four separate occasions, to investigate its effectiveness in reducing marital distress. In each of the trials, EFCT was administered faithfully and (surprisingly) had very low attrition rates (Johnson, 2015).

The power of EFCT was confirmed in a recent meta-analysis of the four most rigorous EFCT outcome studies. A meta-analysis allows researchers to compare results across different studies in order to determine the robustness of the treatment gains. According to Johnson (2003), this analysis found that EFT was associated with a 70%–73% recovery rate for relationship distress in 8–12 sessions and an effect size of 1.3. According to Cohen (1988), a small effect size is generally in the 0.2 range, a medium effect size is in the 0.5 range, and a large effect size is in the 0.8 range. Clearly, this finding is robust and considerably better than the 35% recovery rate calculated for couples receiving behavioral interventions or the 42% recovery rate found for couples receiving a combined cognitive and behavioral treatment (Johnson, 2003). In addition, when couples were contacted posttreatment, the treatment effects were found to be either stable or improved over time (Johnson & Best, 2003). Again, this is a significant improvement over the findings of other schools of couple therapy (Schwartz & Johnson, 2000). Johnson and Best (2003) sum up these effects as follows: "Studies on the process of change in EFT supports the notion that engagement with emotional experiences and interactional shifts are the active ingredients of change in this approach" (Johnson & Best, 2003, p. 179).

More recently, Weibe, Johnson, Moser, Dalglesh, and Tasca (2017) investigated predictors of long-term outcomes in relationship satisfaction. They assessed relationship satisfaction across 24 months in a sample of 32 couples who received EFT sessions (average of 21). They reported that decreases in attachment avoidance were most predictive of higher relationship satisfaction during the follow-up period. They asserted that the findings supported the theoretical assumption that the mechanism of change in EFT is the process of facilitating secure attachment bonds which, in turn, helps couples foster lasting change in relationship satisfaction.

Gottman Couple Therapy

John and Julie Gottman created Gottman Method Couple Therapy as an outgrowth of John Gottman's research about what makes marriages and relationships last, as well as what predicts divorce (Gottman, 1993, 1995, 2015). According to Gottman and Gottman (2017), they

> began with no theory at all, but we were led by our data and our clinical work to become systems therapists, to become behavior therapists, to become emotionally focused therapists, to become psychodynamic

> therapists, to become narrative therapists, and to become existential therapists. We began with none of these theories, but we were forced by the data to adopt parts of them all.
>
> (p. 24)

The metaphor for what they developed was called the "Sound Relationship House," which resulted from both clinical work and research. The Sound Relationship House model has two "walls" and several "levels" or "floors." The two walls that surround the relationship are (1) trust and (2) commitment. Without these, the relationship cannot stand up. As a result, a big part of Gottman Method Couple Therapy focuses on building trust vs. mistrust and building commitment and loyalty vs. betrayal (Gottman & Gottman, 2017).

The "Sound Relationship House" has several overarching areas of focus. Specifically, they are the friendship levels, issues around conflict, and then higher order levels (dealing with shared meaning and dreams). Table 8.4 lists the levels for the Sound Relationship House.

The first level of the model is *building love maps.* Gottman and Gottman (2017) define love maps as one partner's conceptualization of the other partner's internal world, specifically, "the partner's emotion of interest, about feeling known, and about feeling like one's partner is interested in continuing to know one" (p. 15). In session, couple therapists can help couples develop this by asking open-ended questions about the (using a structured interview called the Oral History Interview) and then helping them to remember the answers to connect with each other.

The second level of the Sound Relationship House is nurturing the *fondness and admiration system.* This is a series of skills and habits that are designed to help the couple better communicate the affection and respect they have for one another. Highly successful couples tend to develop "a habit of mind that scans their world for things their partner is doing right and to admire and appreciate specific qualities in their partner" (Gottman & Gottman, 2017, p. 15). It requires couples to cherish each other and communicate this to their partner, rather than to criticize their partner (which is one of Gottman's "Four Horsemen").

The third level of the Sound Relationship House is called *turning toward bids for connection rather than away or against.* A "bid for connection" is when

Table 8.4 Gottman Sound Relationship House

Trust	7 Create Shared Meaning	Commitment
	6 Making Life Dreams Come True	
	5 Managing Conflict	
	4 The Positive Perspective	
	3 Turn Toward Rather Than Turn Away	
	2 Share Fondness and Admiration	
	1 Build Love Maps	

Note: Taken from Gottman and Gottman (2017).

one partner tries to engage the other and let them know what their needs are. This can be done verbally (saying “I love you” or “I had a lousy day”) or nonverbally (e.g. resting their head on their partner’s shoulder, holding their partner’s hand). The second part of the bid is how the partner responds to their partner’s bids. There are three options: *Turning away*, *turning toward*, and *turning against*. According to Gottman and Gottman (2017), “Turning away is when there is no response, turning toward is a minimal response or more, and turning against is a negative response” (p. 15). Turning toward is the preferred option, creating a “virtuous cycle” or positive feedback (where turns toward one’s partner inspires reciprocal turning toward). The key for partners is to be mindful of what a bid “looks like” as well as recognizing and responding to it in a positive way. In addition, Gottman and Gottman note that very small turns toward can have a lasting positive impact on a partner’s behavior, while failing to respond positively will result in the partner being unwilling to “re-bid” or try again. They use the metaphor of an “emotional bank account” to describe the buildup of positive feeling for the other person, which can either facilitate successful repairs from unsuccessful bids or not.

Positive and Negative Sentiment Override is the next level in the Sound Relationship House. This is important for the success of repairs in relationships (which happen when a bid for connection is not accepted, or when a partner does something hurtful to the other partner, whether purposefully or accidentally). According to Gottman and Gottman (2017):

> If a couple is in the state of positive sentiment override, then the positive sentiments they have about the relationship and the partner override negative things the partner does. People then do not take their partner’s negativity as personally, but merely as evidence that the partner may be stressed. The theory claims that when we are in positive sentiment override, repair is effective, and we start repairing earlier, before the interaction gets too negative. In negative sentiment override, the negative sentiments one has about the relationship and the partner override anything positive the partner might do to repair.
>
> (p. 16)

When a couple is in negative sentiment override, people will distort their perceptions for things that are neutral and even positive (in extreme situations), and see them as negative. This gets translated into heightened sensitivity to (perceived) criticism. When couples are in negative sentiment override, friendship and intimacy are not working and the partner is seen as an adversary, rather than just a friend who is situationally annoying (which will pass).

The next level is *Managing Conflict Constructively*. This is one of the more difficult areas that couples counselors need to deal with but one that is crucial in Gottman Method Couple Therapy. In fact, Gottman and Gottman (2017) describe their approach to dealing with conflict as *managing* conflict as opposed to *resolving* conflict (which is often futile as most conflicts are intractable or unresolvable). In addition, they state that conflict is *inevitable* in conflicts, and a natural occurrence that can actually be beneficial to couples, if managed appropriately. Gottman and Gottman have three classifications (or "blueprints") for managing conflict depending on the type of conflict that is presented: Current conflict, conflicts over past emotional injuries, or perpetual conflicts. We will discuss each in the following.

Conflict Blueprint 1: Current Conflicts

When couples have a current conflict, each partner is trying to influence the other to abandon their viewpoint or solution and adopt the other partners. For example, if a couple are trying to decide what chores need to be done first, and they have a limited amount of time, one partner may want to prioritize cleaning the bathrooms, while the other may want to prioritize yard work. Or they may have a conflict about whether to go out with friends or visit family. The point is that both have to agree on a course of action; otherwise, they will not be able to accomplish either task. Gottman and Gottman (2017) have found that one way to manage this type of conflict is to use something called the Gottman-Rapoport blueprint. Named, in part, for game theorist Anatol Rapoport, before attempting to persuade one's partner to adopt their solution to the conflict, they must state their partner's position, to their partner's satisfaction. Much like active listening techniques, each person takes turns stating their partner's position, while the other person takes notes. This approach allows for each partner to feel that the other truly understands their position, and it allows them to be open to influence if they clearly understand what is underlying their partner's viewpoint and if they feel that theirs has been honored and validated. (This technique is described in more detail in Chapter 10.)

Conflict Blueprint 2: Reprocessing Past Emotional Injuries

In their work with couples, Gottman and Gottman (2017) found that they needed an approach to

> reprocess emotional injuries from the past, so that they do not fester. Emotional injuries that are not "processed" become like a stone in the shoe. Over time they hurt the relationship more and more. By *processed*, we mean being able to talk about the miscommunications in the regrettable incident without getting back into the processes.
>
> (p. 17)

What they also found was that the majority of individual's emotional injuries are actually failed bids for connection, or a failure of one person to "be there" for another. As a result, these "regrettable incidents" are really breaches in trust. Gottman and Gottman (2017) have a five-step process for processing these "regrettable incidents" that is effective, which includes (a) discussing the feelings they had, (b) exploring each partner's subjective realities,

(c) understanding triggers that uncover "enduring vulnerabilities," (d) taking responsibility and apologizing, and (e) developing constructive plans for dealing with potential future examples.

Conflict Blueprint 3: Perpetual Conflicts

In his work with couples, Gottman (2015) found that of all the conflicts that couples discussed in laboratory, 69% of conflicts were over issues in which the couple was deadlocked. These deadlocked problems were issues that couples had ongoing disagreements about, where there was no solution and would never fully go away. According to Gottman and Gottman (2017):

> (t)hese perpetual problems concerned fundamental differences between a couple, differences in personality, or needs that are fundamental to their core definitions of self. These are conflicts that the couple has often been dealing with for many years.
>
> (p. 18)

Since these conflicts are perpetual, couples are either "gridlocked" in a stalemate, or in "dialogue" about these issues. The couples in gridlock are at a stalemate. They feel that they either have to be endlessly in an argument, or they have to deny the problem and "sweep it under the rug" (thus avoiding the problem at all costs). Most times, partners in gridlock feel that they don't want to try to compromise because they believe that they are giving up a part of themselves in the process. This became a key insight for Gottman and Gottman as they realized that "in gridlocked conflict each person's position has a deeper purpose in it, a 'dream' of how he or she wanted the world to be with respect to this issue" (p. 18). They developed an intervention called "dreams within conflict" where each person examines the underlying *meaning* of each partner's position and finds ways to honor each person's dreams and core needs with respect to his or her position on the issue. This is what couples in dialogue are able to do. They have learned to accept their differences, which is not necessarily the same thing as resolving the difference (in fact, they may continue to have minor conflicts about them), but they are able to tolerate the difference and understand its relative importance for their partner. As a result, the goal for therapy is to teach couples to have an ongoing, respectful dialogue about the issue.

The next level of the Sound Relationship House, following the ability to manage conflict and understanding the underlying dreams within the conflict, is to *make life dreams come true.* According to Gottman and Gottman (2017):

> We are all dreamers, meaning makers; we are all story tellers; all searching for meaning, for adventure, for playfulness, for having our lives fulfill our own personal dreams that give life meaning and make it worth

> living. A crucial aspect of any relationship is to create an atmosphere that encourages each person to talk honestly about his or her dreams, values, convictions, and aspirations, and to feel that the relationship supports those life dreams.
>
> (p. 19)

They echoed Cherlin's (2010) conclusion that helping one's partner to achieve their life dreams has become an important criterion by which people judge the success or failure of a marriage. Helping couples to have a discussion on this level also becomes an important intervention to foster connection and closeness.

The final level to the Sound Relationship House is *creating shared meaning*. In addition to building a life together, a successful relationship is concerned with creating a life that has a sense of shared purpose and meaning, rather than just being happy. According to Gottman and Gottman (2017):

> Everyone is a storyteller and a philosopher, trying to make some sense out of this brief journey we have through life. Even 4-year-olds are asking questions about whether they have to die, why they were born, where they go when they die, and what life is for, what it's all about. This is part of what our species is all about, making meaning. In this sense every marriage is a cross-cultural experience, since culture is about how we create meaning, and we do that in the values and symbols we have, the rituals of connection, the shared life goals, and shared philosophies of life.
>
> (p. 19)

Therefore, creating shared meaning requires couples (and by extension, families) to create rituals that concretize or foster this. Examples of this can include annual retreats or honeymoons, weekly meetings to discuss wishes and goals, or daily routines of connection. Gottman and Gottman state that, paradoxically, at this level of the Sound Relationship House, the couple actually returns to the first level (love maps) but now at a more profound, existential level. At this level, couples talk about not merely what their likes and dislikes are but how they "create narratives that include the creation of shared purposes, such as shared ethics, shared values, shared philosophy, shared community and shared spirituality" (p. 19). We present a case next to highlight some of these points.

Recall the case from Chapter 7 of Paula and Gene. They came to couple therapy after having been married for 12 years, with presenting problems of work conflict and intimacy. As a result of this and other issues, they have grown apart and "just don't feel it" anymore. Looking at the patterns of interaction for Paula and Gene, they work together well when tension is low because Paula craves control and Gene craves involvement. Therefore, when Paula feels that Gene is attentive to her needs and wishes or agrees with her plans, she is satisfied. Additionally, she values Gene's participation in her life, which increases her level of warmth and caring toward him. For his part, Gene craves the attention and the feeling that he belongs with Paula. Therefore, he works hard to please her and to be seen in a positive light by her. He doesn't like for her image of him to be tarnished in any way. However, when he cannot meet her needs, or if she becomes tense and overbearing, he may try to hide his irritation with her. Often, this can work for a while, but when he disappoints her or feels that she is displeased with him, then he becomes very moody and anxious and may try to overcorrect to make up for his shortcomings. Paula generally sees this as Gene trying to take over the situation, which gets her upset because she feels that her point of view is not being validated. Therefore, she will either try to reassert control over the situation or withdraw and give Gene the cold shoulder. Likewise, Gene may begin to withdraw or invest his attention elsewhere, such as in work.

For a Gottman Method Couple Therapist, the first step would be a thorough assessment. In particular, the couple therapist would assess how the couple is doing in each of the Sound Relationship House. For Paula and Gene, the first area to work on would be to "update" their Love Maps for one another. Much like using an outdated map to get somewhere can be a problem if the roadways have been changed, not updating each other's Love Map makes it hard for Paula and Gene to connect with one another effectively. It has also made it difficult to build up goodwill toward one another when the "hurts" and "slights" come into their relationship. Next, Paula and Gene need to work on building fondness and admiration for one another. In particular, turning toward rather than away from one another when they are making bids for connection. This would require a conscious effort and commitment, especially when Gene is on the road, but with technology to make video calls, this could reduce the sense of distance.

Next, a couple therapist using a Gottman Method approach would work with Paula and Gene on managing their conflict. They would need to see first that their conflict is not problematic, but their way of handling it is. Conflicts would then be separated into solvable (current conflicts and reprocessing past emotional hurts) and perpetual (gridlocked) conflicts. The first kind of conflicts may include things like feeling hurt or abandoned when the other turns away or when there is distance due to Gene's traveling or emotionally shutting down. Teaching the couple about things like emotional flooding and positive vs. negative sentiment override would also be beneficial here. The more gridlocked conflicts might include the expectations each has for the other, and themselves in the relationship. In this instance, seeking ways to understand (but not necessarily change) the other person and their motivations is the goal.

Finally, a Gottman Method Couple Therapist would help Paula and Gene work on helping to make each other's life dreams come true, and finally creating shared dreams together that they can achieve. For Paula and Gene, these would likely be centered around their needs to be involved with each other, and have a sense of autonomy and control. Helping them to balance these would help them to build a life of shared purpose together that each can be satisfied with.

Certification as a Gottman Method Couple Therapist

Gottman and Gottman (2017) have created a training regimen for certification as a "Gottman Certified Therapist." This includes three levels of professional development training that can be conducted live or in a video-based format. Then, couples counselors can enter into a supervision track whereby they demonstrate their proficiency working with couples using the Sound Relationship House theory, and many of the key interventions described earlier. Information on this can be found at the Gottman Institute website: www.gottman.com.

Research

Gottman (2015) detailed the over 45 years of couples research that went into the creation of the Sound Relationship House approach. Specifically, they conducted research that was atheoretical, and allowed the data to guide their interpretation. Subsequently, Gottman and his colleagues created mathematical representations of the dynamics within couples (Gottman, Murray, Swanson, Tyson, & Swanson, 2002) which provided the ability to make predictions about the success or failure of relationships. These findings were replicated for gay and lesbian relationships, as well as relationships for couples from low socio-economic strata. Longitudinal research (over 20 years) provided confirmation for these findings, and has separated Gottman Method Couple Therapy as an empirically vetted approach (Gottman, 1993, 1995; Gottman & Gottman, 2017). In fact, Gottman and his associates continue to pursue research to validate their approach working with couples dealing with affairs and trauma.

Mindfulness-Based Approaches

Although mindfulness has its roots in Buddhist traditions, it has only been in the last two decades that a clinically useful definition has emerged. In

2004, Bishop and his colleagues defined the two components of mindfulness thusly:

> The first component involves the self-regulation of attention so that it is maintained on immediate experience, thereby allowing for increased recognition of mental events in the present moment. The second component involves adopting a particular orientation toward one's experiences in the present moment, an orientation that is characterized by curiosity, openness, and acceptance.
>
> (Bishop et al., 2004, p. 232)

Thus, practitioners (including couple therapists) who work within a mindfulness-based approach stay focused on the present and invite the client to do likewise. The therapist helps clients become aware of their own experiences, without distracting themselves or running away from their experience in the present (regardless of what it might be stirring up). Bishop et al. (2004) conclude that mindfulness is "a kind of non-elaborative, nonjudgmental, present-centered awareness in which each thought, feeling, or sensation that arises in the attentional field is acknowledged and accepted as it is" (p. 232).

Philosophically, many of these mindfulness-based approaches are based on "Relational-Frame Theory" (RFT), which, according to Hayes (2004/2016),

> According to RFT, the core of human language and cognition is the ability to learn to relate events under arbitrary contextual control. Non-arbitrary stimulus relations are those defined by formal properties of related events. If one object looks the same as another, or bigger than another, a wide variety of animals would be able to learn that relation and then show it with new objects that are formally related in the same way...Human beings seem especially able to abstract the features of such relational responding and bring them under contextual control so that relational learning will transfer to events that are not necessarily related formally but rather are related on the basis of these arbitrary cues ("arbitrary" in this context means "by social whim or convention"). For example, having learned that "x" is "smaller than" "X," humans may later be able to apply this stimulus relation to events under the control of arbitrary cues (such as the words "smaller than"). A very young child will know, say, that a nickel is bigger than a dime, but a slightly older child will learn that a nickel is "smaller than" a dime by attribution, even though in a formal sense it is not.
>
> (p. 874)

RFT provides the framework for mindfulness-based approaches to take the principles of mindfulness and change the perspective of the client or their "relationship" to their particular emotional states. Many mindfulness-based approaches help clients attain a level of emotional soothing by teaching some basic relaxation (and mindfulness) techniques. With couples, this is done in the presence of the other person so that both partners can learn to be present, aware, and soothed together without being distracted. There are three essential elements in this process: (1) Being in a relaxed state (usually by focusing on one's breathing), (2) practicing *choiceless awareness* as distractions occur to the client (which they inevitably will), and (3) gently returning to the breathing and breath focus when distracted without any blame or judgment. This is the posture that the clinician also takes toward her own feelings, which, in turn, are modeled for the couple (Mozdzierz, Peluso, & Liseckei, 2014). We discuss how this is reflected in two empirically supported approaches that have recently been applied to couple therapy: Acceptance and Commitment Therapy (ACT) and Dialectical Behavioral Therapy (DBT).

Acceptance and Commitment Therapy

ACT was created by Steven C. Hayes and his colleagues in the 1980s and 1990s. They began with the idea that pathology is due to psychological inflexibility, and placed mindfulness as part of its core constructs to combat this. According to Hayes, Luoma, Bond, Masuda, and Lillis (2006), psychological problems are the result of a lack of values or clarity, the avoidance of unpleasant experiences or emotions, and high impulsivity; and are encased in a belief that they are fused with, they are damaged, the past is negative, and the future is certain (and usually bad). Couples in distress also have each of these qualities, and usually focus the negativity either on the relationship or on each other. However, instead of trying to teach couples to merely control their thoughts, feelings, and behaviors (like many of the cognitive behavioral approaches do), ACT for couples teaches them to increase their psychological flexibility by noticing, accepting, and embracing their internal thoughts and feelings (Lev & McKay, 2017). These are viewed as "positive psychological skills, not merely a method of avoiding psychopathology" (Hayes et al., 2006, p. 8). There are six core clinical principles that ACT clinicians utilize, which include acceptance, cognitive diffusion, being present, viewing the self-as-context, values, and committed action. We discuss these in the following.

Acceptance

In ACT, *acceptance* is the substitute to experiential avoidance. "Acceptance involves the active and aware embrace of those private events occasioned by one's history without unnecessary attempts to change their frequency or form, especially when doing so would cause psychological harm" (Hayes et al., 2006, p. 8). Such individuals are in synch with their emotional feelings and are accepting of what they are feeling, regardless of whether it is positive or negative (Mayer & Stevens, 1993). In couples, acceptance means that neither their thoughts and feelings, nor their partner's thoughts and feelings arouse defensiveness. Instead, thoughts are allowed to come and go without struggling with them. This is one of the most important ACT core principles, as it allows couples to take a different perspective on their emotional states.

Cognitive Diffusion

According to Mayer and Stevens (1993), individuals who habitually feel overwhelmed or swamped by their emotions (to the extent to which they feel like their feelings take over) are "engulfed." Paradoxically, these couples are not very aware of their feeling states (despite feeling their feelings so fully), cannot easily identify what they or their partners are feeling, and don't feel that they can influence or control either their own or their partner's emotions (Lev & McKay, 2017). These couples are seemingly chronically stressed by a feeling of being overwhelmed and emotionally out of control but don't seem to be aware of it (i.e. the person that yells at the top of their lungs "I'm not emotional!!"). In ACT couple therapy, cognitive diffusion (a cognitive behavioral technique) is used to counteract this engulfed style of emotional reaction. According to Hayes et al. (2006):

> Cognitive diffusion techniques attempt to alter the undesirable functions of thoughts and other private events, rather than trying to alter their form, frequency or situational sensitivity. Said another way, ACT attempts to change the way one interacts with or relates to thoughts by creating contexts in which their unhelpful functions are diminished.
>
> (p. 9)

In relationships, it could mean just observing, such as "I am thinking: We are not healthy for each other. This relationship is going nowhere," which weakens the power of the thought or feeling has over the couple. In ACT, cognitive diffusion teaches couples to learn how to change how their experiences impact themselves or their partners.

Contact with the Present Moment

"Contact with the present moment" is an element of ACT that is characterized by developing an awareness of the here and now. According to Hayes et al. (2006), "the goal is to have clients experience the world more directly so that their behavior is more flexible and thus their actions more consistent with the values that they hold" (p. 9). This is accomplished by showing the couple that they have the ability to exert control over their behavior. By using "language" as a tool to note and describe events (like Narrative Therapy), couples can discover that they are not "sentenced" to their previous beliefs or ideas but can be authors who rewrite their own reactions and feelings. In couples work, it is possible that one partner may be better than the other. Finally, it can be helpful to explore the "cost" for avoiding feelings (i.e. "you cannot be fully present with your partner, and vice-versa").

Observing the Self as Context

Observing the self as context is an advanced step in ACT for recognizing emotions that comes about as a result of the elements described earlier. For couples, it also includes understanding the couple as a "transcendent unit" that does not change, compared with emotional states that are changing, based on their circumstances (Hayes et al., 2006; Lev & McKay, 2017). When couples can observe the couple in context, partners have an acute sense of their boundaries, and in general enjoy good psychological flexibility. As a result, bad emotional moods don't concern them for long, and the couple can let these pass without becoming embroiled in them (Goleman, 1995; Hayes et al., 2006; Mayer & Stevens, 1993). According to Hayes et al. (2006), self as context

> is important in part because from this standpoint, one can be aware of one's own flow of experiences without attachment to them or an investment in which particular experiences occur: thus diffusion and acceptance is fostered. Self as context is fostered in ACT by mindfulness exercises, metaphors, and experiential processes.
>
> (p. 9)

Values and Committed Action

In ACT, couples that have a high level of psychological inflexibility are not clear on what their values are and how to achieve them in life. According to Hayes et al. (2006), "Values are chosen qualities of purposive action that can never be obtained as an object but can be instantiated [exemplified] moment by moment" (p. 9). In ACT, the goal for couples is to be able to act in a way that is consistent with their values. When this occurs, the emotions that come with disappointment do not have devastatingly negative consequences for the client (Lev & McKay, 2017). According to Hayes et al. (2006):

> ACT encourages the development of larger and larger patterns of effective action linked to chosen values… ACT looks very much like traditional behavior therapy, and almost any behaviorally coherent behavior change method can be fitted into an ACT protocol, including exposure, skills acquisition, shaping methods, goal setting, and the like. Unlike values, which are constantly instantiated but never achieved as an object, concrete goals that are values consistent can be achieved, and ACT protocols almost always involve therapy work and homework linked to short, medium, and long-term behavior change goals. Behavior change efforts in turn lead to contact with psychological barriers that are addressed through other ACT processes (acceptance, diffusion, and so on).
>
> (pp. 9–10)

ACT uses a variety of exercises that short-circuit cognitive processes that might lead a person to make choices based on avoidance, social compliance, or fusion rather than from their own values (e.g. "I *should* be like..." or "A 'good' person would...." or "My parents would want me to..."). In addition, couples discuss how each person tends to respond reflexively to the other or what they imagine the other person's expectations are for themselves (regardless of whether they are true or not). We present a case study to illustrate some of these points.

Recall the case of Mark and Alex, originally presented in Chapter 5. They had moved in together after dating for a few months, which was now causing tension in the relationship. Both partners were upset about the amount of fighting they were doing, and that it was a "bad omen" for the relationship and that moving in was a mistake. They both care deeply about each other, and are committed to the relationship, but both realize that they have differences in their styles and preferences. This has brought up serious doubts about the other person's commitment to the relationship.

A course of couple therapy with ACT may be very effective with Mark and Alex's case. First, the basic tenet of ACT, *acceptance*, would give them a powerful tool to develop the flexibility and tolerance for the other person's differences without arousing fear of commitment. Instead, building tolerance and teaching *cognitive diffusion* would be a way for each other to separately and together be aware of the feelings and thoughts that they are having about their difference without acting on them or negatively evaluating them (and thus giving them power to disrupt them). In place of this, *observing the self (and the couple) in context* and *being in contact with the present moment* can provide lenses to change their perspective on themselves and the argument they are having. Finally, *acting in a committed fashion within their shared values* can provide a roadmap for moving beyond the particular impasse. For example, when they have arguments during their unstructured time, instead of feeling angry and upset because one person is making demands about what to do (that the other person doesn't want to, which breeds resentment), they can become mindful of the thoughts and feelings, and choose not to act on them, feel defensive about them, or attempt to stuff them down. Then they can, either separately or together, begin to work within the present moment and decide how they want to act in accordance with their needs and values, and dialogue about their particular difference of opinion. For Mark and Alex, this was a particularly appealing approach.

Research

From its inception, Hayes and his colleagues have been committed to subjecting ACT to empirical study and validation (Hayes et al., 2006). As a result, ACT has been widely studied over the past two decades. Recently, A-Tjek et al. (2015) reported the results of a meta-analysis comparing ACT to various control conditions. ACT was superior to wait-list control conditions, as well as "psychological placebo" conditions, and "treatment as usual (TAU) or the standard treatment. Clients also showed significant improvement from pretreatment to posttreatment as well as improvement to be secondary outcomes like life satisfaction and therapy process variables. At the same time, in head-to-head comparisons to cognitive behavioral therapy, A-Tjek et al. found that ACT and CBT were not different in the level of client improvement. It should be noted that all of these findings were with individual clients. To date, there have not been any peer-reviewed empirical studies published using ACT with couples (the reader should note that several dissertations have been conducted but have not been subjected to the peer-reviewed process and will not be presented here).

Dialectical Behavioral Therapy

Mindfulness is also one of the core concepts of another modern approach, called DBT. It is the foundation for the skills taught to clients in DBT because it helps them accept their emotions when they are faced with upsetting situations and ultimately to tolerate them (Mozdzierz et al., 2014). DBT was developed originally as a treatment for clients with borderline personality disorder. Just as with other mindfulness approaches, the capacity to nonjudgmentally attend to the present moment and experience one's emotions and senses fully, without distortion is fundamental in DBT (Linehan, 2003, 2015). According to Freuzzetti and Payne (2015):

> Unfortunately, the couple and family relationships of people with BPD have mostly been neglected. However, recent advances involving adaptations and extension of the principles and practices of DBT to couples and families have shown promise...Adding a DBT couples intervention to ongoing individual DBT has resulted in substantial individual and relationship improvements.
>
> (p. 606)

With DBT for couples, the focus is to develop skills that shift from emotional dysregulation to effective communication, increased emotional regulation, and distress tolerance. In addition, couples develop skills to express each partner's needs, wants, and yearnings as well as problem-solving skills (Fruzzetti, 2006; Linehan, 2015).

Skills acquisition in DBT is the chief intervention. Clients are taught *what* skills and *how* skills. According to Mozdzierz et al. (2014),

> The *what* skills include teaching clients to *observe* (nonjudgmentally) what is going on in a given circumstance); *describe* (explain simply what has been observed); and *participate* (becoming fully focused and involved in the events around them). The *how* skills give instruction about *nonjudgmentally* (describing the facts and not thinking about what's good or bad, fair or unfair, which helps to get the point across in an effective manner to someone else); *one-mindfully* (maintaining focus without becoming distracted by the emotional reactions that may be occurring); and *effectively* (doing what works and avoiding what does not).
>
> (p. 282)

The primary purpose of both of these categories of skills is to help couples discern (1) if they can recognize the emotions they are experiencing and (2) if the emotions are adaptive or maladaptive. If emotions are adaptive, they are considered "authentic" and are accepted and supported. On the other hand, in the case of intense negative emotions, they must be subjected to a process of examination to determine if they are maladaptive. For example, with couples dealing with conflicts, if one partner is feeling extreme anger about the other partner not listening to them, those feelings are examined to see if they are adaptive or not. If one partner is making attempts to listen to the other, but the partner is "negative mind reading," then the feelings may not be adaptive and would be described as so (Linehan, 2015).

Distress Tolerance

Distress tolerance skills are some of the more important mindfulness skills in DBT. Distress tolerance is the ability to accept both oneself and the partner in a nonjudgmental and nonevaluative way (Fruzzetti, 2006; Linehan, 2015). It is important to note that acceptance and tolerance are not signs of approval or rejection but acknowledge the reality of a situation as it is. This is important for couples in therapy, as often the fear (in the early stages) is that "acceptance" is synonymous with accepting or endorsing behavior (which they may not be willing to do). Rather, the goal is to help couples to become capable of calmly recognizing when they find themselves in negative situations, and their potential impact, rather than hiding from or becoming overwhelmed by them. DBT works with couples to help them learn how to bear pain and how not to make poor choices about taking action or responding to the other person in anger. Responding to each other based on an inability to tolerate distress and painful emotions often creates more problems than it solves (Fruzzetti, 2006; Linehan, 2015).

A primary distress tolerance skill that couples are taught is distraction. Distraction entails (1) recognizing the unpleasant reaction or situation, and then (2) distracting one's attention temporarily instead of acting out. DBT counselors teach clients the acronym ACCEPTS, in order to help couples remember distress tolerance skills, which stands for:

Activities – Use positive activities that you enjoy.
Contribute – Help out others or your community.
Comparisons – Compare yourself either with people that are less fortunate or to how you used to be when you were in a worse state.
Emotions (other) – Cause yourself to feel something different by provoking your sense of humor or happiness with corresponding activities.
Push away – Put your situation on the back burner for a while. Put something else temporarily first in your mind.
Thoughts (other) – Force your mind to think about something else.
Sensations (other) – Do something that has an intense feeling other than what you are feeling, like a cold shower or a spicy candy (taken from Linehan, 2015).

So, for a couple in therapy, when dissatisfaction with the relationship creates tension between the partners, each person can be coached to utilize one of the techniques from the previous list in order to tolerate the distress without lashing out at the other person.

Another important distress tolerance technique that DBT therapists teach is *self-soothing*. Although DBT is not the only approach that utilizes self-soothing, in DBT, it becomes a powerful tool to teach couples who have difficulty handling powerful or strong emotions (Frezzutti & Payne, 2015). The process of learning self-soothing begins in childhood and is facilitated by good parenting. It requires that a person takes responsibility for their feelings and reactions, and must find ways to calm one's self down. It is a skill in which one behaves in a comforting, nurturing, kind, and gentle way to oneself. If there was poor or inconsistent parenting, individuals can learn to self-soothe, but it is more difficult. The objective of self-soothing is to provide feelings of emotional comfort to one's self as a counterpoint to negative thoughts, urges, and feelings. DBT methods of self-soothing include promoting a "dialogue" with one's self and engaging in a healthy feeling experience (e.g. a warm bath, listening to one's favorite relaxing music, or engaging in nature through a walk). Promoting self-soothing allows for a disengagement from emotions that are temporarily overwhelming (Linehan, 2015).

Self-soothing also shows clients that they have control over their emotional life. For example, if one member of a couple is having difficulty handling their emotions because they are upset with their partner or not feeling very satisfied with the relationship, rather than lash out at them and damage the bond between them, they may decide to go to the gym and work out, or take the dog for a walk. This allows both partners time to consider their reactions, and decide what they want to do about them (Linehan, 2015).

Interpersonal Effectiveness

All of the aforementioned DBT skills (mindfulness, distress tolerance, and emotion regulation) are important for the individual to help manage his or her emotions. However, there is one more, interpersonal effectiveness, which is particularly salient for couples. Specifically, interpersonal effectiveness is the choice of behaviors that the client makes in relation to another person and their choice of behaviors. People get themselves into a bad emotional state because they either compromise their values or give up their power to someone else, hoping for a good result. Many times, the person may even know that they will not get their needs met by their partner but will still make bad decisions. Interpersonal effectiveness focuses on teaching skills to handle situations when a person needs to make a request of someone, ask someone to do something, request that someone make a change, or say no to someone. The purpose of these skills is to help clients achieve their desired outcome for a particular situation, while simultaneously not damaging either of the relationships. Three acronyms encapsulate the skill sets that are taught to increase interpersonal effectiveness. They are DEARMAN, GIVE, and FAST (Linehan, 2015).

First, DEARMAN is an acronym that is used to help clients remember the steps they need to do in order to be successful in making a request of another person. They are:

Describe your situation.
Express why this is an issue and how you feel about it.
Assert yourself by asking clearly for what you want.
Reinforce your position by offering a positive consequence if you were to get what you want.
Mindful of the situation by focusing on what you want and ignore distractions.
Appear confident even if you don't feel confident.
Negotiate with a hesitant person and come to a comfortable compromise on your request (from Linehan, 1993).

GIVE is the next acronym which focuses on steps for maintaining relationships when making requests. They are *gentle* (being courteous and nonjudgmental; using appropriate language), *interested* (asking questions of the other person, etc.), *validate* (communicating verbally and nonverbally that you are engaged with the other person), and *easy manner* (being clam, using humor, not pressuring, etc.). Finally, FAST is an acronym for a series of skills that help clients maintain self-respect when engaging interpersonally with another person (and is used in combination with the other two skill sets). It stands for *fair* (to one's self and others), *apologies* (don't apologize more than once for something that was effective), *stick to your values* (don't allow others to manipulate you to do something that goes against your values), and *truthful* (lies will only damage relationships and self-respect). The interpersonal effectiveness skills are very similar to assertiveness skills classes that help individuals to appropriately advocate for what they need (Linehan, 1993, 2015; Lynch, Chapman, Rosenthal, Kuo, & Linehan, 2006; Mozdzierz et al., 2014). We present a case next to illustrate some of these points.

Recall from Chapter 2 the case of Ellen and Matt, who have been dating for about three years. They met in college and are beginning their careers in separate states (she is in graduate school, while he is beginning his first job in an investment firm). They have had to go for long periods of time without seeing one another, which has led to some tension in the relationship. They both express a desire to be with one another but acknowledge that this cannot happen right now. In terms of the future, both Ellen and Matt have said that they have talked about the prospect of marriage one day but have not committed to this idea, yet.

What is most salient about Ellen and Matt's case, and where a DBT approach would be most beneficial, is in dealing with their pattern of arguing whenever they get together. Ellen stated that the argument usually starts over something small and escalates until they stop speaking to one another. It usually lasts for an entire day, and eventually one person apologizes to the other. They acknowledge that their fights are silly, but it wastes the little time that they have together (which is frustrating). In addition, their arguments have grown in frequency and intensity.

The most recent conflict was when Matt was scheduled to visit Ellen. When she was not there to meet him, as planned, he left and drove back, thinking that she had "stood him up" following a fight on the phone the night before. The reality was that Ellen got called into an impromptu meeting with her professor in order to correct some last-minute information on an important grant. While she did try to reach Matt, she was not able to get through to him. As he drove back home, Matt refused to take her calls. Ultimately, he found out about the miscommunication, and was embarrassed. However, he still held Ellen responsible for ruining the weekend because she didn't try hard enough to reach him.

A DBT couple therapist would first conduct a "chain analysis" of the sequence of events and (most importantly) decisions that each person made along the way, as well as their feelings about it. Each decision is in a long chain of decisions that brought each of them to the conflict point. At any point, each person could have made a different choice, which could have changed the outcome. Next, the DBT couple therapist would work with the couple on building their skills around distress tolerance (which is clearly an area of struggle for them). For Matt and Ellen, this would help them to accept each other in a nonjudgmental and nonevaluative way, which, in turn, would help to de-escalate their conflict. The goal would be to help them calmly recognize when are in a negative situation (like with the miscommunication over the weekend), and the potential impact ("What would happen if I chose to stay and find out what went wrong, vs. leaving?"), rather than hiding from or becoming overwhelmed by it (and thus leaving). A DBT couple therapist would also work with Ellen and Matt to help them learn how to bear pain and how not to make poor choices about taking action or responding to the other person in anger. Additional skills using the acronyms DEARMAN, GIVE, and FAST would also help Ellen and Matt to communicate their needs and wants to each other in a nondefensive, nonreactive way as well.

Research

There have been several randomized clinical trials of DBT conducted over the past 20 years that have demonstrated its effectiveness as a treatment approach, particularly with borderline personality disorder (Robbins & Chapman, 2006; Stoffers et al., 2012). However, research with couples and DBT has been, thus far, limited. Fruzzetti and Payne (2015) reported the effects of a pilot study on DBT and couple therapy that found significant improvements in satisfaction and communication, as well as improvements in coping with distress and dysregulation of emotion. More extensive research investigating the long-term effectiveness of DBT as a couple therapy approach is planned.

Concluding Note

In this chapter, we have introduced four additional theories of couple therapy that emphasize the central role of emotion in the treatment of couples issues. Such integrative and affect-oriented approaches are a powerful tool for effecting change with clients. At the same time, we are gaining an understanding of the complex, interrelated dynamics of internal emotional responses and their impact on one's partner. Creating change on this level produces profound and lasting benefits. Clearly, however, as past emotive interventions have shown, focusing here is not enough. Instead, a modern, mature, and inclusive approach that pays attention to behavior, cognitions, and emotions is required in order to be successful. Some of the approaches already presented (insight-oriented couple therapy, integrative behavioral couple therapy, Adlerian couple therapy, EFCT, and various family systems therapies) do this.

References

A-Tjak J. G., Davis M. L., Morina N., Powers M. B., Smits J. A., & Emmelkamp, M. P. (2015). A meta-analysis of the efficacy of acceptance and commitment therapy for clinically relevant mental and physical health problems. *Psychotherapy and Psychosomatics, 84*(1), 30–36. doi:10.1159/000365764

Bishop, S. R., Lau, M., Shapiro, S., Carlson, L., Anderson, N. D., Carmody, J., … Devins, G. (2004). Mindfulness: A proposed operational definition. *Clinical Psychology: Science & Practice, 11*(3), 230–241.

Bowlby, J. (1969). *Attachment and loss: Vol. 1 attachment.* London, England: Hogarth Press.

Cherlin, A. (2010). *The marriage-go-round.* New York, NY: Vintage.

Christensen, A., Atkins, D. C., Berns, S., Wheeler, J., Baucom, D. H., & Simpson, L. E. (2004). Traditional versus integrative behavioral couple therapy for significantly and chronically distressed married couples. *Journal of Consulting & Clinical Psychology, 72*(2), 176–191.

Cohen, J. (1988). *Statistical power analysis for the behavioral sciences* (2nd ed.). Hillsdale, NJ: Erlbaum.

Fruzzetti, A. (2006). *The high conflict couple: A dialectical behavior therapy guide to finding peace, intimacy, and validation.* Oakland, CA: New Harbinger Publications.

Fruzzetti, A. E., & Payne, L. (2015). Couple therapy and borderline personality disorder. In A. S. Gurman, J. Lebow, & D. Snyder (Eds.), *Clinical handbook of couple therapy* (5th ed., pp. 606–634). New York, NY: Guilford.

Goleman, D. (1995). *Emotional intelligence: Why it can matter more than IQ.* New York, NY: Bantam.

Gottman, J. (1993). *What predicts divorce: The relationship between marital processes and marital outcomes.* Hillsdale, NJ: Erlbaum.

Gottman, J. M. (1995). *Why marriages succeed or fail: And how you can make yours last.* New York, NY: Fireside.

Gottman, J. M. (2015). *Principia amoris: The new science of love.* New York, NY: Routledge.

Gottman, J. M., & Gottman, J. S. (2017). The natural principles of love. *Journal of Family Theory and Review, 9*, 7–26. doi:10.1111/jftr.12182

Gottman, J., Murray, J., Swanson, C., Tyson, R., & Swanson, K. (2002). *The mathematics of marriage: Dynamic nonlinear models.* Cambridge, MA: MIT Press.

Greenberg, L. S., & Johnson, S. M. (1988). *Emotionally focused therapy for couples.* New York, NY: Guilford.

Gurman, A. S. (2015). The theory and practice of couple therapy: History, contemporary models, and a framework for comparative analysis. In A. S. Gurman, J. Lebow, & D. Snyder (Eds.), *Clinical handbook of couple therapy* (5th ed., pp. 1–18). New York, NY: Guilford.

Gurman, A. S., & Fraenkel, P. (2002). The history of couple therapy: A millennial review. *Family Process, 41*(2), 199–260.

Hayes, S. C. (2004/2016). Acceptance and commitment therapy, relational frame theory, and the third wave of behavioral and cognitive therapies – republished article. *Behavioral Therapy, 47*(6), 869–885. doi:10.1016/j.beth.2016.11.006

Hayes, S. C., Luoma, J. B., Bond, F. W., Masuda, A., & Lillis, J. (2006). Acceptance and commitment therapy: Model, processes and outcomes. *Behaviour Research and Therapy, 44*(1), 1–25. doi:10.1016/j.brat.2005.06.006. PMID 16300724

Hoyt, M. F. (1998). *The handbook of constructive therapies.* San Francisco, CA: Jossey-Bass.

Johnson, S. M. (1996). *The practice of emotionally focused marital therapy: Creating connection.* New York, NY: Guilford.

Johnson, S. M. (2003). Couple therapy research: Status and directions. In G. P. Sholevar (Ed.), *Textbook of family and couple therapy* (pp. 797–814). Alexandria, VA: American Psychiatric Publishing.

Johnson, S. M. (2015). Emotionally focused couple therapy. In A. S. Gurman, J. Lebow, & D. Snyder (Eds.), *Clinical handbook of couple therapy* (5th ed., pp. 97–128). New York, NY: Guilford.

Johnson, S. M., & Best, M. (2003). A systemic approach to restructuring adult attachment: The EFT model of couple therapy. In P. Erdman & T. Caffery (Ed.),

Attachment and family systems: Conceptual, empirical, and therapeutic relatedness (pp. 165–189). New York, NY: Brunner-Routledge.

Johnson, S. M., & Denton, W. (2002). Emotionally focused couple therapy: Creating secure connections. In A. S. Gurman & N. S. Jacobson (Eds.), *Clinical handbook of couple therapy* (3rd ed., pp. 221–250). New York, NY: Guilford.

Johnson, S. M., & Whiffen, V. (1999). Made to measure: Adapting emotionally focused couple therapy to partners attachment styles. *Clinical Psychology: Science and Practice, 6*, 366–381.

Lev, A., & McKay, M. (2017). *Acceptance and commitment therapy for couples: A clinician's guide to using mindfulness, values, and schema awareness to rebuild relationships.* New York, NY: New Harbinger Publications.

Lewis, W. A., & Bucher, A. M. (1982). Anger, catharsis, the reformulated frustration-aggression hypothesis, and health consequences. *Psychotherapy, 29*, 385–392.

Linehan M. M. (1993). *Skills training manual for treating borderline personality disorder.* New York, NY: The Guilford Press.

Linehan, M. M. (2015). *DBT skills training manual* (2nd ed.). New York, NY: Guilford Press.

Lynch, T. R., Chapman, A. L., Rosenthal, M. Z., Kuo, J. R., & Linehan, M. M. (2006). Mechanisms of change in dialectical behavior therapy: Theoretical and empirical observations. *Journal of Clinical Psychology, 62*(4), 459–480.

Mann, B. J., & Schwartz, R. C. (2002). Internal systems therapy. In F. W. Kaslow & T. Patterson (Eds.), *Comprehensive handbook of psychotherapy: Integrative/eclectic, Vol. 4* (pp. 455–474). New York, NY: John Wiley & Sons.

Mayer, J. D., & Stevens, A. (1993). *An emerging understanding of the reflective (meta) experience of mood* (Unpublished manuscript).

Mozdzierz, G., Peluso, P. R., & Liseckei, J. (2014). *Principles of counseling and psychotherapy: Learning the essential domains and nonlinear thinking of master practitioners* (2nd ed.). New York, NY: Routledge.

Nolen-Hoeksema, S., McBride, A., & Larson, J. (1997). Rumination and psychological distress among bereaved partners. *Journal of Personality and Social Psychology, 72*, 855–862.

Robbins, C. J., & Chapman, A. L. (2006). Dialectical behavior therapy: Current status, recent developments and future directions. *Journal of Personality Disorders, 18*, 73–89.

Schwartz, R. C., & Johnson, S. M. (2000). Commentary: Does couple and family therapy have emotional intelligence? *Family Process, 39*, 29–33.

Stoffers, J. M., Vollm, B. A., Rucker, G., Timmer, A., Husband, N., & Lieb, K. (2012). Psychological therapies for people with borderline personality disorder. *Cochrane Database of Systematic Reviews,* (8), Article No. CDC005652. doi:10.1002/14651858.CD005652.pub2.

Wiebe, S. A., & Johnson, S. M. (2017). Creating relationships that foster resilience in emotionally focused therapy. *Current Opinion in Psychology, 13*, 65–69.

Wiebe, S. A., Johnson, S. M., Burgess Moser, M., Dalgleish, T. L., & Tasca, G. A. (2017). Predicting follow-up outcomes in emotionally focused couple therapy: The role of change in trust, relationship-specific attachment, and emotional engagement. *Journal of Marital and Family Therapy, 43*, 213–226. doi:10.1111/jmft.12199

Section 3

The Practice of Couple Therapy

9 Assessment and Case Conceptualization in Couple Therapy

LEARNING OBJECTIVES

In this chapter, the reader will learn the following:

1 Indications/contraindications for couple therapy.
2 A comprehensive and integrative approach to couples assessment.
3 Components of a couples case conceptualization.
4 Instruments useful in assessment.

The way in which therapists think about and carry out a couples assessment is based upon their "model" of how couples relationships become functional and dysfunctional (Gurman, 2015; Sperry, 2012). Chapters 4–9 surveyed the most common and current theoretical models. Such models can be useful guides in making sense out of the complex, sometimes confusing mixture of information, behavior, and communication elicited and observed during the assessment. Nevertheless, these models tend to be reductionistic or limiting since therapists tend to ignore some inputs and focus primarily on data that "fit" their case conceptualization and treatment plan.

During the course of their careers, many couple therapists develop their own personal theory or model of couples functioning and dysfunction, so it is not too surprising that the way in which therapists conduct assessment interviews changes. Often, couple therapists either do not employ a comprehensive and integrative assessment model or employ a model that assesses only some of the pertinent domains of relational or individual functioning. Unfortunately, too many clinically focused couple therapy books reflect this non-comprehensive perspective (Taibbi, 2017).

The purpose of this chapter is to advocate for couples assessment that is both comprehensive and integrative. This approach is based on a biopsychosocial perspective and can be useful for couple therapists to assess all couples, particularly the nontraditional couple. This chapter begins with our perspective on couples assessment and the indications/contraindications for couple therapy. Then it describes an integrative approach to couples assessment. This is followed by a discussion of the components of a couples case conceptualization. An extended case example illustrates these considerations. Finally, an Appendix includes descriptions of common instruments useful in the assessment of couples.

Perspective on Couples Assessment

A common perception among most trainees and some therapists is that a couples assessment is a formal, verbal evaluation that is performed face-to-face with the couple by the therapist in the first interview(s). A corollary to this perception is that the same therapist who completes the assessment will undertake therapeutic interventions. In our experience, this is a rather limited view of assessment. We view the assessment phase as an ongoing process that begins with the couple's first contact with the therapist or clinic, usually by phone, extending over the course of treatment and including follow-up after treatment is formally terminated. As we shall point out later, initial telephone contact prior to the first appointment offers important assessment information. Also important are nonverbal behaviors, data from forms and inventories that the couple completes before or after the first sessions, and medical and psychological reports from other professionals.

Before formal therapeutic interventions are initiated, the therapist must make at least three decisions. The first regards the relative indications for a couples assessment and therapy. Are the presenting symptoms the result of personality dynamics of a partner or couple dynamics, i.e. relational interaction? Even though the couples system is relevant in considering the partners' concerns or symptoms, there are instances in which other factors may be more important. Physical overlays and symptoms such as medication side effects, medical conditions such as hypothyroidism, and a number of neurological and psychiatric disorders are conditions that can greatly impact couple functioning (Sperry, 2013). Usually, when these physical conditions are appropriately treated, the couple relationship improves, probably without formal therapeutic intervention. But couple therapy may also be needed for predisposed couples in which medical conditions are extraordinarily stressful. With a few exceptions, the couple therapy literature has largely ignored the indications and contraindications for such therapy. The assumption is made that couple therapy is a treatment of choice whenever a partner seeks help. Besides being somewhat cavalier, this attitude can be harmful to the couple or partner. It has and may continue to be the basis of malpractice suits brought against such therapists.

The second decision is based on the results of the evaluation. Which of the modes of couple therapy (collaborative; couples groups; family or couple therapy alone, or in conjunction with couples sessions) is the optimal treatment for a particular couple? These modalities will be discussed in the following chapter.

If couple therapy is the treatment of choice, the third set of decisions involves the type, duration, focus, and particular strategies utilized in the treatment of a particular couple. This effort to match treatment to a couple's needs and styles, strengths, and previous positions is called differential therapeutics (Frances, Clarkin, & Perry, 1984). These differential therapeutic considerations will be discussed in the next chapter.

Indications and Contraindications for Couple Therapy

An initial question that the therapist must answer is whether a couple is appropriate for couple therapy. Often, there are strong indications that couple therapy is the treatment of choice or that the opposite is true. Chagoya and Cameron (1998) listed six clinical indications and nine contraindications for couple therapy. The indications they list are:

1 Interactional difficulties in the relationship with a partner are the primary complaints of an individual (i.e. communication with partner, problems of commitment, sexuality, etc.).
2 The couple is confronting a developmental crisis in the relationship that requires significant adjustment (i.e. differentiating from family of origin, parenting, illnesses, children leaving home, etc.).
3 There is a loss of the original bond or purpose for the couple (i.e. infidelity and disclosure of the affair, career change or relocation, developing outside interests, etc.).
4 One partner has a psychiatric or medical illness.
5 One partner adopts an alternative lifestyle or sexual orientation.
6 There is conflict about whether to have children (inclusive of medical conditions that prevent the couple from having children).

While these represent circumstances when couple therapy would be a superior form of treatment over individual therapy, there are also several situations when couple therapy is not appropriate. According to Chagoya and Cameron (1998), these are:

1 When couple therapy leads to a deterioration of a couple's function (recriminations from one partner to another, session material leads to escalation of conflict outside of session).
2 When the primary motivation for therapy is for one partner to use the therapist's opinion to gain a legal or financial advantage over another.
3 When the couple has rigid culture-bound patterns or roles that are not subject to change (therapeutic interventions run the risk of alienating one or both partners).
4 When one partner is too disabled by a psychiatric illness to participate fully in session without potentially deleterious effects.
5 Couples who arouse strong, negative countertransference feelings in the therapist (entangling therapist in triangles, secrets, and degrading therapist effectiveness).
6 When couples have persistent, negative transference feelings toward the therapist that cannot be resolved.
7 When one partner cannot (or will not) acknowledge and examine his or her part in the conflict.

8 When there is a threat of domestic violence without the deterrence of legal punishment (i.e. when the victim will not press charges). Couple therapy is contraindicated since the session material will either be strictly censored or used against the victim.
9 There is no trust or positive feeling between partners and any attempt to instill it is defeated.

Integrative Approach to Couple Assessment

A clinician who has any question about the value of a comprehensive assessment would do well to seriously consider the statistics on treatment failure in couples and family therapy. In *Failures in Family Therapy*, Coleman (1985) noted that 83% of treatment failures were primarily due to inadequate initial assessments. These data confirm our own clinical and supervisory experience. For this reason we have advocated a comprehensive and integrative assessment. Currently, there are various models of couples assessment. Some focus tightly on certain aspects of the couple relationship, while others are more broad and comprehensive. However, one shortcoming that we noted was that they did not include a biological domain. As the field becomes more and more biologically savvy, we believe that including the biological domain is essential.

We wish to present a model that combines many of the aspects described earlier as well as some additional domains. This model integrates the work of Sperry (1989) into a comprehensive biopsychosocial relationship assessment. It provides an integrative and comprehensive model for planning a couples assessment. Briefly stated, the model is:

Integrative Couples Assessment = Situation + Partner + System
+ Suitability for Treatment

Situation refers to the symptoms, stressors, circumstances, and demographics that form the context for the couple's presenting concerns, complaints, or problems.

Partner refers to the individual system dimension, including the physical and psychological health of each partner as well as cognitive and constitutional style.

System refers to the relational subsystem – that is, the relationship between partners.

Suitability for treatment refers to the couple's qualification for couple therapy.

Until recently, the systems approach to couples and family therapy has tended to focus on the marital/couple subsystem at the expense of the individual subsystem (Gurman, 2015). Because this view is reductionistic, we suggest a more comprehensive and integrative view. Sperry and associates (2003) provide an integrative assessment format covering six content areas: Presenting Problem and Context, Mental Status Assessment, Developmental History and Dynamics, Social History and Cultural Dynamics, Health History and Behaviors, and Client Resources. Table 9.1 modifies this format which deletes one and adds two domains: ***relationship dynamics*** and ***suitability for treatment.***

Table 9.1 Domains of an Integrative Couples Assessment

Domain	*Questions/Information Gathered*
Presenting Problem and Context	Clarify type of symptom and stressors Elicit coping skills, social support, and related client resources Elicit previous treatment history and family history of symptom Assess impact on daily functioning
Relational History and Dynamics	Clarify current self-view, level of self-esteem, personality style and dynamics Brief developmental history (family-of-origin issues will be developed further with genogram), developmental milestones or delays, educational history and school experiences
Social History and Cultural Dynamics	Current living situation/legal status Employment status and financial security Ethnic identity, race, age, religion, SES, gender, sexual orientation Assess level of acculturation (assimilated, traditional, bicultural, etc.) Asses impact of cultural status on sense of self or relationship dynamics/norms
Health History and Behaviors	Identify medication or nutrient usage Identify any substance abuse issues Assess general medical condition, chronic medical conditions Assess overall health habits Refer to physician as indicated
Relational Dynamics and-Interaction Pattern	History of the relationship Stage of relationship and degree of synchronicity Compatibility of cognitive and constitution styles Boundaries, power, intimacy Sexual functioning Financial issues Family-of-origin issues and genogram Commitment to and expectations for the relationship Relational interaction pattern
Clients Resources	Probe client's own efforts to change, past efforts and successes in making changes Clarify clients' explanatory model for problem
Suitability for Treatment	Motivation for treatment Expectations for treatment Level of couple functioning and discord Prognostic factors (indications and contraindications)

Following is a description of these seven domains of couples assessment.

Presenting Problem and Context

This part of the assessment addresses the client's reason for coming to therapy and the reason why the client has chosen the present time to make changes. This information may be crucial to determine the impetus for beginning therapy, as well as the motivation to follow through. It also assesses the impact (destructive or facilitative) that the presenting problem is having on the client's life. Asking questions about when the client does not experience the problem (the "exception") also helps to clarify the scope of the problem. Again, as with uncovering the impetus to assess motivation, understanding the role that the problem plays in the function or dysfunction of the client's life may help the therapist to hypothesize about any secondary reinforcement for the problem behavior. In addition, questions about previous mental health treatment and family psychiatric history help to determine the chronicity and scope of the problem. Finally, because psychiatric disorders in one or both partners can complicate the therapy process (Sperry, 2019), a diagnostic evaluation to specify such DSM-5 diagnoses may be indicated (American Psychiatric Association, 2013).

Developmental History and Dynamics

This history is the client's story about his or her life. The therapist should assess for normal developmental milestones common to most people and note any deviations from it. If there were developmental delays or deviations, how did the client handle them? Did he or she strive to persevere and overcome or become overwhelmed and unable to compensate? Are there any lingering effects? In addition, any early traumas, abuse, or deficits in caregiving should be noted. In addition, assessing the client's educational history, attitudes toward school, and career choice is a part of the overall story. Relevant themes may begin to emerge that could help to explain the atmosphere in which the symptom or presenting problem has developed. Early recollections as a part of assessing the client's view of him or herself may also be collected (Sperry et al., 2003).

Social History and Cultural Dynamics

Typically, therapists focus on three elements of cultural dynamics when performing an assessment (and subsequent report): Age, gender, and race (e.g. "Client is a 23-year-old African-American female."). Yet the impact of cultural origins on individual behaviors and couples issues is ubiquitous and frequently underestimated (McGoldrick, 2003). Sperry (2010) lists nine cultural factors recommended by the Group for the Advancement of Psychiatry (GAP, 2002) in addition to the three already discussed. These additional factors are ethnic identity, sexual orientation, religion, migration and country of origin, socioeconomic status, acculturation (viz., assimilation into dominant culture), language, dietary influences, and education.

McGoldrick (2003) asserts that cultural origins generally have positive influences in people's lives but that there can also be attitudes and prejudices that can create feelings of being devalued and alienation. These can contribute to an individual and a couple's dysfunction, particularly for couples who come from different cultural backgrounds. Therapists can create an open and honest atmosphere for discussing these issues if they "assume that no one can ever fully understand another's culture, but that curiosity, humility, and awareness of one's own cultural values and history contribute to sensitive interviewing" (McGoldrick, 2003, p. 257).

Health History and Behaviors

This domain covers a variety of health-related concerns from diet and exercise to hospitalizations. According to Sperry et al. (2003),

> whether this information is elicited in the interview or is provided on ... a form, it is imperative for the therapist to briefly review the health conditions, surgeries, and various medical treatments to ascertain *how* these have impacted a client's life.
>
> (p. 62)

This includes any chronic medical conditions and ongoing relationships with physicians.

Another related area that is assessed by this domain is the use of any prescription medication, over-the-counter (OTC) medication, and any substance use or abuse. Prescription medications (such as antidepressants) can affect mood, behavior, blood pressure, and sex drive, which could contribute to a couple's presenting problem. It also goes without saying that clients who take prescription medication probably have some underlying medical condition, or may have some dependency to medications that are no longer necessary. Similarly, understanding the client's usage of OTC medication or herbal supplements may uncover untreated medical conditions or unacknowledged substance abuse. Likewise, any information about substance use (alcohol or illegal drugs) needs to be investigated at this point. The treatment issues related to this topic will be discussed in Chapter 12. With all of these issues, the impact on couple functioning and on the partner not using substances (prescribed or not) is important to ascertain.

Also included in this domain is assessing the client's regular health-related activity. This is particularly important in understanding clients' attitudes about fitness, proper diet, and overall wellness. These strengths can be used as potential resources or, if the overall pattern is poor, can be developed in the therapy to contribute to success.

Relational Dynamics

Assessment here begins with the history of the relationship in its present stage of functioning and focuses on important system factors, such as boundaries, power, and intimacy, and includes the families of origin of the partners (via genogram), boundaries and power in the relationship, relational interaction pattern, sexual and money issues, and relationship satisfaction.

Relationship History

Eliciting the history of the relationship begins with questions such as, "How did you meet? As best you know, what attracted you to each other? How did your dating go? How did you decide on getting married (if applicable)? How did things go when you were first married? How have things changed since then?" Continuation of this initial relationship can be explained by the bonding that occurs at a deeper and unconscious level. In this view, people are attracted to one another and remain in a relationship because they represent one half of a total personality, and staying in the relationship is the way in which they seek to grow and attain personal integration. Projective identification and collusion often emerge as important clinical indicators of a couple's presenting problems. Issues of attachment style and other personality dynamics enter into the relationship and become salient for assessment at this point as well.

Families-of-Origin Issues

Exploration of the couple's history in relationship to their families of origin often proves useful. Such exploration is frequently helpful in explicating issues and bringing them into the therapeutic arena. This can be accomplished in several ways. A common method is the use of the *genogram*. Genograms are a powerful tool for both understanding the influence of a couple's families of origin and providing feedback to the client about these dynamics. Utilized almost exclusively by family therapists, the genogram was first introduced by Murray Bowen in the 1950s as an assessment tool for family therapy (McGoldrick, Gerson, & Petry, 2008). It is a simple, graphic way to trace the multigenerational influences on an individual or family's present-day functioning.

Bowen and subsequent systems theorists believed that family processes tend to repeat themselves, particularly with regard to unresolved emotional issues (McGoldrick et al., 2008). Genograms have also been used to trace addiction history, patterns of divorce, abuse, and diseases within the family of origin (McGoldrick et al., 2008). Additional information about influential life events, significant deaths in the family, and coalitions in the family of origin, which may be difficult to directly assess in an interview, is readily discussed in a genogram.

Basic and important information reported on the genogram includes names, ages, marital status, divorces, separations, and years of deaths. Typically, the therapist constructs a genogram of one partner and has the other partner fill in information and make comments following the initial disclosures. Then, the process is reversed. Some therapists who operate from an object-relations perspective may collect additional information by asking one partner, "What do you imagine it would have been like to be married to your partner's mother?" and/or "What do you imagine it would have been like for your father to be married to your partner's mother?"

Boundaries, Power, and Intimacy

Another important area of assessment for relationship dynamics involves boundaries, power, and intimacy. For structure or boundaries, questions to be answered include: Who else is considered to be part of the couples system? What is being excluded from the couple's relationship and assigned to children or others? Who and what events or things are intruding into the couple's relationship? For power, the therapist wants to know: Who is in charge? How do the partners deal with power in their relationship? For intimacy, some questions are: How near, how far, and how do the partners tolerate or respond to each other's needs and desires for intimate contact and closeness? How do partners use emotional and geographical distance when struggling with their need for closeness? Answers to such questions provide significant data for the therapist in assessing the couples system.

Relational Interaction Pattern

Couple relational interaction patterns are central to developing an effective couple case conceptualization. When the pattern is negative, the relationship is unable to grow and thrive. At best, that pattern allows the relationship to survive, at least for a while. Presumably, couples work can break and replace these patterns with more adaptive ones. Table 9.2 describes five of the most common negative relational patterns and one positive pattern.

Sexual and Money Issues

The issues of sexual functioning and finances in couples are closely linked to issues of boundaries, power, and intimacy. In an assessment, couple therapists are well advised not to overlook these crucial areas. Decisions about money, how it is spent, and who spends it can often give therapists vital clues to underlying relationship dynamics. For example, if one partner doesn't have control of the checkbook or makes less money than the other, then that person may feel that they always have to defer to the other person. Likewise, sexual issues (which will be covered in more detail in Chapter 13) may have a biological component but often will be a reflection of aspects of the relationship (Schnarch, 1991). Many times, couple therapists will shy away from questions, particularly about sex, mostly due to personal feelings of embarrassment or out of a belief that once sufficient rapport is built with the couple, *then* such personal questions can be asked. The reality is that the tone for the therapy, as well as the unwritten rules of what topics are allowable, is set during the assessment, and unless the therapist encourages an open and frank dialogue with the couple, these issues will be buried to the detriment of the therapy.

Table 9.2 Couple Interaction Patterns

Demand/Withdraw. Develops when one partner blames, criticizes, or demands [*demand*] change from the other partner. In response, the other partner gives in, defers, surrenders, or complies [*withdraw*]. It is also known as the pursuer-distancer pattern and is the most common relational pattern (Christensen & Shenk, 1991). It is correlated with partner hostility and aggression, relationship dissatisfaction, and divorce. All other negative relational patterns are variants of this one.
Demand/Submit. Develops when one partner blames, accrues, criticizes, or demands [*demand*] change from the other partner. Then, the other partner avoids, fails to respond, is defensive or silent, or essentially refuses to discuss the concern [*submit*] (Knobloch-Fedders et al., 2014).
Withdraw/Withdraw. Develops after a couple has exhausted the demand/withdraw pattern. Then, in the face of conflict, both withdraw further. They feel hopeless over their situation and begin to give up (Kasting, 2015).
Attack/Attack. Develops when a partner responds to an attack with an attack which results in an escalation of discord. The escalations are a variant of the demand/withdraw pattern. In response to the demanding partner [*attack*], the withdrawing partner becomes sufficiently provoked and erupts in anger [*attack*]. Also referred to as the "high conflict couple" (Fruzzetti, 2006).
Reactive Demand/Withdraw. Develops when a couple reverses a previous long-standing pattern. Occurs with a role change in one of the partners, as when a demanding wife gradually gives up and limits her investment in the relationship. Increasingly, she withdraws and distances herself [*withdraw*]. In response, the husband will frantically pursue the wife to prevent a separation. When this does not occur, the withdrawer takes on the demand role and aggressively pursues his wife [*reactive demand*] (Knobloch-Fedders et al., 2014).
Constructive Engagement. Develops as partners express issues that bother them in a "non-attacking way that accurately reflects what they feel, think, or want, including accurate expression of primary emotions. The other partner listens, brings curiosity, tries to understand, and communicates understanding, even if he or she disagrees" (Fruzzetti & Payne, 2015, p. 609).

Relationship Satisfaction

Relationship satisfaction is at its highest when the partners' experiences of the other match their expectations. But when hope conflicts with reality, conflict and dissatisfaction usually follow. Thus, it is particularly helpful for the therapist to list the expectations each partner had of the relationship and of the other partner at the beginning of the relationship and the expectations at the present time. Some formal inventories can be used to elicit these data (see Appendix of this chapter), or the therapist can directly question the couple about expectations, divisions of responsibility, decision-making, sharing, recreation, and so on.

In assessing relational issues, a couple therapist begins to put the pieces of the previous domains into the context of the relationship itself and starts to see how there are multiple layers of causality, as well as multiple points of intervention. The sum total of the systemic, relational dynamics assessment should inform the couple therapist as to the best place to start working from if the couple is ready to do the work.

Client Resources

If the relationship dynamics portion of the assessment brings together all the aspects of the couple relationship related to the problem, then the client resources domain looks at what the couple possesses in order to combat the problem. This aspect of the assessment is crucial for tailoring treatment to the strengths of each partner and to the couple as a whole. The couple therapist must assess the level of support, appropriate role models, emotional energy, and cognitive ability to make the kind of changes that are necessary. It includes a chronicle of the couple's past successes and failures, their understanding of the causal determinants of the problem, and each partner's sense of personal responsibility for the condition of the relationship. In addition, clients' level of readiness for change, resistance to treatment, and expectations for therapy are raised.

Suitability for Treatment

It is common for couples and family therapists to assume that couple therapy is the treatment of choice for most conditions and circumstances and that most couples are suitable for couples treatment. Research by Lambert and Barley (2002) has indicated, however, that suitability for treatment is a function of motivational readiness for change and realistic expectations for the outcome of therapy. Clarification of the motivation of each partner in collaborating with the therapist and in a course of couple therapy is crucial. Commitment to a relationship is not synonymous with motivation to change or commitment to engage in couple therapy. Therefore, it is necessary for the therapist to observe the partners' behaviors and verbalizations concerning their relationship, themselves, and therapy, noting the degree of congruence between their behavior and their statements.

Couples should also be queried on their treatment objectives: Do they want rebalancing or symptom relief, divorce mediation, relationship enrichment, and so on? It is also helpful to elicit each partner's explanation for what went wrong with the relationship. Although blame is the common first response, the therapist who probes beyond that level uncovers miscommunications and deep-rooted fears as well as information useful for treatment formulation.

The therapist must be able to determine if any variables that are prognostic of poor treatment outcomes are present. These include a long history of problems and a persistent major symptom; previous treatment based on the individual rather than on the family system; a relatively severe diagnosis; and an external, rather than self-generated, motivation for treatment. It is also helpful to make an early determination of the partners' responses to external control and correction as well as their level of resistance. For instance, the therapist can assess the partners' receptivity to interpretations as compared to directives. All of these factors can be useful in making the three major decisions involved in the assessment phase. At this point, the clinician has all the information necessary to specify a diagnosis for the couple and make a prognosis for the therapy.

Case Conceptualization

Case conceptualization is a "clinical strategy for obtaining and organizing information about a client, explaining the client's situation and maladaptive patterns, and focusing treatment, anticipating treatment challenges and roadblocks, and preparing for termination" (Sperry, 2010, pp. 84–85). When the client is a couple or family, it reflects how a therapist thinks about or conceptualizes the couple's or family's presenting problems and concerns. It also informs all aspects of treatment, including who should attend sessions, the type of therapeutic relationship, and the choice of therapeutic interventions (Gehart, 2017)

Case conceptualizations that are clinically useful and valuable provide therapists with a coherent treatment strategy for planning and focusing treatment interventions that will effect change. Effective case conceptualizations emphasize the unique context and the needs and resources that the individual or couple brings to treatment. Such case conceptualizations can be informed by a theoretical framework (e.g. Strategic, Solution-focused, Narrative, etc.), which incorporates biological, psychological, and sociocultural factors (Sperry & Sperry, 2012).

Clinically useful case conceptualization includes the client's presentation, precipitant, predisposition, maladaptive pattern, and personality dynamics. *Presentation* is the client's presenting problem, often a response to a precipitant that is congruent with the client's pattern. It can include specific symptoms and their severity, personal and social functioning, and medical and DSM diagnoses as well as the history and course of symptoms. *Precipitants* are the triggers that activate the client's pattern, leading to the presenting problem. The maladaptive pattern is the client's consistent style of problematic thinking, feeling, and behaving. *Predispositions* are factors that foster and lead to either maladaptive or adaptive patterns. Biological, psychological, and social factors can all contribute to the predisposition. *Perpetuants* are those factors that maintain the presenting problem.

Many therapists consider case conceptualization to be one of the most challenging clinical competencies to master (Sperry & Sperry, 2012). This may be a major reason why many therapists neither develop nor use case conceptualizations, or lack confidence in their ability to conceptualize cases. Experience with both experienced therapists and trainees can easily and confidently begin to master this competency in as little as two to three hours of formal training in an integrative model of case conceptualization (Sperry, 2016).

A basic premise of this integrative model is that individuals unwittingly develop a self-perpetuating, maladaptive pattern of functioning and relating to others, and that this pattern underlies the individual's, couple's, or family's presenting issue(s). A second premise is that effective treatment will involve a change process in which the client and therapist collaborate to identify this pattern, break it, and replace it with a more adaptive pattern. Two outcomes result from this change process: The first is increased well-being, and the second is resolution of the presenting issue(s).

Centrality of Pattern

Basic to an individual, couple, or family case conceptualization is the pattern which is its central and defining feature. Pattern is defined as the predicable, consistent, and self-perpetuating style and manner in which individuals think, feel, act, cope, and defend themselves (Sperry, 2010). It can either be maladaptive or adaptive. Maladaptive patterns are those that are inflexible, ineffective, and inappropriate, and cause symptoms and impairment in personal and relational functioning. Patterns that are sufficiently distressing or impairing may be diagnosed as a personality disorder. By contrast, an adaptive pattern reflects personality dynamics that are flexible, effective, and appropriate.

Effective therapy requires changing maladaptive patterns (Livesley, 2003). A prerequisite for this change is for clients to become adept at recognizing patterns, particularly their maladaptive patterns. Clients readily accept the idea that there is a "pattern" underlying their behavior. The word pattern is reassuring, because it suggests that there is order and meaning to behavior. Learning about such patterns helps clients distance themselves from activating events, increases self-observation, and promotes "integration by connecting, events, behaviors, and experiences that were previously assumed to be unconnected" (Livesley, 2003, p. 274).

Individual Patterns

Individual patterns in couple therapy involve the long-standing problems and maladaptive patterns that partners bring to and enact into their relational interactions. Their faulty thinking and negative affective reactions can negatively impact one partner's efforts to enjoy intimate contact and maintain a positive attachment with the other partner. These individual patterns inevitably reflect a partner's personality style or DSM-5 personality disorder (APA, 2013).

Relational Patterns

Relational patterns, whether adaptive or maladaptive, are learned, in part, by modeling the relational patterns of the parents of both partners, and appear to be part of the attraction process of the couple. Relational patterns reflect from the personality patterns of each partner. Accordingly, an effective case conceptualization specifies and explains how these factors operate and explain the couples' relational interactions.

Such maladaptive patterns are evident in all aspects of the relationship, including the amount of time spent together, the type of communication, amount, type, and timing of sexual intimacy, how problems and challenges are handled, etc. It should be no surprise that relational patterns have predictable outcomes.

Unfortunately, when fully operative, as in a major disagreement, these patterns can polarize partners so that the situation seems hopeless when their differences are only a matter of degree. Or, they can protect and insulate the partners from getting too close to each other. Maladaptive relational patterns make the partners appear to be more incompatible than they might otherwise seem by polarizing the partners until they seem to represent opposite ends of the continuum of intimacy.

Partner Case Conceptualizations

When working with couples, it can be most useful to develop three case conceptualizations: Individual case conceptualizations for each partner and a couple case conceptualization for the relationship. A clinically useful individual case conceptualization includes the personality style/disorder and maladaptive pattern of a partner. For instance, a partner with an attention-getting pattern usually reflects a histrionic personality style or disorder, while an overly conscientious and perfectionistic pattern is likely to reflect an obsessive-compulsive personality style or disorder.

Couple Case Conceptualizations

Implicit or explicit in every therapeutic approach is a unique method of case conceptualization. Many couples approaches include relational interaction patterns in the couple case conceptualization. "Specifically, therapists focus on identifying the problems interaction cycle around the presenting problem. Typically, couples and families have one or two basic patterns of interaction that characterize the presenting problem" (Gehart, 2017, p. 256). Presumably, the couple case conceptualization reflects and emphasizes the couple's relational pattern(s) and explains their presenting problem or concern with this pattern.

Research reports that partners enact a role and narrative in their relationship, and displays one or two habitual and cyclical patterns of coping relationally. These patterns are referred to as couples interaction patterns or relational patterns (Christensen & Shenk, 1991). Six such patterns are discussed in the Relational Dynamics section and in Table 9.2. We now present a case that will demonstrate aspects of assessment and case conceptualization.

Tom (41) and Lynn (42) came to couple therapy following several heated conflicts that led to Tom temporarily leaving the house for a weekend. Lynn complained that Tom's outbursts have grown in intensity and frequency over the last six months and that she was feeling less and less trustful of him. In the past six months, Tom's father died suddenly in an automobile accident, leaving him to be his mother's primary caretaker (despite having other siblings in the area). His mother has demanded that he come by to do something at her house several times a week. Tom agrees to go over, often after work or on the weekend, which is beginning to be a point of contention between him and Lynn. Although Tom agrees that his mother's demands are becoming unreasonable, he feels that he owed it to his father to take care of his mother.

In addition, his job as a systems engineer has been another source of stress. His employer has required Tom and other engineers to work around the clock to finalize a proposal for a government contract that will determine whether or not his unit will be downsized. These time demands mean that Lynn must shoulder the burden of their two children (a daughter, aged six, and a son, aged four). The final straw for Lynn came when Tom slapped their daughter in the face when she talked back to him: "He's never done that before, and I'll be damned if I ever let him do that again! I can excuse a lot, but that is something I cannot excuse."

An integrative assessment interview conducted with the couple in the initial session yielded the following information.

Presenting Problem and Context

The couple is presenting with symptoms of anger outbursts, communication dysfunctions, and an overall lack of spending time with one another as a result of Tom's demands from work and his mother. Tom's issues seem to have stemmed from the loss of his father, though he downplays any grief issues. Lynn has a previous history of therapy in her early 20s for depression and dealing with her family-of-origin issues; Tom has no previous history of treatment. In terms of their respective families of origin, both Lynn and Tom's mothers have histories of psychiatric treatment. Lynn's mother had been diagnosed as bipolar, and Tom's mother had a "nervous breakdown" 25 years ago. In looking at the day-to-day impact of these issues, it would seem that their problems are acute and require immediate treatment. No DSM diagnoses were made.

Developmental History and Dynamics

Tom came from what he calls working-class roots. His father worked in a local factory, while his mother was a homemaker. He excelled in school (especially science and math), but his parents did not have the money to send him to college, and he had to go to work right out of high school. He eventually went back to complete his bachelor's degree and is in the process of getting his master's in engineering. He states that he had a normal childhood, with only one remarkable medical event when he was hospitalized at age eight for a severe respiratory infection that left him physically weaker than his peers. This was the point where he began to devote more time to school. In general, Tom wants more out of life but feels left back.

Lynn finished high school but did not continue to college. She never felt comfortable at school and struggled to keep a C average. When she graduated, she left home and began to work with a local dentist. She eventually became the office manager but had to leave once the children were born. She continues to work at that office part-time to this day. She is most proud and fulfilled by her role as a mother and caretaker. However, she is finding it very difficult to not be able to understand or help Tom during this time.

Social History and Cultural Dynamics

Both clients are heterosexual, Caucasian individuals raised in the southeastern U.S. Both share a conservative Christian worldview and place their religion (Southern Baptist) as very important in their lives, and it plays a big part in their social activities and peer group. Tom and Lynn have been married for almost 16 years and have lived together continuously during that time (except for the two-day separation two weeks earlier). They both state that they have a strong desire to stay married to one another.

Tom and Lynn are working middle class in terms of their financial and social status. They are both employed (he full-time, she part-time), although Tom has been more preoccupied with employment status and financial security. They do not report any arguments about money, however, as they have established a long-term, collaborative financial plan. This is evidence of their ability to work together amicably.

Health History and Behaviors

Neither client uses or abuses substances (alcohol, over-the-counter or prescription medications, or illegal drugs) on religious grounds. Lynn attends a regular aerobics class. Tom used to engage in outdoor activities (hunting, fishing, etc.) but has not since the death of his father. Both clients appear to be in overall good health and are not overweight. Neither partner has any chronic conditions, although at his last physical four months ago, Tom's blood pressure was elevated. His doctor was not alarmed but recommended that it be monitored.

Relational Dynamics

Lynn and Tom met in high school but did not interact in the same peer group. Lynn states that she barely knew Tom, while Tom remembered that Lynn was "one of the most beautiful girls in school," but he thought that she was "out of my league." After high school, both Lynn and Tom dated, and Lynn was even briefly engaged but called off the engagement because her fiancée was a recreational drug user, and "I didn't want that for my life." It was a few years later, while they were both in their early 20s, that they met up again. Lynn was living independently, and Tom was still living at home and going to school part-time. They were introduced by a mutual friend and were instantly attracted to one another. Tom recalled how beautiful she was in high school and was amazed that she was interested in him. Lynn appreciated how serious he was, unlike the other men she had been dating. She liked that he "knew where he was going" and had a kind of "stability about him." They dated for about three years, until Tom finished his bachelor's degree, before marrying. Despite having some offers to move, both Lynn and Tom decided to stay in the same area where they grew up so that they could be close to family. Both wanted to raise a family but not right away. However, when they decided to have children, they had difficulty conceiving and Lynn was diagnosed with endometriosis, resulting in considerable pain. Treatment was successful and she was able to become pregnant.

Sexually, Lynn and Tom report that they have had an average sex life but that it has been impacted by Lynn's experience of physical pain as well as the stresses of having the children. However, Lynn reported that recently Tom has been avoiding having sex with her. In the past, he would initiate sex, but now she has had to entice him sexually. Tom was embarrassed to admit to her that he had been having difficulty getting or maintaining an erection, which he assumed was related to his high blood pressure or stress at work. Lynn was surprised to hear this. She assumed that he was seeing someone else but couldn't imagine that he was "that kind of man."

In exploring their family-of-origin dynamics, a genogram of Lynn and Tom's families was constructed (see Figure 9.1). Tom was the third of five children and the only son. He states that he was very close to his father, whom he looked up to as a role model and called "a man's man, kind of like John Wayne." They shared many activities in common, and Tom said that in the last few years, "he became like my best friend." Of his siblings, he is closest to his next younger sister, who lives in another state but phones frequently. He refuses to have any contact with his youngest sister, who "was always mom's favorite" and got away with whatever she wanted. Tom claims that he had to cut his ties with her because she is actively addicted to amphetamines and has refused all of his efforts at getting her treatment. In addition, his next older sister is an alcoholic and a divorcee, though Tom has some contact with her and confided in her when he was growing up. Tom is not very close with his oldest sister, whom he described as "bossy and always mothering me." Lastly, Tom has a conflicted relationship with his mother, whom he describes as "fragile" and who had a "nervous breakdown," requiring a brief hospitalization, when he was five years old. He did not know what her diagnosis was, and the family never talked about her condition, though it was rumored that she may have tried to overdose with pills. Despite having two siblings who are substance users, Tom claims that neither of his parents abused substances.

In terms of Lynn's family of origin, she is the older of two children. Her parents divorced when she was three years old. Her mother remarried twice, once when she was five to a man whom she was very close to ("He was like my real father, and I adored him"), but they were divorced when Lynn was 16 years

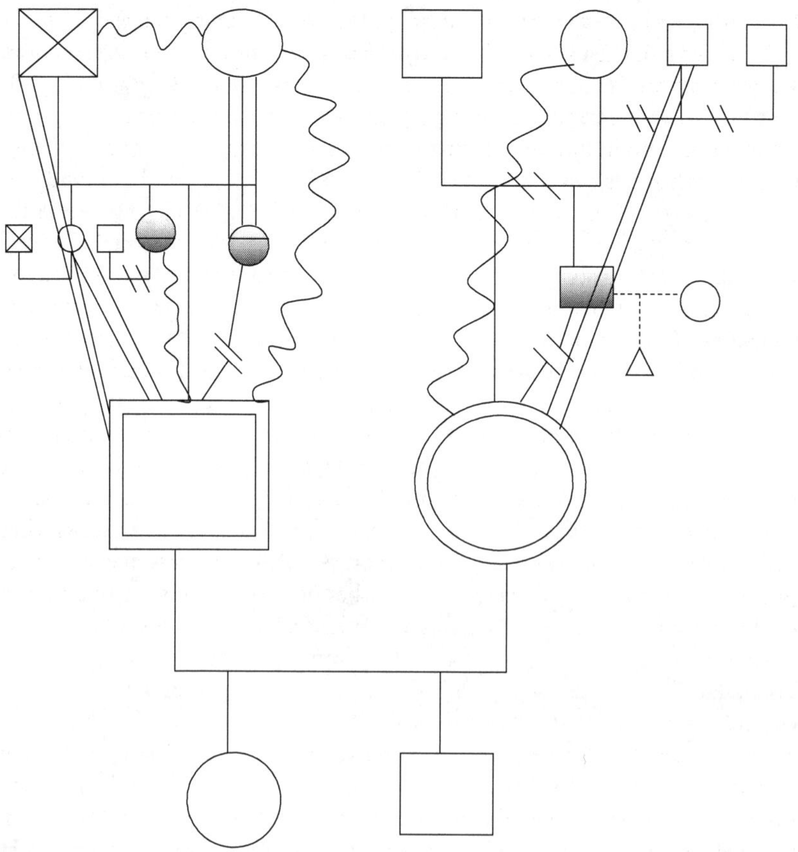

Figure 9.1 Genogram of Lynn and Tom.

old. She states that her mother's "craziness" drove him off, and Lynn became very angry with her. "I decided then that as soon as I was out of high school, a little over a year later, I was going to get out of the house." Lynn remains close with her stepfather to this day; she feels that she might have been able to go to college if her mom and stepfather had stayed married. Lynn frequently was (and still is) in conflict with her mother, who married her third husband when Lynn was 19 but was married for less than four years to a man who treated her "like a queen." Lynn decided, "At this point, I knew that my mother had serious issues with men." She also learned that her maternal grandfather (who had died before she was born) was physically abusive to her mother. When she was younger, Lynn said, "I didn't grasp how that impacted her, and how her behavior impacted me." Lynn described her as moody, controlling, dependent, and unpredictable, and stated that she has been diagnosed with bipolar disorder. Lynn admitted that she saw some similarities between herself and her mother, particularly around feeling moody and being controlling. When she left home after high school, she felt depressed and anxious and sought therapy. She saw a psychiatrist on and off for about six years but stopped shortly before she married Tom. Lastly, like Tom, Lynn is currently estranged from a sibling, her younger brother, because of his rampant marijuana and heroin use.

The interaction between Lynn and Tom's families of origin and their present relational functioning presents some insights into their present conflict. It is clear that Lynn was attracted to Tom because of his "strong but silent" qualities, which were reminiscent of her lost relationship with her stepfather. In contrast, Tom was attracted to Lynn because she did not remind him of his mother. She was independent, confident, and understood him. He felt like she met his needs without him even having to ask for it. At the same time, the seeds of discord are also evident. Tom's calm and steady approach to life can also seem cold and distant when Lynn needs to be emotionally reassured or understood. At the same time, his anger outbursts have shown a wild side that arouses Lynn's fear of the instability that she lived with when she was at home with her mother. When Lynn's moodiness and anxious, controlling behavior is activated, Tom feels that he is dealing with some of the women in his family of origin (i.e. mother, sisters) who were unstable. When these connections were addressed, both Lynn and Tom became extremely defensive of the characterizations of themselves in this frame but acknowledge that the descriptions of their own perceptions of the other person are valid.

Clients Resources

Tom has been frozen in his grief since his father's death. He neither wants to deal with it nor let go of it. He attempted to speak with his pastor about it but could not address the subject with him. Lynn states that whenever the conversation goes toward the topic of his father, he gets very quiet. Lynn, either out of weariness or a lack of understanding about the grief process, questions whether grief is the underlying issue: "After all, it has been six months already, shouldn't he be over it now?" She inappropriately compares her grieving over her father's death (whom she admittedly was not close to) to Tom's experience, which exacerbates Tom's unwillingness to discuss it. In addition, Tom feels that he must bear the burdens of his grief, his mother's demands, and the work pressure "like a man," which doesn't allow him to show weakness or feel vulnerable. On the other hand, Lynn feels that Tom is being too stubborn and unwilling to make his family a top priority. She feels that she has been as understanding as she can be but that his outbursts at her are unacceptable. Tom's promises to do better merely reinforce his belief that he cannot even express his frustration, let alone any deeper emotions.

Suitability for Treatment

Despite this assessment of Tom and Lynn's present dilemma, the indications for couple therapy had a positive prognosis. Both clients have a significant past with one another but have inadvertently settled into a pattern of interaction that has been less than satisfying, though not overtly evident to them until the recent events in their lives. Both Lynn and Tom state that they want to stay together, they acknowledge that the present situation is not acceptable for either of them, and that they are both willing to make some changes.

Couples Case Conceptualization

The couple is caught in a "demand-withdraw" interaction pattern that is understandable, given their respective individual dynamics. Lynn is independent, moody, and controlling, while Tom is strong but silent and emotionally reserved. Their interaction pattern is triggered and reinforced by Jennifer's need for control and emotional support, and Tom's predictable nonresponse to Lynn's demands, particularly his emotional reserve. Accordingly, as Lynn seeks intimate contact in a demanding fashion, Tom withdraws emotionally and excuses his physical absence because of increased work hours and the needs of his recently widowed mother.

Concluding Note

This chapter has described and illustrated an approach to couples assessment and case conceptualization that is both comprehensive and integrative. We believe that such an assessment is a necessary ingredient in the planning and execution of effective couple therapy. Based on the biopsychosocial model, this approach to assessment targets key factors subsumed under seven domains of relationship function. In addition, information was provided about diagnostic models of relational functioning along a clinically relevant continuum. The Appendix reviews nine commonly available assessment instruments useful in the assessment, monitoring, and evaluation of couple therapy.

References

American Psychiatric Association. (2013). *Diagnostic and statistical manual of mental disorders* (5th ed.). Alexandria, VA: Author.

Beavers, W., & Hampson, R. (2003). Measuring family competence: The Beavers systems model. In F. Walsh (Ed.), *Normal family processes* (3rd ed., pp. 549–580). New York, NY: Guilford Press.

Beavers, W., Hampson, R., & Hulgus, Y. (1985). Commentary: The Beavers systems approach to family assessment. *Family Process, 24*, 398–405.

Boen, D. (1988). A practitioner looks at assessment in marital counseling. *Journal of Counseling & Development, 66*(10), 484–486.

Chagoya, L., & Cameron, P. (1998). Guidelines for the practice of couple and family therapy. In P. Cameron, J. Ennis, & J. Deadman (Eds.), *Standards and guidelines for the psychotherapies* (pp. 181–198). Toronto, ON: University of Toronto Press.

Christensen, A., & Shenk, J. (1991). Communication, conflict, and psychological distance in nondistressed, clinic, and divorcing couples. *Journal of Consulting and Clinical Psychology, 59*(3), 458–463.

Coleman, S. (1985). *Failures in family therapy.* New York, NY: Guilford Press.

Epstein, N., Baldwin, L., & Bishop, D. (1983). The McMaster's family assessment device. *Journal of Marital and Family Therapy, 9*, 171–180.

Frances, A., Clarkin, J. F., & Perry, S. (1984). *Differential therapeutics in psychiatry: The art and science of treatment selection*. New York, NY: Brunner-Routledge.

Fredman, N., & Sherman, R. (1987). *Handbook of measurements for marriage and family therapy*. New York, NY: Psychology Press.

Fruzzetti, A. (2006). *The high-conflict couple: A dialectical behavior therapy guide to finding peace, intimacy, and validation*. Oakland, CA: New Harbinger Publications.

Fruzzetti, A., & Payne, L. (2015). Couple therapy and borderline personality disorder. In A. Gurman, J. Lebow, & D. Snyder (Eds.), *Clinical handbook of couple therapy* (5th ed., pp. 606–434). New York, NY: Guilford.

Gehart, D. (2017). Clinical case conceptualization with couples and families. In J. Carlson & S. Dermer (Eds.), *The SAGE encyclopedia of marriage, family, and couples counseling* (pp. 256–260). Thousand Oaks, CA: Sage Publications.

Gottman, J. M. (1994). *Why marriages succeed or fail?* New York, NY: Simon & Schuster.

Group for the Advancement of Psychiatry. Committee on Cultural Psychiatry. (2002). *Cultural assessment in clinical psychiatry*. Washington, DC: American Psychiatric Publishing.

Gurman, A. S. (2015). The theory and practice of couple therapy. In A. Gurman, J. Lebow, & D. Snyder (Eds.), *Clinical handbook of couple therapy* (5th ed., pp. 1–18). New York, NY: Guilford.

Kasting, A. (2015). *Withdraw-withdraw pattern*. University of Tennessee. Retrieved from https://relationshiprx.utk.edu/2015/05/19/withdraw-withdraw-pattern/

Knobloch-Fedders, L. M., Critchfield, K. L., Boisson, T., Woods, N., Bitman, R., & Durbin, C. E. (2014). Depression, relationship quality, and couples' demand/with draw and demand/submit sequential interactions. *Journal of Counseling Psychology, 61*(2), 264–279.

Lambert, M. J., & Barley, D. E. (2002). Research summary on the therapeutic and psychotherapy outcome. In J. C. Norcross (Ed.), *Psychotherapy relationships that work: Therapist contributions and responsiveness to patients* (pp. 17–32). New York, NY: Oxford University Press.

Lee, R. E., Jager, K. B., Whiting, J. B., & Kwantes, C. T. (2000). Clinical assessment using the clinical rating scale: Thomas & Olson revisited. *Journal of Marital and Family Therapy, 26*, 523–534.

Livesley, W. J. (2003). *Practical management of personality disorder*. New York, NY: Guilford Press.

Locke, H. J., & Wallace, K. M. (1959). Short-term marital adjustment and prediction tests: Their reliability and validity. *Journal of Marriage and Family Living, 21*, 251–255.

McGoldrick, M. (2003). Culture: A challenge to concepts of normality. In F. Walsh (Ed.), *Normal family processes* (3rd ed., pp. 375–398. New York, NY: Guilford Press.

McGoldrick, M., Gerson, R., & Petry, S. (2008). *Genograms: Assessment and intervention*. New York, NY: Norton.

Miller, I. W., Ryan, C. E., Keitner, G. I., Bishop, D. S., & Epstein, N. B. (2000). Why fix what isn't broken? A rejoinder to Ridenour, Daley, & Reich. *Family Process, 39*(3), 381–384.

Olson, D. H. (1990). *Clinical rating scale for the Circumplex Model*. St. Paul, MN: Family Social Science, University of Minnesota.

Olson, D., Fournier, D., & Druckman, J. (1986). *PREPARE-ENRICH inventories: Counselor's manual*. Minneapolis, MN: Life Innovations.

Olson, D. H., & Gorall, D. M. (2003). Circumplex Model of marital and family systems. In F. Walsh (Ed.), *Normal family processes* (3rd ed., pp. 514–548). New York, NY: Guilford Press.

Olson, D. H., Gorall, D., & Tiesel, J. (2002). *Family inventories package.* Minneapolis, MN: Life Innovations.

Prouty, A. M., Markowski, E. M., & Barnes, H. L. (2000). Using the dyadic adjustment scale in marital therapy: An exploratory study. *The Family Journal: Counseling and Therapy for Couples and Families, 8*, 250–257.

Ridenour, T. A., Daley, J. G., & Reich, W. (1999). Factor analyses of the family assessment device. *Family Process, 38*(4), 497–510.

Schnarch, D. (1991). *Constructing the sexual crucible: An integration of sexual and marital therapy.* New York, NY: W. W. Norton.

Snyder, D. K. (1997). *Manual for the Marital Satisfaction Inventory–Revised (MSI–R).* Los Angeles, CA: Western Psychological Services.

Snyder, D. K., & Aikman, G. A. (1999). The Marital Satisfaction Inventory–Revised (MSI–R). In M. E. Maruish (Ed.), *Use of psychological testing for treatment planning and outcomes assessment* (2nd ed., pp. 1173–1210). Mahwah, NJ: Erlbaum.

Snyder, D. K., & Schneider, W. J. (2002). Affective reconstruction: A pluralistic, developmental approach. In A. S. Gurman & N. S. Jacobson (Eds.), *Clinical handbook of couple therapy* (pp. 151–179). New York, NY: Guilford Press.

Spanier, G. (1984). *Dyadic adjustment scale: Users manual.* Willowdale, ON: Multi-Health Systems.

Sperry, L. (1989). Assessment in marital therapy: A couples-centered biopsychosocial approach. *Individual Psychology*, 45, 446–451.

Sperry, L. (2010). *Core competencies in counseling and psychotherapy: Becoming a highly competent and effective therapist.* New York, NY: Routledge.

Sperry, L. (2012). Family assessment: An overview. In L. Sperry. (Ed.), *Family assessment: Contemporary and cutting-edge strategies* (2nd ed., pp. 1–16). New York, NY: Routledge.

Sperry, L. (2013). Family case conceptualization and medical conditions. *The Family Journal, 21*(1), 74–77.

Sperry, L. (2016). Educating the next generation of psychotherapists: Considering the future of theory and practice in Adlerian Psychotherapy. *Journal of Individual Psychology, 72*(1), 4–11.

Sperry, L. (2019). Assessment, diagnosis and case conceptualization with couples. In L. Sperry, K. Helm, & J. Carlson (Eds.), *The disordered couple* (2nd ed.). New York, NY: Routledge.

Sperry, L., Carlson, J., & Kjos, D. (2003). *Becoming an effective therapist.* Boston, MA: Allyn & Bacon.

Sperry, L., & Sperry, J. (2012). *Case conceptualization: Mastering this competency with ease and confidence.* New York, NY: Routledge.

Taibbi, R. (2017). *Doing couple therapy: Craft and creativity in work with intimate partners.* New York, NY: Guilford.

Thomas, V., & Olson, D. H. (1993). Problem families and the Circumplex Model: Observational assessment using the clinical rating scale. *Journal of Marital and Family Therapy, 19*, 159–175.

Weiss, R. L., & Cerreto, M. (1980). The marital status inventory: Development of a measure of dissolution potential. *American Journal of Family Therapy, 8*(2), 80–86.

Whiting, J. B., & Crane, D. R. (2003) Distress and divorce: Establishing cutoff scores for the marital status inventory. *Contemporary Family Therapy: An International Journal, 25*(2), 195–205.

Appendix
Couples Assessment Instruments

As we have indicated earlier, different couple therapists utilize different approaches to assessment. Assessment instruments have been used to enhance the effectiveness of couple therapy. Boen (1988) described a three-step process for effectively integrating marital instruments into the assessment process. First, the therapist meets with the partners to determine the type of problems they have been experiencing, what they have done to resolve the problems, and what brings them for treatment at this particular time. Next, an instrument is chosen that will more adequately clarify the couple's problems, illustrate the couple's needs, and give additional insight into the current relationship. According to Boen, selection of an instrument should be based on several factors: Socioeconomic status, the couple's ability to comprehend the results, the partners' awareness and understanding of each other, and how well they understand the presenting problems. The couple is then asked to complete this instrument after the first session. In the next session, the results of the testing information are discussed with the couple and copies of any helpful testing material (scale description, client profiles, etc.) are distributed to each partner. Finally, Boen recommends that the therapist recheck the couple at a further point in the therapy process to gauge their progress or explore other issues.

However, there are some limitations in utilizing self-report measures, including client bias toward looking more favorable (or unfavorable) than is actually the case, differences or errors in recollection of past events, and a lack of thorough validation and norming (Snyder et al., 2002). In this final section of this chapter, we will focus on nine commonly used assessment instruments for measuring specific couple variables: Eight are self-report scales, and one is an observation scale rated by the therapist.

Dyadic Adjustment Scale (DAS)

This 32-item instrument is designed to assess the quality of the relationship as perceived by married or cohabiting couples. It is one of the most widely used self-report questionnaires in both clinical practice and research. The instrument was designed to serve a number of needs, including use as a general measure of overall satisfaction in an intimate relationship. There are 13 items that measure consensus between partners in finances, religion, friends, and decision-making. In addition, there are four subscales: Dyadic satisfaction, dyadic cohesion, dyadic consensus, and affectional expression. The DAS has consistently demonstrated good reliability as well as good discriminant validity (Fredman & Sherman, 1987). Most recently, Prouty, Markowski, and Barnes (2000) revised the instrument from 32 items to 14 items.

Primary References

Spanier (1984); Prouty et al. (2000).

Marital Satisfaction Inventory–Revised (MSI–R)

The MSI–R is a comprehensive, psychometrically sound self-report and partner-report instrument containing both global and specific measures of marital interaction. The original MSI contained 280 true/false items. The revised MSI contains 150 true/false items that are divided into two validity scales, one global distress scale, and ten additional scales addressing the nature and intensity of distress in a relationship. The scales are conventualization, global distress, affective communication, problem-solving communication, aggression, time together, disagreement about finances, sexual dissatisfaction, role orientation, family history of distress, dissatisfaction with children, and conflict about child-rearing. The MSI–R has good reliability and validity (Snyder & Aikman, 1999). The instrument can be hand scored, although a computerized scoring and test report is also available. The report focuses specifically on identification of areas in which a couple may be satisfied or dissatisfied. It prioritizes those areas and produces a narrative as well as a graphic report and summary of issues to consider in work with the couple. This report is helpful for couples and therapists who are at a loss about where to begin in dealing with their issues and formulating differential treatment interventions.

Primary References

Snyder (1997); Snyder and Aikman (1999).

PREPARE-ENRICH Inventory

The PREPARE-ENRICH Inventory is part of a comprehensive package of assessment devices designed to meet the needs of professionals engaged in marriage preparation, enrichment, or marital therapy. (PREPARE stands for Premarital, Personal, and Relationship Evaluation; PREPARE-MC stands for Premarital, Personal, and Relationship Evaluation–Marriage with Children; ENRICH stands for Evaluating and Nurturing Relationships Issues, Communication, and Happiness.) These inventories are all based on Olson's circumplex model discussed earlier in this book.

PREPARE and PREPARE-MC can be used preventively with premarital couples so that they become aware of potential problem areas in their relationships. ENRICH is designed for couples seeking marital therapy or marriage enrichment. The goals of these programs are to explore relationship strengths and growth areas, strengthen couple communication, resolve couple conflict, explore family-of-origin issues, develop workable budgets and financial plans, and set workable couple and family goals (Olson & Gorall, 2003). The PREPARE/ENRICH scales tap into 20 individual and couple content areas related to healthy couple functioning. They each contain ten items (for a total of 200 items for the instrument) and are grouped by personality (four scales), interpersonal (five scales), intrapersonal (five scales), external (two scales), and couple and family system (four scales).

Primary References

Olson, Fournier, and Druckman (1986); Olson and Gorall (2003); Olson, Gorall, and Tiesel (2002).

Clinical Rating Scale (CRS)

The CRS was initially developed in 1980 to operationalize the dimensions of the circumplex model (communication, flexibility, and closeness). It went through several revisions to the present version by Olson (1990). It is designed for therapists to rate a couple's level of functioning based on observed interactions. It has also been used as a training device for couples and family therapists (Lee, Jager, Whiting, & Kwantes, 2000).

Primary References

Lee et al. (2000); Olson (1990); Thomas and Olson (1993).

Family Assessment Device (FAD)

The FAD is a 60-item questionnaire designed to evaluate an individual's subjective assessment of the couple and family functions according to the McMaster's model. The FAD is made up of seven subscales. Six measure the dimensions of the McMaster's model: Problem-solving, communications, roles, affective responsiveness, affective involvement, and behavioral control. The seventh subscale measures general functioning. In recent years, some research has been presented questioning the factor structure of the FAD (Ridenour, Daley, & Reich, 1999); however, Miller, Ryan, Keitner, Bishop, and Epstein (2000) disputed the idea that the items and scales on the FAD should be rescored into fewer scales and reasserted that the FAD was theoretically sound with the seven scales listed.

Primary Reference

Epstein, Baldwin, and Bishop (1983).

Self-Report Family Instrument (SFI)

The SFI is a 36-item instrument based on the Beavers-Timberlawn model of family competence and is designed to distinguish levels of competence in marriages and families. The five dimensions of the SFI are family conflict, communication, cohesion, health, and directive leadership. Beavers and Hampson (2003) report adequate reliability and validity for the instrument.

Primary Reference

Beavers, Hampson, and Hulgus (1985).

Marital Adjustment Test (MAT)

The MAT is a 15-item questionnaire that asks partners to rate their global happiness in their relationship as well as the extent of agreement in key areas of relationship interaction (Locke & Wallace, 1959). Although it is one of the oldest instruments in use, it has been widely used and repeatedly validated. In addition, it is used to validate other instruments. However, some of its items are considered out-of-date (Whiting & Crane, 2003).

Primary Reference

Locke and Wallace (1959).

Marital Status Inventory (MSI)

The MSI is a measure of high distress in a relationship and has been found to be useful in divorce prediction (Gottman, 1994). It has good discriminant validity (higher scores indicate couples seeking treatment for distress rather than marital enrichment), as well as adequate reliability.

Primary Reference

Weiss and Cerreto (1980).

10 Interventions in Couple Therapy

LEARNING OBJECTIVES

In this chapter, the reader will learn the following:

1 The different elements of couple therapy that a clinician must consider.
2 The importance of the initial stage of couple therapy.
3 How to categorize couples according to readiness to change.
4 The various strategies and techniques for working with couples.

Now that we have introduced the major theoretical orientations to couple therapy and the process for assessing the relationship, we turn our attention to the actual practice of couple therapy. The purpose of the assessment process is to give the therapist the necessary information to make these decisions. The first was whether the couple was appropriate for therapy. In addition, assessment must include a through understanding of whether the couple is dealing with issues that may require specialized or tailored treatment (i.e., substance abuse, intimate partner violence, or infidelity). As mentioned in Chapter 9, if a thorough assessment is not made, then the effectiveness and efficacy of any course of couple therapy will certainly be in jeopardy. The second decision is which of the modes of couple therapy (conjoint, collaborative, couples groups, family or couple therapy alone, or in conjunction with couples sessions) is the optimal treatment for a particular couple. If conjoint couple therapy is the treatment of choice, the third set of decisions involves the type, duration, focus, and particular strategies utilized in the treatment of a particular couple. This effort to match treatment to a couple's needs and styles, strengths, and previous positions is called differential therapeutics. Because psychotherapy is as much an art as a science, different clinicians approach couples in different fashions, depending on the clinician's orientation, training, experience, and personality style. Thus, the purpose of this chapter is also to provide the reader with an overview of the various strategies and techniques of treatment process for couples.

Treatment Modalities

There are many different treatment modalities used in couple therapy. According to Sholevar (2003), the most common approaches are individual couple therapy, conjoint couple therapy, co-therapy, concurrent couple therapy, couples group, and family-of-origin intervention.

Individual Couple Therapy

In individual couple therapy, one partner is seen and the focus is on relational issues or conflict with the partner. During a crisis, the therapist may wish to consult with the partner. This modality is recommended for couples where there is a resistant partner or where the client has concomitant issues, such as phobias, or where there is overall a lack of severe psychopathology (Sholevar, 2003).

Concurrent Couple Therapy

Concurrent couple therapy is a treatment modality where both partners are seen individually by the same therapist. The therapist establishes strong, individual relationships with each member of the couple, which can promote client self-disclosure (Sholevar, 2003). However, issues of confidentiality may become a problem between the spouses and the therapist.

Conjoint Couple Therapy

Conjoint couple therapy is the modality in which one therapist meets with husband and wife together. This is to be differentiated from co-therapy, in which there are two therapists with the couple. According to Sholevar (2003), it is the most commonly used mode of couple therapy and has the advantage of allowing the therapist to experience the couple's interaction with one another, as well as to make targeted interventions that encompass both partners.

Couples Groups

Working with several couples at once in a group setting is a popular and, according to outcome research, an effective approach for dealing with marital discord. Kaslow and Lieberman (1981) have presented the rationale, dynamics, and process of using couples group therapy. Many therapists prefer this approach and feel that it is a good use of time for all participants. We have found this to be a very effective intervention approach for the right couples at the right stage of treatment.

Family-of-Origin Intervention

Framo (1983) and Napier (1988) are among the proponents of this technique. It often involves two therapists meeting with clients and the members of their families of origin and is frequently an adjunct to couple therapy. Framo has described a pattern in which a therapist meets with the client and his or her nuclear family for two hours on a Friday night and then two hours on the next Saturday morning as a supplement to marital sessions. This can be a very powerful intervention technique. Skilled couple therapists use it whenever occasions develop in which family members are together, such as at holidays (Nichols, 2003).

Adjunctive Modalities

There are many useful adjunctive modalities. These include various types of skill training such as relationship enhancement efforts (Dinkmeyer & Carlson, 1989) and communication facilitation (Gottman, 1999). Bibliotherapy (Dinkmeyer & Carlson, 1989; L'Abate, 1999; Sperry & Carlson, 1990) is also a helpful procedure for learning skills and preventing future problems. Self-help groups such as Alcoholics Anonymous, Al-anon, and Adult Children of Alcoholics are all helpful adjuncts, as are sexual therapy and financial counseling.

Combining Techniques

All of the previous techniques can be executed in conjunction with one another as well as in conjunction with individual therapy. Many therapists routinely use a combination of weekly individual and conjoint sessions. Therapists with an intrapsychic point of view who are attempting to change characterological structure often use a combination of sessions. One major drawback to this type of an intervention is the financial cost of multiple individual sessions.

We routinely see couples conjointly for assessment and then meet with each individually before beginning couple therapy (see Chapter 8 for an example of this – Gottman Method Couple Therapy). The individual sessions allow us to better understand each person. Sometimes, this process involves more than one session as histories are often complex. During individual sessions, the therapist is able to prepare the individual to participate effectively in couple therapy. Sometimes, clients are confused about whether to continue the relationship and ambivalent about participation in therapy. Other times, individuals need to work through grief from the ending of an extramarital relationship or loss of a parent. If the client's presenting problem involves concerns that do not directly involve the partner, couple therapy would not be appropriate. A final consideration for individualized couples treatment is when partners are so dysfunctional that they are unable to be with their partners without hurting and attacking.

Practice Elements of Couple Therapy

Gurman (2015) extensively reviewed many of the practical elements of the practice of couple therapy, and provided discrete elements within the practice of couple therapy for couple therapists to consider. They encompass the entire scope of the practice of couple therapy, specifically the structure of the therapy process of couple therapy, the role of the therapist, the process and technical aspects of couple therapy, and the curative factors and mechanisms of change within couple therapy.

The Structure of the Therapy Process of Couple Therapy

Each couple therapist must decide how he or she will conduct couple therapy. Gurman (2015) provides some helpful reflection questions for the reader to consider (see Table 10.1).

Specifically, they include questions of who should come to therapy and how often they should come, as well as what is the *focus* of the therapy (as well as what is not). According to Gurman, "How therapist policies and procedures about this decision are addressed and implemented carry profound implications for the maintenance of the therapeutic alliances and even basic portions on what (or who) is (or has) 'the problem.'" (2015, p. 9).

The Role of the Therapist

The role of the therapist in couple therapy is perhaps as important (if not more) than in individual therapy. Since the therapist is responsible to make a relationship with two individuals (as well as with the couple itself), the stance that the therapist takes is vital. As a result, there are some important decisions that need to be made ahead of time.

> The kind of therapeutic relationship required by each approach to couple therapy includes the overall 'stance' the therapist takes toward the experience (e.g., how working alliances are fostered; how active, self-disclosing, directive, and reflective the therapist is). Different models of couple therapy call forth and call for different therapist attributes and interpersonal

Table 10.1 Questions for the Couple Therapist to Consider Regarding the Structure of the Therapy Process of Couple Therapy

1	Besides the couple, are children or extended family members ever included?
2	Are psychotropic medications ever used within this method of couple therapy? What are the indications and contraindications for such use?
3	Are individual sessions with the partners ever held? If "yes," under what conditions? If "no," why not?
4	How many therapists are usually involved? In this approach, what are the advantages (or disadvantages) of using co-therapists?
5	Is therapy typically time-limited or unlimited? How long does therapy typically last? How often are sessions typically held?

Note: From Gurman (2015, p. 9).

Table 10.2 The Role of the Therapist

1	What is the therapist's essential role? Consultant? Teacher? Healer?
2	What is the role of the therapist-couple alliance? How is a working alliance fostered? In this approach, what are the most common and important errors the therapist can make in building early working alliances?
3	To what degree does the therapist overtly control sessions? How active/directive is the therapist? How should the therapist deal with moments of volatile emotional escalation or affective dysregulation in sessions?
4	Do clients talk predominantly to the therapist or to each other?
5	Does the therapist use self-disclosure? What limits are imposed on therapist self-disclosure?
6	Does the therapist's role change as the therapist progresses?

Note: From Gurman (2015, p. 10).

> inclinations. For instance, therapists with a more or less 'take charge' personal style may be better suited to practicing therapies that require a good deal of therapist activity and structuring than to those requiring a more reflective style.
>
> (p. 10)

Table 10.2 provides some helpful reflection questions for the reader to consider regarding the stance of the therapist.

Process and Technical Aspects of Couple Therapy

The decisions that couple therapists must make about the process and technical aspects of couple therapy may seem overwhelming. Whether to focus on the individual level or on the dyadic level, as well as what techniques are appropriate (and why) are all elements that the clinician must consider. According to Gurman (2015), "(m)ost couple therapists are multidirectional in their thinking; that is, they believe that change can be initiated in any domain or at any level of psychosocial organization" (p. 13). Table 10.3 provides some helpful reflection questions for the reader to consider regarding the processes and technical aspects of couple therapy.

In the termination phase, the therapist reviews with the couple the course of treatment beginning with the original problems and goals and the degree to which they have or have not been achieved. Glick, Berman, Clarkin, and Rait (2000) offer four criteria suggestive of successful treatment outcomes. First, the couple shows new coping patterns and enhanced empathy. Second, nonproductive quarreling and conflict are reduced and replaced by productive conflict and management skills. Third, the couple is more flexible in its marital rules and organization and appears more able to grow and develop. Fourth, individual partners are symptomatically improved, and positive channels of interaction and increased agreement about each spouse's role and function exist. During the termination phase, there may be an exacerbation of presenting symptoms that often represents a temporary response to the

Table 10.3 Process and Technical Aspects of Couple Therapy

1 How structured are therapist sessions? Is there an ideal (or typical) pacing or rhythm to sessions?
2 What techniques or strategies are used to join the couple or to create a treatment alliance? How are "transference-countertransference" reactions dealt with?
3 What techniques or strategies lead to changes in structure or transactional patterns? Identify, describe, and illustrate major commonly used techniques.
4 Is psychoeducation (e.g. about parenting or sexuality) part of this approach?
5 How is the decision made to use particular techniques at a particular time? Are some techniques more or less likely to be used at different stages of therapy?
6 Are different techniques used with different types of couples? For example, are different or additional techniques called upon when the therapy is addressing problems involving individual psychopathology, difficulties, or disabilities, in addition to interactional/relational problems? Or alternatively, in work, with more dysfunctional, distressed, or committed couples?
7 What kinds of cultural adaptations of the usual assessment process, treatment techniques/strategies, or therapeutic relationship-building approach are used in work with couples whose ethnic, racial, socioeconomic, or other backgrounds differ from those with whom this approach was originally created?
8 Are "homework" assignments or other out-of-session tasks used?
9 What are the most commonly encountered forms of resistance to change? How are these dealt with?
10 If revealed to the therapist outside conjoint sessions, how are "secrets" (e.g. extramarital affairs) handled?
11 What are both the most common and the most serious technical or strategic errors a therapist operating within this approach can make?
12 On what basis is termination decided, and how is termination effected? What characterizes "good" vs. "bad" termination?

Note: From Gurman (2015, pp. 12–13).

anxiety of termination rather than a sign of treatment failure. This indicates that separation is a key issue that should be addressed in the termination phase (Glick et al., 2000).

Curative Factors/Mechanisms of Change in Couple Therapy

Housed in the wider debate regarding the role of common factors that are inherent in all therapeutic approaches (e.g. the therapeutic relationship) or if specific ingredients are responsible for change, couple therapists must also have their own understanding of the mechanisms for change within a dyad. According to Gurman (2015),

> Identifying mechanisms of change that are shared by different methods of couple therapy is of both academic interest in practical value. Gurman and Burton (2014) have suggested the operation of several such mechanisms: enhancement of partners systemic awareness of the circularity and contextual embeddedness of their conflicts; establishment of the premise of partners' shared responsibility for bringing about change; improved mutual acceptance; interruption of maladaptive conflict-maintaining

Table 10.4 Curative Factors/Mechanisms of Change?

1	Do clients need insight or understanding in order to change?
2	Is interpretation of any sort important, and if so, does it take history into account? If interpretation is used, is it seen as reflecting a psychological "reality" or as a pragmatic tool for effecting change (as in shifting perceptions or attributions)?
3	Is the learning of new interpersonal skills seen as important? If so, are these skills taught didactically, or are they shaped more in process?
4	Does the therapist's personality or psychological health play an important part in the process and outcome of therapeutic approach?
5	Are there certain kinds of therapists who are ideally suited to work according to this approach, and others for whom the approach is probably a poor "fit"?
6	How important are techniques compared to the client-therapist relationship?
7	Must each member for the couple change? Is change in an "identified patient" (where relevant) possible without interactional or systemic change? Does systemic change necessarily lead to change in symptoms? Or vice versa?

Note: From Gurman (2015, p. 14).

> interactions, allowing for more adaptive sequences; refinement of communication and problem-solving skills; and normalization of couple conflict via psychoeducation about intimate relationships.
>
> (p. 14)

Table 10.4 provides some helpful reflection questions for the reader to consider regarding the mechanisms of change in couple therapy.

The therapist also must link each partner's experience, including past events and inner thoughts, to the relationship. This is accomplished in several ways. The therapist may prescribe tasks that encourage the spouse to differentiate between the impact of the other's behavior and the other's intent. Another task may have one partner focus his or her awareness on the concrete behavior of the spouse that contradicts past perceptions of that partner. Or the therapist can encourage each spouse to acknowledge behavior changes that are incompatible with the maladaptive ways each has seen himself or herself and been seen by the partner. Behavioral techniques including communication and problem-solving training are utilized to help the partners reintegrate denied aspects of themselves and of each other. Specific strategies and techniques that are used in this stage will also be discussed in the next section of this chapter.

Strategies in Couple Therapy

The Importance of the Initial Stage of Couple Therapy

Glick et al. (2000) have indicated that the first stage of treatment is usually the most difficult for the trainee to master. There are several reasons for this. First, the initial face-to-face meetings of the couple and therapist are crucial in determining whether therapy will continue. According to a recent study by Masi, Miller, and Olson (2003), the attrition rate for couples is just as high as for individuals and families. In their study of all three groups, 25% of couples didn't show up to the first appointment, and more than 25% did not stay in treatment past the second appointment. Second, in the first stage, the trainee has to contend with a rather large number of treatment tasks and goals that must often be addressed in the first interview. Not only must the therapist complete an adequate assessment, he or she must formulate the case so as to understand the individual and systems dynamics and develop some treatment goals and strategies in order to negotiate a treatment plan with the couple. Finally, as previously noted, the therapist must make a series of decisions about treatment format and treatment interventions. Should the couple be seen in a conjoint format, in individual couple therapy, in concurrent therapy, or in couples groups? What to do if a partner is unwilling to participate or decides to drop out? This is where reflecting on the processes of couple therapy outlined earlier in this chapter, as well as having a clear strategy for helping the couple, comes in.

Strategy

According to Simon, Stierlin, and Wynne (1985), "Strategy is a plan of action, a modus operandi in more or less predictable situations that allows one to make decisions likely to facilitate reaching a specific goal" (p. 338). Strategies can be composed of many techniques or systematic procedures by which a task is accomplished. A couple therapist uses strategy when intervening in a couple's relationship. The number of techniques and combination of techniques are unlimited. Nevertheless, techniques and interventions can be grouped according to strategic intent. The following six categories of strategies, identified by Glick et al. (2000) as basic to family therapy, are also basic to couple therapy intervention. They note that all six incorporate aspects from the various schools of couple therapy. They are:

1. Use of adaptive mechanisms to impart new information, advice, suggestions, and so on (the so-called psychoeducational approach).
2. Expansion of individual and couple emotional experiences.
3. Explicit development of specific interpersonal skills.
4. Reorganization of the relational structure.
5. Increase in insight and fostering of conflict resolution.
6. Help the couple understand and modify its narrative.

According to Glick et al. (2000), the six basic strategies, as listed, reflect an increasing depth of involvement. The earlier strategies are simpler and less involved, and if they work should be used alone. As the marital problems become more complex and complicated and the couple shows resistance to change using simpler techniques, the more involved techniques are probably needed. In practice, it is hard to separate these techniques in a clear, pure fashion. At any given session, a therapist may use all six strategies. Next, we will discuss strategies in the initial stage of couple therapy.

Differential Use of the Six Basic Strategies

Therapists continually wonder about which basic strategy to use and where to utilize it. This is an unresolved area not only in the field of couple therapy but in all psychotherapy. In order to choose a strategy, the therapist must consider both motivation and the couple's relationship style. Assessing and working with client levels of motivation have been reviewed previously. In terms of overall relationship style, couples that are more analytical may enjoy dynamic therapeutic intervention, while clients that are more action-oriented may want a more strategic or behaviorally oriented approach. Another differential factor for employing the basic strategies is speed – both how fast the couple wants to move and how quickly they can implement change in the relationship. Finally, the therapist must determine where along the continuum of the six strategies the couple needs to work (Glick et al., 2000). For example, couples who are wrestling with the immediate aftermath of an affair may not be ready to deal with how to incorporate the rupture in the relationship into the overall narrative. Thus, the couple therapist must be sensitive to a number of issues simultaneously in order to implement the best strategy and techniques that will be maximally effective for the couple. This is where understanding what stage of change the couple may be in is important in tailoring treatment and what strategies to choose.

Strategies for Tailoring Treatment and the Processes of Change

Most theories focus on why people do *not* change rather than on how people do change. They also do not provide models for how insights and ideas from diverse therapies might be integrated into their approach to change, and how they can be used to tailor treatment. The transtheoretical model (TTM) approach sets out to consciously construct a model of therapy and change that draws from a variety of major theories. The following are the ten processes of self-change that have received the most empirical support to date (Prochaska & DiClemente, 2002):

1. Consciousness-raising
2. Dramatic relief
3. Self-reevaluation
4. Environmental reevaluation
5. Self-liberation
6. Social liberation
7. Counterconditioning
8. Stimulus control
9. Reinforcement management
10. Helping relationship

This is an eclectic set. Consciousness-raising has roots in the psychoanalytic tradition; dramatic relief or catharsis has roots in the Gestalt tradition;

self-reevaluation and environmental reevaluation have roots in the cognitive and experiential traditions; self-liberation and social liberation have roots in the existential tradition; counterconditioning, stimulus control, and reinforcement management have roots in the behavioral tradition; and the helping relationship has roots in the person-centered tradition (DiClemente & Wiprovnick, 2017).

Prochaska and his colleagues realized that most systems of psychotherapy typically use only two or three of these processes. They believed that in order for it to be helpful, an approach was needed that could use all ten processes of change. Traditionally, the TTM approach has been used in individual therapy, but recently, clinicians and researchers have adapted it to couple therapy as well (Bradford, 2012; Cordova, Warren, & Gee, 2001; DiClemente & Wiprovnick, 2017; Schneider, 2003).

Stages of Change

The appropriate use of change processes involves the stages of change through which people progress (DiClemente & Wiprovnick, 2017; Prochaska & DiClemente, 1982). Change unfolds over a series of six stages: Precontemplation, contemplation, preparation, action, maintenance, and termination. Each stage of the change process requires the therapist to use different skills.

Among the stages of change, individuals apply the least number of change processes during *precontemplation*. Clients in the precontemplation stage process less information about their problems, spend less time and energy reevaluating themselves, experience fewer emotional reactions to the negative aspects of their problems, are less open with significant others about their problems, and do little to shift their attention or their environment in the direction of overcoming their problems. When these individuals come into therapy, they are often coerced or pressured by the threats of their partners. In therapy, these clients are often labeled resistant. The next stage, *contemplation*, is a shift in the client's awareness of the problem behavior but not a shift in the motivation to change the behavior (DiClemente & Wiprovnick, 2017; Prochaska & Norcross, 2002).

In the *preparation* stage, clients are on the verge of taking action and need to set goals and priorities. However, individuals can stay in the preparation stage. Clients in this stage may even convince themselves that they are doing something about the problem, when all they are doing is thinking about or merely preparing to change. They often need to develop an action plan for new behaviors and find that counterconditioning and stimulus control are useful in reducing the problem behaviors. Yet, these individuals have not made the leap to the action stage (DiClemente & Wiprovnick, 2017).

The *action* stage is characterized by overt behavioral change and a significant commitment of time and energy on the part of the client. If the targeted dysfunctional behavior has been successfully altered for a period from one day to six months, then those clients are considered to be in the action stage (DiClemente & Wiprovnick, 2017; Prochaska & Norcross, 2002). As action proceeds, the therapist works as a consultant or coach to help them fine-tune their life change. Supportive counseling can also be helpful as times of change also produce uncertainty. Knowing that there is another person who cares helps to reduce some of the predictable stress of change.

If clients are able to be free of their problem for more than six months, they are considered to have moved into the *maintenance* phase. Successful maintenance involves assessing the conditions under which one is vulnerable to relapse to the previous ineffective behaviors. Clients consolidate the gains they have received from arresting the problematic behavior, which helps them put into place a relapse-prevention plan. Depending on the behavior, clients may need to be considered in the maintenance stage for the rest of their lives (DiClemente & Wiprovnick, 2017; Prochaska & Norcross, 2002). Finally, when clients no longer have to work at preventing relapse, they can be considered to be in the termination phase. However, any person is vulnerable to relapse and may have to re-engage the change process again.

Adapting Stages of Change to Couple Therapy

In adapting the TTM to couple therapy, Bradford (2012) reported in her survey of couples some interesting gender differences. Specifically, men tended to be in the precontemplation stage, while women were more likely to be in the contemplation stage. She suggested that "women were generally thinking more about making changes in their relationships then were men" (p. 498) and that this result is consistent with previous findings where women seek treatment and recognize relationship problems earlier than men do.

In terms of using intervention strategies to move clients from one stage to another, clients in different stages require different intervention approaches. For example, movement from precontemplation to contemplation and movement through the contemplation stage involve the use of cognitive, affective, and evaluative processes of change. Bradford (2012) suggested that for couples,

> preventative educational interventions might be selected that are appropriate for clients at earlier stages, and specifically, any interventions for men might best be geared toward the precontemplation stage (e.g., consciousness raising), in order to maximize retention and improve outcomes.
> (p. 498)

Consciousness-raising and dramatic relief help to increase awareness and emotional release that relate to problems. Clients in contemplation are mostly open to consciousness-raising interventions and bibliotherapy. As they become more aware of themselves and the nature of their problems, they are willing to evaluate themselves both cognitively and affectively. To better prepare individuals for action, changes are required in how they think and feel about their problem behaviors and how they value their problematic lifestyle. More information about developing strategies for working with clients stuck in the precontemplation, contemplation, or preparation stages will be presented later in this chapter.

The transtheoretical approach integrates processes of change from across leading theories of therapy. However, there are several practical considerations that couple therapists must be aware of in utilizing the transtheoretical approach as they treat couples. These are assess the client's stage of change, beware treating all patients as though they are in the action stage, set realistic goals to move clients from one stage at a time, tailor the processes to the stage, apply the appropriate therapeutic relationship stance to the stage, and avoid mismatching stages and processes. Effective interventions involve matching change processes to the client's current stage of change. Research is supportive of using this approach with a wide population level, including those who are not interested in change at this time (DiClemente & Wiprovnick, 2017; Prochaska & Norcross, 2002).

Resistant Partners

Lastly, all couple therapists have to deal with resistant partners. It would be wonderful if every couple came in agreeing that they needed help, but it simply isn't always the case. An approach for dealing with unresponsive clients, developed by Miller and Rollnick (1991), is called *motivational interviewing.* This approach is frequently used in conjunction with Prochaska and DiClemente's (1982, 2002) transtheoretical stages-of-change model (Bradford, 2012; DiClemente & Wiprovnick, 2017).

Motivational interviewing is designed to help individuals increase their intrinsic motivation to change from one stage (i.e. precontemplation) to the next (i.e. contemplation) by being persuasive and encouraging, and not argumentative. The method for changing a person's level of motivation is through the presentation of objective assessment information and educating the individual or couple about the problems identified. This information is usually quite different than what the unmotivated couple or individual believes, and this discrepancy should create some motivation to change.

According to Miller and Rollnick, the feedback to the clients should have six active ingredients in order to be most successful: Providing structured feedback of current status, highlighting the partner's personal responsibility for change, providing clear advice, offering a menu of alternative choices, demonstrating appropriate empathy, and emphasizing the partners' self-efficacy to pursue change on their own. The feedback is presented in person and should also have a written component to it (either from assessment measures, a standard form, or a treatment overview letter). We believe that a thorough and well-developed case conceptualization will give a couple therapist more data to successfully conduct a motivational interviewing exercise and get the couple to engage in therapy. Clients are free to choose to accept or reject the conclusions and to decide on whether to act. Miller and Rollnick (2002) have demonstrated success using motivational interviewing with a variety of couple presenting problems and across the various transtheoretical stages.

Recall the case from Chapter 9 of Tom and Lynn, who have been married for 16 years and have two children. The couple has been having an increasing number of arguments leading to Tom becoming more and more verbally aggressive. The final straw for Lynn came when Tom slapped their daughter in the face when she talked back to him. Tom's outbursts have grown in intensity and frequency over the last six months, and Lynn is feeling less and less trustful of him. In the past six months, Tom's father died suddenly in an automobile accident, leaving him to be his mother's primary caretaker (despite having other siblings in the area). In addition, his work (he is a systems engineer for a local aviation company) has been another source of stress as the company has been working on a proposal for a government contract, which will determine whether or not his unit will be downsized.

It is clear that Lynn was attracted to Tom because of his strong-but-silent qualities, which were reminiscent of her lost relationship with her stepfather. In contrast, Tom was attracted to Lynn because she did not remind him of his mother. She was independent, confident, and understood him. He felt like she met his needs without him even having to ask. At the same time, the seeds of discord are also evident. Tom's calm and steady approach to life can also seem cold and distant when Lynn needs to be emotionally reassured or understood. In addition, his anger outbursts have shown a wild side that arouses Lynn's fear of the instability that she lived with when she was at home with her mother. When Lynn's moodiness and anxious, controlling behavior is activated, Tom feels that he is dealing with some of the women in his family of origin (i.e. mother, sisters, etc.) who were "unstable." When these connections are addressed, both Lynn and Tom become extremely defensive of the characterization of themselves in this frame but acknowledge that the descriptions of their own perceptions of the other person are valid.

Lastly, Tom refuses to acknowledge that he has any emotional needs resulting from his feelings of grief or the pressures placed on him. Lynn believes that Tom needs to express himself emotionally but has lost patience with him and now questions his commitment to his family, especially when he fails to live up to her expectations. This subtle attack on his masculinity causes him to withdraw more from her emotionally and leaves him feeling more alone and helpless. As a result, a cycle of resentment, outburst, and repentance is set up that has marked their relationship in the last year. The escalation of the behaviors is indicative of a negative cycle that requires outside intervention.

Considering the six basic strategies presented earlier in the chapter by Glick et al. (2000), it is clear that all six strategies will likely need to be utilized at some point in therapy with this couple. In addition, in considering the stage of change of each partner, Tom seems to be in-between the precontemplation and contemplation phases, while Lynn is further advanced (probably in the preparation for action stage). As a result of this, the couple therapist will want to adopt a stance that will be slow (but not too slow) so as to ensure Tom's "buy in" without causing Lynn to "check out" of the therapy. As we mentioned before, each couple therapist needs to approach couples from their own theoretical orientation, but the strategies used to effect changes can be more universal to couple therapy itself.

Techniques in Couple Therapy

The therapist needs to know how to make interventions in the here and now and in the future that will lead to the desired goal. Interventions are suggestions for action made within the therapy hour that are to be taken in the couple's life before the next meeting. On the other hand, techniques are often thought of as moves, prescriptions, or suggestions made by the therapist that require the client to perform a series of actions that yield greater understanding or stimulate change. Techniques may be very complicated or very brief interactions or tactics such as changing the seating order, asking a simple question, or making an empathic or encouraging comment. Sherman and Fredman (1986) have identified eight common variables used in developing techniques.

1 Expansion or reduction of the number of members in the therapeutic system.
2 Variation of the time frame for meeting or tasks.
3 Change in the place in which therapy meeting or tasks occur.
4 Alteration of the activity or introduction of a new one.
5 Engaging of different levels of consciousness and thought processes.
6 Structuring of the patterns of communication.
7 Alteration or reversal of the places or roles of members of the system.
8 Variation of the therapist's mode of interacting with clients.

Many variables and tactics make up techniques, and many techniques are used in a strategy. These decisions are often arbitrary and depend upon the therapist, his or her skills, and the current situation. However, highly effective couple therapists will often go into a session with a strategy already in mind. The therapist needs to feel comfortable with the medium and the style of the technique to be used as well as the theoretical rationale for using it. If the therapist is unassertive, for example, prescriptive behavior may be difficult. If the therapist is structured, the use of more ambiguous projective methods may present problems, whereas a passive type of therapist may have difficulty with more action-oriented methods. The techniques must fit the user, just like a shoe must fit the wearer. We will present these strategies as well as some of the most common techniques that are used with them.

Psychoeducational Techniques

Every couple has some healthy habits and some strengths. These should be recognized and actively encouraged. The therapist uses many skills and techniques to support these coping mechanisms. Active listening and concern, positive feedback about healthy behaviors, education about poor procedures, and advice are all helpful to couples in distress. The therapist is constantly modeling the role of teacher, either directly or indirectly. The therapist models the mood, tempo, and levels of interpersonal acceptance. Much of what the therapist teaches is done implicitly. The therapist shows respect by listening carefully to what each partner says. This, in turn, shows each partner how to respect the other. As the therapist listens and reflects what each partner is saying, the couple begins this important practice. The therapist also models an encouraging attitude that is contagious.

There has been a growing emphasis on prevention and skill training. These approaches provide information that all couples need in order to cope and perform effectively in marriage (Carlson & Sperry, 2010). This approach is most obvious in the skill-training or marriage enrichment programs (Carlson & Dinkmeyer, 1999; Cavedo & Guerney, 1999; L'Abate, 1999). Information can be communicated through written material, lectures, discussion in groups, and workshops. This approach also involves bibliotherapy and the use of directed study as homework assignments.

Many therapists find it helpful to involve couples in ongoing marriage enrichment groups along with therapy to help ensure that the couple has high-level skills. Marriage enrichment is a relatively new area. Many credit its beginnings to the early work of Dreikurs in the 1930s in Europe, in which study groups were set up and focused on the book *The Challenge of Marriage* (Dreikurs, 1946). The modern marriage encounter movement began in 1961 in Italy with Father Gabriel Calbo. Currently, the Association of Couples for Marriage Enrichment coordinates and facilitates the various skill-training programs in this important area. In addition to the TIME approach, there are several other programs, such as PREPARE/ENRICH (Olson & Olson, 1999), COUPLE COMMUNICATION (Miller & Sherrard, 1999), PREP (Stanley, Blumberg, & Markman, 1999), and Relationship Enhancement (Cavedo & Guerney, 1999), to name a few.

Enactments

Psychotherapy has many techniques to help individuals and couples expand their emotional experiences. These techniques, which focus on the here-and-now experience in the sessions, are designed to help members become aware of their feelings and how to express them effectively. These procedures also help couples to slow down and learn important relaxation skills. Furthermore, they help each person live in the present. An enactment is a therapeutic technique that is used to help couples interact with each other in a way that facilitates deeper connection or communication. It can be used regardless of theoretical background, though traditionally it was a structural family therapy technique (Aponte, 2017). According to Davis and Espinoza (2017), enactments "can be used as a vehicle for initiating change, facilitating emotional expression, and practicing communication skills in couple therapy" (p. 41). Enactments can be used at any phase in couple therapy, whether it is in the early initiation or assessment phase, the intervention phases, or the evaluation phase of couple therapy.

> Broadly speaking, an enactment occurs in couple therapy when both partners are speaking with each other...Enactments are used as an intervention to shape interaction as it is occurring rather than didactically teaching the couple communication skills and then sending them home to practice without the safety provided by the therapist's structure and guidance.
>
> (Davis, 2017, p. 37)

While enactments are a powerful technique for couples to experience how to communicate effectively, they must be structured appropriately. Without proper structure, the couple will likely drift back into old (dysfunctional) patterns of interaction, and with too much structure, the dialogue can seem unnatural to the couple and too constricting. As a result, the impact is lessened because it is not genuine (Aponte, 2017; Davis & Espinoza, 2017).

Doubling Technique

One type of enactment is the "doubling" technique created by couple therapist Dan Wile as a part of Collaborative Couple Therapy (Wile, 2002, 2008, 2011, 2017). Doubling can be used when couples are having a problem "in the moment" and turning the couple's immediate concern into an enactment of an intimate conversation. Originally a technique from Psychodrama, in couple therapy, the therapist takes turns speaking as if they were one of the partners talking to the other partner. It allows the therapist to facilitate the conversation the couple *needs* to have but can't rather than the (destructive) conversation that they often have. The primary purpose for doubling is to replace a partner's inflammatory or angry comments for one that is less so. When doubling, the couple therapist "assumes" the voice of each of the partners, speaking out loud the "replacement" statement, while checking in with the person that is being spoken for. Then, the counselor checks with the other partner to see how the reformatted message was received. The couple therapist will often move around the room to crouch or kneel next to the person he is speaking for in order to seem less threatening, and to appear "on their side." Along the way, Wile created six core principles for doubling that will be discussed here (see Table 10.5).

Table 10.5 Six Core Areas of Doubling Technique

1 *Changing the tone.* This principle is focused on both the verbal and nonverbal communications. By repeating the same words but changing the tone, with a softer or more emphatic tone, the counselor can either (a) ask the partner who is experiencing the emotion to reflect on how they perceive it or (b) ask the partner (who the counselor is doubling) to reflect on if this is what they *mean* to say (but may lack the ability to express it clearly). Changing the tone can also take an ambiguous statement, and reinterpret it to give it a new meaning. For example, if a partner says, "I don't know," they may mean that they truly do not know the answer to something (or *how* to answer something), or they may mean that they *know* but don't know how to directly say it. Again, having the counselor make a statement (one way or the other) to clear up the ambiguity gives each partner to experience what an unambiguous statement would be and then react to that.

2 *Confide Vulnerable Feelings/Turn Complaints into Wishes and Fears.* Confiding vulnerable feeling or turning complaints into wishes and fears is a way to get at the emotional core of statements that may be made in anger (or fear), and "soften" them. Confiding vulnerable feelings/Turning complaints into wishes and fears is a way to address deeper attachment longings as well, which helps couples navigate around these conflicts. This is particularly salient when one or both partners are withdrawing from each other. It can help to re-engage them by revealing what might be underlying their more sensitive feelings.

3 *Make Acknowledgments.* According to Wile (2017) during a fight, neither partner wants to concede anything to the other, even in the face of a partner's valid point. They are often afraid that if they do it will undermine *their* argument, and ultimately they will lose the battle that they are having. A typical strategy is to restate their position as if they hadn't even heard their partner. Unfortunately, it also means that opportunities to come to a consensus and navigate difficulty disagreements are lost. When counselors make acknowledgments (and, again, have each partner "check" the validity and the reaction to the response), the counselor is not saying "I'm entirely right and you're entirely wrong" which prolongs the power imbalance. Rather, the counselor is saying "maybe we both have a point here" or "I can see that you have a point" or "You're right that…" in the hopes that hearing an acknowledgment of acceptance of each other's perspective will get the couple to feel less frustrated with one another and back away from or defensive positions. Making acknowledgments (and teaching this to couples) is a way to dissipate the most common tactics that shut down conversation: Namely, criticism, blaming, accusing, and defensiveness (i.e. many of Gottman's "Four Horsemen"). Combining this with "changing the tone" is also very helpful.

4 *Report Rather Than Unload Anger.* When couples are in a conflict, anger is the predominant emotion. By using the principle of reporting, rather than unloading anger, the emotion is given its rightful expression, but it is also put into its proper context. Examples of this include "As you can see, I am very upset" or "I am so hurt by what you said to me," which are better alternatives to shouting, name-calling, or stunned silence/stonewalling. For the couple, hearing the counselor speak from theses vantage points allows for the emotionally flooded person to hear *their highly* emotionally charged thoughts come out of another person's mouth while they can take a detached perspective on it ("Yes, that's exactly what I *wanted* to say" or "Wow, did I *really* sound like that?"). In this approach, it is important for the counselor to make sure that they are actively voicing both partner's viewpoints on this, as well as providing a calm "broker" for their perspectives.

(*Continued*)

5 *Describe the Couple Predicament.* This principle is used to help the couple see their joint situation or predicament. It is a way of explicating the system dynamic, particularly if it is an old or negative one that is trying to assert homeostasis. For example, if a couple is getting gridlocked in a frustrating conversation about their disagreements about sex, where one person usually asserts dominance (i.e. because they have the "stronger drive"), and the other acquiesces but becomes sullen or withdrawn, the counselor may describe their predicament by using a "Look at us…" or "Here we are again…" statement. So for the couple being described the counselor may say "Look at us, we are back to our old fight where you are trying to do what you want physically, and I am feeling powerless to have any influence. This never goes well for us." Making a statement like this gets the couple to commiserate. It is analogous to the Narrative Therapy approach of "externalizing the problem" and, at the same time, also shows mutual awareness.

6 *Turn Monologues into Dialogues.* When partners begin to monologue (go into long descriptions of their position or lengthily diatribes where they detail their – often long – history of gripes or complaints), it is a tactic to "run out the clock" or filibuster during a therapy session. By using doubling, turning monologues into dialogues is the counselor's way of breaking the monologue and getting the other partner's voice into the conversation. The goal is not to shut the partner up but to build in space for the other partner to get their point of view into the conversation in order to spark a dialogue. This might be in the form of stopping the person monologuing, summarizing, and adding a question at the end. Or it might be saying "You know, when I listen to you talk, here is what I hear." It may also be a place to add in a "report" of anger (principle 4), or a description of the couple's predicament (principle 5).

How Doubling Helps a Couple to Navigate Power Issues

In using doubling, the couple therapist is like the director of a play (hence, the original use in Psychodrama), and guides the "action" in the enactment. There are three strategic approaches that are used to direct the conversation: *Going within, going between,* and *going above.* These navigating tactics can be thought of as either being a "first-person" narrator of a story, creating character dialogue, or taking a "third-person" narrative position. In a novel, an author takes a "first-person" perspective when she wants you to know someone's inner thoughts. When using a doubling technique, "going within" is the couple therapist's attempt to take both partners inside the head (or heart) of the partner. For example, "When I hear you say that, it makes me wonder if I am really that important to you?" Or, "I can't help but think, 'are you really going to be there for me'?" When the counselor "goes between" the couple, the conversation is guided more directly. This is more transactional, in order to shape the conversation or navigate it away from distraction or destruction, and less revelatory. It forces the couple to "slow down" their conversation and be more reflective in the dialogue than they might normally be. Finally, going above is the "third person" narrative that takes a "30,000 foot" view of the situation. It elevates a couple's discourse beyond the "street level" conflict, and either universalizes the conflict ("see everyone else goes thought this") or provides feedback on their systems dynamics ("and here is where you get dragged back into your same pattern..."), which can break many impasses. The goal is to help the couple navigate the power issues that perhaps cannot be balanced, by allowing each person to be able to be more authentic in their statements and more vulnerable in their feelings.

One of the pitfalls of doubling that one partner may feel that the couple therapist is not on their side. However, if done properly, each partner's perspective will feel equally and fairly represented. It does require the couple therapist to shift positions (literally and figuratively) throughout the session. If successful, the result is to turn the conflict into a conversation (Peluso, 2018).

Sculpting

The master therapist Virginia Satir (1982) frequently used sculpting with couples as a type of enactment technique. In this procedure, she created a physical representation of the relationship the couple was having by arranging the spouses' bodies in space. Both the content of the sculpture and the way the sculpture used mass and form were examined. This is an excellent procedure to use with couples who may have difficulty expressing themselves verbally.

Communication Techniques

Communication is crucial for all relationships. As a result, when relationships are not functioning well, it is likely that communication between partners is disrupted or ineffective. Conversely, when communication is lacking, the relationship is likely suffering as well. According to Weeks and Gambescia (2017), "One of the most recurrent complaints in couple therapy is the lack of communication between partners; consequently, it is one of the most common issues in treatment" (p. 47). Communication problems can run the gamut from a complete lack of effective communication, to misconstrued communication.

It is important to realize that these communication difficulties are at the heart of most dysfunctional relationships. Often, couples will report, "We don't communicate." This statement is really a mistake, since communication occurs all the time in relationships. Every action or inaction communicates a message. Unfortunately, in troubled relationships what is communicated is generally negative feedback. In other cases, communication problems stem from the fact that one partner is trying to send a message to the other that is not interpreted correctly or is distorted. For example, one partner feels that she is the one who is always demonstratively affectionate and wants desperately for her partner to be more physically affectionate. She withholds any physical contact, and the partner misinterprets this as a rejection rather than as an invitation to demonstrate intimacy. According to Weeks and Gambescia (2017), the problem is that

> the partners fail to understand each other because the intent of the communication is not what the other hears...one partner is trying send a

> message with the particular meaning and the other partner interprets the meaning of the message differently. When intent and effect are very dissimilar, the result is misunderstanding, which can rapidly erupt into conflict.
>
> (p. 47)

It is important that the therapist interprets distorted or hidden messages so that the couple can learn to express them more congruently.

Another problematic communication dynamic has to do with monopolization of time. Often in relationships, one partner talks the majority of the time and the other lets him or her do so. It is important to balance communication time. The couple therapist must not allow either partner to monopolize a session, or to speak for the other. This is a tacit reinforcement of the dysfunctional communication styles that the couple came in with, and will make changing them difficult (if not impossible). Instead, the couple therapist works at teaching the more verbal partner to listen and the less verbal partner to speak.

Another important communication skill is specific, direct, and clear speaking. Vague, generalized speaking makes it impossible to resolve conflict and to achieve understanding. The therapist looks for any dysfunctional patterns in communication, points them out, and helps the couple see how these patterns and the resultant attitudes cause problems. This allows couples to open up blocked channels of communication and repressed feelings. We will present one technique to demonstrate how to do this.

Gottman-Rapoport Technique

Gottman (2011) created a communication technique that couples can use *before* trying to persuade their partner that their approach is correct. It borrows from the work of mathematician and systems thinker, Anatol Rapoport. Rapoport believed that in order to be successful in trying to persuade someone to change their views, this person needs to feel that they are fully understood. Therefore, the Gottman-Rapoport technique teaches couples a method to have a conversation about an area of conflict where the objective is that they must be able to state (to their partner's satisfaction) their partner's position before any persuasion about changing their point of view occurs. There are two "roles" to be played: The role of the speaker and the role of the listener (see Table 10.6).

This technique gives the listening partner the power to ensure that they are being understood before they are asked to consider an alternative point of view. If done correctly, it also can provide both the listener and the speaker with a new appreciation of their partner's viewpoint, and can often lead to areas of compromise, because of the accurate empathizing that they do while going through this exercise.

Table 10.6 Gottman-Rapoport Technique

The Speaker: Requires a mental transformation, and shift to their partner's point of view
• No blaming, no "you" statements • Talk about your feelings • Only use "I statements" about a specific situation • State your positive need. Remember that behind every negative emotion there is a longing, and a wish, and therefore a recipe for your partner to be successful with you. That is your positive need. What do you want and need from your partner?
The Listener: Don't respond defensively
• Postpone your own agenda. Hear and repeat the content of the speaker's needs and perspective (the story) • Listen to your partner's pain with compassion • Hear the speaker's affect (name the affects, and feel a bit of them) • Validate the speaker by completing a sentence like "It makes sense to me that you would feel that way and have these needs, because…" • OK to ask questions

Source: The Gottman Institute (www.gottman.com).

Techniques for Reorganizing the Relational Structure

In each couple and family system, there is a balance that keeps relationships the same (homeostasis). This balance is maintained by structured behavioral sequences that contribute to the maintenance of symptomatic problems and behaviors (Peluso, 2018) The following are techniques that enable the couple therapist to interrupt and change structured couple/family behaviors.

Reframing

Everything can be recapitulated as something else. Each individual sees his or her reality from a unique perspective. When two people come together in a marital situation with both perceiving reality from their own frames of reference, difficulties often occur. Sometimes, one partner has an unhealthy view; sometimes, both have an unhealthy view. It is helpful when the therapist can counter with or enter into the relationship with another competing view. This process is reframing. Reframing can be sudden, dramatic, and even humorous.

Structural Techniques

According to Minuchin and Fishman (1981), boundary marking can be used to focus on and change the distance between partners. In this procedure, a therapist stops one partner from speaking for the other and requires each person to speak only for him- or herself. Boundaries can be made by verbal reconstructions, tasks, spatial rearrangements within the session, nonverbal gestures, and eye contact. Unbalancing is used to change the hierarchical relationship between the couple. The therapist can unbalance by affiliating more closely with one partner than the other, ignoring one member, or taking sides. Another structural procedure is complementarity. This involves using mainly cognitive interventions to help each partner perceive and understand the workings of the marital relationship. Partners usually see themselves acting and reacting to one another, rather than seeing the larger picture of the relational system.

Paradoxical Techniques

Paradoxical procedures are used with the couple to overtly strengthen or promote the homeostatic defenses while not arousing resistance. Paradoxical prescriptions are also called therapeutic double binds. A paradox contains two (or more) statements that cannot simultaneously coexist but do anyway (Mozdzierz, Peluso, & Lisiecki, 2014). Therapeutically, in this procedure, the therapist orders a partner to intensify the occurrence of a symptom. Subsequently, the symptom begins to lose its mystery and power. Whereas the symptom previously seemed out of control, it now seems to come under the therapist's control. Mozdzierz et al. detailed that there are four broad categories of paradoxical interventions: Neutralizers, Tranquilizers, Energizers, and Challengers. For example, a married couple that often stonewalls each other and is not speaking may find that their therapist asks them to continue spending one hour each evening looking at one another but *not* speaking. The injunction jars the continuing process, and both partners may rebel against the order. It is important for the therapist to follow through to make sure that the directions have been followed in the intended manner. This is done by asking the couple each week if they have completed their homework.

Emotional ATTUNEment

According to Gottman (2011), there is a critical set of skills that successful couples demonstrate that are a "blueprint for building trust in long-term committed relationships" (p. 178) that he called "ATTUNEment." The word "ATTUNE" is an acronym that stands for the following six skills: *Awareness* of the emotion; *Turning toward* the emotion; *Tolerance* of the emotional experience; *Understanding* the emotion; *Non-Defensive Listening* to the emotion, and *Empathy* toward the emotion (Gottman, 2011). Table 10.7 defines each of the six skills.

Couples who could do this successfully are called "emotion coaching." They empathize with their partner and can help the other partner understand the emotions they are feeling without taking responsibility for their partner's negative emotion. By contrast, a partner who – in the face of their partner's negative emotion – would either try to take over and take responsibility for the problem (hence, try to "fix" it) or be unable (or unwilling) to "fix" it and dismiss it out of hand as "stupid" are referred to as "emotion-dismissing." This dismissing would often lead to feelings of being uncared for or disregarded.

Table 10.7 ATTUNEment

1. *Awareness of the Emotion.* This skill is designed to have individuals assess their partner's emotional state without blaming or judging the partner. It means accurately labeling and identifying the emotion. It also requires some soothing of the partner by processing the emotion and helping them to "air out" their emotion by letting them talk. The negative emotion in question may be about external forces or entities (work, boss, family, kids), or it may be internally focused (irritation with the partner, or something the partner did or did not do).
2. *Turning Toward the Emotion.* When the negative emotion is about someone or something else, this is an easier skill to master, but when it is focused on the partner, this is more difficult and requires skill in self-soothing (as well as soothing the partner!). By turning toward the (negative) emotion, the partner looks for the "positive" need that is underlying the complaint or criticism that is the impetus for the negative emotion. "In general, in sadness something is missing. In anger there is a frustrated goal. In disappointment there is a hope, and expectation. In loneliness there is a desire for connection" (Gottman, 2011, p. 193). Once the need is found, the couple can work toward providing for that need, rather than argue about being blamed for the negative feeling.
3. *Tolerance of the Emotional Experience.* The idea of "tolerance" for their partner's (negative) emotional experience is not the same as agreeing with the emotion (especially if the negative emotion is directed at them). It also means that they do not try to change the emotion or try to persuade the partner to stop having the emotion as well. In tolerating one's partner's emotion, it also does not mean that they have to also feel the same way as their partner. Instead, it means to "sit with" the partner in the midst of their negative emotion, and be present with them.
4. *Understanding the Emotion.* This skill incorporates both eliciting information from the partner about their experience, and being able to intuit the underlying issue or motivations behind the negative emotion. According to Gottman (2011), "they postpone their own agenda in a search for understanding their partner's point of view" (p. 194). The individual goes on a "mission" to seek out what their partner's experience is, and how *they* understand it (rather than base it on their perspective). Again, when directed externally, it is easier to do in a calm and nonjudgmental way. When it is directed at *them* it can be very challenging (though ultimately rewarding).
5. *Non-Defensive Listening to the Emotion.* Proceeding from the understanding skill, non-defensive listening is the process by which an individual can listen to their partner in a fully present way (especially when they may be the target of their negative emotion) without reacting or "jumping to conclusions." There are several methods to help achieve this. The first is to regulate one's emotions through self-soothing and deep breathing. The second is to cognitively reframe their experience and their partner's experience. This might take the form of "self-talking" where the individual says to themselves, "I have to listen as if this is not about me" or "I know this is upsetting to hear, but I don't have to get upset because of it."
6. *Empathy Toward the Emotion.* The final skill in *attunement* is empathy. Empathy is the ability to "see with the eyes of another" and not just view their experience as they see it but feel their experience as they feel it. In doing so, the individual is able to resonate compassionately with their partner's experience and accurately reflect back to them that they understand it. It is not the same as saying "I know how you feel, because I once felt like..." but rather, "If I were in your shoes, and that happened to me, I would probably feel (like you are feeling now)." It validates the partner's experience and interpretation of their experience, and it builds trust in the other person.

Note: From Gottman (2011).

The skill set in attunement is powerful for any couple because it builds up a sense of connection (i.e. "you get me") between the partners and encourages each partner to feel that the other will be able to help *them* work through the feelings, rather than try to jump in, take over, and "solve" the problem for them. It also allows them to make *choices* about how to react to their partner (similar to Carlson & Dinkmeyer's work, see earlier) and not just impulsively react. This is especially powerful when the conflict is centered as between the couple (when the desire to take over or tamp down the problems is strong) as opposed to a conflict with an external context or person (i.e. work, friends, school, kids, etc.). The good news is that these are skills that can be learned. However, for emotion-dismissing couples, this requires a "shift" in their thinking around negative emotions. Lastly, attunement helps couples to build trust as they competently work through difficult situations, harsh negative feelings, and the inevitable ups and downs of living life together.

Let's return to the case of Tom and Lynn from earlier in this chapter. Recall that central to their dynamic are his anger outbursts, which activates her childhood fear of instability, like the kind she saw with her mother, and precipitates her controlling behaviors. These, in turn, bring up defensiveness and fear in Tom based on his childhood experiences with women in his family.

Utilizing ATTUNEment with Tom and Lynn as an appropriate technique helps them better understand each other's emotional reactions and more effectively help each other work through the emotion. First, awareness of the emotion. Tom and Lynn could be taught how to become more aware of their own emotions (fear, anxiety, anger, sadness, grief, etc.) when they arise. Next is turning toward the emotion. While Tom is more obvious in his "turning away" by refusing to acknowledge his grief reactions, Lynn also "turns away," so both partners could be helped in finding ways to turn toward each other and their emotions when they are feeling them. Tolerance of the emotional experience would take place in the context of each person staying with the emotion, and possibly practicing self-soothing techniques that allow them to experience the emotion in each other's presence without distorting it. Understanding the emotion would mean that each person would help the other process the underlying causes or origins of the emotion (each other's family of origin as well as other relationship-specific events). Finally, non-defensive listening would mean helping Tom and Lynn hear what the other is saying regarding their own (and each other's emotional experience), rather than lashing out defensively. The goal would be to replace the negative interaction cycle with one that helps each person individually, as well as the couple.

Concluding Note

This chapter has highlighted the various strategies and techniques available to the couple therapist. The differential use of these procedures was discussed, and although couple therapy is in the process of becoming more scientific, much of it is still an art. It is hoped that with continued exposure to the various strategies and couples, the couple therapist will develop the intuition necessary to know when strategies can be used effectively.

References

Aponte, H. J. (2017). Enactments: From the perspective of the use of self. In G. R. Weeks, S. T. Fife, & C. M. Peterson (Eds.), *Techniques for the couple therapist* (pp. 33–36). New York, NY: Routledge.

Bradford, K. (2012). Assessing readiness for couple therapy: The stages of relationship change questionnaire. *Journal of Marital and Family Therapy, 38*(3), 486–501. doi:10.1111/j.1752-0606.2010.00211.x

Carlson, J., & Dinkmeyer, D. (1999). TIME for a better marriage. In R. Berger & M. T. Hannah (Eds.), *Preventative approaches in couple therapy* (pp. 149–168). Philadelphia, PA: Brunner-Mazel.

Cavedo, C., & Guerney, B. G. (1999). Relationship Enhancement(R) enrichment and problem prevention programs: Therapy-derived, powerful, versatile. In R. Berger & M. T. Hannah (Eds.), *Preventative approaches in couple therapy* (pp. 73–105). Philadelphia, PA: Brunner-Mazel.

Cordova, J. V., Warren, L. Z., & Gee, G. K. (2001). Motivational interviewing with couples: An intervention for at-risk couples. *Journal of Marital and Family Therapy, 27*, 315–326.

Davis, S. D. (2017). Enactments in five developmental stages. In G. R. Weeks, S. T. Fife, & C. M. Peterson (Eds.), *Techniques for the couple therapist* (pp. 37–40). New York, NY: Routledge.

Davis, S. D., & Espinoza, S. A. (2017). Effectively structuring enactments. In G. R. Weeks, S. T. Fife, & C. M. Peterson (Eds.), *Techniques for the couple therapist* (pp. 41–44). New York, NY: Routledge.

DiClemente, C. C., & Wiprovnick, A. E. (2017). Action as a stage of change in couple and family therapy. In J. Lebow, A. Chambers, & D. Breunlin (Eds.), *Encyclopedia of couple and family therapy*. Cham, Switzerland: Springer. doi:10.1007/978-3-319-15877-8

Dinkmeyer, D., & Carlson, J. (1989). *Taking time for love*. New York, NY: Prentice-Hall.

Dreikurs, R. (1946). *The challenge of marriage*. New York, NY: Hawthorn.

Framo, J. L. (1983). *Workshop on couple therapy*. Bay City, MI: Michigan Psychological Association.

Glick, I. D., Berman, E. M., Clarkin, J. F., & Rait, D. S. (2000). *Marital and family therapy* (4th ed.). Washington, DC: American Psychiatric Press.

Gottman, J. M. (1999). *The marriage clinic*. New York, NY: W. W. Norton.

Gottman, J. M. (2011). *The science of trust: Emotional attunement for couples*. New York, NY: Norton.

Gurman, A. S. (2015). The history and practice of couple therapy: History, contemporary models and a framework for comparative analysis. In A. S. Gurman, J. Lebow, & D. Snyder (Eds.), *Clinical handbook of couple therapy* (5th ed., pp. 1–22). New York, NY: Guilford.

Kaslow, F. W., & Lieberman, E. J. (1981). Couples' group therapy: Rationale, dynamics, and process. In G. P. Sholevar (Ed.), *The handbook of marriage and couple therapy* (pp. 21–34). New York, NY: Medical and Scientific Press.

L'Abate, L. (1999). Taking the bull by the horns: Beyond talk in psychological interventions. *The Family Journal: Counseling and Therapy for Couples and Families, 7*(3), 206–220.

Masi, M. V., Miller, R. B., & Olson, M. M. (2003). Difference in dropout rates among couple and family therapy clients. *Contemporary Family Therapy, 25*(1), 63–75.

Miller, S., & Sherrard, P. A. D. (1999). COUPLE COMMUNICATION: A system for equipping partners to talk, listen, and resolve conflicts effectively. In R. Berger & M. T. Hannah (Eds.), *Preventative approaches in couple therapy* (pp. 125–148). Philadelphia, PA: Brunner-Mazel.

Miller, W. R., & Rollnick, S. (Eds.). (1991). *Motivational interviewing: Preparing people for change.* New York, NY: Guilford.

Miller, W. R., & Rollnick, S. (Eds.). (2002). *Motivational interviewing: Preparing people for change* (2nd ed.). New York, NY: Guilford.

Minuchin, S., & Fishman, H. C. (1981). *Family therapy techniques.* Cambridge, MA: Harvard University Press.

Mozdzierz, G., Peluso, P. R., & Lisiecki, J. (2014). *Advanced principles of counseling and psychotherapy: Learning, integrating, and consolidating the nonlinear thinking of master practitioners.* New York, NY: Routledge.

Napier, A. Y. (1988). *The fragile bond: In search of an equal, intimate, and enduring marriage.* New York, NY: Harper & Row.

Nichols, W. C. (2003). Family-of-origin treatment. In T. L. Sexton, G. R. Weeks, & M. S. Robbins (Eds.), *Handbook of family therapy: The science and practice of working with families and couples* (pp. 83–100). New York, NY: Brunner-Routledge.

Olson, D. H., & Olson, A. K. (1999). PREPARE/ENRICH Program: Version 2000. In R. Berger & M. T. Hannah (Eds.), *Preventative approaches in couple therapy* (pp. 196–216). Philadelphia, PA: Brunner-Mazel.

Peluso, P. R. (2018). *A systemic guide for counselors to understand and work with couples recovering from infidelity.* New York, NY: Routledge.

Prochaska, J. O., & DiClemente, C. C. (1982). Transtheoretical therapy: Toward a more integrative model of change. *Psychotherapy: Theory, Research & Practice, 19*(3), 276–288.

Prochaska, J. O., & DiClemente, C. C. (2002). Transtheoretical therapy. In F. W. Kaslow (Ed.), *Comprehensive handbook of psychotherapy: Integrative/eclectic* (Vol. 4, pp. 165–184). New York, NY: John Wiley & Sons.

Prochaska, J. O., & Norcross, J. C. (2002). Stages of change. In J. C. Norcross (Ed.), *Psychotherapy relationships that work* (pp. 110–125). New York, NY: Oxford Press.

Satir, V. (1982). *Conjoint family therapy.* Palo Alto, CA: Science & Behavior Books.

Schneider, W. J. (2003). *Transtheoretical model of change with couples* (Unpublished doctoral dissertation). Texas A & M University, College Station, TX.

Sherman, R., & Fredman, N. (1986). *Handbook of structured techniques in marriage and family therapy.* New York, NY: Brunner/Mazel.

Sholevar, G. P. (2003). Couple therapy: An overview. In G. P. Sholevar (Ed.), *Textbook of family and couple therapy* (pp. 417–438). Alexandria, VA: American Psychiatric Publishing.

Simon, F. B., Stierlin, H., & Wynne, L. C. (1985). *The language of family therapy: A systemic vocabulary and source book.* New York, NY: Family Process Press.

Sperry, L., & Carlson, J. (1990). Hypnosis, tailoring, and multimodal treatment. *Individual Psychology: Journal of Adlerian Theory, Research & Practice, 46*(4), 459–465.

Stanley, S. M., Blumberg, S. L., & Markman, H. J. (1999). Helping couples fight for their marriages: The PREP approach. In R. Berger & M. T. Hannah (Eds.), *Preventative approaches in couple therapy* (pp. 279–303). Philadelphia, PA: Brunner-Mazel.

Weeks, G. R., & Gambescia, N. (2017). Expanding levels of communication. In G. R. Weeks, S. T. Fife, & C. M. Peterson (Eds.), *Techniques for the couple therapist* (pp. 47–50). New York, NY: Routledge.

Wile, D. B. (2002). Collaborative couples counseling. In A. S. Gurman & N. S. Jacobson (Eds.), *Clinical handbook of couple therapy* (3rd ed., pp. 281–307). New York, NY: Guilford Press.

Wile, D. B. (2008). *After the honeymoon: How conflict can improve your relationship* (Rev. ed.). Oakland, CA: Collaborative Couple Therapy Books.

Wile, D. B. (2011). Collaborative couple therapy. In D. K.Carson & M. Casado-Kehoe (Eds.), *Case studies in couple therapy: Theory-based approaches* (pp. 303–316). New York, NY: Routledge.

Wile, D. B. (2017). *Doubling in collaborative couple therapy: Chapter 3 from solving the moment: Theory and method of collaboative couple therapy (in preparation).* Retrieved December 2, 2017 from http://danwile.com/writings/downloadable-articles/

11 Professional and Ethical Practice of Couple Therapy

LEARNING OBJECTIVES

In this chapter, the reader will learn the following:

1 Elements of relational ethics, principle ethics, and virtue ethics.
2 Special topics in ethics relevant to couple therapy.
3 Similarities in ethics codes that apply to couple therapy and counseling.
4 Ethical decision-making and understanding decision-making styles.
5 Ethical and professional decisions and evidence-based practice.
6 Ethical teaching and supervision of couple therapy.

Over the years, the practice of couple therapy has continued to evolve and is now a mature mental health profession. One indicator of this is the emphasis on sound, ethically informed practice. However, perhaps because of the seemingly punitive nature of the ethics codes, anxiety over possible malpractice, or an ethics review by a state licensing board or professional association, many therapists view ethics as an unwelcome burden designed to impinge on the right to practice therapy effectively. This attitude may be an outgrowth of the training that a therapist received, personal philosophy, or as the result of direct experience with the corrective function of an ethics board. It can result in a toxic split in a therapist's attitude about ethics as either fear producing or aspirational, i.e. caring, appreciative, inclusivity, and excellence. The toxicity results from the belief that by attending to the first part of the split, the second part can be easily forgotten or buried (i.e. "I don't have to worry about that ethics stuff. I write my notes properly, follow the treatment plan, and I don't have sex with my clients."). Unless they are subpoenaed, these therapists think explicitly about ethics when they renew their licenses and get continuing education credits. Hence, ethics is a topic that is relegated to keeping up with paperwork, and managing risk, with limited sense of fulfillment associated with making a real difference in the lives of clients and the involvement in civic and professional organizations.

This chapter overviews ethical issues and considerations that are common in the practice of couple therapy. To set the stage for the discussion of these ethical considerations, we first describe relational ethics as well as principle ethics and virtue ethics. Then we focus on the ethical issues of confidentiality, secrecy, privacy, dual relationships, and online therapy. Next, we briefly compare the ethical codes of the American Association of Marital and Family Therapy (AAMFT) and the International Association of Marriage and Family Counseling (IAMFC). The final section focuses on ethical decision-making.

Relational Ethics

We began this chapter by identifying the split-view therapists can have of ethics. In this section, we introduce another way of looking at ethics – one that integrates the earlier split. We believe that ethical practice is inextricably linked with sound, professional practice. The ethical values (beneficence, non-malfeasance, fidelity, justice, and autonomy) should guide and inform the clinician as to the best way to proceed. In doing so, these values are also at the heart of all best practices. We also believe that ethical practice is a lived relational experience. According to Sperry (2007a), this is referred to as Perspective III ethics. Contrasted with Perspective I ethics, wherein a clinician's focus is solely on ethical codes, risk management, and avoiding sanctions out of a sense of fear, Perspective III (or relational) ethics are reflected by an integration of ethical codes, higher ethical principles (beneficence, non-malfeasance, justice, autonomy, and fidelity), and personal values. This means that ethics do not, and cannot, reside in isolation locked away in file cabinet but must be expressed in the relationship with (and to) clients. These clinicians view ethics as a means of creating connections with a couple rather than put up barriers to them. In addition, a relational ethical practice is a process that evolves over time for the clinician. As with all aspects of practicing couple therapy (assessment, intervention, and case conceptualization), ethical practice should *never* be learned once and not revisited. Instead, ethical practice is shaped by the therapist's growth, exposure to new ideas and concepts, developed in concert with client interaction, and reflective of broader organizational dynamics. These dynamics can be both broadly universal (i.e. professional associations) and uniquely individual (i.e. agency or practice culture). In short, we view ethics as a positive endeavor from a health-based, holistic perspective (rather than from a negative, fear-based one), which allows therapists to consciously incorporate and implement these principles in the practice of therapy. Couple therapists who view ethics from this perspective have the potential to grow and mature as clinicians with powerfully efficient tools for effecting change (see Peluso, 2007; Sperry, 2007a for a more thorough discourse on this topic).

In terms of the practice of couple therapy, a number of specific ethical concerns are involved in the work of couple therapy. Which partner is the therapist ethically bound to serve? Should the therapist begin working with one partner and try to involve his or her spouse? What is done in the case of a reluctant partner? Should the therapist lie to a couple in order to help solve their problems? Should the spouses attempt to reveal all secrets, even to the extent that they may suffer embarrassment, great anxiety, and loss of respect?

What about the role of technology in the delivery of services? What are the implications for couple therapists in the future? How do couple therapists employ a relational ethics (Perspective III) approach to these issues? These are some of the many thorny and complicated ethical issues that affect the work of a couple therapist. In this chapter, we touch on some of these and present the current code of ethics. In addition, we present a discussion of the prevalence of ethical complaints and their resolution within the professional association. Lastly, we end with a discussion of the process of ethical decision-making and the personal factors that can shape it.

Principle Ethics and Virtue Ethics

The practice of couple therapy routinely involves ethical considerations. If all a therapist had to do was consult an ethics code for "the" answer, professional practice would be relatively easy and straightforward. Unfortunately, it is seldom the case that an ethics code can deliver without some deliberation – and possible consultation – before making an ethical decision. The reason is that ethics codes provide guidance instead of absolute directives. Occasionally, a code will provide clear directives, such as get informed consent, don't have sex with your clients, or keep clients from harming themselves or others. However, many cases are much more difficult to understand and resolve, particularly when ethical dilemmas are involved (Kleist & Bitter, 2014). An ethical dilemma is a "situation involving an ethical consideration that confuses a professional either because there are competing or conflicting ethical standards that apply, or because there is a confect between ethical and moral standards" (Sperry, 2007a, p. 486).

So, what guides a couple therapist's ethical decision, particularly when ethical dilemmas are involved? Is it personal virtue, principle ethics, virtue ethics, or a combination of these? Let's look briefly at all three of these.

Personal virtue is the therapist's personal disposition or quality of being morally good or righteous (Sperry, 2007b). Principle ethics is a way of applying a system of ethical rules and principles to determine the right decision when an ethical dilemma arises. It focuses on actions and choices based on predetermined values (Corey, Corey, Corey, & Callanan, 2014). The emphasis is on doing. Ethics codes typically reflect principle ethics.

In contrast, virtue ethics focuses on the character traits of individuals or the profession (Sperry, 2007b). Here, the emphasis is more on being than doing. Accordingly, while principle ethics poses the question, "What shall be *done*?" virtue ethics asks, "What kind of person shall the couple therapist *be*?" A not so obvious question for a couple therapist to ponder is might it be that your ethical behavior as a couple therapist is more about personal moral *being* than about just understanding and applying a set of ethical principles and an ethics code (Kleist & Bitter, 2014)? With time and experience with different ethical considerations, therapists arrive at an answer to this question of what guides a therapist's ethical decisions.

Orientation to Therapy and Informed Consent

As a part of sound, professional practice, couples need to be oriented to therapy in an ethically responsible fashion. According to Margolin (1998), for this to be thoroughly accomplished, the following five points should be covered:

1. A full explanation of the procedures of therapy and their purposes.
2. A clear discussion about the qualifications of the therapist and the role to be taken by the therapist in the sessions.
3. A disclosure of anticipated discomforts and risks as well as benefits of treatment.
4. Alternative treatments and available referral sources that may be better suited to the needs of the couple.
5. A firm understanding that each individual and the couple as a whole may discontinue treatment whenever they wish.

In addition to orienting the clients to therapy, it is the cornerstone of ethical practice to gain the client's consent before treatment begins. From a relational ethics perspective, it does two things: (1) demonstrates to the clients exactly what is going to happen in the therapy so that they are not surprised and can fully participate, and (2) allows the therapist to begin to set a collegial and collaborative tone with the client. This orienting of the couple includes thoroughly going through the points mentioned earlier, as well as addressing any issues, fears, or questions that clients may have. Often, structural issues of how often the sessions will be or how much the therapy will cost will need to be addressed, but there may also be more subtle questions as to the client's overall safety (psychological, confidentiality, and physical). It may seem that the requirement for a therapist to provide accurate, honest descriptions or informed consent can be overwhelming, if not impossible. Keep in mind that (except in extreme situations) it is in the best interests of the client to be able to make the determination for him- or herself, especially from a relational ethics perspective. Indeed, informed consent should never be a single event but rather an ongoing process as the therapy evolves and goals develop more fully or even change (Margolin, Shapiro, & Miller, 2015; Sperry, 2007a).

Special Case of Consent: Lack of a Common Purpose

In couple therapy, it may not be clear who the patient is. Often, the troubled partner is viewed as the patient by the couple, or one partner may unilaterally label the other as the problem, but it is important for the therapist to designate the couple as the patient. Many come to therapy hoping to help their partners. The couple therapist needs to be aware of the issues involved in implying that a non-symptomatic partner is the patient when he or she originally did not think so or even need to contract for treatment. Properly orienting clients to the process of couple therapy and providing some brief education about systems can be beneficial.

Another common challenge to the couple therapist occurs when one person wants divorce (or separation) counseling and the other is coming to the sessions under the expectation of saving the marriage or improving the relationship.

> While the therapy may begin with a common goal that appears to serve the best interests of both partners, the situation may evolve to a point in which individual interests take precedence and what best serves one client actually undermines the interests of the other.
>
> (Margolin, 1998, p. 79)

In this situation, who is the primary client? How does the therapist carry out his or her ethical responsibility when the two people in the relationship have differing expectations? What happens when one partner refuses to attend, but the other continues to come? Attempts to balance therapeutic responsibilities toward one partner and toward the couple relationship involve intricate judgments. Because neither of these responsibilities cancels out the importance of the other, the couple therapist cannot afford blind pursuit of either extreme (Margolin et al., 2015). Instead, couple therapists have the responsibility to communicate clearly the boundaries and limitations of therapy, what the policy is on conjoint vs. individual therapy, and how and at what point does the nature or purpose of therapy change (e.g. from reconciliation to separation).

Confidentiality, Secrecy, and Privacy

Like any type of therapy, couples are guaranteed a certain level of confidentiality. Confidentiality should be discussed at the beginning of therapy, as a part of informed consent and a thorough orientation to therapy (Wilcoxon, Remley, & Gladding, 2013). The limits of confidentiality related to any mandated reporter or duty-to-warn statutes should be covered. In addition, unlike individual therapy, complete confidentiality cannot be guaranteed in couple therapy since the therapist cannot assume that both clients will keep confidential the information disclosed in sessions (i.e. talking to a friend or a family member). All that the therapist can guarantee is that she or he will not disclose any information about the couple, pursuant to the laws and ethics of sound, professional practice. Lastly, therapists should also disclose their position on the confidentiality of information gleaned through any individual meetings that may be an adjunct to the couple therapy (Margolin et al., 2015).

In light of the ethical principles, confidentiality requires couple therapists to balance the needs of all clients involved, much as beneficence means doing good for each of the partners. This is not always easy to do. Many times, the principles of beneficence and non-malfeasance are at odds, as what may be best for an individual or for most members of the family may not be best for one member. For example, if a person requires substance abuse treatment, it may be good for the family, but it may be bad or uncomfortable for the substance user. In addition, if the substance abuser is the sole provider for the family, a recommendation for substance abuse treatment may place an undue economic burden on the family. Likewise, ethical values like beneficence and autonomy can be in conflict, as what is best for the family may infringe on the ability of one person to make decisions for him- or herself. At this point, a relational context is necessary to overcome these issues, as most straightforward methods of resolving ethical dilemmas begin to break down. Opening a dialogue (or even better, continuing a dialogue that was started from the first session) about how it is difficult to achieve a balance and an outcome for all members may be helpful. Discussing the need for cooperation from all family members to help the family surmount the challenge can be a good consensus builder.

For the therapist, discussing the particular ethical principles openly with the family can help the family to see the therapist's struggle as not merely one of taking sides in a battle but really striving to effect the best outcome for the family (Caldwell, 2016). Also, discussing the concept of privacy vs. secrecy can help foster a more honest discussion, where the clients can process information openly. In this framework, issues of confidentiality (particularly where confidentiality cannot be kept) can be resolved. Some therapists extend confidentiality to the individuals and agree not to share any information in the individual meetings with the partner, while other therapists hold the position that the couple is the client and that to hold secrets in confidence would be counterproductive (Margolin, 1998; Woody, 2000).

Often, therapists are confused about the difference between privacy and secrets, and how each might affect a relationship. Privacy is information held by a person that they would rather not share but that does not affect his or her relationship with other people (Sperry, 2007b). Examples of this might be how they voted in the last election, the fact that they always dreamed about being a sports hero, their secret fantasy about having a billion dollars, or their first crush from kindergarten. These are personal fantasies, or aspects of the self that are not necessary to share in order to participate fully in a relationship. Secrecy, by contrast, is characterized by information or feelings that a person has that might influence a relationship (Wilcoxon et al., 2013). These might be feelings of fear, ambivalence about the relationship, or shame about their own actions or behavior (e.g. having an affair). Therefore, the therapist's view of keeping secrets is intertwined with issues of confidentiality, whereas privacy might not necessarily be.

There are pros and cons to couple therapists agreeing to keep secrets. The pros to having a policy of keeping secrets includes being able to get more reliable information from clients about what they are thinking or feeling and would be reluctant to offer if they knew it would be shared with their partners. This avoids the case of couple therapists being blindsided by a hidden agenda from one of the partners that might sabotage treatment. The cons for this policy are that it requires the therapist to remember what information is accessible to the couple and what information is to remain confidential. In addition, it potentially puts the couple therapist in the position of working against the best interests of the other partner and the couple as a whole (Margolin, 1998). As a result, an increasing number of therapists apparently have made the decision that he or she will not assure confidentiality regarding matters that vitally affect the marriage unit or where there is evidence of criminal behavior and intent.

Special Case of Confidentiality: Extramarital Affairs

One commonly encountered dilemma for therapists is the confiding by one spouse of involvement in an extramarital affair. In addition to being a treatment issue all its own, it often puts therapists in an ethical bind when deciding how to handle the information with the clients (in the case of a secret) and how to handle the behavior (as a threat to the therapy). The disclosure is often made to the therapist alone, and the partner asks the therapist not to divulge it. In fact, the client often demands secrecy. Unless the therapist has clarified his or her position on secrets, revealing the affair would violate confidentiality, even if the therapist believes that dealing openly with the issue of the affair would benefit the couple in the long term. A therapist who assures confidentiality is obligated to maintain it for each partner. If the policy is full sharing, the couple should be informed. When a couple therapist is confronted with a secret (like an affair), it should be assessed for how damaging the disclosure to the other person would be, and the therapist should seek to minimize the injury from the disclosure (Snyder & Doss, 2005). Ideally, the transgressing partner should be the one to make the disclosure. However, this is seldom the case, and it is up to the therapist to decide how to proceed.

Therapists can be confused about how to handle an ongoing sexual relationship outside of the marriage that the partner does not wish the therapist to reveal (Snyder & Doss, 2005). It is helpful if therapists do not get involved in doing couple therapy in this situation. The therapist must be trustworthy and therefore cannot keep secrets. If the other spouse knows of this relationship, the couple can perhaps proceed toward the goal of mutual satisfaction and trust. This applies only to current extramarital sexual relationships. Past events are the property of the individuals involved, and whether they are shared is the decision of the owners of the memory, not the therapist. Generally, a therapist will need to say something like:

> I don't think I can help you develop intimacy with your spouse if you are seeking a similar goal with your lover. You may wish to continue this unsatisfying marriage because of power, position, children, or other reasons and find what intimacy you can elsewhere. That is surely a respectable and perhaps viable choice, but if you wish to promote growth in your life with your spouse, letting go of your lover will be necessary in order not to become entrapped in unresolved ambivalence.

The therapist may agree to work with either or both on an individual basis but not conjointly (Peluso, 2018).

Dual/Multiple Relationships

The therapeutic relationship is infused with a great deal of trust in the clinician, coupled with a heightened sense of vulnerability in the client. When a therapist has more than one relationship with a client (i.e. business relationship, friendship, etc.), the ability to remain neutral or act in the client's best interest is compromised (or at least can be called into question). Thus, the prohibition against therapists having more than one relationship (that is, the professional, therapeutic relationship) is designed to protect both the clinician and the client(s) from manipulation, collusion, boundary confusion, and exploitation (Sperry, 2007a). Explicit in this ethical prohibition is the ban against having a sexual relationship with a client while she or he is under a therapist's care. A therapist engaging in inappropriate sexual behavior with one partner while treating the couple constitutes one of the greatest betrayals of the therapeutic relationship in a couples format (Margolin, 1998; Woody, 2000). However, because of the ban on sexual contact between a client and a therapist, all dual relationships are suspect. It is a slippery slope argument which contends that any relationship outside of the professional realm has the potential to gradually (and inexorably) lead to sexual misconduct (Zur, 2002). This is not to say that this code has been put in place without reason. It is a sad commentary on our profession that several of our own colleagues have fallen prey to inappropriate behavior or (even worse) have exploited a client at a vulnerable moment. Regardless, however, any dual roles/relationship now "carries with it a connotation of sexual or other exploitative malfeasance" (Coale, 1998, p. 101). In fact, some experts even go as far as suggesting that practitioners engaging in any kind of dual roles should have their licenses and professional association memberships suspended (Coale, 1998; Lazarus, 2002; Pope & Vasquez, 1998).

Unfortunately for those who wish to see all dual relationships banned, it is impossible for the therapist not to operate in two or more roles. Both interpersonally and intrapsychically, therapists must face dealing with clients on multiple levels. Interpersonally, therapists may have social settings in common with their clients (especially in small town settings), such as church or religious communities, school or children's athletics leagues, or shopping areas, where they may have to interact with their clients. In addition, they may have to occupy multiple professional roles as evaluator for court cases, or job functioning, and mandated reporter in the case of abuse issues. Intrapsychically, when working with a client, therapists must contend not only with their role as a professional but also with their role as a male, a parent, a spouse, a son, etc. All of these are dual roles that are not sexual in nature, which necessarily raises the question: Are there instances where a dual or multiple relationship is healthy or useful?

There are dangers in both maintaining the strict boundary about dual relationships and of not paying attention to the potential for the exploitation of clients. "Relationships are messy and there are circumstances in which not participating in a dual role can be more destructive than doing so" (Coale,

1998, p. 105). There are also dangers in sending these relationships underground by making *any* dual relationship suspect in all situations (Zur, 2002, 2005, 2011).

Sometimes, it's impossible for therapists to completely avoid multiple relationships. Dealing with multiple relationships is commonplace for therapists practicing in a small community some distance from a major metropolitan area. For example, that therapist could decide to buy a car from a therapy client because buying one elsewhere might signal that the car dealer was in therapy. A useful question to consider when facing dual and multiple relationship situations is this: Whose needs are being met? If the answer is the needs of the therapist, that is when the therapist needs to proceed with great care and seek consultation.

Prohibiting all dual relationships, however, does provide an elegant solution. One does not need to sort out the good dual relationships from the bad ones (a process which could be unbearably burdensome in a legal sense) but rather simply to examine whether duality exists. If so, it is bad and the practitioner is punishable. If not, there is no harm. Context and circumstance have no place here. However, then the question is "Who is this process best for – the client, the therapist, or the evaluating bodies?" If it is the first, then it can be ethical and justified. If it is for the other two, then it does not meet the principle of beneficence, or justice, and instead borders on non-malfeasance (Coale, 1998).

In terms of the ethical principles, it should be noted that those dual relationships that are exploitative (including sexual relationships) are not good, just, or truthful. In addition, these relationships are always bad (for both client and practitioner), and they deny the client the ability to make a free choice. Hence, they are in violation of all the ethical principles (beneficence, non-malfeasance, autonomy, justice, and fidelity). However, what about the nonexploitative dual relationships? Can they be beneficial, respect the client's autonomy, promote justice for the client, and allow for truth to be maintained? In other words, can a therapist have nonsexual dual roles/multiple relationships with clients *and* operate within the framework of the ethical principles? Again, it depends on the therapists' ability to clearly define and maintain boundaries, as well as be able to negotiate these with the client's best interests at heart while openly admitting the ways that the therapeutic relationship is meeting their own personal, emotional, and even financial needs. Then, perhaps, the relationship can be viewed as ethical. From a principles-based and relational-ethics perspective, this is a much higher standard than any specific code can ever hope to attain. It is also the starting point of any good, ethical practice of couple therapy (Peluso, 2007).

Online Therapy and the Use of Technology in Couple Therapy

In a curious juxtaposition, we introduce a discussion of an emerging area in the practice of couple therapy that is, on the one hand, designed to create greater connectivity by delivering new avenues of access to therapists; on the other hand, the very nature of the technology removes the human connection for the individuals using it. The use of technology, and especially the Internet, in the practice of couple therapy is an evolving frontier of the field. Some therapists conduct couples sessions via Skype of FaceTime, and the prediction is that therapeutic robots will begin to play a role in counseling (Fulmer, 2018).

Since the explosion of the Internet in the late 1990s – and particularly since the last edition of this text – the use of cyber technology in work settings and social life has increased exponentially. So, how many couple therapists use it in their clinical practice? Unfortunately, its use is unknown since no national survey results have been reported. However, two small studies have been reported that offer some hints. The first looked at the extent to which couple and family therapy journals published articles on the integration of the Internet in couple and family life. It found that from 1996 to 2010, there were only 79 of 13,274 articles that appeared in 17 couple and family therapy journals focused on Internet use (Blumer, Hertlein, Smith & Allen, 2014).

The second study looked at the frequency and ways in which couples and family therapists communicated online with their clients. It also identified the therapists' level of comfort with online treatments. The researchers surveyed 169 practicing couples and family therapists in 28 states. They found that the majority (83.4%) of these therapists reported that they communicated with clients via e-mail occasionally. This compares with research showing that 72% of psychologists communicated with their clients via e-mail. It is noteworthy that the majority of couples and family therapists surveyed expressed discomfort treating couples and families exclusively online. This is similar to the outlook of those in other mental health profession. Finally, twice as responders indicated that online therapy should be used in rural areas rather than in suburban or urban areas (Hertlein, Blumer, & Smith, 2014).

Both of these studies suggest that the use of technology in therapy is just beginning and is frontier area for the profession. Like other frontiers, there are still more questions than answers for therapists who are considering the use of these technological advances to improve their services to clients. The AAMFT and the IAMFC have provisions in their code of ethics for online counseling (AAMT, 2015; IAMFC, 2017). Other associations have position papers and statements about online therapy but often with some *caveat emptor* (let the buyer beware). We will briefly outline some of the concerns.

The first question about therapy online is "Is it legal?" The answer is yes and no. The legality of online counseling varies from state to state. However, this brings up the first (and oft-cited) problem in the debate over online therapy: Where does the therapy take place? More specifically, what body of laws is enforced to protect either the practitioner or the client? Are they the laws in the state where the client resides or the counselor? According to Leslie (2002), "the majority view is that the health service is performed in the state where the patient is at the time of treatment" (pp. 39–40). The same principle applies to licensure, as not all states recognize the licensees of other states. Hence, online counselors may run the risk of being charged with the crime of practicing without a license in the state where the client is, regardless of their status in their state (Leslie, 2002). In addition, since many of the professional associations have not made ethical determinations about the use of the Internet in couple therapy, the risk of running afoul of the ethical codes is increased.

Other ethical issues related to online counseling are informed consent (written vs. oral), handling e-mail communication from clients, and whether physically being present with the clients and observing nonverbal behavior affect the quality of therapy. However, perhaps one of the most serious ethical issues has to do with assuring the confidentially and security of online counseling. The security of communication over the Internet, whether written, voice, or video, cannot be guaranteed unless encrypted or conducted on a secure network (Shallcross, 2011). Even then, the occurrence of hacking or the transmission of sensitive information over public telephone lines makes it impossible to absolutely guarantee complete confidentiality. The risks to clients from all these issues must be disclosed as a part of good clinical practice. However, there are some potential benefits to online counseling, such as increased access to quality services (especially in remote areas), reduction in travel costs, and overall inconvenience as well as the potential for greater continuity of care (Shallcross, 2011). Obviously, technology, in one form or another, will continue to play a part in the practice of therapy. The use of faxes, voicemail, and electronic reimbursement of claims has not ended but rather enhanced the practice of therapy. As with any new growth area, however, the expansion of technology has outpaced the ethical and legal regulation of it.

Research on Ethical Issues with Online Therapy

While technology use has advantages and benefits in the practice of couple therapy, its use also involves a number of ethical concerns and drawbacks. A study of ethical concerns and drawbacks of online therapy is thought-provoking. It surveyed 226 licensed marriage and family counselors, students, and supervisors (Hertlein, Blumer, & Mihaloliakos, 2015).

Five themes emerged with regard to the ethical issues and drawbacks that emerge in online therapy. The first and most frequently cited ethical concern was confidentiality. This included concerns about privacy, who could view the video or feedback, and the authenticity of the user. Other concerns included the risk that others, besides the couple, could gain access to the computer account.

The second theme involved the therapeutic relationship. Concerns were expressed that messages sent might be misunderstood or misinterpreted and thereby compromise the therapeutic process. Another concern was that online therapy does not provide opportunities for physical interaction, like offering a tissue or appropriate therapeutic touch to a crying or distressed client. Similarly are boundary-related concerns complicated dual relationships issues since clients might be able to contact their therapist on social media.

The third theme involved working therapeutically with individuals who are at risk, i.e. those who are suicidal or experiencing other crises. Specific concerns were for assessing risk factors, difficulty in monitoring self-injurious behavior, client safety, and therapist inability to intervene immediately.

The fourth theme involved liability and licensing concerns such as meeting HIPAA requirements, record keeping, informed consent, distributing forms and handouts to clients, mandated reporting, and involvement of third-party payers.

The fifth theme involved the necessity of having sufficient training and education to conduct therapies online as well as privacy practices and the use of personal and professional pages on social media sites (Hertlein et al., 2015).

The concerns of the participants in this study are real and deserve consideration by those practicing couple therapy as well as supervisors and instructors. Training programs would do well to discuss these concerns alongside instructions on the applying technology to the practice of couple therapy.

Ethics Codes Informing the Practice of Couple Therapy

A defining hallmark of a profession is the existence of a professional association which represents the profession, and that publishes and enforces a code of ethics. Ethical codes have been developed for all the mental health professions, i.e. social work, counseling, psychology, couple and family therapy, and psychiatry. However, there are two professional organizations that are specifically relevant to the practice of couple therapy: The AAMFT and the IAMFC. This section briefly overviews the most recent codes of AAMFT and IAMFC.

2015 AAMFT Ethics Code

This Code became effective on January 1, 2015. Its purpose is to honor the public trust in couple and family therapists by setting standards for ethical practice which define professional expectations for therapists, and which will be enforced by the AAMFT Ethics Committee. The Preamble to the Code includes a brief discussion of the core values that should inform the practice of couple and family therapy. These values are intended to provide an aspirational framework within which couple and family therapists can pursue the highest goals of professional practice. The core values are:

> Acceptance, appreciation, and inclusion of a diverse membership. Distinctiveness and excellence in training of marriage and family therapists and those desiring to advance their skills, knowledge, and expertise in systemic and relational therapies. Responsiveness and excellence in service to members. Diversity, equity and excellence in clinical practice,

> research, education, and administration. Integrity evidenced by a high threshold of ethical and honest behavior within Association governance and by members. Innovation and the advancement of knowledge of systemic and relational therapies.
>
> (AAMFT Code, 2015a, p. 1)

In this edition of the Code, the nine ethical standards are designated as rules of practice for which couple and family therapists are obliged to follow and be judged. Introductory paragraphs provide an aspirational/explanatory orientation for each standard.

IAMFC 2017 Ethics Code

This Code became effective on January 1, 2017. Because IAMFC is a division of the American Counseling Association (ACA), the guidelines presented in the IAMFC Ethical Code were developed to supplement the current ethical standards of ACA (IAMFC, 2017, 2018). The Preamble to the IAMFC Code indicates that IAMFC members are dedicated to advocating for their clients, the counseling profession, and the professionalism of counselors. The Preamble also notes that IAMFC members "commit themselves to enhancing family relationships and advocate for the healthy development of families while also considering the uniqueness of individuals within family systems" (IAMFC Ethics Code, 2015a, p. 1). The Code specifies guidelines for the practice of couple and family counseling. It is divided into ten sections which are identified in Table 11.1.

This table provides a brief comparison of the standard or sections of these two codes. Links to these and other ethics codes are available in the Appendix to this book.

Prevalence of Ethical Breaches

Often, beginning clinicians and the denizens of Perspective I risk management use sanctions by governing boards and professional associations to justify a restrictive (and possibly unethical) approach to ethics because of an unwarranted fear of prosecution and sanction. We hope this information is helpful in providing some much-needed context to the debate.

There are three types of complaints: Legal (malpractice), regulatory, and ethical (Woody, 2000). According to Woody, it is impossible to obtain precise numbers of legal complaints, since many cases are settled out of court or are in protracted litigation and are not reported anywhere. However, Peterson (1996) asserts that malpractice suits are on the rise. Likewise, the occurrence of complaints about therapists' unethical behavior brought before state licensing boards is increasing.

The AAMFT, like many other professional associations, maintains a committee on ethics and professional practices. Operating under the AAMFT

Table 11.1 Side-by-Side Comparison of AAMFT and IAMFC Ethics Codes

AAMFT 2015 Code of Ethics	*IAMFC 2017 Ethics Code*
Preamble	*Preamble*
I Responsibility to Clients	A The Counseling Relationship & Client Welfare
II Confidentiality	B Confidentiality & Privacy
III Professional Competence & Integrity	C Competence & Professional Responsibilities
IV Responsibility to Students & Supervisees	D Collaboration & Professional Relationships
V Research & Publication	E Assessment & Evaluation
VI Technology-assisted Professional Services	F Counselor Education & Supervision
VII Professional Evaluations	G Research and Publication
VIII Financial Arrangements	H Ethical Decision-Making and Resolution
IX Advertisings	I Technology Assisted Couples & Family Counseling
	J Diversity & Advocacy

Source: IAMFC (2017, 2018); AAMFT (2015a).

bylaws, the ethics committee interprets the code of ethical principles, considers allegations of violations of this code made against AAMFT members, and, if judicial counsel hears the case, adjudicates the charges against the member (AAMFT, 2015b).

In a report of the AAMFT Ethics Committee of ethical violations, a total of 1,120 ethics cases have been reported in the last 50 years (AAMFT, 2001). The committee reported that they receive approximately 50–60 complaints each year, referred by a state licensure board, a fellow member or practitioner, or a client. The most frequent part of the ethics code violated by members included the aspects of the code that were related to dual/multiple relationships. This accounted for 40% of the cases reported. In addition, of this group, 65% involved sexual attraction or sexually inappropriate behavior. The second largest group of violations (13%) was for issues related to competency and impairment of the therapist. Many of these issues dealt with operating outside of one's area of training or expertise or where personal deficiencies weaken one's ability to practice ethically or professionally. Nine percent of cases were related to disciplinary actions by state regulation boards (a violation of AAMFT ethics), and 6% were due to violations of confidentiality, advertising, and termination (Principle 1). The remaining 20% of categories include being convicted of a felony or misdemeanor, noncompliance with the ethics committee (refusing to comply with an investigation), and financial impropriety. Each of these categories represented 5% or less of the overall cases reported. Clearly, however, therapists have the greatest problem dealing with the boundary between professional and personal relationships (sexual or otherwise). This is an area where further training must be targeted.

Given the aforementioned percentages, a therapist might feel discouraged about the occurrence of ethics violations. However, once these issues were identified, what were the results of the investigation? Most of the cases that are identified to the Ethics Committee are not followed up with the necessary waivers of confidentiality (approximately 65%), and the case must be closed. Hence, only 49% of initiated complaints proceed to the Ethics Committee. According to AAMFT (2001), from 1990 to 2001, only 281 cases were adjudicated, and of these, 17% resulted in termination from membership (the ultimate sanction under the AAMFT Ethics Committee). Over half of the cases (52%) resulted in no action being taken because either the charge was dismissed, the charge was investigated and found to have no merit, or the violation was so minor that no disciplinary action was warranted. Twenty-seven percent of the cases are found to have ethics violations and require some rehabilitative action for the therapist. Often, this includes personal therapy, temporary suspension of practice, or practicing under continuing supervision.

Making Ethical Decisions

What the findings of the study by AAMFT's Ethics Committee seem to indicate is that the remedy for helping therapists who violate the codes is to focus on the therapist's ethical decision-making process. It is crucial for avoiding sanctions and, more importantly, the truly ethical, professional practice of couple therapy. The ethical codes are the profession's mechanism for policing itself and providing guidance in these difficult matters. Often, however, the situations that therapists face require some interpretation of the ethical codes, which can be ambiguous and inconsistent for the providers who must wrestle with complex situations (Corey et al., 2014; Haber, 1996; Kitchener, 1986). This struggle is often due to the emotional reaction of the therapist, which often clouds his or her ability to understand the event and the issues surrounding it. Indeed, it has been noted that

> ethical issues arise when existing guidelines do not provide direction … When faced with ethical dilemmas or new issues, counselors must be able to critically evaluate and interpret the relevant codes, as well as evaluate their feelings as appropriate or inappropriate bases for ethical behavior.
>
> (Kitchener, 1986, p. 306)

From the relational ethics perspective, we feel that understanding, addressing, and incorporating the therapist's emotional and intellectual perspectives denote the hallmark of Perspective III ethics (Peluso, 2007).

One of the most difficult aspects of being a therapist is understanding and acting in accordance with the ethical codes (Robson, Cook, Hunt, Alred, & Robson, 2000). Attempts to synthesize the process of making ethical decisions have traditionally been divided into two categories, one that focuses on a step-by-step approach to resolving dilemmas, while others look at broader moral or ethical issues involved in the process (Corey et al., 2014). Kitchener (1984) proposed a model that includes both aspects of the ethical decision-making process. Her model contains two levels of ethical decision-making: The intuitive and the critical-evaluative levels of ethical justification. The intuitive level consists of an individual's personal moral beliefs as well as the immediate facts of the situation, while the critical-evaluative level is based on the specific ethical codes and larger principles of ethics: Beneficence, non-malfeasance, justice, autonomy, and fidelity (Haber, 1996; Kitchener, 1984). Kitchener's model of ethical decision-making has been adapted for use in clinical, medical, and research contexts, and is considered one of the more comprehensive and versatile models (Haber, 1996; Robson et al., 2000).

According to Kitchener (1986), the intuitive level consists of immediate feelings and reactions to the situation as well as personal ethical beliefs. This intuitive level is further described by Robson et al. (2000) as a "pre-reflective response to an ethical dilemma, which is informed by the set of knowledge, beliefs and assumptions that individuals carry with them" (p. 542). Thus, the intuitive level is where therapists make a decision to proceed further in determining whether additional action is needed (Haber, 1996). However, many practitioners focus solely on the critical-evaluative level of ethical decision-making and not enough on the intuitive level:

> Decision making is based not only on the facts of the decision-making but also on our feelings surrounding the facts and upon the values we hold that shape those feelings. All too often, our emotional, value-driven responses to decision-making are undervalued and we "rationalise" [*sic*] our intuitive process—post factum.
>
> (Robson et al., 2000, p. 534)

Yet, to be unaware of or ignore the influence of these initial gut feelings or intuitions can lead to either underreaction or overreaction by therapists, which can lead to ethical problems (Peluso, 2007; Robson et al., 2000).

Family therapists have claimed that these emotion-level responses are formed, in part, by the influences of the individual's family of origin (Aponte, 1994; Haber, 1996; Minuchin, 1974; Peluso, 2003). According to Aponte (1994), therapists – particularly those in training – should seek to understand their own families of origin as a matter of sound, ethical practice. At present, practitioners or educators have not paid enough attention to this level of ethical decision-making. However, to better understand one's basic philosophical assumptions and intuitive reactions to ethical dilemmas, an exploration of the family-of-origin dynamics that may have influenced them seems to make sense (Peluso, 2003).

Peluso and his associates (Bilot & Peluso, 2009; Peluso, 2003, 2006) developed an extension of the genogram for understanding the influence of family-of-origin dynamics on present-day ethical decision-making styles. The *ethical genogram* is created in the same way as a regular genogram. Once the family of origin is drawn, and the relationship between the supervisee and her family members is established, additional questions related to overall ethical decision-making styles that were present in parents, siblings, and others can be discussed (for a full review of the procedure, please see Peluso, 2003, 2006).

In working through this process, a picture should begin to emerge that can indicate what types of ethical dilemmas might be difficult for the supervisee or therapist to recognize. Additionally, working through the ethical genogram can help determine whether a supervisee may have difficulty with gray areas vs. black-and-white ethical decisions. When these underlying family-of-origin dynamics are uncovered, the therapist or supervisee can appreciate the context for, and the impact of, these forces on the initial appraisal of ethical decisions. Because of the exercise, some therapists may discover the source of strengths or influences that they have never realized. Others may come to an understanding of how a particularly negative pattern resulting from unresolved conflicts within the family of origin might impact ethical decision-making. Therapists can process any insights that may arise or develop strategies to make better ethical decisions when certain potentially problematic conditions arise (Bilot & Peluso, 2009; Peluso, 2003, 2006).

Ethical Decisions and Evidence-Based Practice

Practicing therapy with couples creates unique ethical considerations. These include difficulties in identifying treatment goals in the face of partners' conflicting desires, deciding when to discuss information obtained in private from one partner, and managing risk in order to maintain partner safety. Therapists can minimize these ethical dilemmas by clearly articulating their policies when obtaining consent and over the course of treatment (Margolin et al., 2015). They would do well to also base treatment decisions on evidence, client need, and ethics.

In the not so distant past, it was common for therapists to make treatment decisions based on their espoused orientation and experience rather than on evidence that the treatment provided would be safe, effective, and ethical. That began to change in the early 1990s with the appearance of evidence-based practice. As originally described, evidence-based practice is a process of inquiry whose purpose is to help therapists and their clients make important decisions about treatment. It is a process, in which therapists decide which interventions to provide by considering research evidence, their clinical experience and expertise, client preferences and values, professional ethics, situational circumstances, and the availability of resources (Gambrill, 2011; Sackett, Richardson, Rosenberg, Haynes, & Brian, 1997).

Two kinds of evidence can be delineated: *External evidence*, which is quality empirical research, and *internal evidence* or clinical expertise, which involves gathering information from the client or couple and then tailoring the external evidence to a specific client or couple. In other words, it is "the ethical responsibility of all clinicians regardless of orientation to be guided by current empirical research as well as their own specific areas of competence, experience, and limitations when making treatment recommendations" (Sookman, 2015, p. 1295).

Recall from the descriptions of the various couple therapy approaches in Chapters 4–8 that only a small number of these approaches report empirical support. One practical implication we suggested was that many of these approaches would likely lose eligibility for third-party reimbursement, given the increasing demand for utilizing evidence-based interventions. Another implication is that only a few of these approaches would provide sufficient external evidence to warrant being incorporated in clinical decision-making.

The key premise in developing evidence-based practice was to design a decision-making tool to support clinicians in promoting the well-being of their clients and avoiding harm, malpractice, and unethical practice in the process. It is important to note that this premise reflects and supports the first principle in the ethics code of the ACA: "The primary responsibility of counselors is to respect the dignity and promote the welfare of clients" (American Counseling Association, 2014, p. 2).

Ethical Instruction and Supervision in Couple Therapy

The history of couple and family therapy reveals a strong anti-empirical research bias. Despite this,

> a new generation of family therapy students is emerging that is thirsty for scientifically informed strategies. In almost every class we teach, students are asking the question 'What does the research say about that treatment approach or intervention approach in addressing problem X?' Their assumption is that there should be research to support what we do.
>
> (Williams, Patterson, & Edwards, 2014, p. 206)

So what does this all mean for instructors and supervisors who train couple therapists? According to Gambrill (2011):

> Evidence-based practice as viewed by its originators is as much about the ethical obligations of educators and researchers to be honest brokers of knowledge and ignorance as it is about the obligations of practitioners and administrators to honor their professional codes of ethics, for example, to integrate practice and research and honor informed consent obligations. Ethical obligations emphasized in original sources include the obligation to help clients and avoid harming them and the obligation to involve them as informed participants.
>
> (p. 33)

Presumably, it means that instructors and supervisors, irrespective of their preferred orientation, will assist students or supervisees in assessing client needs and values, reviewing pertinent empirical research, and tailoring treatment in light of these factors as well as their current level of expertise. Basically, "educators are encouraged to help students use EBP principles when students are searching for ways to help their clients. Students will be most motivated to learn EBP when the EBP skills help them with their own clients" (Williams et al., 2014, p. 236). In doing so, instructors and supervisors serve as role models of effective and ethical clinical practice.

Concluding Note

This chapter introduced some of the most common ethical issues that couple therapists face. In addition, we have attempted to introduce a less punitive and more relational perspective on ethics, which views ethics as a means of fostering connections with a couple rather than put up barriers to them. We presented the ethics codes of the major organizations for couple therapists (IAMFC and AAMFT), some statistics on the prevalence of ethical violations, and a discussion about the process of making ethical decisions. Finally, we reviewed ethical decision-making in terms of evidence-based practice and some implications for instructors and supervisors who train couple therapists. Essentially, we endorsed a perspective of ethics whereby the sound practice of ethics by a couple therapist is as entwined with sound practice of couple therapy as the twin strands of DNA.

References

American Association of Marriage and Family Therapy. (2001, June/July). Do all ethics complaints end in termination of membership? *Family Therapy News,* 8–9.

American Association for Marriage and Family Therapy. (2015a). *Code of ethics.* Retrieved from http://www.aamft.org/iMIS15/AAMFT/Content/Legal_Ethics/Code_of_Ethics.aspx

American Association of Marriage and Family Therapy. (2015b). *AAMFT procedure for handling ethical matters.* Author. Retrieved from http://dx5br1z4f6n0k.cloudfront.net/imis15/Documents/Legal%20Ethics/AAMFT-Ethics-Procedures.pdf

American Counseling Association. (2014). *ACA code of ethics.* Alexandria, VA: Author.

Aponte, H. J. (1994). How personal can training get? *Journal of Marital and Family Therapy, 20*(1), 3–15.

Bilot, J., & Peluso P. R. (2009). The use of the ethical genogram in supervision. *The Family Journal: Counseling and Therapy for Couples and Families, 17*(2), 175–179.

Blumer, M. L., Hertlein, K. M., Smith, J. M., & Allen, H. (2014). How many bytes does it take? A content analysis of cyber issues in couple and family therapy journals. *Journal of Marital and Family Therapy, 40(*1), 34–48.

Caldwell, B. (2016). *User's guide to the 2015 AAMFT Code of Ethics.* Create Space Independent Publishing Platform.

Coale, H. W. (1998). *The vulnerable therapist: Practicing psychotherapy in an age of anxiety.* New York, NY: Hawthorne Press.

Corey, G., Corey, M., Corey, C., & Callanan, P. (2014). *Issues and ethics in the helping professions* (9th ed.). Belmont, CA: Brooks Cole.

Fulmer, R. (2018). Counseling with artificial intelligence. *Counseling Today*. (January). Retrieved from http://ct.counseling.org/tag/technology/

Hertlein, K. M., Blumer, M. L., & Mihaloliakos, J. H. (2015). Marriage and family counselors' perceived ethical issues related to online therapy. *The Family Journal: Counseling and Therapy for Families and Couples, 23*(1), 5–12.

Hertlein, K. M., Blumer, M. L., & Smith, J. M. (2014). Marriage and family therapists' use and comfort with online communication with clients. *Contemporary Family Therapy, 36*(1), 58–69.

Haber, R. (1996). *Dimensions of psychotherapy and supervision: Maps and means*. New York, NY: W. W. Norton.

International Association of Marriage and Family Counselors. (2017). *IAMFC Code of Ethics*. Alexandria, VA. Author.

International Association of Marriage and Family Counselors. (2018). International association of marriage and family counselors ethics code. *The Family Journal, 26*(1), 5–10.

Kitchener, K. S. (1984). Intuition, critical-evaluation and ethical principles: The foundation for ethical decision in counseling psychology. *Counseling Psychologist, 12*(3), 43–55.

Kitchener, K. S. (1986). Teaching applied ethics in counselor education: An integration of psychological processes and philosophical analysis. *Journal of Counseling and Development, 64*(1), 306–310.

Kleist, D., & Bitter, J. R. (2014). Virtue, ethics, and legality in family practice. In J. Bitter (Ed.), *Theory and practice of family therapy and counseling* (2nd ed., pp. 71–94). Belmont, CA: Brooks/Cole.

Lazarus, A. A. (2002). Psychologists, licensing boards, ethics committees and dehumanizing attitudes: With special reference to dual relationships. In A. A. Lazarus & O. Zur (Eds.), *Dual relationships and psychotherapy* (pp. 239–248). New York, NY: Springer.

Leslie, R. S. (2002). Practicing therapy via the internet: The legal view. *Family Therapy Magazine, 1*(5), 39–41.

Margolin, G. (1998). Ethical issues in marital therapy. In R. M. Anderson, T. L. Needels, & H. V. Hall (Eds.), *Avoiding ethical misconduct in psychology specialty areas* (pp. 78–94). Springfield, IL: Charles C. Thomas Publishers.

Margolin, G., Shapiro, L. S., & Miller, K. (2015). Ethics in couple and family psychotherapy. In J. Sadler, B. Fulford, & C. Van Staden, (Eds.), *Oxford handbook of psychiatric ethics* (Vol. 2., pp. 1306–1314). New York, NY: Oxford University Press.

Minuchin, S. (1974). *Families and family therapy*. Cambridge, MA: Harvard University Press.

Peluso, P. R. (2003). The ethical genogram: A tool for helping therapists understand their ethical decision-making styles. *The Family Journal: Counseling and Therapy for Families and Couples, 14*(3), 286–291.

Peluso P. R. (2006). Expanding the use of the ethical genogram: Incorporating the ethical principles to help clarify counselors ethical decision making styles. *The Family Journal: Counseling and Therapy for Couples and Families, 14*(2), 158–163.

Peluso, P. R. (2007). The professional and ethical practice of couples and family counseling. In L. Sperry (Ed.), *The professional and ethical practice of counseling and psychotherapy* (pp. 285–351). Boston, MA: Allyn & Bacon.

Peluso, P. R. (2018). *A systemic guide for counselors to understand and work with couples recovering from infidelity*. New York, NY: Routledge.

Peterson, C. (1996). Common problem areas and their causes resulting in disciplinary actions. In L. Bass, S. DeMers, J. Ogloff, C. Peterson, J. Pettifor, R. Reaves … R.

Tipton (Eds.), *Professional conduct and discipline in psychology* (pp. 79–81). Washington, DC: American Psychological Association.

Pope, K. S., & Vasquez, M. J. T. (1998). *Ethics in psychotherapy and counseling: A practical guide* (2nd ed.). San Francisco, CA: Jossey-Bass.

Robson, M., Cook, P., Hunt, K., Alred, G., & Robson, D. (2000). Toward ethical decision making in counseling research. *British Journal of Guidance and Counseling, 28*(4), 532–547.

Sackett, D., Richardson, W., Rosenberg, W., & Haynes, R., & Brian, S. (1996). Evidence based medicine: What it is and what it isn't. *British Medical Journal, 312*, 71–72.

Shallcross, L. (2011). Finding technology's role in the counseling relationship. *Counseling Today*. (October). Retrieved from http://ct.counseling.org/2011/10/finding-technologys-role-in-the-counseling-relationship/

Snyder, D. K., & Doss, B. D. (2005). Treating infidelity: Clinical and ethical directions. *Journal of clinical psychology, 61*(11), 1453–1465.

Sookman, D. (2015). Ethical practice of cognitive behavior therapy. In J. Sadler, B. Fulford, & C. Van Staden (Eds.), *Oxford handbook of psychiatric ethics* (Vol. 2., pp. 1293–1305). New York, NY: Oxford University Press.

Sperry, L. (2007a). The professional and ethical practice of couples and family therapy: An overview. In L. Sperry (Ed.), *The professional and ethical practice of counseling and psychotherapy* (pp. 3–19). Boston, MA: Allyn & Bacon.

Sperry, L. (2007b). *Dictionary of ethical and legal terms and issues: The essential guide for mental health professionals*. New York, NY: Routledge.

Wilcoxon, A., Remley, T., & Gladding, S. (2013). *Ethical, legal, and professional issues in the practice of marriage and family therapy* (5th ed.). Upper Saddle River, NJ: Pearson.

Williams, L., Patterson, J., & Edwards, T. M. (2014). *Clinician's guide to research methods in family therapy: Foundations of evidence-based practice*. New York, NY: Guilford.

Woody, R. H. (2000). Professional ethics, regulatory licensing and malpractice complaints. In F. W. Kaslow (Ed.), *Handbook of couple and family forensics: A sourcebook for mental health and legal professionals* (pp. 461–474). New York, NY: John Wiley & Sons.

Zur, O. (2002). The truth about the codes of ethics: Dispelling rumors that dual relationships are unethical. In A. A. Lazarus & O. Zur (Eds.), *Dual relationships and psychotherapy* (pp. 55–63). New York, NY: Springer.

Zur, O. (2005). The dumbing down of psychology: Faulty beliefs about boundary crossings and dual relationships. In R. Wright, & N. Cummings (Eds.) *Destructive trends in mental health: The well-intentioned path to harm* (pp. 253–282). New York, NY: Routledge.

Zur, O. (2011). *Dual relationships, multiple relationships & boundaries in psychotherapy, counseling & mental health*. Retrieved from http://www.zurinstitute.com/dualrelationships.html.

12 Substance Abuse and Intimate Partner Violence

LEARNING OBJECTIVES

In this chapter, the reader will learn the following:

1 Specific treatment issues related to couples and substance abuse.
2 The efficacy of couple therapy in treating substance abuse.
3 An understanding of the underlying dynamics of domestic violence and its impact on relationships.
4 The differential treatment options for couples in abusive relationships.

While every couple is unique in their development and their stories, couple therapists are confronted with several common problems and issues. In the next two chapters, we will highlight a few of these topics. In this chapter, we present two common and perhaps most challenging areas in treating couples: Substance abuse and domestic violence.

Alcohol and Substance Abuse

According to the National Institute on Drug Abuse, it is estimated that over 26 million Americans engage in illicit drug use every month. In addition, the lifetime prevalence of alcohol use disorder (SUD) ranges from 17.5% for men to 8.0% for women (Schumm, O'Farrell, Kahler, Murphy, & Muchowski, 2014). The cost of drug abuse, alcohol abuse, and tobacco use combined is estimated at over $700 billion annually in costs related to lost productivity, criminal activity, and medical care. This cost is on par with costs associated with obesity and cancer, according to the Centers for Disease Control and Prevention (CDC, 2011). However, the cost to couples and families can be even greater as partners and children often bear the burden of dealing with the negative behaviors associated with substance abuse, or cope with the health and other consequences that result from it. Couples in which there is substance use generally have lower levels of relationship satisfaction, poorer interpersonal communication skills, and sexual dysfunction and dissatisfaction (Klosterman & O'Farrell, 2017; McCrady & Epstein, 2015; O'Farrell, Schumm, Dunlap, Murphy, & Muchowski, 2016). In this section, we will discuss some of the diagnostic, assessment, and treatment issues related to the treatment of substance abuse in couple therapy.

Table 12.1 DSM-5 Diagnostic Criteria for Substance Use Disorder

1	Taking the substance in larger amounts and for longer than intended
2	Wanting to cut down or quit but not being able to do it
3	Spending a lot of time obtaining the substance
4	Craving or a strong desire to use substances
5	Repeatedly unable to carry out major obligations at work, school, or home due to substance use
6	Continued use despite persistent or recurring social or interpersonal problems caused or made worse by substance use
7	Stopping or reducing important social, occupational, or recreational activities due to substance use
8	Recurrent use of substances in physically hazardous situations
9	Consistent use of substances despite acknowledgment of persistent or recurrent physical or psychological difficulties from using substances
10	Tolerance as defined by either a need for markedly increased amounts to achieve intoxication or desired effect or markedly diminished effect with continued use of the same amount. (Does not apply for diminished effect when used appropriately under medical supervision)
11	Withdrawal manifesting as either characteristic syndrome or the substance is used to avoid withdrawal (Does not apply when used appropriately under medical supervision)

Source: Diagnostic and Statistical Manual (APA, 2013).

Diagnostic Issues

In the most recent edition of the *Diagnostic and Statistical Manual of Mental Disorders* (*DSM-5*; American Psychiatric Association, 2013), there were significant changes in the "Substance Use and Addictive Disorders" section. In previous editions, there were delineations between *substance abuse* and *substance dependence*, but in DSM-5, these have been combined into one diagnosis: Substance use disorder. While the list is nearly identical to earlier versions of the DSM, now all substances are assessed using the same 11 criteria (see Table 12.1). However, in order to receive a diagnosis for a substance use disorder, only two out of 11 of the criteria must be met.

The criteria themselves are further broken down into four subcategories. Criteria 1–4 deal with impaired control due to substance use. Criteria 5–7 assess social impairment due to substance use, while Criteria 8 and 9 investigate risky use behaviors. Finally, Criteria 10 and 11 are pharmacological criteria that assess tolerance or withdrawal symptoms. In place of the separate abuse and disorder categories, DSM-5 includes a severity rating based on the number of criteria that are met. A mild substance use disorder is diagnosed if two to three criteria are met. If a client has met four to five criteria, then a moderate disorder is diagnosed. If an individual meets six or more criteria, then a severe substance use disorder is diagnosed.

Assessment

As indicated in Chapter 9, the purpose of assessment is to evaluate the immediate needs of the couple and get a complete biopsychosocial relational picture of the client. In addition to the diagnostic process outlined earlier, this includes a history and prevalence of any substance abuse. If a couple explicitly states that substance abuse is a presenting concern, or if the therapist suspects that it may be more of an issue than is being reported, the therapist will want to get more in-depth information. First, it is important to assess the severity of the substance abuse and determine the appropriate level of care (acute detox, inpatient, outpatient, couple therapy, group meetings, or some combination). Next, the therapist should assess the extent of the abuse and its consequences on the substance abuser (e.g. loss of job, arrests, decreased cognitive functioning).

It is also important to assess the impact of the substance abuse on the couple. This usually starts with a history of the substance abuse problem, whether it was before or after the relationship began. According to McCrady and Epstein (2015), conceptualizing a couple with a substance use disorder from a behavioral coupes approach incorporates three distinct areas: The *identified patient* perspective, the *significant other's* perspective, and the *overall couple functioning*. These are detailed in Table 12.2.

Additionally, the couple therapist may want to assess whether the partner was aware of drinking problems prior to the start of the relationship, and/or whether the substance abuse became problematic after the marriage. Did the non-abusing partner also engage in the behavior but stop at some point? Another aspect of the assessment is the abuse's effect on the couple – particularly, if the abuse is causing relational problems or distress or if the substance abuse is a way to avoid problems with the relationship. It is also helpful to assess the family history and to see the intergenerational patterns of substance

Table 12.2 Case Formulation of Couples with Substance Use Disorders

Questions for the Identified Partner (IP)

1 What is maintaining the IP's drinking* problem? To what degree do physical dependence, psychological issues, and interpersonal issues appear to maintain the drinking?
2 What are the IP's major triggers?
3 What positive consequences seem to be most important in maintain the drinking, and what negative consequences might serve as sources of motivation to change?

Questions for the Significant Other (SO)

1 How effectively is the SO coping with the drinking?
2 In what ways does the SO's behavior serve as a trigger for the drinking?
3 In what ways does the SO reinforce the drinking?
4 In what was does the SO create appropriate consequences for the drinking?

Questions About the Couple Functioning

1 How well are the members of the couple working collaboratively or against each other in coping with the drinking?
2 How is the couple functioning in general as a collaborating unit?
3 Is the overall quality of the relationship more positive or more negatively?
4 To what degree do the partners support each other?
5 What are specific strengths and deficits in their communication?

Source: McCrady & Epstein (2015).

* "Drinking" here implies substance use in general.

abuse. In addition, it is important to assess whether the couple has ever functioned without the presence of the problematic substance. It is likely that if the abuse is a recent problem, the appropriate relational patterns have already been established. Otherwise, a more educational approach will have to be utilized to teach the couple to function at a new skill level. It is also important to assess the current status of the marital relationship and its use of alcohol. Is it possible for the individual to stop on his or her own, or will it be necessary to provide support?

Couple therapists can access this information in a variety of ways, either through conjoint or individual interviews, physiological tests (blood tests, urine screens, breath analysis), or projective tests to assess the level and impact of substance abuse. In addition, the use of techniques, like the genogram, can quickly provide this information to the couple therapist. Once this process is complete, treatment decisions about the best course of action are shared with the couple. Many times, one or both partners will be resistant to the treatment decisions, deny there is a problem, and/or refuse to comply. In this instance, the motivational interviewing techniques (outlined in Chapter 10) are appropriate in order to provide objective information to the clients for the purpose of making a fully informed decision (Epstein & McCrady, 2002; McCrady & Epstein, 2015). According to a study by Kelly, Epstein, and McCrady (2004), only 29% of eligible callers to an outpatient substance abuse facility entered treatment. They also note that in couples in which one partner did not use, the abuser was more likely to enter treatment.

Treatment

When one or both partners engage in disordered drinking or other substance abuse, the relationship issues can either be a precipitating factor, or can be a perpetuating factor (Klosterman & O'Farrell, 2017; McCrady & Epstein, 2015; O'Farrell et al., 2016). However, there does not appear to be any one acceptable method to help the problem user arrive at a decision to stop using. Many authors feel that it is necessary to have the problem user "hit rock bottom" (i.e. to experience severe consequences if he or she continues to abuse substances) before treatment will be sought or accepted. Couple therapists who work with substance abusers need to develop their own answer to this question. Ultimately, the therapist's job is to help the couple return to a previous level of functioning. As a result, we feel that it is important to have the problem user stop all substance abuse, not just to moderate use in controlled amounts or abuse another substance instead of the primary drug of choice.

Currently, the most well-researched method for working with couples that have a substance abuse disorder is Behavioral Couple Therapy (BCT) or Cognitive Behavioral Couple Therapy (CBCT). As detailed in Chapter 5, most couples-based substance abuse treatment is grounded, in part, by Bandura's (1997) social learning theory and his concept of self-efficacy or the belief that a person has it in their power to accomplish some task or goal

(McCrady & Epstein, 2015). In addition, BCT is often heavily utilized in working with couples dealing with a substance use disorder (O'Farrel et al., 2016). McCrady and Epstein (2015) note that this approach conceptualizes the etiology of both the disordered drinking and the dysfunctional dyadic issues, which can be co-related or independent (i.e. due to personal reasons outside of the relationship) but share several assumptions:

1 External antecedents to drinking have a lawful relation to drinking through repeated parings with positive or negative reinforcement or through the anticipation of reinforcement.
2 Internal physiological, cognitive, and affective states mediate the association between external antecedents and drinking behavior.
3 Expectancies about the reinforcing value of alcohol play an important role in determining subsequent drinking behavior.
4 Drinking is maintained by its more immediate, positive consequences, and these consequences might occur at a physiological, individual, or interpersonal level.
5 Negative consequences of drinking tend to be delayed and therefore have less impact on drinking behavior (p. 558).

Systems therapists also know that once the decision to stop using has been reached, it is necessary to assist the nondrinking partner in not engaging in actions that maintain the problem drinking and in dealing with his or her codependent issues. Working with the couple in the conjoint fashion is the usual strategy employed (Klosterman & O'Farrell, 2017; McCrady & Epstein, 2015; O'Farrell et al., 2016). In BCT for substance abuse, there are four hypothesized mechanisms for behavior change: Identified patient (IP) motivation, identified patient coping skills, significant other (SO) support, and couple interactions. For the IP, "interventions should help the IP develop (1) a better ability to identify high-risk situations, (2) better coping skills to respond to these high-risk situations, and (3) a greater sense of self-efficacy in using these coping skills" (McCrady & Epstein, 2015, p. 572). For the SO, the interventions include:

> (1) identify his or her own behaviors that are cues for drinking, (2) develop better skills to cope with drinking related high risk situations, (3) develop better support the drinker's efforts at change and provide more frequent reinforcement of abstinence, and (4) provide less attention to drinking.
>
> (McCrady & Epstein, 2015, p. 572)

Finally, changes should impact the couple at the relationship level in "(1) a greater frequency of positive reactions, (2) greater reciprocity of positive interactions, (3) increased positive and supportive communication in the dyad, (4) decreased negative communication, and (5) better problem-solving skills"

(McCrady & Epstein, 2015, pp. 572–573). The longer-term goal is to help the couple to develop a new couple system with changed attitudes, values, and behaviors. According to Trepper, McCollum, Dankoski, Davis, and LaFazia (2000), "since relationship difficulties can reinforce drug abuse, it stands to reason that amelioration of such difficulties can reinforce sobriety" (p. 203). It is important to note that these changes are not made by the counselor. The control of substance abuse rests in the hands of the individual and his or her relational system (Klosterman & O'Farrell, 2017; McCrady & Epstein, 2015).

Nevertheless, a variety of formats may be needed in order to break up the impact of substance abuse on the relationship. The intervention strategies depend on the particular problem, as well as the stage of treatment. It is not unusual to see each partner separately in order to change the marital system by helping the non-using partner to be less enabling or the substance using partner to stop using. Therapists have a variety of additional therapeutic resources at their disposal, such as behavioral contracts. In addition, therapists have also found it useful to augment treatment with family therapy, couples group therapy, Alcoholics Anonymous, Narcotics Anonymous, Cocaine Anonymous, and Alanon, as well as inpatient and day hospital stays (O'Farrell et al., 2016). We have found it helpful in treating substance abuse problems to utilize these existing programs as an adjunct to treatment. In particular, we encourage individuals to work the 12-step program, in conjunction with the relationship issues.

Research Findings for Couple Therapy Treatment of Substance Abuse

In terms of the efficacy of couple therapy and substance abuse treatment, there are encouraging findings. Raytek, McCrady, Epstein, and Hirsch (1999) found that there was a link between conjoint therapy and substance abuse treatment. Specifically, they discovered that if couple therapists working with substance abusing clients were able to successfully maintain a therapeutic alliance with the couple, then treatment completion rates were better. They noted that these therapists

> were able to be more active with their clients, acknowledge and address issues the client initiated, and be very flexible in how they followed the manual guidelines. They were able to do this even if the couples raised very difficult issues such as ambivalence about abstinence, lack of trust of each other, physical violence, and sexual problems. The more experienced therapists were able to manage the negativism and hostility at those times in ways that continued to contribute to the building of the therapeutic alliance.
>
> (Raytek et al., 1999, p. 328)

Trepper et al. (2000) reported that treatment that included spouses or partners had retention rates nearly double the individually focused treatments.

They also reported that participation by the addict in treatment is also enhanced when the partner is involved, too. Epstein and McCrady (2002) reported that couples interventions that include behavioral methods aimed at "self-control training and skills training to facilitate abstinence, better coping by the nonalcoholic partner with drinking related situations, and communication techniques" (p. 597) are more successful in achieving treatment goals. In fact, Kuenzler and Beutler (2003) found that family systems-based couple therapy with a substance abusing partner not only benefited the impaired partner but also modified the substance use behavior of the other partner. They did not find the same results, however, when they utilized a cognitive behavioral treatment modality. The relational system can effectively change to accommodate this shift toward healthy behavior.

Schumm et al. (2014) conducted a Randomized Clinical Trial (RCT) comparing BCT to individual therapy for women with alcohol dependence. They found that participants who had the couples component had a higher percentage of days abstinent at the one-year follow-up period and fewer related problems as well. In addition, male counterparts reported greater levels of satisfaction as a result of going through the treatment with their female partners. O'Farrell et al. (2016) reported the results of their RCT conducted to investigate whether a BCT group therapy would have a better effect on couples dealing with substance abuse compared to BCT alone. The couples group condition did not show any benefits above what was observed with BCT. In fact, couples in the couples group condition had worse outcomes, whereas couples in the couple therapy-only condition maintained their gains up to one year posttreatment. While this was contrary to their original hypotheses, the results provided potential support for couple therapy as a superior format to substance abuse treatment than group counseling, though not the most economically beneficial for many treatment settings (O'Farrell et al., 2016). We present the following case to illustrate some of these points:

Tracy (28) and Jan (25) have been together for about four years. They met in a bar one night when they were introduced by mutual friends. They got "way drunk" and slept with each other that night and have been together ever since. Their dating life has been centered around partying and getting drunk every weekend and sometimes during the week as well. This pattern has caused some problems for them in the past. Two years ago, Jan lost an entry-level executive training job due to the number of days that she was absent from work because she was hung over, which has had a negative impact career-wise. Their friends are all "heavy partiers" and their social activities seem to revolve around alcohol consumption. This pattern has begun to exact a cost on Jan and Tracy's relationship.

Last year, Tracy's father died at a young age (59) from liver failure complicated by a lifetime of alcohol abuse. Jan was not much support for Tracy and did not even attend the funeral, saying, "I just don't do death well." This hurt Tracy deeply and caused some doubts about Jan's investment in the relationship. Tracy had been hoping for more of a commitment from Jan but hadn't broached the subject. Now, there was less certainty about the future. As a result, or perhaps as a test, Tracy began to stay home more and party less. At first, Tracy made excuses to not go out, claiming to be ill or working, but eventually, he began to question why they always had to drink when they did something together. Jan teased Tracy about getting old but was not willing to change the old pattern. Eventually, they began to argue more and became dissatisfied with the relationship.

Tracy felt that couple therapy was their last hope for the relationship. Jan expressed concerns that couple therapy was going to be unfair and judgmental and was clearly unwilling to make any changes. Recall from Chapter 11 the discussion of the Stages of Change model from Prochaska and DiClemente (1982). This couple was clearly not at the same stage in terms of their readiness for change. Tracy is most likely somewhere between the contemplation and preparing-for-action stages since he has realized that there is a problem and made some attempts to change, though not enough to constitute action (the phase where lasting change occurs). Jan, on the other hand, is more likely to be in the precontemplation stage, meaning that there is not much motivation to change since she does not feel that they have a problem.

This presents a dilemma for the counselor: Should he or she try to treat the couple together, treat Tracy alone for the substance abuse, or work with Jan on her reluctance to enter treatment? According to Prochaska and DiClemente (2002?), for clients who enter therapy in the precontemplation stage, if there is no movement toward the contemplation stage in the first three sessions, there is not much chance that the treatment will be successful. The therapist may try the motivational interviewing technique (Miller & Rollnick, 1991), which was also presented in Chapter 10. By using a combination of testing and questioning, the therapist may be able to get Jan to consider the possibility that there is a problem. In addition, it may help Tracy to make a more informed decision about the future of the relationship, the decision to seek help, or both. At that point, a decision about what kind of treatment would be appropriate (outpatient, inpatient, 12-step, etc.) can be made.

Intimate Partner Violence

Intimate Partner Violence (IPV) is one of the most devastating and pervasive problems confronting families and society in the 21st century. Simply put,

IPV is the physical, sexual, verbal, or emotional maltreatment of one family member or partner by another. The origins of IPV against women go back as far as recorded civilization and are rooted in patriarchal attitudes (Gelles & Cornell, 1985; Walker, 1979). Historically, in Western culture, wives were considered to be the property of their husbands. This classification was codified in Greek and Roman societies, in the definitions of citizenry, property holdings, and inheritance, which only recognized the rights of men under law. These attitudes also dictated that a husband was obligated to chastise his wife for misbehavior in any manner he saw fit, which often led to the beating, mutilation, and death of many women, with the approval of the society (Gelles & Cornell, 1985; Pagelow, 1984). The use of physical force to subdue wives was likewise legally sanctioned across a wide variety of cultures, including Russian, Central European, French, and British (Pagelow, 1984; Sonkin, Martin, & Walker, 1985). One such example of this was the "Rule of Thumb," which allowed a husband to hit his wife with a stick no larger than the width of his thumb. Moreover, women who were beaten by their husbands were not allowed to sue because, ironically, such a suit would destroy the peace of the home. Law enforcement officials and judges were often unwilling to pursue charges in these cases ("family squabbles"), even though the same crimes would be severely punished under law if they had been committed by someone outside the family (Walker, 1979).

Today, society's response to IPV is different. Many states have adopted family violence statutes, and the federal government adopted the Violence Against Women Act in the 1990s, which has toughened the stance taken against perpetrators of IPV. These changes have resulted in the mandating of some form of treatment for batterers and state prosecution – rather than victim prosecution – of family violence crimes. While laws have changed recently, attitudes about the treatment of women have responded more gradually (Peluso & Kern, 2002). Indeed, the issue of IPV provides unique challenges to couple therapists.

Prevalence of IPV

The impact of IPV is felt directly by approximately 16% of couples each year or about 8.7 million couples (Straus, 1999). In addition, over the entire course of a marriage, it is estimated that close to 25%–30% of couples will experience at least one episode of IPV (Horst, Stith, & Spencer, 2017). In general, violent couples are more likely to have pushed, grabbed, and shoved each other (24%); slapped or threw something at each other (18%); or kicked, bit, or tried to hit each other (approximately 10%). Between 2% and 5% of couples have either threatened to use or used a gun or knife on each other (Straus, Gelles, & Steinmetz, 1980). One of the more horrifying statistics related to IPV is that it accounts for almost 10% of all homicides in the U.S. (Epstein, Werlinich, & LaTaillade, 2015). Most often, the victims of IPV are women, and the perpetrators are men (Glick, Berman, Clarkin, & Rait,

2000; Holtzworth-Munroe, Meehan, Rehman, & Marshall, 2002; Horst et al., 2017). However, women are violent about as often as men in a family, although a great deal of their aggression is self-defensive or retaliatory (Epstein et al., 2015). According to Straus et al. (1980, 2003), when women are violent, they are more likely to throw something at their partner, kick or bite their partner, or try to hit their partner with something. When men are violent, they are more likely to push, grab, shove, slap, beat, and use a knife or gun against their partner. Conflict over children is the form of disagreement most likely to lead to physical violence.

Types of Violence

IPV is a complex phenomenon to study. Several researchers have noted that there are different types of violence, and while no amount of violence is appropriate or tolerable, understanding the different types can assist in appropriate treatment planning (Horst et al., 2017; Karakurt, Whiting, van Esch, Bolen, & Calabrese, 2016). There is agreement that there are two types of violence. The first is situational couple violence, which is characterized by

> less frequent and less severe forms of violence. Often this type of violence is bidirectional, meaning both partners are violent toward one another. Situational couple violence is typically the result of a stress response or emotional reaction rather than a calculated move by the perpetrator toward control or manipulation.
>
> (Horst et al., 2017, p. 454)

The second type of violence is more severe. Commonly referred to as "intimate terrorism" or characterological violence, it is characterized by "moderate to severe, chronic, highly injurious violence and male-to-female violence. The violence used in intimate terrorism is typically a means to exert power and control over a partner" (Horst et al., 2017, p. 454). Much of the available research and writing is centered around the more severe version (intimate terrorism), even though it does not occur as frequently as the more common situational violence (Horst et al., 2017; Karakurt et al., 2016). Clinicians and researchers maintain that these couples may be amenable to conjoint therapy, whereas the dangers to the victim associated with couples involved with the more severe physical violence are not (Armenti & Babcock, 2016; Epstein et al., 2015).

Cycles of Violence

Social learning theorists explain violence as a learned response to stress, which is reinforced by the reduction in stress following a battering incident. Gender roles are also a contributing factor, particularly as men are typically socialized from a very early age to inhibit their emotions and to act out physically instead of verbally (Bandura, 1973). Expanding upon this, in 1979,

Table 12.3 Cycle of Violence

1 *The tension-building phase.* This phase is marked by constant arguing or the escalation of conflict. It may last from days to years and frequently leads to a battering episode.
2 *The violent incident.* In this phase, some form of physical abuse takes place to relieve the tension. It often results in police intervention, the woman's voluntary departure from the home, or hospitalization.
3 *The conciliation or honeymoon phase.* In this phase, the battering partner is typically remorseful, contrite, and begging for forgiveness. He may buy the partner gifts and promise it will never happen again. Some may seek treatment at this point.

Source: Adapted from Walker (1979).

Lenore Walker published *The Battered Woman*, a seminal book that began to change the way that therapists thought about the occurrence and the consequences of IPV. Among Walker's breakthrough ideas was the concept of the cycle of violence (see Table 12.3). Walker observed that during the incidents of IPV, there appears to be a predictable cycle of violence with three phases that vary in length and intensity. The first, or tension-building, phase may be marked by constant arguing or the escalation of conflict. It may last from days to years and frequently leads to a battering episode. The second phase, the violent incident, often results in police intervention, the woman's voluntary departure from the home, or hospitalization. The final, or conciliation, phase finds the battering man typically remorseful, contrite, and begging for forgiveness. He may buy his partner gifts, promise her it will never happen again, and in some cases (but not many) may seek treatment on his own. This phase provides the glue that keeps the couple together, as both partners get a sense of the intimacy they crave and convince themselves that they have things under control. Sadly, as violent couples continue over time, especially with the more savage physical abuse, the honeymoon phase gets shorter in duration or disappears altogether, leaving just an alteration between the tension-building and violent-incident phases (Peluso & Kern, 2002).

Victims of IPV

The need to understand the root causes of IPV, and the treatment of the families affected by it, has been a source of serious investigation in the last two decades. Oftentimes, unfortunately, victims of IPV are portrayed as either meek and servile or shrewish and provocative. These generalizations are shortsighted and unfair. Rather, these individuals have often been abused as children, and many suffer low self-esteem and believe in the myth that they somehow create the beatings and are responsible for the batterer's actions. In addition, many battered women become so used to abuse that when the partner is not abusing them, they can become initially depressed and fear that the partner no longer cares for them. Abused women also tend to subscribe to traditional sex roles and values. Women in violent relationships are more likely to report symptoms of clinical depression and less marital satisfaction than women in nonviolent relationships (Holtzworth-Munroe et al., 2002) and tend to make more demands of their partners (Berns, Jacobson, & Gottman, 1999). However, Berns et al. (1999) explain it thusly:

> Although battered women also made more demands than did women in nonviolent marriages, it is reasonable to hypothesize that, for them, demanding behavior serves a different function. After all, they are being abused, both physically and emotionally, and one would expect them to want the abusive behavior to stop.
>
> (p. 672)

As a result, women in violent relationships are sometimes seen (fairly or not) as co-contributors to the violence. However, while the rates of violence between the sexes are considered to be relatively equal, Stets (1988) noted two important reasons for focusing on violence against women over violence against men. First, women typically use violence as a measure of self-defense against aggression from their spouses, rather than as a means of controlling the other person. Second, women are more likely to suffer physical damage from physical abuse than men. In addition, in light of Holtzworth-Munroe et al.'s (2002) description of the types of violence, it also seems that these women are more likely to be in the mild physical violence category.

Another factor that is generally present in the victims of IPV and abuse is prior (childhood) trauma. Susan Johnson (who developed the emotionally focused couple therapy (EFCT; see Chapter 8 for details on treatment) has recently written about the successful treatment of couples in which one partner has experienced trauma. According to Johnson (2002):

> Trauma intensifies the need for protective attachments and often, simultaneously destroys the ability to trust that is the basis of such attachments ... Trauma survivors are more likely to experience distress in their close relationships and to have fewer resources with this distress. Much of their energy is consumed in facing a world infused with danger and uncertainty. They are more likely to get stuck in the cycles of pursue-withdraw and criticize-defend that consume relationships and make separation so likely.
>
> (p. 10)

As a result, these individuals are more likely to end up in relationships that echo and compound these traumatic relationships, based on the client's *working model of self and others.* Recall from the discussion in Chapter 2 that the working model is the individual's schema or template for relating to the world and the people around them based on early attachment experiences (Fraley & Shaver, 2000; Johnson, 2002; Peluso, Peluso, White, & Kern, 2004). While they are usually adaptive (even if they are negative and based on insecure attachment relationships), these models become problematic if they are rigid and closed. As a result, the victims of IPV get trapped in their old response sets – whether they are hypervigilant, overly anxious about abandonment, or jealous – which set up negative cycles of couple interaction, like the cycle of violence. Therefore, couple therapists must not only "lessen the distress in a survivor's relationship, but to create the secure attachment that promotes active and optimal adaptation to a world that contains danger and terror, but is not necessarily defined by it" (Johnson, 2002, p. 10). This can be tricky when dealing with IPV, but in a couple that is sincerely motivated to do the work to stop their violence and address all of the contributing factors, the issues of trauma and attachment *must* be included.

Perpetrators of IPV

Jacobson and Gottman (1998) conducted one of the most comprehensive research studies on the assessment and categorization of batterers. They studied 63 couples that had engaged in battering, which was operationally defined as any aggression, physical or emotional, that had the purpose to control or intimidate a spouse through the use of fear or terror. In a laboratory setting, readings of each couple's heart rates, blood flows, and galvanic skin responses (sweating) were collected. In addition, videos of the couples discussing an area of continuing disagreement were made and synchronized with the physiological data. Their results revealed two distinct patterns of batterers: cobras and pit bulls.

When examining the videos and physiological data from the couples, Jacobson and Gottman (1998) found that approximately 20% of the men in their sample of batterers evidenced a pattern of physiological responses that showed a *decrease* in heart rates as they became verbally aggressive with their spouses during arguments. Externally, they appeared aggressive (e.g. tone of voice, actions, etc.), but internally, they became calm. Jacobson and Gottman also found that these individuals were more aggressive at the beginning of an argument, starting out defensive or belligerent: "They were so stirred up that you would probably pick them up as good candidates for a stroke or heart attack" (p. 29). However, they remained internally calm like a cobra, waiting to strike its victim in a swift attack. Dutton (1995) referred to these individuals, who become internally calmed and focused, as vagal reactors (referring to the vagus nerve that controls heart rate). In terms of their battering, these individuals were more likely to have used weapons (e.g. gun, knife, etc.) or to have threatened to do so. They were likely to be more severe in their use of violence and to instill a strong sense of fear and sadness in their spouse rather than anger, which is indicative of individuals in Holtzworth-Munroe et al.'s (2002) severe physical abuse category. They are seen as solitary characters, not seeming to need anyone, and also more likely to be violent or aggressive with others, not just their spouses (Jacobson & Gottman, 1998).

In contrast, batterers in the pit bull category had heart rates that increased as they became angry. Their level of anger seemed to increase slowly over time (described as a "slow burn"), eventually dominating and becoming more threatening until they attacked. They resembled pit bulls, becoming angry gradually but attacking with ferocity and not letting go. Emotionally, they are dependent and fear being abandoned. These individuals will accuse their wives of having affairs based on little or no evidence, which can lead to violently jealous rages if denied or not answered satisfactorily (Dutton, 1995). They frequently check on their wives, expect them to account for their every movement, or forbid them to be outside of the home (no jobs, friends, etc.) as a way of ensuring their fidelity (Jacobson & Gottman, 1998). However, the wives of pit bulls frequently fight back, and these relationships are more likely to be unstable and collapse as the wife finds it increasingly intolerable to live under these conditions, unless there is some outside intervention. These relationships seem to correspond to the mild physical violence category of Holtzworth-Munroe et al. (2002).

Additional research on batterers has found differences similar to that of Jacobson and Gottman (1998) between groups of batterers seeking treatment. Peluso and Kern (2002) found that batterers who drop out of treatment have different personality characteristics than clients who complete treatment. Specifically, the dropout group is more likely to be rebellious, unwilling to follow the rules, highly rigid, cautious, and untrusting of others. They speculated that individuals who completed treatment seemed to have personality styles that were more indicative of mild physical violence, which could be addressed in the context of a therapeutic setting rather than jail. This is especially salient as most participants in IPV treatment do so in order to avoid incarceration.

In addition to understanding the types of violence that can occur, clinicians are also confronted with questions as to the origins and purposes of violent behavior. Holtzworth-Munroe et al. (2002) reviewed the research on factors (i.e. age, socioeconomic status [SES], race and ethnicity, marital status, childhood influences, and head injury and neurophysiological deficits) that correlated with the background of violent men. Specifically, they found that men under 30 with low incomes, unemployed, or lower educational background were more likely to be violent. In terms of race and ethnicity, the findings are unclear and there is some evidence that race disappears as a factor when SES variables are controlled (Holtzworth-Munroe, Smutzler, & Sandin, 1997). Cohabitating couples seem to be at greater risk statistically than married couples as are individuals who were exposed to violence in the home growing up or had insecure parental attachments. Lastly, head trauma, particularly to the frontal lobes (which play a role in impulse control), seemed to have a strong relationship to an individual's tendency toward violence. While these elements cannot be targeted for treatment, they can inform the clinician as to what to look for in assessing the client's propensity for violence (Epstein et al., 2015; Horst et al., 2017). However, they also identified factors that may be amenable to treatment. These factors included deficits in social skills and social support, issues of power and gender, stressful life events, anger and hostility, attitudes, jealousy and attachment, alcohol use, and psychopathology. Straus et al. (1980, 2003) found that younger couples were the most violent and that spouse abuse was higher among lower-income families and in situations in which there was unemployment and economic stress (though not exclusively so), which seems to correlate with Holtzworth-Munroe et al.'s (2002) data.

Appropriateness of Conjoint Couple Therapy and IPV

The idea of conducting conjoint couple therapy when there is IPV remains a controversial subject. Many therapists will not see a couple together if there is violence because of their concern for the victim's safety due to reprisals for things said in sessions, a concern that the victim will not feel comfortable telling the truth about the extent of the violence, or a concern that responsibility for the violence will be displaced from the perpetrator to the couple (Holtzworth-Munroe et al., 2002). Traditionally, many therapists will not see couples who have engaged in violence for theoretical reasons, believing that issues of violence are bound up with issues of gender and power and must be dealt with in gender-specific groups (Dutton, 1995; Glick et al., 2000; Jacobson & Gottman, 1998). However, the evidence that batterers-intervention groups are successful in preventing future violent behavior has not been evidenced (Karakurt et al., 2016). In fact, systemic reviews of the literature find that these groups tend to have high dropout rates, and even help to normalize the use of violent behavior in a relationship (Armenti & Babcock, 2016; Horst et al., 2017; Karakurt et al., 2016).

Many couple therapists have begun to see conjoint therapy for couples that are violent as uniquely suited to address the couple's issues. Primarily, they see violence as the result of couples' interactions, which can only be halted if both partners make a concerted effort. These therapists believe that mild physical violence where both partners engage in violent behavior is most amenable to this approach. Conjoint therapy has an advantage over gender-specific therapy, which can pit treatment against treatment without solving the problem ("My group says that I don't have the problem, you do!"). Instead, the couple therapist can get a more balanced picture of the couple's dynamics and direct interventions to both partners, thus ensuring treatment compliance (Epstein et al., 2015; Holtzworth-Munroe et al., 2002; Horst et al., 2017; Pittman, 1990).

The decision to initiate couple therapy when IPV is an issue is best made after a thorough assessment of the severity of violence. The question of whom to treat and whom not to treat is difficult, and there are no empirically derived rules for when to refer to gender-specific groups. Holtzworth-Munroe et al. (2002) summarized the literature on making the decision to treat when violence is an issue thusly:

> Most authors agree that severity of violence and danger to the woman are important factors; they concur that conjoint treatment is only appropriate if levels of aggression are low to moderate and if the woman is not perceived to be in danger of imminent physical harm. Related to this, the woman must not fear the man, must feel comfortable in therapy with him, and must not feel so intimidated or dominated by him that she cannot be honest in therapy. In addition, both partners must be interested in staying in the relationship. A conjoint format is most suitable for partners who believe that physical aggression is a problem and are willing to work toward a nonviolent relationship; it is inappropriate if one partner does not acknowledge the existence or problematic nature of the violence, or is not willing to take steps to reduce it (e.g., removing weapons from the home, seeking drug/alcohol treatment, temporarily separating).
>
> (p. 453)

Armenti and Babcock (2016) put forth the following consideration for conducting couples counseling when there is the issue of IPV:

> Couples-based approaches are only suggested for couples with strong evidence of situational violence, or violence that is not largely motivated by a desire to control and dominate one's partner, with little risk of physical injury, where there are no substance or mental health issues that coupe compromise safety, where accountability for violence is taken without blaming one's partner, and where violence results from maladaptive responses to situational conflicts.
>
> (p. 119)

Lastly, in a meta-analysis of the existing empirical research on the use of couple therapy for IPV, Karakurt et al. (2016) found a moderate effect ($d = 0.84$) for couple therapy, concluding that "couple therapy is a slightly better treatment approach than standard treatment when working with violent couples" (p. 578). At the same time, the researchers caution that this is appropriate for couples with situational violence patterns, and not the characterological/"intimate terrorism" type of violence.

Conducting Conjoint Couple Therapy

Once the decision is made that couple therapy will be engaged, several initial steps must be taken. These include setting goals, setting the therapy contract, and clarifying the expectations about violence. Epstein et al. (2015) created a protocol for therapists to use in the context of CBCT (as outlined in Chapter 5). They describe several components that

> Focus on decreasing aggressive behaviors through psychoeducation about partner aggression and its consequences, as well as promotion of

> personal responsibility for behavior toward one's partner. Emotional regulation is fostered though training in anger management and stress reduction techniques. Reduction in aggressive behavior and increase in constructive couple conflict management are targeted with training in communication and problem solving skills; use of cognitive restructuring techniques to modify negative attributions and beliefs that foster psychological and physical abuse; strategies for relationship recovery from prior domestic abuse; and enhancement of positive couple interaction that both reduce risk for aggression and increase tach partner's satisfaction with the relationship.
>
> (pp. 399–400)

Meanwhile, Stith, Rosen, and McCollum (2003) reviewed the existing literature and treatment models, and recommend several core ingredients for any couples treatment for IPV (see Table 12.4). The primary message to communicate to the couple is the absolute need for any violent behavior (physical, emotional, verbal, or sexual) to end immediately. In addition, as a part of the therapeutic contract, both partners should acknowledge their responsibility for their violent actions. The therapist should facilitate the creation of safety plans for the couple and should also get a "no violence" contract from each of the partners with the consequences for violations clearly spelled out. At this point, two broad, immediate goals of therapy can be discussed: Managing the couple's anger and violent behavior, and increasing the couple's communication and problem-solving skills (Holtzworth-Munroe et al., 2002; Horst et al., 2017).

Once the treatment contract and goals are in place, the next phase of treatment is devoted to addressing and managing the couple's behaviors related to anger and the use of violence. Specifically, the therapist teaches the couple how to recognize the physiological, cognitive, emotional, and behavioral cues for their anger. Patterns to the couple's anger are identified, particularly the

Table 12.4 Common Core Ingredients of Successful Domestic Violence Treatment

- Clients are carefully screened into the program.
- Clients who have seriously injured their partners are excluded.
- Both clients (in separate interviews) must report that they want to participate in couples treatment and that they are not afraid to express their concerns to their partners.
- The primary focus of treatment is on eliminating all forms of partner abuse (physical, emotional, verbal), not on saving marriages.
- Most programs emphasize taking responsibility for one's own violence and include a skill-building component, including teaching skills such as recognizing when anger is escalating, de-escalating, and taking time-outs.
- Effectiveness in all the successful programs reviewed here is measured by reduction or elimination of violence.

Source: Adapted from: Stith et al. (2003).

typical events, words, or topics that trigger violent episodes. Finally, couples are taught time-out procedures and other anger-management techniques to be able to avoid destructive, violent acting-out behaviors.

The next goal deals with communication skills and problem-solving skills. These include nonverbal listening, verbal listening and paraphrasing, expressing feelings, problem-solving, problem defining, and problem solution. Proper communication and problem-solving skills provide the couple with new, constructive choices for relating to one another and resisting the need to use anger or violence against each other. These are all skills that will require the therapist to take a more active role in sessions demonstrating the techniques and evaluating the extent to which the couple understands and implements the new behaviors (Holtzworth-Munroe et al., 2002).

Once these initial goals have been met, it is appropriate to deal with more traditional couples issues that may have arisen or which the couple would like to address. However, the couple therapist must continue to monitor for violent episodes and provide support for the couple's nonviolent behavior choices. In terms of treatment benefit, Jacobson and Gottman (1998) have expressed doubts as to whether treatment is an option for cobras: "We doubt whether any of the current education and rehabilitation programs will ever rehabilitate Cobras. But it is entirely possible that a substantial number of Pit Bulls may benefit from an intervention" (p. 234). It seems, however, that for the majority of batterers, as well as for the majority of couples, treatment of violence in some form is possible and can often be successful (Peluso & Kern, 2002).

Sara (53) and Richard (54) have been married for 21 years. They have an older son (20), a daughter (18), and a younger son (17). Sara and Richard have been separated for the past six weeks following an incident that forced Richard to leave the house after being arrested and briefly incarcerated for simple battery (IPV). At present, there was an injunction against him coming to the house until both were evaluated for IPV treatment.

Richard was indignant at having to come to therapy and spent the first 15 minutes of the intake session complaining that the government has no right to interfere with his life or his family and that the lawyers, judges, and therapists were all in league with one another to make money off innocent people like him. During the initial phone call to the counseling center, the couple was instructed to bring a copy of the police report of the incident. This provides a less biased account of the event and is frequently helpful for focusing a couple on the task at hand. Richard was asked about the specifics of the report, and he began to comply. Sara remained quiet for the most part until questioned directly. The full scope and purpose of the three-session assessment period was explained to them, including the joint interview, separate interviews with each of them, and the feedback and recommendation session. It was also made clear that they may be recommended for group, individual, or couple therapy, or a combination of the treatment modalities.

The information gleaned in the intake interviews (both joint and individual) revealed a marriage plagued by verbal and emotional abuse. Richard frequently used verbal put-downs like "fat" and "dumb" and frequently referred to his wife in the individual interview as "that bitch." Sara responded that "his name-calling used to bother me so much, but now I look at him, fat, bald, and ugly, and think 'what a loser.' So, no, it doesn't really bug me anymore." The physical violence started approximately 13 years ago when Sara started to argue back rather than to "cower before him like a slave." The physical abuse started as shoving and restraining, which was "only on a couple of occasions." However, in the past three years, the fights have started to become more intense and frequent. At that time, Sara started to go back to school to finish her bachelor's degree (which she abandoned when the children were born). Frequently, she would not be at home at night when she was taking classes, and Richard would have to accommodate his schedule to hers or the children's. She said, "It was all a part of the bargain that I'd go back to school when the kids got to high school. The youngest one did, and I went back. He's just jealous that I actually did it and am now working, too!"

Although the police had been called to their house on several occasions, Sara never pressed charges, so nothing legally could be done. She even had to go to the hospital emergency room one time for a broken wrist after a fight with Richard where he knocked her to the ground and she braced herself with her hand, breaking her wrist. "He wouldn't even go to the hospital with me. I had to drive with a broken wrist!" However, a recent change to the law in their state now allows for "victimless prosecution" by law enforcement officials in the case of IPV. Therefore, when the police were called out for the last incident, they determined that Richard was the aggressor (although Sara admitted that she slapped him as well). As a result, he was brought to jail. When asked about what their intentions were, Sara expressed ambivalence about continuing the marriage. Richard stated that he just wanted to get back in his own home and "put all of this behind me."

It was clear that at this point, there was not a whole lot of motivation for this couple to work on the marriage. In fact, using the guidelines presented earlier, there was not enough of a commitment to ending the violence (of any kind) to warrant couple therapy first. Instead, a one-year treatment regimen was recommended, beginning with eight weekly individual sessions for Richard, followed by a males-only, 24-week batterers-intervention group that would overlap with the last four individual sessions. Then, upon successful completion of the men's group, the prospect of beginning couple therapy would be reevaluated. The goal of the individual sessions would be to begin to work on Richard's resistance to treatment and on the power and control issues underlying his violence. In addition, the sessions would help prepare him for group. The group treatment would continue to work on the power and control issues and have the added benefit of having other men involved and hearing their stories and struggles with their partners. Sara, meanwhile, would be recommended for both individual and group counseling, which would be timed to match Richard's treatment as well. This would give them the chance to decide, once the violence had been reduced in the relationship, if they were both ready to address their couples issues or if they even wanted to continue the marriage at all.

Substance Abuse and IPV

Given the focus of this chapter, we wish to briefly present the areas of overlap between these two issues. The preponderance of the evidence seems to indicate a strong relationship between substance abuse and IPV (Glick et al., 2000). According to a national survey, Kantor and Straus (1987) found that 31% of husbands who did not assault their wives admitted being drunk one or more times in the past year, compared to 50% of husbands who moderately assaulted their wives, and 70% of husbands who severely assaulted their wives. Among the victims of IPV, researchers found that only 16% of non-abused women reported being drunk one or more times, while 36% of the moderately assaulted women and 46% of the severely abused women surveyed admitted to episodes of substance abuse (Kantor & Straus, 1987). While causality for violence cannot be attributed solely to substance abuse, it is often a precipitating, contributing, or predisposing factor for an episode of violence for both the perpetrator and the victim (Glick et al., 2000). Finally, Schumm et al. (2014) found that couple therapy for substance abuse also provided significant benefit in reducing IPV for couples where this was an issue. As a result, couples counselors who encounter one of these issues will likely, though not always, encounter the other and should understand the complicated relationship between the two. In addition, depending on the severity of the violence or the substance abuse, couples counselors must be ready to actively intervene or refer to appropriate treatment for these issues.

Concluding Note

Working with couples experiencing substance abuse and IPV can be some of the most challenging and difficult therapy in the field. However, the prevalence and devastation of these problems make it essential that couple therapists have some knowledge of the dynamics and relevant treatment issues related to substance abuse and IPV. Next, we will continue to look at the treatment aspects of two additional common issues raised in couple therapy: Sexual dysfunction and infidelity.

References

American Psychiatric Association. (2013). *Diagnostic and statistical manual of mental disorders* (5th ed.). Washington, DC: American Psychiatric Association.

Armenti, N., & Babcock, J. C. (2016). Conjont treatment for intimate partner violence: A systematic review and implications. *Couple and Family Psychology: Research and Practice, 5*(2), 109–123. doi://10.1037/cfp0000060

Bandura, A. (1973). *A social learning analysis.* Englewood Cliffs, NJ: Prentice-Hall.

Bandura, A. (1997). *Self-efficacy.* Englewood Cliffs, NJ: Prentice-Hall.

Berns, S. B., Jacobson, N. S., & Gottman, J. M. (1999). Demand-withdraw interaction in couples with a violent husband. *Journal of Consulting and Clinical Psychology, 67*(5), 666–674.

Centers for Disease Control and Prevention. (2011). *Alcohol use and your health.* Retrieved from http://www.cdc.gov/alcohol/fact-sheets/alcohol-use.htm

Dutton, D. (1995). *The batterer.* New York, NY: Basic Books.

Epstein, E. E., & McCrady, B. S. (2002). Couple therapy in the treatment of alcohol problems. In A. S. Gurman & N. S. Jacobson (Eds.), *Clinical handbook of couple therapy* (3rd ed., pp. 597–628). New York, NY: Guilford.

Epstein, N. B., Werlinich, C. A., & LaTaillade, J. J. (2015). Couple therapy for partner aggression. In A. S. Gurman, J. Lebow, & D. Snyder (Eds.), *Clinical handbook of couple therapy* (5th ed., pp. 389–411). New York, NY: Guilford.

Fraley, R. C., & Shaver P. R. (2000). Adult romantic attachment: Theoretical developments, emerging controversies, and unanswered questions. *Review of General Psychology, 4*(2), 132–154.

Gelles, R., & Cornell, C. (1985). *Intimate violence in families.* Beverly Hills, CA: Sage Publications.

Glick, I. D., Berman, E.M., Clarkin, J. F., & Rait, D.S. (2000). *Marital and family therapy* (4th ed.). Washington, DC: American Psychiatric Press.

Holtzworth-Munroe, A., Meehan, J. C., Rehman, U., & Marshall, A. D. (2002). Intimate partner violence: An introduction for couple therapists. In A. S. Gurman & N. S. Jacobson (Eds.), *Clinical handbook of couple therapy* (3rd ed., pp. 597–628). New York, NY: Guilford.

Holtzworth-Munroe, A., Smutzler, N., & Sandin, E. (1997). A brief review of the research on husband violence: Part II. The psychological effects of husband violence on battered women and their children. *Aggression and Violent Behavior, 2*, 179–213.

Horst, K., Stith, S., & Spencer, C. (2017). Intimate partner violence. In J. Fitzgerald (Ed.), *Foundations for couple therapy: Research for the real world* (pp. 453–463). New York, NY: Routledge.

Jacobson, N. S., &. Gottman, J. M. (1998). *When men batter women.* New York, NY: Simon and Schuster.

Johnson, S. M. (2002). *Emotionally focused couple therapy with trauma survivors: Strengthening attachment bonds.* New York, NY: Guilford Press.

Kantor, G. K., & Straus, M. A. (1987). The "drunken bum" theory of wife beating. *Social Problems, 34*(3), 213–230.

Karakurt, G., Whiting, K., van Esch, C., Bolen, S. D., & Calabrese, J. R. (2016). Couple therapy for intimate partner violence: A systematic review and meta analysis. *Journal of Marital and Family Therapy, 42*(4), 567–583. doi:10.1111/jmft.12178

Kelly, S., Epstein, E. E., & McCrady, B. S. (2004). Pretreatment attrition from couple therapy for male drug users. *The American Journal of Drug and Alcohol Abuse, 30*(1), 1–19.

Klosterman, K., & O'Farrell, T. (2017). Couple therapy in the treatment of substance use disorders. In J. Fitzgerald (Ed.), *Foundations for couple therapy: Research for the real world* (pp. 404–414). New York, NY: Routledge.

Kuenzler, A., & Beutler, L. E. (2003). Couple alcohol treatment benefits patients' partners. *Journal of Clinical Psychology, 59*(7), 791–806.

McCrady, B. S., & Epstein, E. E. (2015). Couple therapy and alcohol problems. In A. S. Gurman, J. Lebow, & D. Snyder (Eds.), *Clinical handbook of couple therapy* (5th ed., pp. 555–584). New York, NY: Guilford.

Miller, W. R., & Rollnick, S. (Eds.). (1991). *Motivational interviewing: Preparing people for change.* New York, NY: Guilford.

O'Farrell, T. J., Schumm, J. A., Dunlap, L. J., Murphy, M. M., & Muchowski, P. (2016). A randomized clinical trial of group versus standard behavioral couple therapy plus individually based treatment for patients with alcohol dependence. *Journal of Consulting and Clinical Psychology, 84*(6), 497–510. doi:10.1037/ccp000089

Pagelow, M. D. (1984). *Family violence.* New York, NY: Praeger Publishers.

Peluso, P. R., & Kern, R. M. (2002). An Adlerian model for assessing and treating the perpetrators of domestic violence. *Journal of Individual Psychology, 58*(1), 87–103.

Peluso, P. R., Peluso, J. P., White, J. F., & Kern, R. M. (2004). A comparison of attachment theory and individual psychology: A review of the literature. *Journal of Counseling and Development, 82*(2), 139–145.

Pittman, F. (1990). *Private lies: Infidelity and betrayal of intimacy.* New York, NY: W. W. Norton.

Prochaska, J. O., & DiClemente, C. C. (1982). Transtheoretical therapy: Toward a more integrative model of change. *Psychotherapy: Theory, Research & Practice, 19*(3), 276–288.

Prochaska, J. O., & DiClemente, C. C. (2002). Transtheoretical therapy. In F. W. Kaslow (Ed.), *Comprehensive handbook of psychotherapy: Integrative/eclectic* (Vol. 4, pp. 165–184). New York, NY: John Wiley & Sons.

Raytek, H. S., McCrady, B. S., Epstein, E. E., & Hirsch, L. S. (1999). Therapeutic alliance and the retention of couples in conjoint alcoholism. *Addictive Behaviors, 24*(3), 317–330.

Schumm, J. A., O'Farrell, T. J., Kahler, C. W., Murphy, M. M., & Muchowski, P. (2014). A randomized clinical trial of behavioral couple therapy versus individually based treatment for women with alcohol dependence. *Journal of Consulting and Clinical Psychology, 82*(6), 993–1004. doi:10.1037/a0037497

Sonkin, D. J., Martin, D., & Walker, L. E. (1985). *The male batterer: A treatment approach.* New York, NY: Springer.

Stets, J. E. (1988). *Domestic violence and control.* New York, NY: Springer-Verlag.

Stith, S. M., Rosen, K. H., & McCollum, E. E. (2003). Effectiveness of couples treatment for spouse abuse. *Journal of Marital and Family Therapy, 29*(3), 407–426.

Straus, M. A. (1999). The controversy over domestic violence by women: A methodological, theoretical, and sociology of science analysis. In X. B. Arriaga & S. Oskamp (Eds.), *Violence in intimate relationships* (pp. 17–44). Thousand Oaks, CA: Sage Publications.

Straus, M. A., Gelles, R. J., & Steinmetz, S. K. (Eds.). (1980). *Behind closed doors: Violence in the American family*. New York, NY: Doubleday/Anchor.

Straus, M. A., Hamby, S. L., & Warren, W. L. (2003). *The Conflict Tactics Scales handbook*. Los Angeles, CA: Western Psychological Services.

Trepper, T. S., McCollum, E. E., Dankoski, M. E., Davis, S. K., & LaFazia, M. A. (2000). Couple therapy for drug abusing women in an inpatient setting: A pilot study. *Contemporary Family Therapy, 22*(2), 201–221.

Walker, L. (1979). *The battered woman*. New York, NY: Harper & Row.

13 Sexual Dysfunction and Infidelity

LEARNING OBJECTIVES

In this chapter, the reader will learn the following:

1 The effect of sexual dysfunction on relationships.
2 The necessity for taking a thorough sexual history.
3 Incorporating sex therapy into couple therapy.
4 Working with couples who are dealing with infidelity in the relationship.

How humans physically relate to each other and how they go about the process of healing a relationship after an infidelity is disclosed are complex and intricate activities. Anyone working as a couple therapist may encounter either or both of these issues on a daily basis and must have an understanding of how to intervene effectively. In this chapter, we present an overview of these common and, at times, very challenging areas in working with couples: Sexual problems and infidelity.

Sexual Dysfunction and Couple Therapy

The role of sex in a relationship is central. It provides a point of emotional and physical connection between partners, as well as a source of mutual comfort and pleasure. It is also a biological function of human beings that is subject to the limitations of the human condition. As a result, frequently, sexual dysfunction is caused by medical issues, although the ramifications for a couple can extend beyond the biological. Therefore, since sexual dysfunction is a relationship issue, there are many overlaps between sex therapy and couple therapy. Particularly, as attitudes and expectations toward sex have changed, many relational problems have occurred.

Sex is often viewed as recreation rather than an obligation or a procreative function. It has long been known that sexual activity is mixed with a variety of motives, such as power, hostility, dependence, and submission. These factors, coupled with new attitudes toward female sexuality and sexual preference in general, have led to a change in sexual relationships and demands between partners. Historically, sexual functioning was largely relegated to the context of heterosexual marriage for the male's pleasure, whereas now women are increasingly expecting to receive pleasure and to achieve orgasm, just like men. Women now participate in sexual activity in a more assertive way and (by and large) have had their sexual interest legitimatized in Western culture. This change in women to a more assertive sexual role disturbs many men, and can be a source of perceived threat and increased dysfunction, particularly if their partners do not reach orgasm. In addition to the changes to women's roles in sex, other changes in society's perceptions of sex and sexuality have caused couples (and couple therapists) to begin to consider the implications of heterosexuality, bisexuality, and homosexuality on the functioning (or dysfunctioning) of close relationships (Glick, Berman, Clarkin, & Rait, 2000).

As a result, researchers have estimated that as many as 75%–80% of all couples seeking couple therapy have sexual difficulties, while approximately 80% of the couples presenting for sex therapy have significant relational problems (Heiman, LoPiccolo, & LoPiccolo, 1981; McCarthy, 2002; McCarthy & Ross, 2017; Schnarch, 1997; Weeks & Gambescia, 2015). According to Glick et al. (2000), approximately 50% of all relationships will experience a sexual problem at some point. This rate is true for homosexual couples as well as heterosexual couples. Therefore, it is important for couple therapists to be well versed in the areas of sexual function, as well as the treatment of sexual dysfunction. The field of sex therapy has emerged out of the shadows of shame and misunderstanding to be recognized by the public as a legitimate treatment modality for couples who experience sexual dysfunction.

Models of Sex Therapy

We will present three historical models of sex therapy, starting with Masters and Johnson's landmark work, Helen Singer Kaplan's model of sex therapy, David Schnarch's sexual crucible approach, and finally Weeks and Fife's Intersystem Approach which blends couple therapy and sex therapy.

Masters and Johnson's Model

William Masters and Virginia Johnson are considered pioneers in the scientific and systematic exploration of human sexual functioning. Their model includes four phases of sexual response (see Table 13.1): *Excitement* (erection, arousal, other physiological responses), *plateau* (a gradual buildup of sensations during sex), *orgasm* (intense, pleasurable buildup and release of sexual tension), and *resolution* (the phase where the body resets to normal or prepares for more sexual stimulation). According to Masters and Johnson (1966), sexual dysfunction is usually the primary or core issue rather than a symptom of a deeper psychological or relational problem. They believed that pressure to perform and fear of failure are often the causes of sexual dysfunction and that good sexual performance is a skill that can be learned. Thus, their treatment focus is on overcoming sexual barriers using educational

Table 13.1 Masters and Johnson Four-Phase Model of Sexual Response

Excitement	Erection, arousal, other physiological responses.
Plateau	A gradual buildup of sensations during sex.
Orgasm	Intense, pleasurable buildup, and release of sexual tension.
Resolution	The phase where the body resets to normal, or prepares for more sexual stimulation.

material and on behavioral techniques designed to progressively reward couples with small victories toward their ultimate goal.

In the initial phase of sex therapy, Masters and Johnson often recommend that couples refrain from sexual intercourse or any type of genital contact. They introduced one of the primary methods for helping couples achieve their sexual goals using *sensate focus*. Sensate focus is the process of relaxing and directing one's attention to pleasurable stimulation at different places on the body. Each partner is responsible for starting and stopping the stimulation from the other partner as they become overstimulated or uncomfortable without shame or guilt. The partner is directed to listen and respond to the other person's desire for more or less stimulation. This serves several purposes: (1) It puts the partner receiving stimulation in control of his or her body as well as the partner's physical contact, (2) it gives both partners the opportunity to feel successful at pleasing one another, and (3) it begins to establish a level of trust between the partners. As couples are successful, they are instructed to progressively move toward sexual contact, while continuing to communicate their needs to their partner. Eventually, they build on success and are able to meet their goal. This approach is especially helpful with premature ejaculation disorders and other inhibited sexual desire or performance disorders.

Kaplan's Triphasic Model

Helen Singer Kaplan (1974) made a significant improvement in developing a comprehensive model of human sexual response (Schnarch, 1991). She created a *triphasic* model of human sexual functioning consisting of *desire*, *excitement*, and *orgasm*. This built upon the work of Masters and Johnson by adding the idea of human desire as a precursor to sexual arousal. In this way, Kaplan's model begins to include a cognitive and emotional dimension to sexual functioning, allowing therapists to concentrate on more than just physiological responses when treating couples. Kaplan was able to distinguish between disorders of desire, arousal, and orgasm, which permits therapists to concentrate different treatment interventions for different complaints. This approach does not exclude one from incorporating sensate focus or any of Masters and Johnson's techniques in working with couples but instead elevates the elements of wish and fantasy to a necessary antecedent to arousal and orgasm, not just a by-product of it (McCarthy, 2002; McCarthy & Ross, 2017; Weeks & Gambescia, 2015).

David Schnarch's Sexual Crucible Approach

Schnarch (1991) noted that previous models of sexual functioning lacked a full explanation of human sexual functioning. In particular, there is an absence of the role of human personality in sex. He questioned the idea that orgasm represents the limit of peak sexual experience. Instead, he believes that there is a vast amount of untapped sexual potential that moves beyond the physical. For Schnarch, the subjective experience of sexual fulfillment is not necessarily correlated with physiological experience. Rather, fulfilling one's sexual potential means experiencing an emotional intensity that comes from being truly vulnerable with one another, while at the same time being alone and satisfied. The capacity for intimacy is directly linked to the ability to tolerate existential loneliness and the relativity of one's perceptions. Differentiation is what permits an individual to participate in a system – whether it is a couple, family, or society – without being overwhelmed and caught up in it. Individuals with low levels of differentiation require other-validated intimacy, which often fails to live up to the individual's expectations. Individuals who have high levels of differentiation are capable of self-validated intimacy, which allows for each partner to be truly present with one another, rather than a projection of the other person's needs (Schnarch, 2010).

One of Schnarch's (1991, 1997) breakthrough concepts is the idea that the sexual relationship can be seen as a metaphor for the entire relationship. He believed that a couple's sexual actions are an expression of that relationship's overall functioning and style of relating to one another and can help guide therapists in making interventions that impact the entire relationship (Schnarch, 1997). As a result, he has challenged the use of sexual exercises because they have a tendency to emphasize a need to be validated sexually by the other partner, which runs contrary to the process of differentiation. Instead, Schnarch advocates a treatment approach that merges couple therapy and sex therapy, which he calls the *sexual crucible*. This approach combines aspects of Bowen's systems theory (differentiation), object-relations theory (projective identification), and existential theory (aloneness and anxiety) into his model of the human expression of intimacy. While this approach fosters self-differentiation and self-regulation as important components to being satisfied in a committed relationship, Schnarch's therapy is far-reaching in its use of confrontation, self-exploration, and personal challenge. Schnarch believes that low and high desire are changeable positions within a relationship system and are not stable characteristics of a single individual. As a result, he is not fatalistic that desire cannot be changed. In fact, he notes that high- and low-desire partners are similar in differentiation, although the low-desire partner always controls sexual frequency and access. And while desire conflicts are inevitable and highly prevalent, they frequently will lead to major rifts in relationships that need to be addressed (Schnarch, 2010).

In the crucible approach, the therapist must act like a crucible and remain nonreactive in the face of the psychological and emotional energy that is produced when couples confront these basic issues of differentiation and sexuality. Because the individuals work through their intimacy needs and become more differentiated, they are transformed (like metal in a crucible). The transformation allows the couple to attain their full sexual potential, moving beyond the physical and into the spiritual (Schnarch, 2010).

Intersystem Approach

Weeks and Fife (2014) created the *intersystem approach* as an integrative approach to assess and treat sexual dysfunctions. The approach takes several different perspectives on sexual dysfunction, including the individual experiencing the problem, the relational dynamics (that may or may not have either created the problem or sustained it – or both), and the influence of each partner's family of origin on their current sexual functioning (Weeks & Gambescia, 2015). The intersystem approach has five different domains that inform the couple therapist's treatment plan for each unique couple's presentation of sexual dysfunction.

The first domain is the *Individual Biological Domain.* In this domain, each person's "medical history, genetic predispositions, health status, physical strengths, illnesses and change throughout the lifespan" (Weeks & Gambescia, 2015, p. 636) provide a multilayered explanation for the physical presentation of symptoms. The next domain is the *Individual Psychological Domain.* Here, the couple therapist assesses the role of sexual identity, personality traits, and any mental health symptoms (i.e. anxiety) that might impact sexual function are considered. The third is the *Couple Relationship Domain.* At this point, the couple's relationship style is assessed including conflict resolution strategies, communication patterns, tolerance for intimacy, and relationship satisfaction. For example, "reduced sexual satisfaction may have an adverse impact on overall relational satisfaction. A sexual problem such as lack of interest/arousal may precipitate a dysfunction in the asymptomatic partner" (Weeks & Gambescia, 2015, p. 637). The fourth is the *Intergenerational Domain.* This domain centers around how each partner's family of origin felt about sex and communicated about sexuality, and how issues related to sex were modeled to each person. Often, misinformation or expressions of disgust about sex are transmitted to children and retained into adulthood. Other times, secrecy about sex (as in the case of parental infidelity) from childhood impacts the individual in his or her own romantic relationship. The final domain is the *Environmental Domain.* Issues that are related to cultural values, religious customs, and other media messages regarding sexuality are assessed for their impact on the couple in the form of (unrealistic) expectations or taboos regarding sex (Weeks & Gambescia, 2015).

The Intersystem Approach "blends and integrates theoretical models, resulting in a cohesive paradigm rather than a series of isolated interventions" (Weeks & Gambescia, 2015, p. 638). As a result, it provides a comprehensive framework for working with couples that present with a wide variety of sexual dysfunctions. By conceptualizing the dysfunction across multiple domains, the intersystem approach provides a nuanced approach to work on couples goals related to sexual functioning and relationship satisfaction.

Assessment for Sexual Dysfunction

Although sexual dysfunction and marital distress can operate independently of each other, they often do not. Therapists need to have good skills in assessment in order to determine which problems are primary and at what point to make an intervention. A thorough sexual history is often needed in order to determine which problems are primary. Exploration of a sexual complaint and the joint sexual history of the couple may or may not lead to the clinical decision that a complete sexual history for each spouse is necessary. The amount of information needed in order to determine the nature and extent of the dysfunction and the kind of treatment required is whatever information the clinician needs. Table 13.2 presents some guidelines for taking a sexual history, which could be done in conjunction with a traditional assessment (see Chapter 9) or separately.

The Diagnostic and Statistical Manual of Mental Disorders (DSM-5, American Psychiatric Association [APA], 2013) has several categories of diagnoses for sexual disorders. The main types of sexual problems include delayed ejaculation, erectile disorder, female orgasmic disorder, female sexual interest/arousal disorder, genito-pelvic pain/penetration disorder, male hypoactive sexual desire disorder, premature (early) ejaculation, substance/medication-induced sexual dysfunction, other specified sexual dysfunction, and unspecified sexual dysfunction. Sexual dysfunctions are a group of disorders that are typically characterized by a clinically significant disturbance in a person's ability to respond sexually or to experience sexual pleasure. An individual may have several sexual dysfunctions at the same time. In such cases, all of the dysfunctions should be diagnosed. In most of these cases, it is essential to refer for a medical evaluation performed by a gynecologist, urologist, or physician. Thus, it is important for

Table 13.2 Guidelines for Taking a Sexual Problem History

1 Description of current problem
2 Onset and course of problem
  a Onset (gradual or sudden, precipitating events, consequences)
  b Course (changes over time: Increase, decrease, or fluctuation in severity, frequency, intensity; functional relationships with other variables)
3 Client's concept of cause and continuation of the problem
4 Past treatment and outcome
  a Medical evaluation (specialty, date, form of treatment, results, current medication for any reason)
  b Other professional help (specialty, date, form of treatment, results)
  c Self-treatment (type and results)
5 Current expectations and goals of treatment (concrete and general)

couple therapists working with sexual disorders to establish a working relationship with such physicians. In addition, therapists would do well to develop a working knowledge of the types of tests that are routinely performed and the implication of their results regarding sexual functioning. Finally, understanding the impact and limitations of medications like Viagra, Levitra, and others for erectile dysfunction or hypoactive arousal, which have been heavily marketed to the public, is crucial as these agents become standard practice in the treatment of sexual dysfunction (McCarthy, 2002; McCarthy & Ross, 2017; Weeks & Gambescia, 2015).

An assessment of sexual function also provides the therapist with the opportunity to set the tone for how sexual issues will be discussed. Couples will generally feel anxious and may be highly defensive about discussing sex with a stranger. If the therapist is anxious and fumbles through a discussion of sexual interactions, asks questions that seem to be provocative, or addresses sex in a coldly clinical manner, this will communicate a message of "I can't handle a discussion about sex" and the couple will not address the issue in much depth. Too often, this will have a negative impact on the therapy, leading to impasses because a key component cannot be brought to light. Thus, it is *imperative* that therapists become facile in their discussions of sex. If there is any hesitancy in addressing sex, then the therapist should seek appropriate training or supervision. Table 13.3 provides some reflection questions for couple therapists regarding their attitudes and feelings about sex.

Table 13.3 Questions to Assist Counselors Reflection About One's Personal Beliefs About Sex

- Am I just a bit resentful when I realize that some couples have a better sex life than I do?
- Am I comfortable with the idea of a woman or a man in late life masturbating to orgasm, self-pleasuring?
- How comfortable am I with the thought of an older couple giving and receiving oral sex? Can I imagine them experiencing passionate deep kissing?
- Do I assume that all the people I work with are heterosexual unless I am told otherwise?
- Can I picture a male couple or female couple enjoying their lovemaking?
- How do I feel about an older widow or widower having sex with a variety of dating partners and not wanting to marry any of them?
- How easy is it for me to assess for sexually transmitted infections and HIV/AIDS when interviewing a couple?
- How easily do I initiate a discussion of the sexuality and intimacy needs of my clients?
- Do I feel secretly relieved when the topic of sex is not mentioned and reassure myself that I am protecting a couple's privacy?
- How do I react when a "sexual situation" presents itself in my work with couples?
- What does my silence, changing of the subject, not taking the hint, laughing, or looking embarrassed communicate to my clients?

Adapted from Moll (2013).

Ultimately, the therapist should demonstrate (1) an attitude of openness and understanding to the couple as they discuss sexual issues, (2) the ability to elicit information in a way that is constructive, and (3) an understanding of the proper role that a healthy sex life plays in a couple's level of functioning. With these skills, the therapist's chances of successfully treating the couple increase dramatically (McCarthy, 2002; McCarthy & Ross, 2017; Weeks & Gambescia, 2015).

Intervention Models for Sexual Dysfunction as Part of Couple Therapy

Sexual problems can be divided into two categories: Primary sexual problems, which are those that arise from sex-related stimuli and occur only in sexual situations, and secondary sexual problems, which are manifestations of a larger personal or relationship dissatisfaction. Classification of cases as secondary or primary helps to determine the appropriate counseling strategy. Primary problems usually respond well to brief therapy, whereas secondary problems require more in-depth, intensive therapy. Table 13.4 presents the interactions between couples and sexual problems, along with some treatment recommendations (traditional sex therapy, traditional couple therapy, or both).

Table 13.4 Interaction between Couple Problems and Sexual Problems and Treatment Suggestions

Interaction	*Treatment Suggestion*
1 The sexual dysfunction produces or contributes to secondary relational discord.	Traditional sex therapy is recommended, with specific strategies focused on the sexual dysfunctions, would be considered the treatment of choice. This is especially true if the same sexual dysfunction occurred in the person's other relationships.
2 The sexual dysfunction is secondary to relational discord.	Depending on the severity of relational discord, some brief sex therapy may provide the couple with the benefit of a shared victory, which could translate into positive momentum in addressing the larger relational problems. Otherwise, traditional couple therapy is considered treatment of choice.
3 Relational discord co-occurs with sexual problems.	Traditional couple therapy would be considered the primary course of treatment. In this instance, sex therapy is discouraged as the initial, especially if the partners are openly hostile to one another. However, if there is significant progress in couple therapy, then some attention can be paid to sexual issues.
4 Sexual dysfunction occurs without relational discord.	Traditional couple therapy would be the treatment of choice as sexual dysfunction may occur as a result of illness or accident where loss of function is organic, or when a partner has a history of sexual abuse.

Source: Adapted from Glick et al. (2000).

Table 13.5 ExP-LI-SS-IT Approach for Brief Sexual Therapy

Ex-P	Extended Permission
LI	Limited Information
SS	Specific Suggestions
IT	Intensive Therapy

Note: Adapted from Annon (1974) and Taylor and Davis (2007).

One successful model of sexual therapy that we endorse is the PLISSIT approach originally developed by Annon (1974), and recently updated and re-branded the Ex-PLISSIT approach by Taylor and Davis (2006, 2007). Ex-P-LI-SS-IT is an acronym for the four progressively intensive levels of the approach. Each letter (or pair of letters) designates a suggested method for handling the presenting sexual concern based on the couples' complaint (see Table 13.5). The four levels are expressed-permission, limited information, specific suggestions, and intensive therapy.

Extended Permission

The first level, Ex-P, is the initial stage of treatment. In the extended, Ex-PLISSIT model, the first step was included as an "extended" permission giving whereby the couple can express any concerns that they might have (hence the "Ex-"). This revision allows for permission to be a more robust and thoughtful process rather than a formality that is often given short shrift. According to Taylor and Davis (2006, 2007), this places permission giving at the core of the treatment approach. Thus, by giving people explicit permission to discuss the concerns they have about their sexuality, couple therapists affirm the individual as a sexual being. Sometimes, all that people want to know is whether they are normal, okay, not perverted, deviated, or abnormal. Once they find this out from someone with a professional background or someone who is in a position of authority, often the problems just disappear. One example of a presenting concern is the person who dreams of having sex with someone of the same sex. This can be dealt with very simply by saying, "Many people have sexual dreams with people of the same sex, opposite sex, groups, or people of different races, and it's perfectly normal. The average person has an average of four or more sexual fantasies each day." Another concern may be when spouses worry about the fact that they are having sex only one time per month. Or another may be, "I can only come when he touches me with his tongue." Or another, "I get an erection when my baby daughter bounces on my lap. Am I some kind of a pervert? Will I try anything with her?" These are all perfectly normal sexual concerns that normal people have (Taylor & Davis, 2006, 2007).

Limited Information

The second level of treatment involves giving the client specific factual information that is directly relevant to his or her sexual concern. This may result in the client's continuing to do what he or she was doing, or it may result in something different. Often, the way to approach this is by providing books or videotapes. Questions can be as simple as, "Can germs be transmitted through oral-genital contact?" To this we suggest you respond with, "Yes, there are many germs in the mouth." Another concern may be, "I have small breasts, and I want to have plastic surgery so that I can have better orgasms." Another came from a gentleman we saw who wanted to have circumcision. He had an uncircumcised penis and was having trouble with premature ejaculation and thought that if he had his penis circumcised, this problem would be solved.

Further information can be very helpful in dispelling many of the sexual myths. Some of the common myths are listed in Table 13.6. Again, it is crucial that therapists feel comfortable discussing these issues, along with having a thorough and accurate understanding of most areas of sexual functioning.

Specific Suggestions

In order to practice the third level of treatment, specific suggestions, the therapist must first obtain specific information, which usually includes a thorough sexual problem history. Once this is completed, and a specific problem has been identified, specific suggestions can be made. These can range from sensate focus activities and progressive relaxation to fantasy fulfillment and role-playing. Suggestions can be made to either partner alone or the couple together (McCarthy, 2002; McCarthy & Ross, 2017; Weeks & Gambescia, 2015).

Intensive Therapy

The fourth stage is used only when the others do not work. Often, sexual problems, as we have indicated, have to do with ignorance of sexual anatomy and physiology, negative attitudes, self-defeating behaviors, or even the use of medication. Sometimes, these problems are a symptom of a mental disorder. Recently, researchers have affirmed the Ex-PLISSIT model as useful with couples where one partner has a chronic illness or disability (Daneshfar et al., 2017; Khakbazan et al., 2016).

Table 13.6 Common Sexual Myths Encountered in Couple Therapy

"It's coitus that counts. That's the normal or right way."
"The search for simultaneous orgasm is worthwhile; the couple that comes together stays together."
"Males need erections to make love."
"Sex must be spontaneous."
"Males are always ready. Females have to be made ready."
"All sexual problems are resolvable."
"Women don't get turned on by fantasies."

In this section, we have attempted to give the reader an overview of the topic of sex in the context of couple therapy, and some of the models for working with couples within the boundaries of couple therapy. However, some states require specific training before therapists can call themselves "sex therapists." AASECT is an accrediting body that regulates the training of certified sex therapists. Readers are encouraged to review the guidelines for training in order to become familiar with the topics and domains within sex therapy.

Working with Infidelity in Couples Counseling

Infidelity is the issue most likely to bring a couple into therapy. Paradoxically, it is also the issue that most therapists say they are the least prepared to treat (Whisman, Dixon & Johnson, 1997; Peluso, 2018). Atkins, Eldridge, Baucom, and Christensen (2005) reported that over 50% of couples in a large randomized clinical sample identified infidelity as an issue in their relationship. In terms of the general, nonclinical population, the reality is that statistics on infidelity in couples is widely varying. Some reports have estimates that range from 25% to over 50% of individuals reporting engaging in an extramarital affair (Starratt, Wekes-Shackelford, & Shakelford, 2017; Weiser & Weigel, 2015). In the dating population, these figures can rise from as high as 70% for women and 75% for men (Shackelford & Buss, 1997), though the generalizability of the findings is very limited (Labrecque & Whisman, 2017). Instead, the best information comes from large, national surveys. The General Social Survey (GSS), a multiwave survey that has sampled households in the U.S. every two years since 1972 and that is conducted by the University of Chicago may provide the closest population estimates. Each wave of participants is new and consists of a cross section of the general adult population (18 years and older), and includes questions on general health and relationship issues. Labrecque and Whisman (2017) examined over 13,000 responses from nine waves of the GSS spanning from 2000 to 2016 to see how people's responses to questions related to extramarital sex have changed, or remained the same over the last 16 years. Overall, 3% of married individuals in a given year will report having extramarital sex. Lifetime rates of infidelity for married couples range from 22% to 25% of men and 11% to 15% of women. Tafoya and Spitzberg (2007) conducted a meta-analysis of 50 studies and found that 24% of women and 34% of men have engaged in extramarital sexual activities over the span of a relationship.

Systems Theory and Infidelity

When an infidelity is the presenting concern in couple therapy, it can seem like an all-consuming issue. For many couples, there is a laser-like focus on the details of the infidelity, the betrayal, and the emotional aftermath. This focus can suck the couple therapist into this as well, and bring productive therapy to a standstill. However, systemically oriented couple therapists conceptualize infidelity from a different perspective than other types of therapists.

According to Peluso (2018), they utilize two important systemic principles regarding the lead-up to infidelity and the aftermath of infidelity:

1 The infidelity is *not* the central issue of concern in the relationship, it's a symptom.
2 Both partners had a contributing role in creating the conditions that led to the infidelity.

Both of these systemic issues are difficult for couples (and many couple therapists) to grasp. It takes a systemic orientation to genuinely understand the implications of the aforementioned principles as they "go against the grain" of finding one person to blame, while the other adopts a victim stance. If, however, a couple therapist can understand these principles, and can effectively communicate them to the couple, the chances of successfully resolving infidelity are greatly improved (Peluso, 2018).

Systematic Principle 1: The Infidelity Is Not the Central Issue of Concern in the Relationship, It Is a Symptom

According to Peluso (2018):

> At the beginning, this may seem like a difficult concept to grasp. After all, an infidelity has occurred, isn't that the worst possible thing that could happen? And if there is an understanding that the relationship was supposed to be monogamous and lifelong, then yes, it does seem that an infidelity is the worst thing that can happen. However, the reality is that an infidelity reveals something much more problematic in the relationship. More than just the betrayal itself and the erosion of trust. An infidelity reveals that the relationship is in much more jeopardy, at a deeper level than is apparent.
>
> (p. 16)

Systematic Principle 2: Both Partners Had a Contributing Role in Creating the Conditions that Led to the Infidelity

According to Peluso (2018):

> This might be the hardest "sell" that a systemically oriented couples counselor has to do. The reason for it is that people always want to assign blame for their pain. They want someone to bear the responsibility, and often (in child-like way) want that person to take the pain away. The reality is that if you view the couple as a system, then no one individual is to *blame,* in the traditional sense of the word. Instead, both partners created the conditions that were necessary for the one partner to stray.
>
> (p. 17)

Systemically oriented couple therapists intuitively understand that the underlying dynamics of the couple system are the cause of the infidelity, but they must win the couple over to this way of viewing the connection between the infidelity and their relationship issues. At the same time, there is a "needle" that the couple therapist must thread. On the one hand, the couple system created the context that allowed for the infidelity to occur, and though both partners had a role to play, it does not mean that the partner who had the affair is *not* responsible for their individual actions nor for the consequences of it. Thus, keeping the two systemic principles described earlier in mind, the individual responsibility for behavior is part of "threading the needle" that systemically oriented couples counselors have to do in order to be effective (Peluso, 2018).

Typology of Affairs

Emily Brown (2001, 2007) produced a typology of affairs. What is so useful about Brown's types of affairs – though derived only from experience and not necessarily by any empirical evidence – is that she does not see all infidelity as the same. Rather, she says that

> the type of affair has to do with the interaction pattern between the two spouses and the issues underlying the affair...By identifying the message encoded in the affair, the therapist can begin to formulate a plan for treatment. The typology is based on the behavior patterns and emotional dynamics of the couple.
>
> (2001, p. 30)

Originally, the five types of affairs were the conflict-avoidance affair, the intimacy-avoidance affair, the sexual addiction affair, the split-self affair, and the exit affair. Each will be described below.

Conflict-Avoidance Affairs. The conflict-avoidance affair is indicative of a couple who try to avoid provoking one another. They may have a perfectionistic idea of what a view of what a "good" relationship should be, which is often defined as the absence of conflict. In terms of their makeup and family of origin, Brown says "(t)hose who were taught as a child that anger was bad, who were instructed to 'look at the positive side of things,' or were punished for disagreeing, are likely to have a hard time expressing dissatisfactions." (2001, p. 33). The couple may view conflict as needlessly destructive or corrosive, and thus are afraid of it. The affair temporarily reduces conflicts (usually about sex), but it is generally a symptom of the deeper issue of not being able to bring up and resolve conflicts. Interestingly, the partner who has the affair (and thus is the person who has become dissatisfied with the status quo) always seems to manage to have the affair "accidentally" discovered. The discovery makes it clear that there are serious problems in the marriage and brings the couple into therapy.

In terms of the infidelity itself, the affair is seldom a real threat to the primary relationship. It usually occurs relatively early in the relationship (though can occur much later): "(t)he threat to the marriage is not the affair, but the avoidance of the conflict. The affair becomes a threat only when its message is misinterpreted or ignored" (Brown, 2001, p. 34). It usually occurs relatively early in the relationship (though can occur much later), and has the best potential for therapeutic success. Some characteristics of the couple's presentation in therapy include extreme guilt, remorse, and responsibility on the part of the partner that has the affair. The other partner may present as hurt or sad, or angry (though usually not openly hostile so as to not provoke conflict). For the couple therapist, the most important therapeutic consideration is keeping the avoidance of conflict at the forefront of the couple therapy and seeing how that dynamic plays out in both the affair and the relationship. Ultimate success for this type of affair is increasing the couples capacity to successfully bring up conflicts, and then resolve them without retreating from them.

Intimacy-Avoidance Affairs. Intimacy is at the heart of this type of affair. The infidelity "protects against hurt and disappointment. It is saying 'I don't want to need you so much (so I'll get some of my needs met elsewhere).' Both spouses fear letting down the barriers and becoming emotionally vulnerable" (Brown, 2001, pp. 34–35). Typically, these affairs begin after the "honeymoon period" of the relationship is over, or a few years into a relationship. The trigger for this type of affair is the fear (or even panic) that the relationship might lead to genuine vulnerability. Thus, the affair is used to perpetuate conflict which acts as a distraction. Unlike the conflict-avoiding couple, the intimacy-avoidance couple looks more hostile in the form of arguments and disagreements. These are all usually "smoke screens" that keep the couple in constant conflict so that they don't have to get close to one another. In the families of origin for these couples, there was usually a lot of chaos (e.g. alcoholic or abusive households), and conflicts and arguments were the norm. As a result, no one modeled appropriate boundaries, or felt any real intimacy or genuine vulnerability (Brown, 2007). The affair becomes a way to find intimacy (or pseudo-intimacy) elsewhere, but then when it is discovered, it can also be a source of continuing conflict (thus perpetuating the cycle of intimacy-avoidance).

For couple therapists, the important therapeutic consideration for treating these couples is getting the couple to see the fighting as a distraction from true intimacy, and then focus on their intimacy needs. Since fear of rejection is predominant, these couples are usually very guarded and hypervigilant about the motives and behaviors of the other partner, this may be difficult at first. However, getting each partner to express their wishes and needs underlying the conflict (and the affair) is also important for getting their commitment to work on the relationship. If the couple can learn how to risk vulnerability without resorting to arguments and anger to mask their loneliness, as well as open themselves up to each other, then the outlook is positive. If they cannot, then the likelihood of getting involved in another high-conflict, intimacy-avoiding relationship (with the associated need for affairs) is the likely outcome (Brown, 2007).

Sexual Addiction Affair. When one partner has multiple affairs with different partners that seemingly have a compulsive aspect to them, they are usually Sexual Addiction Affairs. According to Brown (2001), "these affairs are the province of those who deal with their emotional neediness by winning battles and making conquests in the hope of gaining love. Emotionally deprived, overwhelmed, or abused as children, they haven't finished growing up" (p. 37). The person engaging in the sexual addiction affair may have come from a family of origin where they were considered to be "special" or a favorite child of one of the parents. There may have been addictions (substances, gambling, sex, etc.) where there was a strong ethos of entitlement, secret-keeping, and "don't talk" rules. Partners having the compulsive affairs are often in positions of power (e.g. politics, finance, etc.), having attained some success or fame, or seek power sexually. As a result, the idea of breaking the rules and "getting away with it" becomes very intoxicating. However, the underlying dynamic is a sense of internal emptiness and pain, and the need to fill the emptiness in order to numb the feelings of pain (Brown, 2007).

For the other partner, as children they may have been privy to their parent's affairs and had to carry the secret of them. They often have a sexual abuse or trauma history which inclines them to accept this behavior from their partner, since they do not believe that they deserve a good relationship. Taken together, the dynamics of the relationship that define a sexual addiction affair include a partner that may be cold and indifferent, or compartmentalized and weak and another partner who is charismatic and self-important. So when the affair comes to light, it is usually a high-drama event. Treatment for these couples is often focused on the addictive aspects first, before the couples issues are addressed. If the partner with the sexual addiction has sought treatment, and has adopted a recovery model, then couples-work can focus on the underlying attachment needs and the entitlement needs that often accompany a sexual addiction affair (Brown, 2001). Otherwise, the prognosis is for the relationship to continue, and for continued relapses to happen as the other spouse continues to look away.

Split-Self Affair. The Split-Self affair is centered around the idea that a person has had (or felt that they had) to deny or repress a side to themselves for a long time to keep up a façade of respectability, or perceived social norms for a successful family. Often, these couples are concerned with doing what is "right" in the eyes of society, and have done so at the expense of their own personal happiness or fulfillment. "Personal needs were sublimated as they tried to make their family be what they believed a family should be. This often meant focusing the family resources, financial and emotional, on the children" (Brown, 2001, pp. 40–41). At the beginning of the relationship, these individuals may have believed that getting married to whom, or when they did was the "right" thing to do, or that it would be a way to gain some security. For both partners in the relationship, they "learned early in life that they were supposed to do the right thing, rather than pay attention to their own needs and feelings" (p. 41). Many times, these individuals are successful personally and professionally but are not emotionally or interpersonally. Typically, to the outside world, these relationships look like the "perfect" family, and the partners are considered pillars of the community (which makes the personal revelation of the affair more shocking). However, when that is not satisfying enough, it can produce frustration, confusion, or loneliness. According to Brown (2001):

> In the Split Self Affair, the marriage feels empty, as opposed to the Sexual Addiction where the individual feels empty. The partners may or may not share a bedroom, any sexual relationship is likely to be pro forma, and they lead very separate lives. Communication is limited to practical matters like taking the garbage out or social necessities.
>
> (p. 41)

The affair offers the opportunity for passion and fun that have been denied over the years. While it is often dismissed as part of a "mid-life crisis," this is shortsighted as the affair may reflect a deeper set of issues. Sometimes, the affair has persisted for a number of years, and may represent a significant attachment to the other person. In fact, the partner having the affair may be torn between the two relationships and uncertain which one to end (Brown, 2007). On one side of the equation, when a Split-Self Affair occurs, the marriage is often over 10 or 20 years old – so there is a significant investment of time, resources, and emotions in the relationship. But on the other side, the relationship has become so ossified that the new relationship makes the partner feel alive and excited emotionally. As a result, the straying partner may come to therapy individually to determine which relationship to pursue, deciding how to tell the other partner about the relationship, and perhaps more importantly about the thoughts and feelings that were previously suppressed. In general, in the case of the split-self affair, the outlook is not good:

> Frequently it is too late to create a satisfying emotional partnership between the spouses. The husband may leave to marry the other woman, or may usually stay in the marriage but be emotionally committed to the affair. Women usually choose the latter option. These affairs can continue until death.
>
> (Brown, 2001, p. 45)

Exit Affair. In the Exit Affair, one or both partners know that the relationship is over but don't know how to end it. As a result, the affair becomes the way to get the issue of ending out in the open, and/or force the other partner to make the final decision. Since the affair occurs just before the end of the relationship, it is sometimes mistakenly thought of as the "cause" of the split. However, the relationship has often been "on the rocks" for a long time. In many cases, the straying partner did not want to hurt their spouse, but they have no desire to work on salvaging the relationship, and the affair offered a way "out." The betrayed spouse will typically present with anger and hurt, while the betraying spouse will typically present as regretful but disengaged. Each partner will blame the other for the state of the relationship, as a way to hide from the pain having the relationship fail. Couple therapy in these cases can help each partner see the relational patterns which, if they are not addressed, will often be recreated in the next relationship, thus continuing the cycle.

Brown's typology is just one approach to looking at infidelity, but it fulfills the two important systemic principles outlined earlier. First, it provides a good starting point for sorting out the different system dynamics, from which the symptom of the infidelity emerged. Second, it gives both partners a way to see how they participated in creating the system that allowed the (conflict-avoidance, intimacy-avoidance, etc.) affair to occur. So once you know what type of affair the couple is presenting with, the next question is can it be treated effectively? What kind of hope for success does the research conducted to date give clinicians and couples?

Clinical Research Findings on Infidelity: Can Treatment Really Work?

According to Kroger, Reißner, Vasterling, Schutz, and Kliem (2012), there have only been five reported efficacy studies on the treatment of infidelity using a randomized control trial (RCT), which is considered to be the "gold standard" of empirically supported treatments (Castonguay, 2013). So, is couples counseling effective to treat infidelity? The short answer is "yes," but there are some important qualifications.

In 2005, Atkins et al. found that couples who were in counseling because of an affair had lower overall satisfaction scores than couples who sought couple therapy for other reasons at pretreatment. But at posttreatment those differences were no longer there, indicating that couple therapy was successful. These results were replicated in a European sample seeking couples counseling, with couples maintaining satisfaction gains at six months posttreatment (Atkins, Marin, Lo, Klann, & Hahlweg, 2010). Atkins et al. (2005) also reported an interesting finding that when couples had one partner who did not disclose an affair during treatment (but had disclosed it in confidential forms), they did not seem to benefit from couples counseling. Greenberg, Warwar, and Maclom (2010) looked at the traumatic "injuries" following an infidelity (as part of larger study of attachment injuries). Not surprisingly, the "injured" (or betrayed) partner reported lower relationship satisfaction and greater personal strain at pretreatment but showed improvement during couple therapy, at the end of treatment, and at follow-up (at three months). In addition, the other partner showed improvement as well, again showing therapeutic success.

Gordon, Baucom, and Snyder (2004) conducted a study that looked at couples who had an affair disclosed within the past six months and who were seeking couples counseling. They investigated a specific approach that focused exclusively on infidelity and not on other couples issues. Their results showed some improvement on anxiety and depression scores pre-post-treatment for the betrayed spouse, and even higher gains for the betraying spouse on the same instruments. But at a six-month follow-up, only the betraying partner continued to show positive effects and improved relationship satisfaction. Lastly, in 2012, Kroger and his associates investigated almost 90 couples in treatment (one group on a waiting list, one group in treatment). Interestingly, they found that over half (56%) of the participants dropped out before the end of treatment (underscoring the emotional volatility). Their results supported the use of couple therapy for the treatment of infidelity, particularly for the trauma and anxiety symptoms that are a part of dealing with infidelity. However, they only found mixed results in depression scores from pre- to posttreatment for the unfaithful partner, and they did not see improvements in relationship satisfaction. Again, like Gordon et al.'s study, their approach focused more on the infidelity-specific issues than on the couples system, which could have accounted for the results.

Finally, in their review, Kessel, Moon, and Atkins (2007) found that "A hybrid approach that includes both infidelity-specific and general couple therapy strategies may provide the most realistic and flexible strategy." (p. 62). Thus, for treatment to be successful, couples need a competent couple therapist, who needs to be able to:

1 Articulate an *explanatory* model which explains *how* the couple got into the situation that they are in with the infidelity. It needs to address both the infidelity-specific aspects of what happened and the couple-wide issues that created the conditions where this happened. This model must contain the two systemic principles discussed earlier.
2 Provide a *treatment* model that will (1) guide the therapist and the therapy process through the turbulent issues that will inevitably arise and (2) give the couple a sense of the course of treatment and that there is a "roadmap" with "light at the end of the tunnel." One such model, developed by Peluso (2018), will be discussed next.

Three-Step Model for Understanding and Treating Infidelity

A critique of previous approaches is that they are often too complicated and too full of "jargon" to be helpful to clients in the midst of the trauma that an infidelity inflicts. Peluso (2018) developed a simple, three-step model following a review of more common treatment approaches (see Peluso, 2007). The three steps are simple enough to understand, and they serve as both an explanatory model and a treatment model that can be easily used by systems-based couples counselors. Each of the steps is an additive "ingredient" that includes the basic components necessary for an infidelity to occur. According to Peluso (2018), they are:

1. Perhaps, with the exception of an infidelity that results from a sexual compulsion or addiction, all infidelities are associated with a decline in *satisfaction with the relationship*. However, not all dissatisfied couples have an affair. Relationship satisfaction can bounce up and down very rapidly. This can be affected by so many factors: Work, children, parents, friends, etc. Much like a volatile stock market, a couple's satisfaction with the relationship might be "up 25 points" some days, and the next day "down 50 points." But focusing on the "day-to-day" satisfaction does not – by itself – indicate whether an infidelity will occur. The key indicator is the overall "trend" over time. The trends, though, can tell you if there is trouble up ahead. But it is not the *only* ingredient.
2. One of the reasons for long-term dissatisfaction in a relationship is an *imbalance of power* in the relationship. It is like being on a "see-saw" when one person is bigger than the other. One person stays up all the time and the other is down all the time. It's no fun for either. Usually, one person feels that they don't have influence over the other person's actions (particularly with regard to decisions that affect the couple), or they feel that they sacrifice their needs and give into the other person's wants. Another way that the power balance is upset in a couple is when one partner brings in (or "triangulates") another person in the relationship (i.e. children, parents, friends, etc.), which makes the other person feel "left out" or "ganged up on" when it comes to major decisions. As a result, an infidelity is often a way of rebalancing the perception of a power imbalance (by bringing in someone else). It is a way to demonstrate to the other person that they have the power also, though it is expressed in a negative and destructive way. However, there are many couples who are dissatisfied with their relationship and feel that there is an imbalance of power but do not have an affair. That is because there is one final ingredient that is needed!
3. Lastly, the role of *unfulfilled fantasies, wishes, and dreams* in infidelity are crucial. When a person in a relationship gets to the point where they think "this is never going to change, this is never going to get any better, and I am never going to get what I want out of my partner," they realize that they have been deluding themselves. Everything that they had hoped for, wished for, and dreamed that they would get in their relationship fails to come true, and the fantasy dies. It is the critical ingredient needed, which makes an affair so tempting. It holds the promise of fulfilling something (fantasy, wish, dream, etc.) for a person that seems to be missing in the relationship, or in the person. By contrast, the *reality* of the individual's present relationship is usually fraught with struggle, negotiation, disappointment, and conflict. In short, making *real* relationships work is hard *work*, while an affair (on the surface) seems to be effortless and enjoyable. Then, this is the point where all three ingredients are present (dissatisfaction, imbalance, and fantasy) and the infidelity occurs (pp. 27–28).

This is the point when an affair is disclosed. It is also a place where a major decision must be made: Do I stay or do I go? If the couple decides to stay together, then the question is: Can we save this relationship or marriage? If each person is willing to go through the process, then they usually can save it. The process for exiting from an affair is the same way that you came in, except in reverse. In other words, it is the same three steps, only in reverse order (see Figure 13.1).

This means that first, the couple must explore the original wishes, reams, and fantasies that they had for each other; *then* find ways of balancing power; and finally create ways to feel more satisfied in the relationship. Unfortunately, the problem with most couple therapists who attempt to treat couples dealing with infidelity without a comprehensive explanatory and treatment model is that they reverse the order and try to work on satisfaction first and dampen the more raw emotions at the beginning of couple therapy.

An important key to ultimately recovering intimacy following an infidelity is to understand the excitement of the fantasy, dream, or wish that was unfulfilled and hence led to the affair. If a person was feeling abandoned, how can they be made to feel wanted? If they need to feel protected, how can they

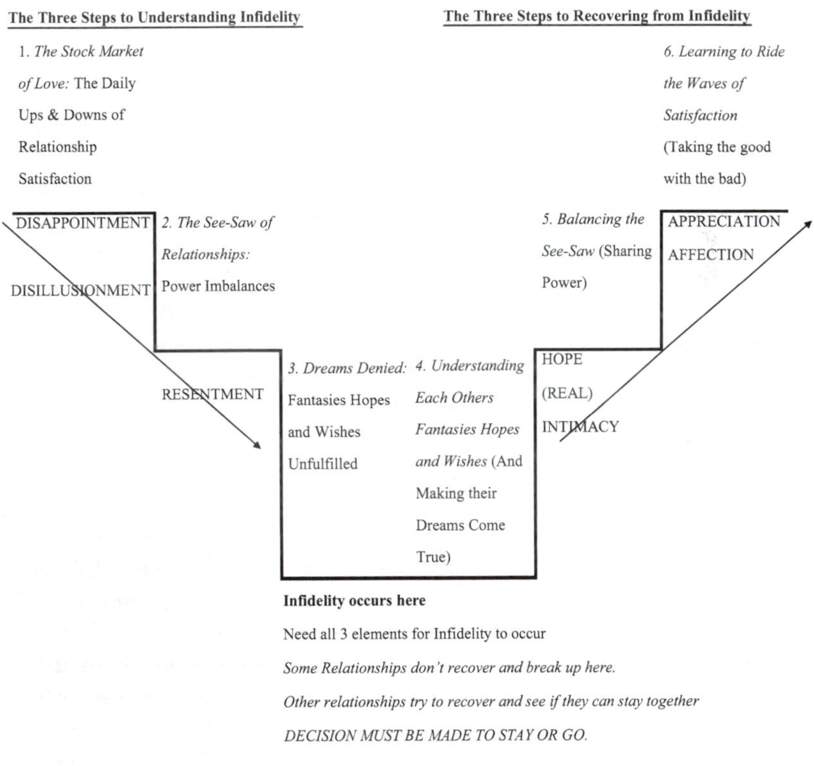

Figure 13.1 Three-Step Model of Infidelity (Peluso, 2018).

be made to feel safe? At the same time, it is crucial to tap into each partner's *original* fantasies about the relationship and how that led to expectations that they placed on each other and on themselves ("I don't ever want to be hurt," "I want to have a happy, joyful family," etc.). In the beginning of therapy, these will probably be connected to feelings of betrayal, disgust, grief, or anger. However, if the couple can be guided *through* those emotions, then there is the possibility of growth and deeper intimacy.

As the fantasies, wishes, and dreams are explored and ultimately renegotiated by the couple, the work through the other two steps can take place. However, not all couples can do this. Many times, couples decide that too much damage has been done, and that the dreams for the relationship are irretrievably broken. But, if a couple can take these three steps together, then the couple will have ways to discuss and rebalance the "see-saw" of power, and the "trend line" in relationship satisfaction will increase within a framework of a shared, explicit wish dream, or fantasy about the relationship (Peluso, 2018). Now let's look at a case example to see this in practice.

In Chapter 6, the case of Jerry and Anna was presented. This couple had been married for 15 years and has a five-year-old daughter and a three-year-old son. Anna was the one who initiated therapy following the discovery of a recent affair between Jerry and a coworker. Anna learned about the affair when she arrived home earlier than expected from a stay at her mother's summer house and discovered Jerry's coworker in a bathrobe. Jerry defended himself by saying that he and Anna had not had sex in more than a year and that they had been growing apart since the birth of their son. Jerry said that the problems between them had actually started at the beginning of the marriage because Anna was "attached at the hip" to her mother. The couple stated that they want to stay together, primarily for the children, if possible.

Since sex was one of the first issues to be raised by the couple, it seemed logical to pursue the matter further. This is a case where the sexual and relational problems are intertwined, and therefore information about the client's sexual relationship will undoubtedly provide needed information about the dynamics underlying the entire relationship. Likewise, information about the clients' relationship (history, family-of-origin dynamics, etc.) will be invaluable for the couple therapist to understand their bids for sexual intimacy. First, we will discuss the intake information about their sex life and then discuss their family-of-origin dynamics relative to their intimacy needs.

It was apparent from the outset that the emotions between the partners were extremely raw. Jerry described their sex life as "lifeless" and angrily called Anna a "frigid bitch." He claimed that he only started the affair at work after he had been abandoned by her in the marriage and only after repeatedly being rejected by her until he stopped trying to initiate sex. He reminisced that in the beginning, their sex life was "hot" and that, before the kids were born, they would frequently make love spontaneously in "kinky spots" (e.g. in the car while in the driveway), watch adult movies and attempt different positions, or even engage in masturbatory fantasy on the phone with each other during the day while at work. Anna was initially embarrassed that Jerry would reveal this information to a total stranger, but when asked about her characterization of the sexual aspect of the relationship, she stated that it was "fun for a while, but then it got old. I grew up." This seemed to hurt Jerry, though he didn't voice the feeling.

In terms of her sexuality, Anna reported feeling that her sex drive had diminished since the birth of her children, which has concerned her. Although she has not had a full physical workup, she reported it to her ob-gyn, who told her that hormonal changes in the body postpartum can have long-term effects. Anna stated that she doesn't really miss sex and was kind of relieved that Jerry stopped pestering her for it all the time. She did admit that she does periodically want Jerry sexually, but it never seems to happen at a convenient time (kids, mealtime, etc.). Anna confessed that she had suspicions that Jerry may have been seeing someone else, which compounded her feelings of sexual inadequacy. In terms of Brown's (2007) typology, the type of affair being described is most likely a "Split-Self" Affair. Each person was suppressing a side to themselves in order to keep up the appearances of normality to the outside world. A picture was beginning to emerge, where a negative feedback cycle was keeping this couple apart, but more information was needed.

Exploration of the couple's families of origin produced the genogram seen previously (Figure 13.2), which revealed that Anna was estranged from her father from her late teens until his sudden death from a heart attack ten years ago. She described him as aloof and clueless about the family's day-to-day functioning. Anna has an enmeshed relationship with her mother and reported that she usually calls her mother several times a day and at least every night (usually when Jerry is home), and they talk at length. Jerry complained that Anna "always makes time for her mother but never puts in that type of effort with me." Anna indignantly retorted that her mother needs her, "and besides, I like her. Is there anything wrong with being friends with your mother?"

Jerry's family of origin revealed that his mother and father divorced following an affair that his father had with a neighbor, which

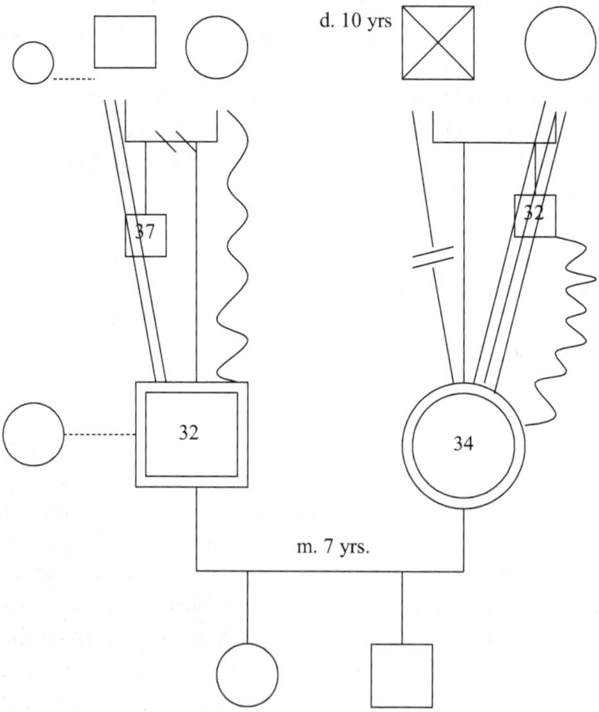

Figure 13.2 Case-study genogram.

he described as devastating to his mother, who was anxious before the divorce and became clinically depressed following it. Jerry recalled that he was 13 years old at the time of the divorce, and that he was close to his father, whom he admired as strong and decisive compared to his mother's apparent weakness. Jerry also revealed that he resented his mother and blamed her controlling behavior for driving his father away from the family (and him). However, although he was close to his father, Jerry also recalled several awkward episodes where he, his father, and his father's girlfriend would go out together. During those times, he would be aware that his father's attention was always on his girlfriend, and on several occasions when Jerry was sleeping over, he could hear his father making love in the next room. "I understand it now. He was still a young man, and he wanted to live life," Jerry said. "But I did wish that he would have thought about me sometimes."

In focusing on the patterns in the relationship dynamics from the family of origin, it was obvious that, like his father, when Jerry no longer felt like he was a contributing member of the family (as evidenced by his wife's over-functioning at home following the birth of their son), he began to withdraw and invest his time and energy at work, which led to a relationship (and subsequent affair) with a coworker. In addition, his disdain for anxious and controlling women like his mother made it difficult for him to hear Anna's pleas for connection with him as anything but demands. This, coupled with her unwillingness to engage him sexually, was intolerable, since it would be akin to his father's relationship with his mother (a pattern he swore that he would not repeat). Finally, seeing the growing influence of Anna's mother on her strengthened Jerry's desire to withdraw from her, and he no longer initiated sex. When he withdrew from her, Anna was very hurt and disappointed and took this as a sign that Jerry was being cold and selfish like her father. This forced her to adopt a position similar to that of her mother, whom she saw as caring, self-sacrificing, and effective at managing her family. This stance exhausted her physically and emotionally, which compounded her decreased desire for Jerry sexually.

Consistent with Schnarch's (1991) sexual crucible approach, and looking at the dynamics of the relationship, the individual with the lowest sexual desire always controls the sex. This was the case between Anna and Jerry. She controlled sex and treated Jerry with the same dismissiveness (cutoff) that she had for other men (like her father) when he was not there for her. Specifically, she recalled an incident when their son was nine months old and their daughter was about three, and she was overwhelmed with caring for the two of them. They had not been on a vacation, which they used to do often, and her husband had been invited to go on a golf weekend for business. She asked him not to go, but he left her anyway. "I had a mommy meltdown, and he didn't give a damn." In her mind, this was the last straw, and she made the decision that since she was no longer the object of his affection, he no longer deserved her attention (or sex). In a very heated way, she recounted,

> I finally realized that I had tried everything from being his 'little whore' in the beginning to trying to be the perfect wife and mother. Then, when I needed him, he just shut me out. I finally admitted that I was never going to get what I needed.

She called her mother, crying, and her mother came to stay with her that weekend. From then on, she cut off Jerry (literally and metaphorically) in the same way she cut off her father from her life. This put the power dynamics of the system way out of balance. Previously, Jerry was used to "having to work for it" (Anna's affection as well as sex), but now, there was nothing he could do to win her over. Jerry's affair was a way to rebalance the system by rupturing the marital bond.

Considering the case from Peluso's (2018) three-step model, Jerry and Anna (1) clearly have overall negative marital satisfaction (and have for some time), (2) have a clear power imbalance that manifested itself in both (a) the control of when they have sex and (b) the amount of time they spend with one another, and (3) the realization that the fantasies that each had for the marriage were not going to be fulfilled. At this point, each person turned to someone outside the marriage (Anna to her mother, Jerry to his mistress) in order to get their needs met. This is because each perceived some hurt or disappointment from the other that caused them to withdraw (in a fashion similar to their parents). Now, however, it has become an issue of boundaries and a test of the marriage, whereby both partners must make a good faith effort to resist using these surrogates and turn their attention to their marriage. In this way, they are both saying that they will seek to meet their needs by relying on themselves (both individually and together). However, it is not enough to say that they will stop seeing other people. In order to complete this process, both must undergo some differentiation. For Jerry, his going outside of the marriage may have been a symbolic way to show Anna that he doesn't approve of her going outside of the marriage for fulfillment (to her mother), which always leaves him feeling felt left out. However, he must develop a more adult view of sex and intimacy that allows him to experience aloneness and vulnerability rather than just pleasure and conquest. Anna must differentiate from mother. She has introjected her mother's viewpoint and role so far into her own life that there is no place for sex anymore. Instead, she must reconnect with her fantasies of fulfillment and self-loving and find some meaning for herself between the images of the "frigid bitch" and the "little whore." This will be hard work for each of them and requires a high level of personal maturity and emotional courage; otherwise, they will revert to their old patterns, which will result in more of the same for both of them.

Concluding Note

Sexual dysfunction and infidelity are common issues that couples face, and initiate couple therapy for help. In this chapter, we have given an overview of historical and current methods of working with sexual dysfunction. In addition, a review of the systems-based principles of conceptualizing infidelity, along with an explanatory and treatment model for infidelity, has been provided. In order to be effective, couple therapists need to have a clear idea of relational systems and how to intervene effectively in these often difficult areas.

References

American Psychiatric Association. (2013). *Diagnostic and statistical manual of mental disorders: DSM-5* (5th ed.). Washington, DC: American Psychiatric Association.

Annon, J. S. (1974). *The behavioral treatment of sexual problems. Volume I: Brief therapy*. Honolulu, HI: Enabling Systems.

Annon, J. S. (1975). *The behavioral treatment of sexual problems: Volume 2. Intensive therapy*. Honolulu, HI: Enabling Systems.

Atkins, D. C., Eldridge, K. A., Baucom, D. H., & Christensen, A. (2005). Infidelity and behavioral couple therapy: Optimism in the face of betrayal. *Journal of Consulting and Clinical Psychology, 73*, 144–150.

Atkins, D. C., Marin, R. A., Lo, T. T. Y., Klann, N., & Hahlweg, K. (2010). Outcomes of couples with infidelity in a community-based sample of couple therapy. *Journal of Family Psychology, 24*, 212–216.

Brown, E. (2001). *Patterns of infidelity and affairs: A guide to working through the repercussions of infidelity.* New York, NY: Jossey-Bass.

Brown, E. (2007). The affair as a catalyst for change. In P. R. Peluso (Ed.), *Infidelity: A practitioner's guide to working with couples in crisis* (pp. 149–165). New York, NY: Routledge.

Castonguay, L. G. (2013). Psychotherapy outcome: An issue worth re-revisiting 50 years later. *Psychotherapy, 50*(1), 52–67. doi:10.1037/a0030898

Daneshfar, F., Behboodi-Moghadam, Z., Khakbazan, Z., Nabavi, S. M., Nayeri, N. D., Ghasemzadeh, S., & Montazeri, A. (2017). The influence of ex-plissit (extended permission, limited information, specific suggestions, intensive therapy) model on intimacy and sexuality of married women with multiple sclerosis. *Sexual Disabilities, 35*, 399. doi:10.1007/s11195-017-9482-z

Glick, I. D., Berman, E. M., Clarkin, J. F., & Rait, D. S. (2000). *Marital and family therapy* (4th ed.). Washington, DC: American Psychiatric Press.

Glick, I. D., Clarkin, J. R., & Kessler, D. R. (1987). *Marital and family therapy* (3rd ed.). Orlando, FL: Grune & Stratton.

Gordon, K. C., Baucom, D. H., & Snyder, D. K. (2004). An integrative intervention for promoting recovery from extramarital affairs. *Journal of Marital and Family Therapy, 30*, 1–12.

Greenberg, L., Warwar, S., & Malcolm, W. (2010). Emotion-focused couple therapy and the facilitation of forgiveness. *Journal of Marital and Family Therapy, 36*, 28–42.

Heiman, J., LoPiccolo, L., & LoPiccolo, J. (1981). The treatment of sexual dysfunction. In A. Gurman & D. Kniskern (Eds.), *Handbook of family therapy.* New York, NY: Brunner/Mazel.

Kaplan, H. S. (1974). *The new sex therapy: Active treatment of sexual dysfunction.* New York, NY: Brunner/Mazel.

Kaplan, H. S. (1995). *The sexual desire disorders.* New York, NY: Brunner/Mazel.

Kessel, D. E., Moon, J. H., & Atkins D. C. (2007). Research on couple therapy for infidelity: What do we know about helping couples when there has been an affair? In P. R. Peluso (Ed.), *Infidelity: A practitioner's guide to working with couples in crisis* (pp. 55–70). New York, NY: Routledge.

Khakbazan, Z., Daneshfar, F., Behboodi-Moghadam, Z., Nabavi, S. M., Ghasemzadeh, S., & Mehran, A. (2016). The effectiveness of the permission, limited information, specific suggestions, intensive therapy (PLISSIT) model based sexual counseling on the sexual function of women with multiple sclerosis who are sexually active. *Journal of Multiple Sclerosis Related Disorders, 8*, 113–119.

Kroger, C., Reißner, T., Vasterling, I., Schutz, K., & Kliem, S. (2012). Therapy for couples after an affair: A randomized-controlled trial. *Behaviour Research and Therapy, 50*, 786–796. doi:10.1016/j.brat.2012.09.006

Labrecque, L. T., & Whisman, M. A. (2017). Attitudes toward and prevalence of extramarital sex and descriptions of extramarital partners in the 21st century. *Journal of Family Psychology.* Advance online publication. doi:10.1037/fam0000280

Masters, W., & Johnson, V. (1966). *Human sexual response.* Boston, MA: Little Brown.

McCarthy, B. W. (2002). Sexuality, sexual dysfunction, and couple therapy. In A. S. Gurman & N. S. Jacobson (Eds.), *Clinical handbook of couple therapy* (3rd ed., pp. 629–652). New York, NY: Guilford.

McCarthy, B. W., & Ross, L. W. (2017). Integrating sexual concepts and interventions into couple therapy. In J. Fitzgerald (Ed.), *Foundations for couple therapy: Research for the real world* (pp. 355–364). New York, NY: Routledge.

Moll, C. (2013). New Aging: Sexuality and intimacy. In P. R. Peluso, R. E. Watts, & M. Parsons (Eds.). *Changing aging, changing family therapy: Pracricing with 21st century relities* (pp. 97–112). New York, NY: Routldege.

Peluso, P. R. (2018). *A family systems guide to infidelity helping couples understand, recover from, and avoid future affairs.* New York, NY: Routledge.

Peluso, P. R. (2007). *Infidelity: A practitioner's guide to working with couples in crisis.* New York, NY: Routledge.

Schnarch, D. (1991). *Constructing the sexual crucible: An integration of sexual and marital therapy.* New York, NY: W. W. Norton.

Schnarch, D. (1997). *Passionate marriage: Love, sex, and intimacy in emotional committed relationships.* New York, NY: Henry Holt.

Schnarch, D. M. (2010). A crucible approach to sexual desire disorders. In Leiblum, S. R. (Ed.), *Treating sexual desire disorders: A clinical casebook* (pp. 44–60). New York, NY: Guilford Publications.

Shackelford, T. K., & Buss, D. M. (1997). Cues to infidelity. *Personality and Social Psychology Bulletin, 23,* 1034–1045.

Starratt, V. G., Weekes-Shackelford, V., & Shakelford, T. K. (2017). Mate value both positively and negatively predicts intentions to commit an infidelity. *Personality and Individual Differences, 104,* 18–22. doi:10.1016/j.paid.2016.07.028

Tafoya, M. A., & Spitzberg, B. H. (2007). The dark side of infidelity: Its nature, prevalence, and communicative functions. In B. H. Spitzberg & W. R. Cupach (Eds.), *The dark side of interpersonal communication* (2nd ed., pp. 201–242). Mahwah, NJ: Lawrence Erlbaum Associates.

Taylor, B., & Davis, S. (2007). The extended PLISSIT model for addressing the sexual wellbeing of individuals with an acquired disability or chronic illness. *Journal of Sexual Disabilities, 25,* 135–139.

Taylor, B., & Davis, S. (2006). Using the extended PLISSIT model to address sexual healthcare needs. *Nursing Standards, 21*(11), 35–40.

Weeks G., & Fife, S. (2014). *Couples in treatment.* New York, NY: Routledge.

Weeks, G., & Gambescia, N. (2015). Couple therapy and sexual problems. In A. S. Gurman, J. Lebow, & D. Snyder (Eds.), *Clinical handbook of couple therapy* (5th ed., pp. 635–656). New York, NY: Guilford.

Weeks, G., & Hof, L. (1987). *Integrating sex and marital therapy: A clinical guide.* New York, NY: Brunner/Mazel.

Weiser, D. A., & Weigel, D. J. (2015). Investigating experiences of the infidelity partner: Who is the "other man/woman"? *Personality and Individual Differences, 85,* 176–181. doi:10.1016/j.paid.2015.05.014

Whisman, M. A., Dixon, A. E., & Johnson, B. (1997). Therapists' perspectives of couple problems and treatment issues in the practice of couple therapy. *Journal of Family Psychology, 11,* 361–366.

14 Aging, Separation, Divorce, and Remarriage

LEARNING OBJECTIVES

In this chapter, the reader will learn the following:

1 The effect of aging on relationships.
2 Working with couples when one partner becomes a caregiver of the other.
3 Preparing to practice with older couples.
4 Helping couples discern whether or not to end the relationship.
5 Working with couples who are ending their relationship.

How couples progress through the life span, and how this changes over time is an often overlooked area of couples counseling. In addition, how couples go about the process of separation and ending relationships are complex and intricate activities. Anyone working as a couple therapist may encounter either or both of these issues on a daily basis and must have an understanding of how to intervene effectively. In this chapter, we present an overview of these common and, at times, very challenging areas in working with couples: Issues of aging as well as issues related to separation, divorce, and remarriage.

Aging and Couple Therapy

On January 1, 2011, the oldest member of the "Baby Boomer" generation turned 65 years old. This generation (who were born in the aftermath of World War II from 1946 to 1960) was one of the largest generational groups of children born in the U.S. (estimated at approximately 79 million people. Every day for the next 19 years, about 10,000 more individuals turn 65 and become "senior citizens." Today, individuals over the age of 65 comprise 13% of all Americans. By 2030, when all Baby Boomers will have turned 65, they will compromise 20% of the nation's population. At the same time, people are living longer (well past 65 years old), which is forcing clinicians and researchers to reconsider what the needs and issues of aging couples will be, and how to best meet them (Peluso, Parsons, & Watts, 2013). According to Fruhauf and Lambert-Shute (2013):

> Aging is, therefore, a relationship rather than a discrete chronological number separate from "self." For example, aging as a relationship might be further described as being retired, losing sensory memory (e.g. hearing, seeing, taste, touch, etc.), being unable to care for ourselves, watching friends die, and, possibly, becoming a parent at age 65. These changes impact individuals' relationship with their selves, their relationship with family, and their relationship with the world. Moreover, who someone is changes his/her view of self, society's view of him/her, others' perception of how he/she can or cannot participate, how family members interact with him/her, and the choices he/she believes he/she has.
>
> (p. 31)

Not only is it a disservice for couple therapists to ignore aging-related topics, but there may be a lost financial opportunity for them as well. According to U.S. Department of Labor (2011) estimates, 3.6 million new jobs will be created in health care and social services to meet the needs of the aging population. With the increased number of older adults, there is a possibility for sustained therapy with the aging population (Fruhauf & Lambert-Shute, 2013).

Unfortunately, the field is not meeting this challenge! Most recently, Lambert-Shute and Fruhauf (2011) conducted a content analysis of 957 articles published in *Journal of Marital and Family Therapy*, *American Journal of Family Therapy*, and *Contemporary Family Therapy*. Surprisingly, they found that only 2.8% ($n = 27$) of the published articles included older adults in their sample or even mentioned aging as an issue. When the topics of aging were discussed, the focus was more often on more contemporary aging issues (i.e. health-related issues, later life marriages, and caregiving), suggesting that the field is beginning to recognize that the unique and emerging issues of aging couples and families are starting to become important issues for clinicians and researchers to pay attention to in the marriage and family therapy literature (Fruhauf & Lambert-Shute, 2013).

At the same time, the response by practitioners in the field regarding the desire to work with older couples and families is somewhat mixed. In a survey of over 1,200 psychologists, Qualls and her colleagues (2002) found that 40% of practitioners wanted to increase their professional work with older clients but hadn't as of yet. The implication of this trend is that if they are not deliberately exposed to the conceptual ideas of working with older couples and do not have the practical experiences of working with them, couple therapists are not likely to want to work with them. This is problematic since they represent one of the fastest growing groups of potential clients in the population. At the same time, couples and family therapists are uniquely suited to help these families by utilizing some of the most basic elements of family systems theory (family life cycle, genograms, intergenerational patterns, etc.). Adding to this gap is the fact that there is a serious lack of specific training for family therapists in the area of aging and age-related issues in family therapy, in light of the overwhelming need. In fact, if couple therapists wish to develop greater competency in working with aging couples, they must seek out this training on their own (Peluso et al., 2013).

The Pikes Peak Training Model for Couple Therapists

As we and others have noted, the lack of attention that has been paid to issues of older adults has also meant a lack of proper training for clinicians (Fruhauf & Lambert-Shute, 2013; Lambert-Shute & Fruhauf, 2011; Peluso, 2013). Shortages in the workforce for geriatric mental health care are predicted to rise significantly. In 2009, a group of clinicians created a comprehensive model for training, called the Pikes Peak model (Knight, Karel, Hinrichesen, Qualls, & Duffy, 2009). The Pikes Peak competencies and related training recommendations are aimed at newly licensed couples counselors that wish to specialize in working with older couples. According to Knight et al., "The Pikes Peak model is offered as an aspirational model for training programs and for individual psychologists and psychologists in training who may seek guidance in selecting programs or creating self-study programs on their own" (2009, p. 206). They noted that due to many of the similarities and overlaps between younger and older couples, not every clinician who works with older couples may need specialized training. Rather, they remark that as the couples' issues become more complicated, couple therapists who work with older couples will need specialized training.

The Pikes Peak training model outlined four broad domains that distinguish it from other areas of psychological practice. They are (1) an emphasis on the developmental aspects of aging and understanding the universal elements of aging vs. the historical time elements of any given cohort; (2) knowledge of psychopathologies that have a higher prevalence late in life (e.g. dementias) or that have unique expression in older populations (e.g. personality disorders, alcohol abuse, depression, etc.) and the skills to distinguish and work with them; (3) understanding the interaction of medical conditions common to older adults on psychological disorders, inclusive of any medication side effects; and (4) understanding the various contexts and embedded systems that older individuals are part of (e.g. residential care, community organizations that serve elder populations, etc.). In addition, Knight et al. (2009) list six competencies that reflect their "aspirational goals for training" (p. 209). We have listed them in Table 14.1.

In terms of practice, proponents of the Pike Peak training model recommend that couples counselors who want to work with older couples should be prepared to provide their services in at least two or more settings. These can include outpatient mental health services, long-term care settings or assisted living facilities, outpatient primary care or medical settings, and inpatient medical or psychiatric service, to name a few. Hartman-Stein (2013) discussed protocols for visiting clients in their home or rehabilitation facility when they were not able to come to the office. In addition, several accessibility considerations must be made when considering clinical practice with older couples (Blando & Lawton, 2013).

Table 14.1 Pikes Peak Model Core Competencies for Geropsychologists

1	Normal aging is taught so that students have a basis for understanding abnormal aging experiences.
2	Bona fide professional geropsychologists using observational methods are employed as supervisors in geropsychology training programs so that students can develop appropriate skills in working with older adults.
3	Training in geropsychology includes facilitated experiences to gain self-awareness about one's responses to aging that vary by health status (e.g. frail as well as healthy aging), cultural and individual identities (e.g. wealthy or poor, rural or urban, ethnic identity, gender identity, sexual orientation, religious identity, disability status), and diverse historical cohort experiences.
4	Experiential professional training with older adults is provided across a variety of settings. Trainees need experience in diverse settings (e.g. nursing homes, assisted living, primary care medical practice, hospitals, and clients' homes).
5	Interprofessional team training is an essential part of professional geropsychology training. Trainees must learn about the knowledge base, scope of practice, and distinct professional work styles of other disciplines.
6	The distinct ethical and legal issues and practice standards that are part of practice with older adults are included in professional geropsychology training programs. Examples include late-life decision-making and functional capacities, advance care planning and surrogate decision-making, communication with caregiving families in a manner that respects the confidentiality of the older client, and end-of-life care.

From Knight et al. (2009).

Another important consideration for clinicians who want to work with older couples is the need to consult effectively with families and other support systems (medical personnel, care agencies, and other professional and nonprofessional geriatric care-providers). Again, here is where trained family therapists may be uniquely suited to helping this population (Peluso, 2013). Specifically important, couple therapists

> must have a working knowledge of these various systems and interface with them as appropriate. How and when to include family members in geropsychological care is a critical issue with ethical and clinical implications...In addition to being able to attend to the complex needs of frail older adults in long-term care, the psychologist working in the long-term care setting must be capable of training all levels of staff from nurses' aides to administrators, organizational consultation, and skilled work within interdisciplinary teams.
>
> (Knight et al., 2009, p. 207)

In the appendix to their article, Knight et al. (2009) present an outline to the full training model, which includes the knowledge, attitude, and skill competencies for professional practice in geropsychology. We recommend that clinicians who are interested in learning more about this should consult this valuable resource.

Even with these advances, however, the field needs to create more awareness of the needs of aging couples and provide education about aging-related issues so that couple therapists can have a better foundation to meet the needs of the older client. It is not feasible for couple therapists to have expertise in all areas of gerontology; however, addressing the essential training needs for competency in working with older couples that includes both couples and family therapy as well as gerontology is essential.

Couple Therapy and Older Adults

Therapeutic work with older couples in late life requires an understanding of the different stages of older individuals. Traditionally, they are broken down into three groups: Youngold, middle-old, and old-old. The "young-old" are couples in their 60s who are likely still working or are close to retirement. These couples may still have young adults in their household and may also be caring for elderly parents. The "middle-old" are couples in their 70s and 80s, and may be in the beginning phases of retirement (if they have not already retired). They may be facing issues of their own health and mortality, as well as negotiating intimacy needs based on personal vulnerability that may not have been discussed previously. These couples may have concerns about financial security or children as they enter adulthood. Finally, there are the "old-old." These are couples in their 80s and 90s (or beyond). The issues that these couples may be facing are issues of mortality and meaning as well as loss (Peluso et al., 2013). In addition, the therapist must be aware of his or her own feelings about aging and mortality:

> (T)herapists who choose to work with old-old couples will be more effective if aware of their own fears about aging and dying. To connect with the old-old the therapist must acquire a degree of comfort dealing with topics such as loneliness, living with memory loss, spirituality, mystical experiences, death, and the purpose of life. Therapists who choose to work with late life couples are bound to develop meaningful connections with some of the clients they serve and consequently experience sadness and loss when the client dies.
>
> (Hartman-Stein, 2013, p. 125)

According to Qualls (1993), therapists encounter two types of late-life couples: Those wanting to resolve a conflict and caregiving couples. An interesting finding about aging couples seeking couple therapy is that despite years of disorder and dysfunction, the couple may have gone decades without any professional involvement (Knight et al., 2009; Lambert-Shute & Fruhauf, 2011). Unless the children in these families acted out or had difficulty in school, the family's dynamics may not have risen to the attention of teachers, principals, or other community members who could intervene (i.e. recommend family therapy). As a result, these families may only come to the attention of professionals when someone's poor support or functioning becomes visible within the agencies and systems that tend to older adults (particularly in the medical field). When couples present with these structural problems, interventions need to be targeted to reorganize the system to better meet aging family members' needs.

As with other crisis points in family development (adolescence, divorce, drug addiction, etc.), couple therapy can address these basic factors and help to "backfill" the areas that were missing. It provides the couple an opportunity to build structures that weren't there before, as well prepare to use them in the care of the aging family member. Couple therapy can be particularly helpful in both the remediation of dysfunctional families and assisting better functioning families who are overwhelmed with the dizzying array of caregiving decisions to cope with them in a productive way (Peluso et al., 2013; Qualls, 2000).

Couples as Caregivers

Spousal caregivers face different challenges from adult children due to the meaning of the historical relationship: "Intimate personal care of the body may be more comfortable for spouses than children because such familiarity is part of their historical roles" (Qualls & Vair, 2013, p. 74). However, acting decisively when a need arises can be a challenge to many spouses who struggle with making decisions for their spouse or partner unilaterally. Another barrier (though one that is becoming less insurmountable) is faced by long-term partners who lack a marriage certificate (e.g. cohabitating couples, gay and lesbian couples, etc.) and encounter distinct challenges of claiming authority within various service systems, though this has changed significantly in the last decade (Qualls & Vair, 2013).

The challenges for couples that must transition into a caregiving arrangement can be fairly significant. For example, when one partner begins to suffer cognitive declines, the other partner becomes involved in caretaking. According to Qualls (2000), this response requires a substantial effort, ranging from three to five hours per day, dealing with widely varying tasks, such as "cooking, management of personal finances, social relationships and ultimately basic activities of daily living (e.g. bathing, dressing, eating)" (p. 194). Some spouses or partners will – either by choice or by default – have to respond and provide some care. Others may ignore the emerging needs of older partners and abdicate any responsibility. Moreover, particularly with older individuals who have suffered from bouts of depression, the need for ongoing treatment is crucial. It is estimated that close to 40% of people over 60 who have had a depressive episode will have a recurrence within three to six years. These will likely require their spouse or partner to be a primary caregiver, as depression in the elderly creates additional challenges. We present a case illustration next.

Joan had always been depressed. As far back as she could remember, she struggled with feelings of sadness, difficulty getting motivated, and sometimes was preoccupied with thoughts of death and suicide. She would often go through periods where she would have plenty of energy, despite sleeping only a few hours a night, then times where she was unable to move from her bed for days at a time. She enjoyed how much she could get accomplished when she was "normal" and was disappointed by her lethargy when she was in her "black hole." Her husband of 47 years, Mike, and her three children (ages 46, 41, and 37) had been there to "weather the storms" of her mood swings and could easily predict when Joan's mental state was beginning to deteriorate. Frequently, she would begin to talk incessantly about whatever crossed her mind, she would begin large projects (but often not finish them), or she would make plans that would affect her (and her family's) life without consulting them. Throughout her life, several doctors misdiagnosed her with borderline personality disorder, dissociative identity disorder, major depression, and bipolar disorder. She was hospitalized three times in her life for suicidal ideation, first as a result of postpartum depression following the birth of her youngest child, second as a result of depression brought upon by the death of her mother, and lastly when her youngest child moved out of the house. Finally, she was properly diagnosed as cyclothymic, and for the last ten years, she has been able to effectively manage her symptoms – with medication and psychotherapy – and has not had any significant events.

However, two years ago, at age 66, Joan was diagnosed with hypertension and an irregular heartbeat. She was put on medication to regulate her blood pressure and heart condition. She informed her cardiac doctors about her medication, and they assured her that there would not be any interaction of interference. Shortly after she began her cardiac medication, she began to feel light-headed and dizzy. At first, she was told that she needed to get used to the medication, and that a drop in blood pressure was a common side effect. It did not go away, and Joan was afraid of losing consciousness and breaking her hip or another bone (something that had happened to her mother, and, in Joan's mind, hastened her death). She began to experiment with her psychiatric medication and found that her dizziness seemed to be reduced when she halved her dosage or took it every other day. Unfortunately, she did this without informing any of her physicians. It was several months when Mike first noticed that Joan didn't seem to be herself. She began to talk constantly about moving to Arizona for a warmer climate. This was odd to him because she had vehemently been against the idea when they discussed it several years earlier. Then he discovered that a credit card that had been long closed was suddenly getting charges on it from a television shopping channel. Finally, he found a closet full of packages that Joan had ordered but never opened. When he confronted her about this, she broke down sobbing and shrieking that she felt like she wanted to die. Mike was astonished to hear her talking about this, and brought her in to her therapist for a consultation.

5R Framework for Helping Aging Couples

In considering cases like the ones described earlier, Peluso (2013) developed a framework for couples and families to utilize when discussing the needs of caregiving spouses or children. Like many families that have to deal with aging parents and a maturing family structure, there were five major underlying (and interlocking) issues. These are the Resources, Residence, Respite, Respect, and Reaction (a "5R Framework") that most families have to cope with, and when there are problems in the family, it is often due to an inability to work out one of these five issues. Briefly, these refer to:

Resources are issues that relate to human and financial resources that are available. *Human* resources can include the cognitive and physical abilities of family members and their availability to participate in the older family member's care, or their proximity to being able to care. It can also include the abilities and functioning of the person in need of care, and the tasks that they can still reliably perform themselves. *Financial* resources, on the other hand, can include money to pay for medical needs, the ability to afford "quality" long-term care, insurance available, as well as other things.

Residence refers to the living arrangements for the older family member. Decisions have to be made regarding whether he or she can continue to live at home unsupervised, live at home supervised, move in with a family member, or move into an assisted living facility. Temporary living arrangements, as well as longer term arrangements often need to be made, which can be daunting for caregivers.

Respite follows from the residence issues. If the spouse or partner takes on the task of physically housing the other member, then decisions with adult children or other relatives about how to give that caregiver respite (or a "break") from the day-to-day caregiving must be made. If the family member is living at their home, there may be periods of time when another family member will stay with them, or have the older family member stay with the adult child. This is dependent on the *resources* issues outlined earlier, as well.

Respect is the overarching element toward this joint decision-making. It values the input of all family members, and creates an atmosphere of "good-faith" when negotiating the other issues. Families that are unable to respect each other will not come to consensus, and there may be lingering bitterness that can sabotage any decisions. Family therapists can help to clarify the issues that may be getting in the way of this, and often family members have to put aside old hurts or feelings of resentment in order to help care for the parent.

Reaction is the understanding that individual family members, especially the spouse or partner, will have an emotional reaction prior to, during, and following these changes to the family. By allowing time for the various family members to process their own feelings, and feed them back into the decision-making, adjustments can be made. If no adjustments can be made, it also gives each family member the opportunity to draw support from other family members' experience and reactions. Again, couples and family therapists trained in geropsychology can be facilitative in this process (Peluso, 2013).

The 5R Framework is helpful in preserving as much function for the spouse or partner who has to be a caregiver. Primary caregivers must be made aware that their health and mental health are at risk, and encouraged to engage in self-care practices. Couple therapists working with these couples must help the spouse or partner to see the necessity of self-care. Imagery exercises can be helpful to caregivers: "I want you to imagine yourself waking up in the emergency room with great pain in your hip which appears to be fractured. As you think about your _____ (loved one with dementia), you realize that no one else may have _________________." By filling in the blanks, caregivers can see the wide range of services that they provide, which can quickly translate into insight as to why self-care is important (as their loved one might be at risk if they were not able to function) (Qualls & Vair, 2013). For example, a spouse or partner may realize that without them, the partner would most likely be home by themselves and unable to take medications or prepare meals. The goal of this type of imagery exercise is used to increase urgency and overcome resistance by the caregiver to engage in self-care (Peluso, 2013; Qualls & Vair, 2013).

Practical Physical Space/Accommodation

One last area in which we wish to provide some guidance for couple therapists who are considering working with older couples is in the area of physical space and accommodations for older individuals. Many of the physical and access issues that clinicians must address are the results of the Americans with Disability Act (ADA) of 1990 and ADA Amendments Act (ADAAA) of 2008. However, there is more than just compliance with physical access. Blando and Lawton point out that:

> In addition to addressing the on a manifest level the particular content issues that are brought up by families with older adults (e.g., stopping driving, dangerous or noxious behaviors related to dementia, alcohol or other substance abuse, psychiatric problems, nursing care), clinicians also communicate to their clients on a latent level. Specifically, these are underlying messages about regard for the client, sensitivity to client needs, etc., that are communicated latently. These messages are communicated

> through such items as how the waiting room is organized, how the consultation room is designed, how information is communicated to clients, how clients are allowed to respond, etc.
>
> (p. 151)

Thus, couples counselors must not only think through how they will arrange the physical space for older couples (including lighting, font size for handouts/paperwork, noise considerations, etc.) but also consider differences in cognitive comprehension and how they will present information to couples.

Adapting Universal Design for Learning Principles to Couple Therapy

Universal design for learning (UDL) is a framework designed to maximize successful learning by designing curricula that meet the needs of every person who receives the curricula, regardless of cognitive or physical differences. It is based upon the understanding that the brain contains three primary networks related to learning: Recognition, strategic, and affective networks (CAST, 2011). These three networks – recognition, strategic, and affective – suggest three areas in which to focus universal design principles: Providing multiple means of representation, of expression, and of engagement (Blando & Lawton, 2013). *Recognition* brain networks are elements that focus on acquiring information and organizing data from sensory input, including seeing, hearing, feeling, and reading. *Strategic* brain networks are elements that focus on planning and performing activities, including managing and communicating ideas through activities such as writing, drawing, or verbalizations. *Affective* brain networks are elements that focus on the motivational aspect of learning, including helping people be stimulated or curious about learning (Blando & Lawton, 2013).

Similar to UDL, a *universal design for counseling* is a framework that is designed to maximize success in the counseling process (regardless of theoretical orientation or counseling approach) by designing and organizing counseling to meet the needs of couples (particularly older couples). Table 14.2 summarizes a checklist of general principles for a universal design for counseling that can be adapted for couple therapists.

By adopting UDL and applying the framework for counseling, couple therapists can make their practices more welcoming and effective for older couples. As this group continues to grow and redefine the issues of aging, couple therapists who receive the necessary training will be in a unique position to be maximally helpful.

Separation, Divorce, and Remarriage

There are varying opinions about the role of couple therapists when working with a couple in the brink of divorce. Some therapists believe that it is

Table 14.2 ADA and Universal Design for Counseling Checklist

General Counseling Elements

- A statement or information is contained in my informed consent form and other forms that specify my willingness to provide accommodation for persons with disabilities or unique needs.
- I provide comprehensive informed consent and other forms that clearly specify requirements for counseling, expectations for counseling, and the estimated length of counseling, subject to change.
- I offer multiple forms of contact (answering service, email, etc.) so clients have varied ways to contact me between sessions, if necessary.

Representation

- I utilize multiple ways of providing psychoeducational content and other counseling approaches that incorporate different communication styles (visual/graphic, verbal/auditory, etc.).
- I provide multiple ways of clearly identifying and explaining essential counseling concepts (transference, collaboration, talk therapy, etc.).
- I support accessibility for all counseling content and materials (accessible websites for web-therapy, captioned videos for video-therapy, e-books for bibliotherapy, etc.).
- I provide examples and/or illustrations of how other clients approach psychoeducational, supportive, or other types of counseling.

Engagement

- I offer various ways to involve clients in the counseling process (conversation, homework, bibliotherapy, journaling, etc.).
- I encourage natural support systems (friends, family, group counseling members, social circles, etc.) for my clients, as appropriate.
- I provide alternatives for clients on how they can participate or complete homework or other counseling assignments.

Expression

- I offer clear and specific feedback on homework or other counseling assignments and on the course of counseling.
- I allow clients to demonstrate what they have learned in more than one way or through a variety of means (verbally, in writing, through role-play, etc.).
- I encourage the use of appropriate technologies to ensure that clients can accurately express what they have learned in counseling.
- I provide clear guidelines and expectations for all counseling activities.

Adapted from Blando and Lawton (2013).

wrong to hold a relationship that is poorly functioning together rather than letting it break apart. Other clinicians (Doherty & Harris, 2017) feel that couple therapists have too quickly helped couples to split up without fully exploring the consequences of a split. He and others believe that couple therapists should work to preserve the relationship at all costs and only contemplate a dissolution of a relationship if all else fails or under certain negative circumstances (i.e. intimate partner violence). Therapists should understand exactly what their position is on marriage and divorce. Ours is very pro-relationship, with the caveat that the ultimate decision must be made by the couple. Some couples hold onto relationships that are not good for them in order to avoid change. At the same time, maintaining a lasting relationship is often more difficult than forming a new one. Nevertheless, not every relationship can be improved, and some relationships are just not healthy for either of the participants. It is often important for partners to learn to change what can be changed and to accept what cannot be changed. As such, we believe that it is the therapist's job to guide the couple through the process to the best possible solution. We will now focus on various counseling aspects of separation, divorce, and remarriage, including how to handle the impact on children.

Separation

Separation is defined as "a formal or informal agreement between partners to remove themselves from their current marital situation" (Hale, 2015, p. 109). There is no one "right" model of separation. It can run the gamut from one partner physically removing him- or herself from the home to remaining and living as roommates. In addition, separation can also take place on an emotional level as each partner detaches from the other and begins to contemplate what life would be like apart from the other person. Sometimes, a separation can be helpful in allowing the spouses to learn more about themselves and what they really want in life. However, for couple therapists, as well as for couples, there can be a great deal of confusion about what a separation is, and what the goals should be during one. According to Hale (2015):

> The ultimate goal of separation should not be reconciliation. It is important that one not make the mistake of making reconciliation the goal of the separation. By establishing reconciliation as a goal of separation, one could act in ways that run counter to actions necessary to "win" someone back. For most, reconciliation is a by-product of the separation and the work that was accomplished during the time apart... Divorce, on the other hand, is also a by-product of separation. Like reconciliation, it too is not the primary goal of separation. Many fear that separation is the final step before divorce. In most cases, it doesn't have to be.
>
> (p. 114)

In order to clear up some of the confusion, we will discuss some pre-separation agreements and outline the protocol for Discernment Counseling as described by Doherty and Harris (2017), which we will outline later.

Pre-Separation Agreements

In order to make the transition time as smooth as possible, the therapist is wise to clarify and structure the separation beforehand. Table 14.3 presents the areas that often need to be clarified and that require agreement between the spouses.

Table 14.3 Areas of Consideration for Couples Thinking about Separation

1 The purpose of the separation. Is it to get away in order to think clearly? Is it to see whether or not the spouses can live apart? Is it a time to work on individual issues?
2 The time limit on the separation.
3 Discretion in not injuring the reputation of the other by imprudent talk with relatives, friends, or others in the community; when necessary, discussion of personal matters away from the relationship.
4 What to tell others about what is going on; confidentiality.
5 No legal action before the separation is ended unless the action is mutually agreed upon.
6 Convenient, regular, and arranged access by the noncustodial parent to the children; no negative use of the children.
7 No one-sided action (such as withdrawal of savings, applications for loans, sale of belongings, relocation, etc.) without consultation with the partner.
8 Meetings with friends; dates.
9 No changes, such as filing for divorce or taking or leaving a lover, without full discussion with a counselor.
10 No sabotage of the other partner's care and discipline of the children.
11 Nature of counseling sessions: Individual or conjoint?
12 How and when the spouses will see/date each other as well as participate (or not) in joint social functions.

Discernment Counseling

Discernment counseling, as developed by William Doherty and his associates, is a brief (one to five sessions) course of structured meetings with a couple that is considering a divorce. The goal of discernment counseling is to help a couple gain greater clarity about their relationship and make a decision about future actions that the couple will take. Through the process of discernment counseling, each member of the couple can explore what has happened to the marriage on a deeper level as well as each person's contributions to the relationship problems. It is intended for couples who are in a committed relationship in which one of the two partners is contemplating ending the relationship. The partner may be ambivalent about taking this step but may also have some reservations about engaging in couples counseling. An important distinction between couples counseling and discernment counseling is that the focus of couples counseling is improving the relationship by addressing the underlying dynamics of it, while discernment counseling helps couples clarify what the next step will be for their relationship and gain confidence about their next step. According to Doherty and Harris, the goal is "not to solve marriage problems but to see whether (the relationship) can be saved" (2017, p. 15). In other words, instead of a binary, forced choice of "saying together forever" or "going right this instant," discernment counseling is a "middle-way" process whereby the possibilities are explored:

> The immediate decision is not framed as whether to divorce or stay married for life, but whether to carve out a 6-month period of all-out effort

> in couple therapy to restore the marriage to health, with divorce off the table during that time. At the end of 6 months, they can reopen the decision about divorce on the basis of what they have learned about the prospect of successfully rebuilding their marriage.
>
> (Doherty & Harris, 2017, p. 14)

For the "leaning-out" partner (the partner that is thinking about leaving), the current relationship dynamic is usually intolerable, making divorce an attractive alternative. At the same time, the "leaning-in" spouse (the partner who does not want the relationship to end) may or may not agree that the relationship is problematic or they may or may not be aware of the leaning-out partner's dissatisfaction. Discernment counseling is not an approach for couples where one partner is committed to the idea of a divorce (Doherty & Harris, 2017).

In order not to get weighed down by an infinite number of possibilities, the decision that is to be discerned is one of three choices (or "paths"). Path 1 is the "status quo" where the relationship stays exactly as it has been with no change. In other words, the partners decide neither to work on the relationship in counseling nor to move toward a divorce. The way that Path 1 (i.e. the status quo) is framed automatically causes the leaning-out spouse to rule it out. Paradoxically, the leaning-in partner is often not in favor of Path 1 either. Many times, this is a surprise to the leaning-out partner. As a result, "the discernment process begins with agreement instead of disagreement—something has to change; the old way of being married is no longer viable" (Doherty & Harris, 2017, p. 15).

Path 2 is the decision to divorce (or separate) and not to work on the relationship. The way that Path 2 is framed places divorce on the table where it has been for the leaning-out spouse, making it a viable option and part of the discerning counseling process, rather than something that is avoided. Talking about it as a possible "path" is not a "threat" to the discernment counseling (as it often is for couple therapy) because couple therapy is not being done.

Path 3 is a six-month commitment to work on the relationship where divorce is "off the table," and instead the partners engage in couples counseling (along with other forms of counseling, such as substance abuse counseling, parenting classes, or individual work). After six months, if satisfactory change has not been made, then consideration of divorce is allowed. Path 3 is framed as a way out of the dilemma that the couples face with Paths 1 and 2. For the leaning-out partner, they may feel pressure to turn from Path 2 and remain committed to the relationship. However, this is often unacceptable because the relationship hasn't changed. At the same time, the couple may feel empowered by the possibilities for change (which may have taken years to muster the courage to ask for or consider). According to Doherty and Harris (2017), Path 3 avoids the "in or out" conundrum by offering a provisional commitment to work hard on the relationship for a period, with divorce not an option but something that can be revisited later if things do not change enough (p. 16).

As a result, the discernment that the leaning-out spouse needs to clarify is whether or not to embrace Path 3 and (potentially) embark on couple therapy

Table 14.4 Sequence of Sessions for Discernment Counseling

1 Time with the couple together,
2 Meeting with one partner alone (while the other partner, usually the leaning-in partner, waits in the waiting room),
3 Both partners together, the first partner summarizes to the other partner the key discussion points from the meeting,
4 Meeting with the other partner alone (while the first partner, usually the leaning-out partner, waits in the waiting room),
5 Both partners together, this time the second partner summarizes to the first partner the key discussion points from the meeting, and
6 The therapist summarizes the entire session, checks in with the couple, and sets up the next session.

From Doherty and Harris (2017).

after the discernment process, or immediately move toward divorce (selecting Path 2). The key for discernment counseling to get couples to choose Path 3 is to address the ambivalence about working on changes in the relationship, and "see whether it's possible to put the marriage into a place that would be good for both partners" (Doherty & Harris, 2017, p. 15).

A central aspect of discernment counseling is that the majority of the work occurs in individuals' conversations with each partner as opposed to couples counseling, where the work is generally done with the couple together (Doherty & Harris, 2017). Each session has six separate segments that proceed the same way each time (see Table 14.4 for details).

According to Doherty and Harris (2017), the themes in the individual conversations are similar, though slightly altered. For both, the main focus is on which "Path" they will ultimately choose. For the leaning-out spouse, exploration of their source of frustration and pain in the relationship is a part of the conversation, while for the leaning-in spouse, the emphasis is on how to manage their needs during the crisis, and not to make things worse by pressing them for a commitment that they are not willing to make just yet. Instead, the couple therapist can work on helping the leaning-in spouse to make personal changes that may be helpful to the relationship in the future.

Divorce

According to Pinsof (2002), prior to the second half of the 20th century, the leading cause of marriages ending was the death of one spouse. He reports that prior to 1940, more than two-thirds of marriages ended because of the death of a spouse, but by 1976, that number was down to about one-third. However, the rate of divorce in the U.S. continues to be high, with approximately 40%–50% of all marriages ending in divorce (Knoester & Booth, 2000; Lebow, 2015; Poladian, Rossi, Rudd, & Holtzworth-Munroe, 2017). In addition, although in the years between 1976 and the beginning of the 21st century, the rate of divorce leveled off, by then, the children affected by divorce had grown up and fashioned relationships of their own. Knoester and Booth (2000) describe that one reason for this is often concern for the well-being of children, which can be a significant, subjective barrier to divorce. However, they also found that objective circumstances (such as wife's income, birth of a new child, and church attendance) were stronger influences on the decision to stay married. This ambivalence is usually a driving force to bringing couples to couple therapy, with the future state of the relationship riding in the balance. It is essential, however, that the therapist be familiar with the stages of separation and divorce and the specific emotional problems related to them (Lebow, 2015; Taylor, 2002).

The specific phases of divorce and separation are *disillusionment* and *distance* (Emery & Sbarra, 2002; Lebow, 2015; Taylor, 2002). *Disillusionment.* The initial phase is one of disillusionment and increasing feelings of dissatisfaction. In this phase, the focus of attention is on the negative aspects of the relationship, and spouses tend to be overly critical of each other. If the partners are able to express their disappointments and are willing to share the responsibility for changing the situation, an improvement of the relationship is possible. If this does not succeed, a specific type of family pathology-relational stagnation is likely to develop, and the relationship increasingly erodes. This state of affairs can last for years because a vague, diffuse hope that things might get better maintains the status quo. Fear of separation and fear of being alone prove to be stronger than the realization that the present situation is unsatisfactory or even hopeless. The desire not to hurt anyone, as well as consideration for the children's well-being, can also lead to denial about the status of the relationship.

Distance. The disillusionment phase is usually followed by increased emotional distance, indifference, and finally the physical and spatial separation of the couple. At this point, the situation can no longer be denied, and the separation now has to be worked out emotionally. This process corresponds to a large extent with what Kubler-Ross (1969) has described as the stages of mourning: Denial and anger, attempt to change the situation through action or compromise, depression, and final acceptance of loss. Once this process of mourning is complete, a second adolescence, an altered identity as it were, may develop. Pinsof (2002) notes that as a consequence of this prevalence of divorce, a variety of new pair-bonding arrangements have emerged and that couple therapists must be ready to deal with these issues.

Recently, Scott, Rhodes, Stanley, Allen, and Markman (2013) studied divorced couples to determine what the "final straw" was that pushed them toward divorce. They found that the most commonly reported major contributors to divorce were lack of commitment, infidelity, and conflict/arguing. However, they found that the most common "final straw" reasons were infidelity, domestic violence, and substance abuse. In addition, more divorced individuals blamed their partners than blamed themselves for the divorce.

Talking to Children

If children are involved, no matter what their ages, the reasons for separation and divorce should be openly and honestly discussed in an age-appropriate and understandable way. Parents need to make clear that the separation and

Table 14.5 Outline for Parents Considering a Separation or Divorce to Talk to Children

1 "We are getting a divorce" and explain it.
2 Explain that they are not to blame (e.g. "You did not cause the divorce.").
3 Explain that they could not have prevented the divorce.
4 Explain what will *not* change (e.g. "I am still your Mommy. I am still your Daddy.") as well as what will change.
5 Explain that your feelings for them will not change. (This cannot be emphasized enough.)
6 Explain specifically what the living arrangements will be to the best of your ability. Children do not have to choose between the parents, at least for now.
7 Where there are areas that you and your spouse don't understand, say so (e.g. "We do not understand all the reasons for the divorce ourselves, but as we find out more, we will try to explain more to you.").
8 Solicit children's feedback.
9 Give permission to discuss the situation at any time (e.g. As time goes on, Mom and Dad may need to talk more about the divorce, and you might need to talk about it, too. Anytime you have any questions or feelings you want to talk about, we will always be ready to listen.).
10 Tell them that it is okay to tell their friends. It is not a secret.

Source: Adapted from Glick et al. (2000).

divorce are taking place because they cannot get along with each other, not because of any primary problems with the children. The children should be aware that both parents are still interested in them and love them, provided that this is true. The ten-item outline in Table 14.5 indicates how to talk to children in these situations (Glick, Berman, Clarkin, & Rait, 2000). Marital therapists may want to have such an outline on hand, as separating and divorcing couples are often wondering what and how to tell the children.

Wallerstein and her associates (Wallerstein & Blakeslee, 1989; Wallerstein & Kelly, 1980; Wallerstein, Lewis, & Blakeslee, 2000) conducted groundbreaking longitudinal research on the effects of divorce on children. They found that the most important element seemed to be what happened after couples divorce and how the children were then treated. In today's world, this includes the influence of social media on the conflicts of ex-partners and the detrimental effects on children (Visser et al., 2017). Effective parenting is important after divorce as are a good relationship with the ex-spouse and an effective relationship with the next mate. If a healthier relationship is established in the next marriage, this can minimize the negative impact of the divorce on the children (Lebow, 2015).

The Postdivorce Crisis

Family conflicts often escalate in the year following divorce, and the parenting skills of the ex-spouses decrease as parents become inconsistent, grow less affectionate, and exert less control over the children. Statistically, the risk of delinquency is much greater if parents separate or divorce than if a parent dies. Parental quarreling and mutual denigration can lead to the child's questioning of a previously positive evaluation of the parents. For example, criticism of the absent father by the mother can lead to disruption of sex-typing for boys and disruption of heterosexual relationships in adolescent girls (and vice versa). As the parents begin to date, the children, particularly preadolescents and adolescents, become aware of their parents as sex objects, and some develop precocious sexual behavior. The fact of divorce does not lead to any pathological consequences; though what happens after the divorce may have lasting effects (Wallerstein, 2005). At the same time, some divorces can be a positive solution to a very destructive family situation.

It was often thought that boys suffer more as a result of divorce. According to Wallerstein and Blakeslee (1989), however, girls suffer, but there appears to be a "sleeper" effect. Wallerstein and Blakeslee's studies strongly indicated that girls experience the serious effects of divorce at the time they are entering young adulthood. The authors also found that some girls tend to become overburdened in taking on responsibility to make sure that their parents are okay, which had long-term consequences in their own lives (Wallerstein, 2005; Wallerstein et al., 2000). More recently, Rudd et al. (2016) found negative effects of parental separation on children. In particular, these children scored lower on social, behavioral, and health measures. Academic performance declines were also observed, compared to children of cohabitating parents (Poladian et al., 2017).

However, it is not just the children who suffer in many divorces. When there is acrimony between parents, fights over custody can lead to one of the parents being effectively shut out of their children's lives. Gardner (1998) defined this alienation of one parent as parent alienation syndrome (PAS). PAS results when a custodial parent levels unsubstantiated or vague charges of sexual or physical abuse against the other parent, questions the fitness of the other parent, or engages in lengthy legal actions that slow down the process of the other parent gaining access to the children (Lowenstein, 1998). These noncustodial parents can often experience extreme psychological disturbance at the separation, feeling like they are missing out on critical experiences with their children that are forever lost. Although PAS was initially seen with fathers, parents of either gender can become the victims of this type of custodial manipulation. This is especially acute in gay and lesbian couples where parental rights are not always granted to nonbiological (or adoptive) parents. Active, ongoing divorce therapy or mediation can be effective in alleviating some of the problems with PAS (Lowenstein, 1998; Visser et al., 2017).

Divorce Therapy

Divorce therapy is a time-limited, usually 6–15-session intervention in which the goal is to provide advice, information, and counseling about the common alternatives, problems, and emotional upsets involved in the divorce process (Lebow, 2015). Divorce therapy attempts to aid families in mastering this crisis situation by investigating the normal phases of a separation process.

Divorce therapy focuses particularly on the well-being of the children and attempts to find acceptable, fair, and functional solutions for all the family members to the problems posed by divorce. The problems in divorce are similar to those observed in the separation process in general and are analogous to the processes of individuation and mourning.

According to Lebow (2015), there is no single, "right" way to work with divorcing couples. The goals for these couples can be widely varying, from making peace with one another following a period of increasing conflict, to taking an in-depth review of the relationship dynamics in order to avoid the mistakes that doomed the present relationship. As a result, the couple therapist must be adept at using various strategies to help couples meet these goals. These strategies are summarized in Table 14.6.

Table 14.6 Strategies for Divorce Counseling

1. *Psychoeducation* – A cornerstone of divorce therapy, providing information about good and bad divorce outcomes. Dispelling inaccurate information can be very helpful to couples.
2. *Negotiation* – This is an essential component but often challenging because the couple was (generally) not able to negotiate with each other in the marriage. Teaching win-win processes can help forestall negative consequences later.
3. *Establishing Reliable, Rule-Driven Methods of Communication and "Good Enough" Collaboration* – This is especially useful in high-conflict relationships and when there are separate households established with different "rules" for children. Formal communication training (i.e. "speaker-listener" techniques) is helpful.
4. *Disengagement Skills and Anger Management* – Skills for respectfully disengaging from conflict in the presence of challenging behaviors or statements by the other partner as well as basic anger management techniques ("time-out" procedures) are important here.
5. *Reattribution and Narrative Change* – Helping partners to resist assigning negative motives for the other person's behavior can help reduce tension and conflict. Cognitive restructuring techniques (such as reality testing, etc.) are helpful in this instance.
6. *Catharsis* – Depending on the couple, this can either be helpful in managing the traumatic aspects of the divorce or not. Expressions of hurt and anger, if managed well, can bring about understanding and resolve differences.
7. *Reviewing the Marriage* – Again, depending on the couple, some review of the dynamics (and what went wrong) can help the partners avoid the same mistakes in future relationships.
8. *Exploring Individual Issues* – Like reviewing the marriage, this strategy is designed to help each partner to see his or her own part of the dissolution of the relationship and what each one can address in their own behavior.
9. *Working with Children* – This can take place directly, by having the children attend sessions, or indirectly, by coaching the parents. The goal is to help children deal with their feelings from the end of the marriage (especially if there was high conflict, and the children feel a sense of responsibility). This can also be a forum for working through the logistics of co-parenting.
10. *Working with Extended Family Members* – The goal of this strategy is to preserve relationships with extended family members, to the degree that this is possible, and help transition to new relationships following the divorce.

From Lebow (2015).

In summary, divorce therapy is a process whereby the therapist helps those in the decision-making phase of divorce to assess their needs, strengths, and shortcomings and thus facilitates their arriving at a satisfactory decision to stay married or to divorce. The therapist further helps couples and families that are facing divorce in the process of restructuring their individual lives, present and future relationships, problems with their children, financial difficulties, and general adjustment to singlehood (Emery & Sbarra, 2002; Glick et al., 2000; Lebow, 2015).

We return to the case of Jerry and Anna from Chapters 6 and 13 (see Figure 14.1). If we are to suppose that one or the other was unable to make the kind of changes that were necessary, then a divorce would be imminent. Jerry would continue to pursue an outside relationship, and Anna would continue to rely on her relationship with her mother. It is also conceivable that she might engage in a new relationship as revenge (rebalance the system) against Jerry. However, regardless of the reason, since there are two children under age six (ages five and three), it is evident that Jerry and Anna will be a part of the kids' – and hence

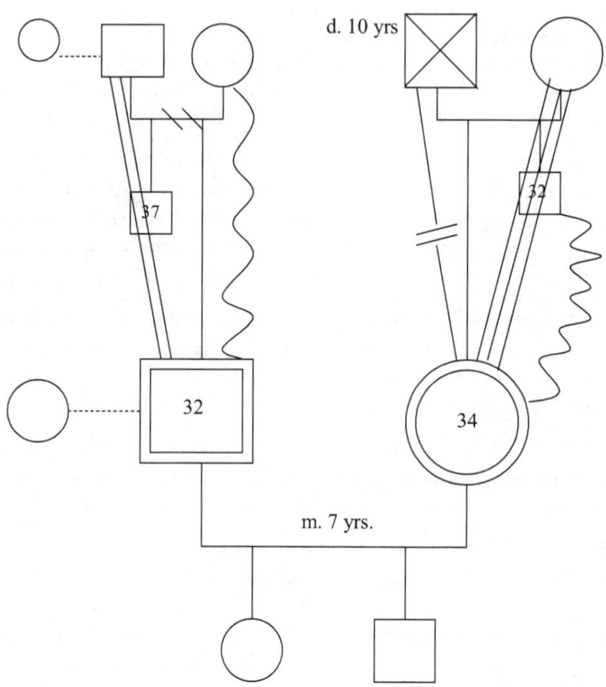

Figure 14.1

each other's – lives for a long time. As a result, they will need to take several active steps to plan and understand the impact of the divorce in order to ensure the well-being of the children. It will be necessary to facilitate the discussion with the children along the guidelines presented in Table 14.5. And Jerry and Anna need to be educated about the fact that in the first year, there are often several crises that will force them to work together at a difficult, emotional time.

Other issues to discuss are the phases of disillusionment and distance that may result in the first few years for each of them. The crucial part is how each of these will be perceived by the children, and how it may negatively impact their development if not handled properly. In therapy, the couple may make some decisions or agreements about how to jointly make decisions and resolve differences. Again, working through the issues of grief and loss may be very useful for the parents and the children, if needed. Lastly, the purpose of divorce therapy with Jerry and Anna will be to orient them toward their own and their children's future. Oftentimes, this is one of the only ways that divorcing couples can divert their attention from the painful memories and wounds of the past.

Divorce Mediation

Divorce mediation is the process by which a couple meets together with a trained mental health professional or an attorney educated in mediation and the psychology of conflict resolution. The differences in issues for the couple are mediated in a task-oriented manner until a settlement is reached. In this process, each person assumes responsibility for his or her actions. Respect for each other's concerns is expressed, and the integrity of the family unit is maintained. Although the husband and wife separate and obtain a divorce, the family continues and the agreement is discussed in terms of the relationships among mother, father, and children. An advisory attorney rewrites the mediated settlement in legal terms and relates impartially to the family as the client, not to two parties in conflict. The settlement task for mediation includes division of marital property, possible spousal maintenance or rehabilitative alimony, required child support, shared parenting responsibilities, and custodial arrangements for the children (Folberg & Milne, 1988; Taylor, 2002).

Couples with children often engage in a mediation process prior to divorce in order to resolve issues such as custody (legal or physical), visitation arrangements, and child support (Emery, 2012). In some jurisdictions, this is a required step before going through a divorce, while in others, it is voluntary. There are several models of mediation, including directive, facilitative, and transformative. In the *directive* model, the mediator takes a more active role and usually will make proposals to the couple about how to handle the various issues as well as how to propose solutions to the court. In the *facilitative* model, mediators adopt a neutral stance and "encourage constructive communication between parties and refrain from recommending solutions, giving advice, or offering opinions" (Poladian et al., 2017, p. 258). Finally, the transformative model focuses more on helping each member of the couple to recognize their partner's point of view and empower them to make their own solutions. It is more of a process mediation, rather than finding specific solutions, in the hope that the couple can then come up with solutions (Poladian et al., 2017).

In this type of intervention, the husband and wife come together with a mediator rather than an attorney to work out an equitable solution for ending their marriage. In this situation, there are no winners or losers. In divorce, once an attorney is hired, it becomes an adversarial system in which the participants need to do battle with one another. Lawyers are subject to malpractice if they do not get the best possible deals for their clients. Most mediators view divorce differently and really work toward a solution that is best for all parties. The mediator works hard to teach people how to cooperate. A communication process is used to resolve practical and emotional issues of divorce in a mutually cooperative manner. Given the two parties' different values, different abilities, and limited resources to face the future, mediation provides a participatory process for them to achieve a successful termination of a partnership that has created children, shared income, and accumulated assets. Table 14.7 presents the six conditions necessary for successful conflict resolution.

In fact, many couple therapists offer mediation services as a part of their practice, as many of the skills necessary in conducting successful therapy significantly overlap with successful mediation (Taylor, 2002). The four areas that a mediator tries to influence in creating a cooperative settlement outcome are communication, attitudes, negotiating methods, and outcome goals (Erickson & McKnight-Erickson, 1988). The overall goal is to negotiate the best settlement possible that will maximally satisfy each partner's needs and interests now and in the future. At the very least, the process consists of systematically isolating points of agreement and disagreement, developing options, and

Table 14.7 Six Conditions Necessary for True Conflict Resolution to Occur

1	The physical well-being of each party involved is maintained during negotiations and in the resolution reached.
2	Each party maintains his or her feelings of self-worth during the negotiating process and in the resolution itself.
3	All involved parties are respected and tolerated as persons but with the understanding that this need not imply approval of others' morals or values.
4	All relevant facts, available options, and technical information are considered and used in reaching any solutions.
5	The consequences of each available option are considered by all parties before any resolution is agreed upon.
6	The resolution that is reached is agreed to by all parties even though other choices were available.

Source: Adapted from Coogler (1978).

considering accommodations (Poladian et al., 2017). Lowenstein (1998) found that couples with children who went through a mediation process came to a resolution faster than couples who did not and reduced the instances of PAS. Even if all the elements of the dispute cannot be resolved, the conflict may be reduced to a much more manageable level (Poladian et al., 2017; Taylor, 2002).

Effectiveness of Mediation

How effective is family mediation? According to Poladian et al. (2017), there have been only three randomized control trials (RCTs) to study the effectiveness of mediation. We will summarize these briefly. Two of the three (Emery, Laumann-Billings, Waldron, Sbarra, & Dillon, 2001; Zuberbuhler, 2001) compared mediation to litigation, and only Emery et al. (2001, as cited in Poladian et al.) conducted follow-up interviews with families. In the third study, Ballard et al. (2013) compared models of mediation to one another. In all three studies, child contact with the noncustodial parent was significantly increased, and that contact persisted well over a decade later (see Emery et al., 2001). In addition, communication and contact between parents were found to be more positive and collaborative (compared to parents who did not participate in mediation), and parental well-being was also found to be improved. While it would seem that in the cases of divorce, family mediation has empirical support for its benefits, Poladian et al. (2017) caution that much more research into this area is warranted in order to determine the overall efficacy of mediation.

Remarriage

A remarried family is a blended or reconstituted family or a stepfamily that is formed by the marriage or living together of two adults, one or both widowed or divorced, with their custodial or visiting children. Remarried, also called step- or reconstituted, families must be recognized as a viable form of a new commonplace American family. Acceptance of this reality is a necessary orientation for working with remarried families. These families have another set of problems, potentials, and options with which they may need professional help. There is very little history for how to live in these new family units, and without set "traditions", these families encounter many problems. According to Papernow (2017), the rates of divorce of remarriages rise steeply as a result of these challenges. This type of living style, however new, is here to stay, and therapists must learn how to deal with it. The special concerns of these families are the roles of step-parents vis-à-vis the children and vice versa. Relationships with the former spouse, financial arrangements, child custody, and visitation are issues that are often determined by the courts.

Psychoeducation is often a preferred method of intervention at this level. *Strengthening Stepfamilies* (Albert & Einstein, 1986) and *New Beginnings* (Dinkmeyer, McKay, & McKay, 1987) are complete educational programs that help people become aware of the special problems and skills needed to live in

Table 14.8 Goals for Working with Blended Families

1	Ensure that children have access and ongoing relationships rather than mere visitations with both their parents and their families in order to define their own identities and identifications.
2	Parents and children remain emotionally attached and responsible to each other.
3	Guilt and anger are reduced for children and parents.
4	A noncustodial parent's participation is increased.
5	Pains are taken by biological parents not to stimulate loyalty conflicts in the children.
6	Children can gain by experiencing two father and mother images and two different family cultures.

blended family units. Many therapists use these programs on an individual basis or offer them in the community as a preventive intervention (Garneau, Higginbotham, & Adler-Baeder, 2015). The major goals for work with this group are shown in Table 14.8 and include fostering ongoing relationships with both parents, addressing guilt and anger, and focusing on the positive aspects of learning from multiple families. There are other goals as well. The primary problems, however, center on how to take people who have been wounded in a prior relationship into a new relationship in which the parents have very strong romantic feelings and are really overly involved in another adult. In this situation, the children often feel neglected and that they are not getting their fair share. There is difficulty for the parent and children in mourning the old relationship as well as in learning how to deal with a new neighborhood, friends, and a new way of life. Another problem involves children from different families now being brothers and sisters. Still another involves establishing new boundaries within the family for what roles a new adult will take (Emery & Sbarra, 2002; Garneau et al., 2015; Papernow, 2017; Sager et al., 1983).

Concluding Note

The theme of endings unites the two broad topic areas covered in this chapter (Aging and Separation; Divorce and Remarriage). A number of common problems and issues of relationships have been discussed. Couple therapists will have to deal with these issues as a common course of couple therapy. Therefore, knowing the unique challenges and strategies for dealing with them is important. We have provided a broad overview of these but invite the reader to follow up on the recommendations presented for further training.

References

Albert, L., & Einstein, E. (1986). *Strengthening stepfamilies.* Circle Pines, MN: American Guidance Service.

Ballard, R. H., Holtzworth-Munroe, A, Applegate, A. G., & D'Onofrio, B. M. (2011). Factors affecting the outcome of divorce and paternity mediations. *Family Court Review, 49*(1), 16–33.

Blando, J., & Lawton, M. (2013). ADA, universal design, and counseling older adults and their families. In P. R. Peluso, R. E. Watts, & M. Parsons (Eds.), *Changing aging, changing family therapy: Practicing with 21st century realities* (pp. 151–173). New York, NY: Routledge.

CAST. (2011). *About UDL*. Wakefield, MA: National Center on Universal Design for Learning. Retrieved June 28, 2011 from http://www.cast.org/udl/index.html

Coogler, O. J. (1978). *Structured mediation in divorce settlement*. Lexington, MA: D.C. Heath.

Dinkmeyer, D., McKay, G. M., & McKay, J. (1987). *New beginnings*. Champaign, IL: Research Press.

Doherty, W. J., & Harris, S. M. (2017). *Helping couples in the brink of divorce. Discernment counseling for troubled relationships*. Washington, DC: American Psychological Association.

Emery, R. E. (2012). *Renegotiating family relationships: Divorce, child custody, and mediation*. New York, NY: The Guilford Press.

Emery, R. E., Laumann-Billings, L., Waldron, M. C., Sbarra, D. A., & Dillon, P. (2001). Child custody mediation and litigation: Custody, contact, and coparenting 12 years after initial dispute resolution. *Journal of Consulting and Clinical Psychology, 69*, 323–332.

Emery, R. E., & Sbarra, D. A. (2002). Addressing separation and divorce during and after couple therapy. In A. S. Gurman & N. S. Jacobson (Eds.), *Clinical handbook of couple therapy* (3rd ed., pp. 508–532). New York, NY: Guilford.

Erickson, S. K., & McKnight Erickson, M. S. (1988). *Family mediation casebook: Theory and process*. Philadelphia, PA: Brunner/Mazel, Inc.

Folberg, J., & Milne, A. (1988). *Divorce mediation: Theory and practice*. New York, NY: Guilford Press.

Fruhauf, C. A., & Lambert-Shute, J. (2013). Systemic integration of gerontology and marriage and family therapy. In P. R. Peluso, R. E. Watts, & M. Parsons (Eds.), *Changing aging, changing family therapy: Practicing with 21st century realities* (pp. 21–45). New York, NY: Routledge.

Gardner, R. A. (1998). Recommendations for dealing with parents who induce a parental alienation syndrome in their children. *Journal of Divorce & Remarriage, 28*(3–4), 1–23.

Garneau, C. L., Higginbotham, B., & Adler-Baeder, F. (2015), Remarriage beliefs as predictors of marital quality and positive interaction in stepcouples: An actor–partner interdependence model. *Family Process, 54*, 730–745. doi:10.1111/famp.12153

Glick, I. D., Berman, E. M., Clarkin, J. F., & Rait, D. S. (2000). *Marital and family therapy* (4th ed.). Washington, DC: American Psychiatric Press.

Glick, I. D., Clarkin, J. R., & Kessler, D. R. (1987). *Marital and family therapy* (3rd ed.). Orlando, FL: Grune & Stratton.

Hale, D. (2015). A model of structured separation in couple therapy: Making the best use of a separation period. *Journal of Divorce & Remarriage, 56*(2), 109–116.

Hartman-Stein, P. (2013). Working with older couples: Tackling problems as a team late in live. In P. R. Peluso, R. E. Watts, & M. Parsons (Eds.), *Changing aging, changing family therapy: Practicing with 21st century realities* (pp. 113–126). New York, NY: Routledge.

Knight, B. G., Karel, M. J., Hinrichsen, G. A., Qualls, S. H., & Duffy, M. (2009). Pikes peak model of training in professional geropsychology. *American Psychologist, 64*(3), 205–214. doi:10.1037/a0015059

Knoester, C., & Booth, A. (2000). Barriers to divorce. When are there effective? When are they not? *Journal of Family Issues, 21*(1), 78–99.

Kubler-Ross, E. (1969). *On death and dying: What the dying have to teach doctors, nurses, clergy and their own families.* New York, NY: McMillan.

Lambert-Shute, J., & Fruhauf, C. A. (2011). Aging issues: Unanswered questions in marital and family therapy literature. *Journal of Marital & Family Therapy, 37,* 27–36.

Lebow, J. (2015). Separation and divorce issues in couple therapy. In In A. S. Gurman, J. Lebow, & D. Snyder (Eds.), *Clinical handbook of couple therapy* (5th ed., pp. 445–456). New York, NY: Guilford.

Lowenstein, L. F. (1998). Parent alienation syndrome: A two step approach toward a solution. *Contemporary Family Therapy, 20*(4), 505–520.

Papernow, P. L. (2017). Therapy with couples in stepfamilies. In In A. S. Gurman, J. Lebow, & D. Snyder (Eds.), *Clinical handbook of couple therapy* (5th ed., pp. 467–488). New York, NY: Guilford.

Peluso, P. R. (2013). Summarizing changing aging, changing family therapy. In P. R. Peluso, R. E. Watts, & M. Parsons (Eds.), *Changing aging, changing family therapy: Practicing with 21st century realities* (pp. 249–266). New York, NY: Routledge.

Peluso, P. R., Parsons, M., & Watts, R. E. (2013). Introduction. In P. R. Peluso, R. E. Watts, & M. Parsons (Eds.), *Changing aging, changing family therapy: Practicing with 21st century realities* (pp. 3–20). New York, NY: Routledge.

Pinsof, W. M. (2002). The death of "till death us do part": The transformation of pair-bonding in the 21st century. *Family Process, 41*(2), 135–157.

Poladian, A. R., Rossi, F. S., Rudd, B. N., & Holtzworth-Munroe, A. (2017). Family mediation for divorce and parental separation. In J. Fitzgerald (Ed.), *Foundations for couple therapy: Research for the real world* (pp. 256–267). New York, NY: Routledge.

Qualls, S. H. (1993). Marital therapy with older couples. *The Family Journal: Counseling and Therapy for Couples and Families, 1,* 42–50.

Qualls, S. H. (2000). Therapy with aging families: Rationale, opportunities and challenges. *Aging & Mental Health, 4*(3), 191–199.

Qualls, S. H., Segal, D. L., Norman, S., Niederehe, G., & Gallagher-Thompson, D. (2002). Psychologists in practice with older adults: Current patterns, sources of training, and need for continuing education. *Professional Psychology: Research and Practice, 33*(5), 435–442. doi:10.1037//0735-7028.33.5.435

Qualls, S. H., & Vair, C. (2013). Caregiver family therapy for families dealing with dementia. In P. R. Peluso, R. E. Watts, & M. Parsons (Eds.), *Changing aging, changing family therapy: Practicing with 21st century realities* (pp. 63–78). New York, NY: Routledge.

Sager, C., Brown, H., Crohn, H., Engel, T., Rodstein, E., & Walker, L. (1983). *Treating the remarried family.* New York, NY: Brunner/Mazel.

Scott, S. B., Rhoades, G. K., Stanley, S. M., Allen, E. S., & Markman, H. J. (2013). Reasons for divorce and recollections of premarital intervention: Implications for improving relationship education. *Couple and Family Psychology: Research and Practice, 2*(2), 131–145. doi:10.1037/a0032025

Taylor, A. (2002). *The handbook o family dispute resolution.* San Francisco, CA: Jossey-Bass.

United States Department of Labor. (2011). *High growth industry profile: Heath care.* Retrieved August 23, 2011 from http://www.doleta.gov/brg/indprof/healthcare_profile.cfm

Visser, M., Finkenauer, C., Schoemaker, K., Kluwer, E., van der Rijken, R., van Lawick, J., ... Lamers-Winkelman, F. (2017). I'll never forgive you: high conflict divorce, social network, and co-parenting conflicts. *Journal of Child and Family Studies, 26*(11), 3055–3066.

Wallerstein, J. S. (2005). Growing up in the divorced family. *Clinical Social Work Journal, 33*(4), 401–418. Winter. doi:10.1007/s10615-005-7034-y

Wallerstein, J. S., & Blakeslee. S. (1989). *Second chances: Men, women, and children a decade after divorce.* New York, NY: Ticknor and Fields.

Wallerstein, J. S., Lewis, J., & Blakeslee. S. (2000). *The unexpected legacy of divorce: A 25 year landmark study.* New York, NY: Hyperion, 2000.

Wallerstein, J. S., & Kelly, J. B. (1980). *Surviving the break-up: How children and parents cope with divorce.* New York, NY: Basic Books.

Zuberbuhler, J. (2001). Early intervention mediation: The use of court-ordered mediation in the initial stages of divorce litigation to resolve parenting issues. *Family Court Review, 39*(2), 203–206.

Conclusion

The Future Practice of Couple Therapy

15 Preparing to Practice Couple Therapy in the 21st Century

LEARNING OBJECTIVES

In this chapter, the reader will learn the following:

1 The training requirements to become a couple therapist.
2 Issues related to licensure and marketability in practice.
3 New areas of practice for couple therapists.
4 Future directions for the field of couple therapy.

The previous chapters in this book were dedicated to providing an overview of the knowledge necessary for a person to understand couple therapy. However, there are practical, structural, or how-to issues that previous chapters have not been able to cover. These include questions such as "How do I get trained in couple therapy?" "What is supervision?" "Why should I get licensed?" and "Where can I work as a couple therapist?" This chapter is devoted to the practical aspects of becoming a couple therapist. It is not our intention to exhaustively answer these questions but rather to touch on the subjects related to the day-to-day practice of becoming a couple therapist and give the reader some basic information to pursue these questions further.

Training

Training is the process of becoming cognitively, behaviorally, emotionally, and personally ready to be a couple therapist (Fraenkel & Pinsof, 2001). The minimum level of training in order to practice as a couple therapist is a master's degree in one of the helping professions (professional counseling, social work, psychology, or couples and family therapy). These degree programs generally range from two to three years in duration. Students in general therapy programs (professional counseling, social work, and psychology) usually will need to seek out additional coursework and specific internship experiences in a couple therapy setting, while students in a couples and family-therapy program will not since the focus is primarily on couples and family work (AAMFT, 2018). Training programs recognized and approved by an accrediting body of their respective profession (i.e. Commission on

Accreditation for Marriage and Family Therapy Education [COAMFTE] for couples and family therapy programs) adhere to a set of standards shared by the profession for proper training of students.

However, despite the standardization of content that is taught to trainees, there is still wide latitude as to how that knowledge is presented. The question that most training programs must face is how to provide students with maximum exposure to the empirically supported approaches and techniques of therapy while also giving them the ability to practice and demonstrate mastery of the necessary skills as well as the clinical judgment and unique mind-set of a couple therapist (Mozdzierz, Peluso, & Lisecki, 2014). Some programs offer training in certain theories with the idea that students will get a depth of training over a breadth of knowledge. Other programs have begun to look at ways of training students from an integrative perspective to give students the essential building blocks of skill, technique, and theory upon which the student will be able to construct (or adopt) a particular theory of practice (Cornille, McWey, Nelson, & West, 2003; Fraenkel & Pinsof, 2001; Norcross & Beutler, 2000).

Norcross and Beutler (2000) have developed ten core principles for psychotherapist development, which underlie any training for couple therapists.

1 *Demonstrate and Model Psychotherapy.* "Trainees should observe the work of clinical supervisors, conduct psychotherapy with more experienced peers, and watch representative videotapes of seasoned clinicians conducting psychotherapy" (p. 250).
2 *Furnish Ample and Diverse Experiences.* "The core principle is to ensure extensive experience in actually evaluating and treating a range of patients and participating under close supervision in treatment assignments. Advocating diverse experiences also invokes the need to appropriately train students to serve clients from diverse and historically undertreated groups" (p. 251).
3 *Coordinate the Training Process.* Often, the training process itself is poorly coordinated or just plain chaotic. Six basic steps for acquiring therapeutic skill are recommended: "First, is the development of an attitude of respect and regard; this is followed in sequence by the development of knowledge of sound psychotherapeutic change principles, understanding of the tools of influence, skill in the application of techniques, appreciation for the importance of time for therapists to season, and the invocation of a creative imagination. Training that makes use of these keys, Attitude, Knowledge, Tools, Techniques, Time, and Imagination, ensures that a trainee will appreciate the importance of therapist attitude and knowledge relative to that of techniques, and will ultimately come to understand the value of informed knowledge in bridling the therapists imagination and creativity" (p. 251).
4 *Impart Technical and Interpersonal Skills.* Any good training program will value the development of technical mastery (i.e. the cognitive behavioral approaches) along with interpersonal understanding (i.e. psychodynamic and humanistic approaches).

5 *Establish Competence.* "[B]ecoming proficient in techniques is of little value if one has not learned the attitudes that will make them credible to patients or if one has not acquired the knowledge of change principles that will allow them to intervene at advantageous moments ... Competence must reflect the ability to communicate, the ability to recognize markers for applying procedures, and the procedures themselves" (p. 252).
6 *Account for Individual Differences.* Just as integration tailors treatment to the client, Norcross and Beutler (2000) suggest that training should likewise take into account the individual variables of the student and develop them to uniquely mesh with sound practice.
7 *Provide Students with Therapeutic Experience.* Training should not be in a vacuum. Instead, training programs should encourage students to explore personal therapy, group experiences, self-help groups, retreats, etc. Norcross and Beutler (2000) believe that if the student develops personally, this will positively impact professional development.
8 *Incorporate Technological Advances into the Training.* Just as the introduction of videotapes of sessions exposed students to real-world examples of therapy for modeling, employing a wide range of technological advances (computer-assisted experience, virtual reality, etc.) can only enhance the student's experience and knowledge base. This requires professors to be as alert to emerging technologies as students, thus continually refining one's skills.
9 *Cultivate Respect for the Empirical Literature.* "There is a disparity between the procedures that have been found to be effective in clinical research and those that are most frequently used in professional practice" (p. 253). Ultimately, this is due to a schism that begins in training when research is devalued or not emphasized. Communication must open up between the researchers and the clinicians in order to develop an appreciation for the benefits of empiricism and its positive impact on practice.
10 *Evaluate Training Outcomes.* The adequacy of training and the competence of graduates is usually assumed but seldom measured. If the field of psychotherapy is to embrace evaluating its outcomes, training institutes must be willing to subject their instruction and supervision methods to the rigors of evaluation.

While Norcross and Beutler (2000) emphasized the structural aspects of an integrative training program, Fraenkel and Pinsof (2001) attended to the characteristics of the trainers of integrative couple therapists. Specifically, they contend that the trainer or supervisor should actively model the qualities of an integrative therapist to students, including having the ability to tolerate ambiguity, confusion, anxiety, and uncertainty. They recommend that trainers have an attitude of humility and self-criticism about their work; pay attention to the therapeutic alliance to experience how to repair rifts in the relationship when things get uncomfortable; be able to channel the anxiety of client criticism or "not knowing what to do next" into a stimulus for creativity; and cultivate a spirit of adventure and openness to new perspectives. They conclude that training to become an integrative couple therapist is a journey with many challenges that is "as much about becoming a more integrated person as about becoming an integrative therapist" (Fraenkel & Pinsof, 2001, p. 83).

A final area of concern for many couple therapy scholars and researchers is the "research-practice gulf." Simply put, this is the propensity for clinicians to either be unaware of the efficacy and effectiveness research (and put into practice many of the findings in their approach), or their unwillingness to do so (Parker, Chang, & Thomas, 2016). This is despite the fact that there have been significant findings that can bolster the effectiveness of couple therapy. Halford, Peppping, and Oetch (2016) point to the fact that much of the research findings on "research-efficacy" trials routinely have large effect sizes, but "practice-effectiveness" trials have moderate-to-small effect sizes. They point out that training and supervision that emphasize the transfer of empirically validated practice elements can predispose couples counselors, from the beginning, to prize empirically based practice elements and be open to incorporating new and emerging research that can increase their effectiveness (Halford et al., 2016; Parker et al., 2016). However, for this to be fully realized, educators and accrediting bodies must shape the standards of training to facilitate this (Blow & Karam, 2017).

Supervision

Most persons involved in the training of couple therapists believe that couple therapists need to continue developing their professional skills and understanding of couples after training is completed. This is accomplished primarily through the provision of clinical supervision. Supervisors act as gatekeepers for the profession, ensuring that new therapists are sufficiently trained to properly treat couples in an ethical, professional, and competent manner (Jordan, 2016).

> Historically, the presence of a supervisor has enabled a partially trained clinician to practice, leading to supervision being a core component of training programs per se, an integral part of couple and family therapists' postgraduate experiences, and an essential component of endorsement for licensure.
>
> (Storm, McDowell, & Long, 2003, p. 432)

Through good supervision, consultation, and review of his or her own videotapes and treatment successes and failures, the therapist can profit tremendously and continue to develop as a couple therapist.

There are several types of supervision: Live supervision where the supervisor and others observe through a one-way mirror or closed-circuit camera, live supervision with the ability for the supervisor to interact with the supervisee (via headphones, a telephone, interrupting the session, etc.), viewing videotaped or listening to audiotaped sessions, or supervisee case report (Jordan, 2016). Researchers have found that live or videotaped supervision is most informative for supervisors and supervisees, but there is often resistance by offsite training institutions fearful of confidentiality breaches and supervisees fearful of negative evaluations of their performance (Storm et al., 2003). Supervisors must work with institutions to develop assurances and mechanisms for overcoming the concerns of confidentiality issues. In addition, supervisees' ambivalence about their performance can be ameliorated by encouraging a supportive, collaborative supervision environment.

Reflecting teams have emerged in the last decade as a new modality for conducting supervision in a collaborative and contextual setting. In this procedure, other supervisees act as additional observers of the one-on-one supervision process and provide feedback to the supervisor/supervisee dyad about their observations of the content of the supervision or the process that emerged between the two. For couple therapists in training, this modality may provide an additional level of understanding of systemic, relational, and contextual dynamics as they receive feedback from the reflecting team about their observations and compare them with their own experiences (Jordan, 2016).

Over the last two decades, many supervisors have been influenced by postmodern and feminist ideas, which have altered the provision of supervision as well as the supervisory relationship. Supervisors now strive for more collaborative, egalitarian supervisory relationships. Most couple therapy supervisors believe that the relationships with supervisees are critically important for providing optimal training. At the same time, while supervisees appreciate the supportive environment, many prefer receiving specific direction from their supervisor as to what they need to do in the context of therapy (Storm et al., 2003). The amount of hands-on direction that a supervisee requires is related to the level of competence that a supervisee has (Skovholt & Ronnestad, 1992). Regardless of the context, however, a warm, encouraging, and supportive supervisory relationship clearly benefits the trainee, much in the same way the therapeutic relationship is the most crucial element to benefit the client. In fact, isomorphism, whereby the similarities between the supervisor/supervisee relationship and the therapist/client relationship are explored to provide training in a specific theoretical model (typically that of the supervisor), plays a dominant role in much of the supervision for couple therapists (Jordan, 2016; Storm et al., 2003).

While the isomorphic approach is widely accepted as a means to provide depth and in vivo modeling of correct therapeutic interventions (as well as the emotional, relational, and cognitive elements of the therapeutic process), overreliance on isomorphism has been criticized as failing to address the aspects of the supervisory relationship that are different than therapy. This is less of a salient issue in the supervision of couple therapists, as the isomorphic dynamics are different because the supervision is conducted with a couple rather than an individual. That is not to say that there are no issues of isomorphism but that they are attenuated with couple therapists. However, the criticism that supervisors who operate solely from an isomorphic approach sacrifice training therapists in a breadth and variety of theoretical modalities is especially salient for couple therapists and needs to be addressed (Jordan, 2016; Storm et al., 2003).

Despite the issues that are frequently raised, supervision continues to be a major element in the training of therapists for practice in the field. As the field of couple therapy begins to move forward, new issues and challenges await supervisors: How should supervisors be trained? What are the developmental issues and needs of beginning therapists? Do present forms of supervision just reproduce more of the same type of therapists and stifle growth? What is the role of technology in the provision of supervision (Jordan, 2016; Storm et al., 2003)?

Licensure

Licensure or certification laws for couple therapists provide a mechanism for the public (and other parties) to identify qualified practitioners of marriage and family therapy (MFT). Couple therapists who obtain a license (the most common titles used for this license are Marital and Family Therapist or Marriage and Family Therapist) have met certain educational and clinical experience criteria. All states require a minimum of a master's or doctoral degree and at least two years of postgraduate supervised clinical experience before becoming eligible for licensure. In addition, applicants for licensure must take a licensure exam designed to test the therapist's knowledge of the practice of MFT (AAMFT, 2018).

Today, MFTs are licensed in all 50 states. By comparison, when the second edition of this text was authored in 2006, only 47 states (including the District of Columbia) had statutes regulating MFT practices in the U.S. By comparison, in 1986, only 11 states regulated MFTs. This represents an era of tremendous growth in the recognition of the field as a separate discipline, as well as the premium that individuals are placing on becoming legitimized and regulated (AAMFT, 2018). Licensure is considered to be crucial for gaining access to third-party payers, parity with other mental health disciplines, and recognition by the federal government (Medicare) and by state governments (Medicaid) for the provision of services to individuals, couples, and families. Specific information about individual state requirements can be obtained by contacting the boards listed through the Association of Marital and Family Therapy Regulatory Boards (www.AMFTRB.org) or the American Association of Marriage and Family Therapy (www.aamft.org).

Portability

Related to the issue of licensure is the issue of portability. As more individuals become licensed in one state and move to another, the need to provide a process for the smooth transition of a license from state to state is evident. At the same time, state licensing boards must be assured that requisite coursework, training, and experience have been achieved or demonstrated in order to protect the public. In addition, some state boards fear an influx to certain regions (e.g. cities, resort areas, etc.) and a depletion of qualified therapists from other regions (e.g. rural areas). At the present time, there is no unified method for providing immediate transfer of licenses, but states continue to work together to address the concerns of the practitioners moving to a new state, the therapists already in practice in the state, and the clients residing in the state (Caldwell, 2017).

Parity

If portability is the recognition of equivalence of licenses between states, parity is the recognition of equivalence of licenses across professions. Specifically, issues of parity are related to the recognition that couples and family therapists who are licensed are on the same level as other, similarly trained mental health professionals for the purpose of providing treatment, being included on insurance panels, and getting reimbursed for the same services. The Mental Health Parity Act of 1996 went a long way toward addressing the discrimination of couples (and family) therapists by insurance providers and other entities. More recently, the Mental Health Parity and Addiction Equity Act of 2008 (MHPAEA) has strengthened provisions of the 1996 Parity Act by requiring

> group health plans and health insurance issuers to ensure that financial requirements (such as co-pays, deductibles) and treatment limitations (such as visit limits) applicable to mental health or substance use disorder (MH/SUD) benefits are no more restrictive than the predominant requirements or limitations applied to substantially all medical/surgical benefits.
>
> (US DOL, 2010, p. 1)

In other words, if a plan provides medical and surgical benefits, it must comply with the parity provisions for mental health and substance abuse. Since the federal government recognizes marriage and family therapists as one of the five core mental health disciplines, this applies to couple therapists. However, much more work needs to be done in this area to bring about effective parity among the disciplines in the eyes of the public and policy makers. Nowhere is this more evident than with Medicare and Medicaid.

Medicare and Medicaid

Medicare is the federal system for providing medical and mental health services for, primarily, elderly citizens. In order for a mental health service to be covered by Medicare, the service must be for the diagnosis and treatment of mental illnesses (AMMFT, 2018). In addition, the mental health service must be delivered by a "covered" practitioner who is legally authorized to perform that service under state law. Since MFTs are licensed in every state, this prerequisite is covered, and many, although not all, of the state laws governing the licensing of couple therapists already grant this power to diagnose and create a treatment plan for clients. Thus, couples and family therapists meet the major educational and practical criteria for inclusion in the Medicare program. However, to date, they (along with professional counselors) are not yet recognized by Medicare. The federal government has designated five mental health disciplines as "core mental health professionals": Psychiatrists, psychologists, mental health clinical nurse specialists, clinical social workers (CSWs), and marriage and family therapists. However, of those only marriage and family therapists are not currently recognized by Medicare. By way of comparison, the education, licensure requirements, and scope of practice of couples and family therapists and CSWs are remarkably similar. Yet, the services of CSWs are reimbursed by Medicare, while services rendered by couples and family therapists are not (AAMFT, 2018).

So why is recognition by Medicare important for couple therapists, and why should the reader care? In addition to providing services to seniors (a rapidly growing segment of the population, increasingly becoming in need of mental health services), recognition under Medicare would allow for couples and family therapists to be included in state and federal Medicaid programs (which provide services to underprivileged and disabled citizens). These, like seniors, are significant groups of people, who are often most in need of the services of couples and family therapists but cannot access them because of the lack of recognition by Medicare. More importantly, there are many areas in the country with an insufficient number of mental health service providers (HRSA, 2018). As a result, couple therapists, who could readily provide the types of services most needed, frequently cannot be hired by state and local social service or community mental health centers since their services cannot be reimbursed. This represents a significant disenfranchisement for couple therapists and places couples and families needing these services but unable to pay for them at a serious disadvantage.

Progress in getting couples and family therapists included in the Medicare program has been encouraging, if incomplete. Over the last 15 years, several efforts have been made to include MFTs in Medicare but have fallen short. However, as of the writing of this text, both houses of the U.S. Congress are considering legislation that would alter the text of the Social Security Act to include covering marriage and family therapist and mental health counselor services under Medicare Part B (Civic Impulse, 2018). Titled Senate Bill 1879 and House Resolution 3032, they both include the same language to include MFTs and MHCs. While it is not certain whether these bills will ultimately be successful, it is only a matter of time and continued effort before couples and family therapists will be included in Medicare and be able to deliver to clients the needed services that couple therapists are uniquely trained to provide.

When it comes to Medicaid, the picture is more complicated. Since Medicaid is a joint federal-state program, where the funding comes from the federal government, but the administration of the services comes from the states. Federal regulations allow for the inclusion of MFTs in Medicaid but do not require it, instead leaving it up to the states. According to the AAMFT (2018), 38 states have *some* reimbursement for marriage and family therapists, which can allow for them to primarily be hired in community behavioral health centers. Readers are encouraged to review individual state guidelines for details.

Practice

Beginning therapists usually hear horror stories that private practice is a dead end and that managed care panels are closed off, thus limiting potential salaries. During training, many students ask, "Can I possibly make a living doing this?" While the landscape for practitioners has radically changed in the last two decades, the news is not all bad or bleak.

According to the Bureau of Labor Statistics (a branch of the U.S. Department of Labor), in 2017 the median salary for couples and family therapists was $48,790 and the average salary was $53,860. The lowest 10% of couples and family therapists made over $31,000, while the top 10% made over $81,000 (BLS, 2018). California, New Jersey, and Florida were the states with the highest employment level, and had annual mean wages of $52,000, $74,000, and $51,000, respectively. In addition, the states with the largest annual mean wages were New Jersey, Colorado, and Hawaii ranging from approximately $67,000 to $74,000.

In addition, the outlook is promising for couples and family therapists. In 2016, there were an estimated 41,500 couples and family therapists. According to the BLS (2018), over the next ten years, the rate of growth expected to exceed most other professions (approximately 23% or almost 10,000 new jobs). How do couple therapists fare compared to other mental health professionals? Again, the U.S. Department of Labor estimates that all of the helping professions will grow in the next ten years, though couples and family therapists will have among the highest rates of growth of professions requiring a master's degree and comparable median salaries (BLS, 2018). However, there are new opportunities that could further shape the way that couple therapists practice in the future. We will present an example of some of these in the following.

New Practice Opportunities

Executive Coaching and Organizational Consulting

One area of new practice opportunities attracting the attention of counselors is the realm of organizational consulting and executive coaching (Kern & Peluso, 1999; Kovacs & Corrie, 2017; Peluso & Stoltz, 2002; Shumway, Wampler, Dersch, & Arredondo, 2004; Sperry, 2004). Therapists, in general, are trained to understand the complexities of human behavior, and couples and family therapists have specialized training in understanding the dynamic interplay between two or more people. Many of the systems-based approaches and skills that couples and family therapists have traditionally used in treating clients (such as reframing, circular causality, hidden loyalties, and intergenerational patterning of behavior) have equal usefulness in work settings where there is dysfunction or chaos. Couples and family therapists can effectively intervene in these areas by recapitulating work issues into family systems dynamics (Kovacs & Carrie, 2017). From this perspective, disagreements and conflict amongst coworkers can be viewed as similar to sibling conflicts, while problems between managers or team leaders and their subordinates can be seen as parent-child conflicts over authority or power (Kern & Peluso, 1999; Peluso & Kern, 1998; Peluso & Stoltz, 2001). Lastly, work teams must be able to function together and overcome gender, cultural, and other obstacles in order to be successful. Couples and family therapists working in organizations can apply their understanding of the impact of larger systems on smaller units and help to overcome these potential obstacles (David & Cobeanu, 2015).

In the area of executive coaching, couples and family therapists can also be especially useful in helping executives gain insights into their work activities, understand their particular strengths, and achieve their goals (Kovacs & Carrie, 2017). Couples and family therapists can use a variety of family-of-origin techniques (e.g. the genogram) to help executives explore the origins of their particular view of life, their motivation and drive, and the areas of potential shortcomings toward the goal of developing strategies to overcome them (Peluso & Kern, 1999; Peluso & Kern, 1998; Peluso & Stoltz, 2001; Sperry, 2004). In the arena of organizational consultation and executive coaching, couples and family therapists have found ways to continue to fulfill their purpose and at the same time expanded the traditional settings for utilizing the knowledge of couples and family therapy (David & Cobeanu, 2015).

Integrated Primary Care/Medical Family Therapy

Couple therapy is increasingly considered a necessary part of multimodal treatment plans implemented by multidisciplinary staffs in medical hospitals and outpatient clinics. From this, a new practice paradigm has emerged. Integrated Primary Care or Medical family therapy (also sometimes called family behavioral medicine) is the practice of family therapy in a medical setting, usually with couples or families dealing with a chronic condition and providing social and psychological support (McDaniel et al., 2014; Sperry, 1992). According to Doherty, McDaniel, and Hepworth (2014):

> Medical family therapy is a form of professional practice that uses a biopsychosocial approach and systemic family therapy principles in the collaborative treatment of individuals and families dealing with medical problems … It differs from traditional family therapy in its explicit

> embrace of the biopsychosocial model (mind, body, family, community), its focus on problems traditionally considered medical as well as mental health conditions, and its use of collaborative teams to deliver care. Medical family therapists work in a wide range of health care settings including family medicine, pediatrics, OB-GYN, and a variety of specialty medical settings... Particular goals of treatment may include better coping with a chronic illness or disability, less conflict about handling a medical regimen better communication with physicians, help with making lifestyle changes, and increased acceptance of a medical problem that cannot be cured.
>
> (pp. 529–530)

Medical family therapy utilizes approaches from virtually all of the various schools of family therapy but operates primarily from a biopsychosocial approach in order to accomplish the following goals (commonly referred to as the "Triple Aim"):

1 Improving the patient experience of care (including quality and satisfaction).
2 Improving the health of populations.
3 Reducing the per capita cost of health care (Doherty et al., 2014).

Although it was not always the case, most physicians now recognize the importance of the interaction between biological, social, and psychological factors in the onset of and recovery from diseases. In fact, approximately 25%–30% of patients in primary care present with a mental health disorder. At the same time, it is estimated that primary-care physicians write approximately 70% of the prescriptions psychotropic medications prescribed annually (Baird, 2002; Ruddy & McDaniel, 2003). Yet, many physicians feel overwhelmed and intimidated by the idea of monitoring and treating their patients psychologically (which is beyond their training). Often, when medical and psychosocial issues are intertwined, these physicians find that they need assistance helping patients who have serious mental health or relational difficulties (McDaniel et al., 2014). Mental health professionals who are trained in integrated medical practice can serve as a resource for physicians, providing backup and sharing patient care when "medical providers delve into psychosocial issues without feeling that they will not know how to manage what they discover" (Ruddy & McDaniel, 2003, p. 366).

Couples counselors working in integrated medical practices must take on several important roles (see Table 15.1). Medical family therapists must be willing to bridge the largely separate worlds of mental health care and medical care. To communicate with medical providers, therapists must learn the language of disease and physical illness and, in return, be able to translate the language of mental health (Ruddy & McDaniel, 2003). Doherty, McDaniel, and Baird (1996) created a structural model for gauging the integration of medical practice and behavioral health care that has direct implications for couples and

Table 15.1 Roles of Mental Health Professionals in Integrated Medical Practice

Track patient medical and mental health outcomes
Track medication and treatment adherence, including any adverse effects
Support the patient's relationship with the primary care clinician and other relevant health professionals
Provide psychoeducation to the patient and family about the diagnoses
Encourage patient activation and self-management in the context of the family
Use motivational interviewing techniques to clarify patient's motivation for change and treatment
Negotiate a mutually agreeable treatment plan among patient, family, and health professionals
Facilitate family support
Encourage psychiatric or other consultation if mental health problems do not improve

Note: From Doherty et al. (2014).

family therapists in the future who want to specialize in medical family therapy. Specifically, they outlined five levels of integration between physicians and therapists that address the coordination of care for complex cases, delineate the functions for each of the professionals, and establish the parameters of client benefit. They note that their model "assumes that the greater the level of systemic collaboration, the more adequate the management of very demanding cases is likely to be. Conversely, very demanding cases will generally challenge less collaborative settings beyond their ability to manage adequately" (Doherty et al., 1996, p. 25). A description of the levels is detailed next.

LEVEL 1: MINIMAL OR NO COLLABORATION

At this level, mental health and other health-care providers work in separate facilities and rarely communicate about cases. This is the predominant model for practitioners working in agencies and private practices and can be effective with couples who have more basic or routine problems (either psychosocial or medical) and where there is little case management required.

LEVEL 2: BASIC COLLABORATION AT A DISTANCE: "REFERRAL"

At this level, providers view each other as resources, but each operates independently in their own sphere. There is very little sharing of power, responsibility, or understanding of each other's professional culture. In addition, they have separate systems (medical model vs. educational model) and practice at separate sites but do periodically communicate via telephone and letters about shared clients. This kind of collaboration takes place in settings where there are active referral linkages and works best in cases where there is moderate biopsychosocial interplay (e.g. a patient with diabetes and depression) and the management of both problems proceeds reasonably well. Couples for whom this level of collaboration does not work are those that require closer monitoring of medical and mental health treatment (e.g. substance abuse treatment).

LEVEL 3: BASIC COLLABORATION ONSITE "COORDINATION"

At this level, mental health and other health-care providers share the same facility but have separate systems. These practitioners may engage in regular communication about shared patients (again, mostly through phone or letters with occasional face-to-face contact). There is appreciation of the importance of each other's roles, as well as a sense of being part of a larger team. However, these practitioners do not share a common language or an in-depth understanding of each other's practices. As with the previous levels, medical physicians have considerably more power and influence over case-management decisions than the other practitioners, which may cause resentment. Examples of where this is practiced include HMO settings, medical clinics that employ therapists, and rehabilitation centers whereby collaboration is facilitated by proximity but where there is no systemic structure for collaboration.

LEVEL 4: CLOSE COLLABORATION IN A PARTLY INTEGRATED SYSTEM "CO-LOCATION"

At this level, providers from different disciplines share the same sites and have some systems in common (e.g. charting, scheduling, or billing). The level of contact includes regular face-to-face interactions about clients, mutual consultation, coordinated treatment plans for difficult cases, and a basic understanding and appreciation for each other's roles and cultures. There is a shared commitment to a biopsychosocial/systems paradigm. However, there are likely to be unresolved but manageable tensions over medical physicians' greater power and influence or parity issues. This level of collaboration is found in some HMO centers, rehabilitation centers, hospice centers, and some family practice training programs. Clients who have significant biopsychosocial issues that are complicated to manage seem to respond well to this level, while clients with greater need for closer coordinated responses may require further integration.

LEVEL 5: CLOSE COLLABORATION IN A FULLY INTEGRATED SYSTEM

At this level, mental health and other health-care professionals seamlessly share the same sites and systems and have similar visions for the provision of care. All professionals are committed to a biopsychosocial/systems paradigm and have been cross-trained with an in-depth understanding of each other's roles and cultures. Regular collaborative team meetings are held to discuss both patient and team collaboration issues. Power and influence are balanced among the professionals according to their roles and areas of expertise. Hospice and other special training and clinical settings are the prototypical facilities where this model is employed. In addition, the most difficult and complex cases (having biopsychosocial problems) with challenging management problems respond well to this level of collaboration.

Medical family therapy has been found to be particularly efficacious in helping a couple or family cope with a disease. As Ruddy and McDaniel (2003) have noted:

> Obviously, the family's own characteristics affect adaptation to illness. The stress of an illness can serve to pull a somewhat disengaged family together or to heighten tensions in an already struggling family. Pre-existing patterns of communication and roles become more rigid when the family is stressed by illness. The pre-illness role of the ill family member impacts how stressed the family is by the potential loss of function, and how able family members are to replace the functions that the person is no longer able to perform.
>
> (p. 368)

Medical family therapists can evaluate the level of pre-illness dysfunction and ascertain the degree to which a family will be able to overcome and adapt to the stresses of the illness. Issues such as differing levels of acceptance among family members, withdrawal from outside support, and disruption of normal activities (e.g. sexual intercourse between spouses) can create conflict. Treatment can be planned around these psychosocial factors in order to maximize benefit for the patient and the family or at least to minimize the negative impact of dysfunctional family patterns (Doherty et al., 2014). Often, just heightening family members' awareness of problems and fostering communication about problematic issues can be enough to encourage families to make needed changes (Ruddy & McDaniel, 2003).

In terms of training, McDaniel et al. (2014) chaired an APA Presidential Task force to detail the "Competencies for Psychological Practice in Primary Care." They centered around six "clusters" including science, synthesis, professionalism, relationships, application, and education. Table 15.2 details the "competency groups" associated with each of the clusters. Couple therapists who are interested in a more detailed review of these, including specific behavioral anchors to each of the competency groups, are strongly recommended to review McDaniel et al. (2014). In addition, specific training for mental health professionals to work in integrated medical practices is becoming more available.

In conclusion, medical family therapy represents a new and viable modality of practice for couple therapists. Changes in disease patterns have created opportunities for couples and family therapists, as threats to a person's health have shifted from sudden illnesses, such as influenza, to chronic illnesses often arising from lifestyle variables. At the same time, changing demographics (e.g. a growing percentage of people over 65, people living longer) guarantee that, for the foreseeable future, there will be work for couple therapists who wish to specialize in medical family therapy (Baird, 2002; Doherty et al., 2014; McDaniel et al., 2014). Closer collaboration with physicians, especially as both couple therapists and medical personnel embrace a shared, comprehensive biopsychosocial approach to managing client issues, allows

Table 15.2 Integrated Medical Practice Cluster and Competencies for Behavioral Practitioners

Cluster	*Competency groups*
Science	Science related to the biopsychosocial approach Research/evaluation
Systems	Leadership/administration Interdisciplinary systems Advocacy
Professionalism	Professional values and attitudes Individual, cultural, and disciplinary diversity Ethics in primary care Reflective practice/self-assessment/self-care
Relationships	Interprofessionalism Building and sustaining relationships in primary care
Application	Practice management Assessment Intervention Clinical consultation
Education	Teaching Supervision

Note: From McDaniel et al. (2014).

for a synergistic application of effective treatment for many complicated cases (McDaniel et al., 2014). It also represents a complementarity relationship between medical and psychological professionals, whereby each can address issues that the other is not equipped to do. There are many issues that need to be addressed related to shared vision and missions of care, equality and a balance of power between professionals, and issues of payment for services (Doherty et al., 2014). However, this approach has the potential to provide the greatest level of care for the couple in the most efficient way.

Future Challenges to Couple Therapists

Although there have been great strides made in legitimizing the practice of couples counselors in the larger realm of psychotherapy, there is still much more work that remains. Sexton, Weeks, and Robbins (2003) have identified eight specific challenges that couples (and family) therapists face in the early part of the 21st century. The way that couple therapists respond to these challenges will determine how the field as a whole will evolve and grow.

1 *Avoid simplicity and embrace complexity.* Sexton et al. note that couples and family therapy, by virtue of working with multiple perspectives at the same time in session, has an inherent complexity to it. Couple therapists are required to be able to conceptualize and communicate with each individual in the couple as well as to the couple as a whole, which can require subtle (or gross) shifts in thinking and attending. In order to be

effective, this must be done in the moment and be conveyed seamlessly to the couple. However, it is a natural human characteristic to simplify matters by using a heuristic approach. Most theories provide the tools to do this without sacrificing such complex concepts as multi-determinism or circularity. Unfortunately, when faced with ambiguity or intense emotionality, too often couple therapists will foreclose on deeper understanding and relegate complex interactions to a simple declaration in the mistaken belief that simplicity is the best approach. Seldom do couples find relief in five steps or less, nor should couple therapists try to shoehorn these interactions into a preconceived mold. Frequently, when this is done, what is lost in order to make the couple fit are the most salient and clinically powerful aspects of the relationship. Therefore, it is those couple therapists who are able to maintain an effective working alliance in the face of complexity, ambiguity, or intensity who are truly successful.

2 *Embrace the era of evidence and accountability.* As mentioned throughout the text, research was traditionally eschewed by many practitioners as studies of elements that were too far removed from relevant clinical work to be useful. However, with the push to show evidence of the benefit of couple therapy, and studies supporting the efficacy and effectiveness of couple therapy, this criticism has receded. This has resulted in what Sexton et al. call a new "era of evidence" in couple therapy. At the same time, research methodology has been developed or incorporated from other disciplines (e.g. anthropology, epidemiology, etc.) to look at complex change processes and outcomes. As an emphasis on accountability and best practices becomes the sine qua non of couple therapy, practitioners may find new areas of linkage with the scholarly community and new venues for the dissemination of emerging areas of research and applications of treatment.

3 *Rediscover the relationship in couple therapy.* Despite the fact that couple therapy ushered in the idea that relationships between two people can become an effective focus of therapy, according to Sexton et al. (2003) and Johnson (2003), there has been very little attention given to relationship issues. Most clinical theories are derivatives of individual psychotherapy extended to two people, but which do not address the basic concepts of couples relating to one another. This includes alternative forms of relationships (i.e. unmarried, homosexual, or multiple relationships). Couple therapists must begin to refocus on patterns of interaction as a basic unit of couple therapy and understand the "noncausal, dialectical process of mutual influence in which all parties are involved" (Sexton et al., 2003, p. 461) if this is to be accomplished.

4 *Identify and incorporate the common mechanisms of successful change.* Sexton et al. describe change mechanisms as "specific activities of the family and couple therapist that lead to specific experiences of the family/couple that result in therapeutic change in a specific direction" (p. 462). Sprenkle and Blow (2004) outline several common factors that couple therapists share with other forms of psychotherapy (i.e. therapeutic alliance,

expectancy, client factors, etc.), as well as some that are unique to couple therapy (i.e. relational conceptualization, expanded direct treatment system, expanded therapeutic alliance, etc.). Some critics of this approach cite the lack of research, lack of complexity, and the failure to consider the differential effects of these factors in different settings as major limitations of the common factors approach, to date (Sexton, Ridley, & Kleiner, 2004). Agreement on the specific factors that help facilitate change and treatment will come with further refinement and research.

5 *Expand evidence-based models of practice that are clinically responsive and systematic.* This is one of the areas of deficit in the field of couple therapy identified by Johnson (2003), Pinsof and Wynne (2000), and others. Well-researched theories that have been shown to have clinical usefulness are greatly outnumbered by theories that have not been rigorously investigated. The latter group of theories, often viewed as faddish or tied to a cult of personality revolving around a guru, was indicative of earlier eras in the field (Bevcar, 2003). Unfortunately, this will continue to be seen as a shortcoming of the field until more comprehensive, clinically relevant research is conducted.

6 *Integrate diversity and culture into the core of theory, research, and practice.* Falicov (2003) and Sexton et al. argue that issues of culture and diversity have yet to be made central to the practice of couple therapy. Sexton et al. note that the attempts of the larger field of psychology to make multiculturalism a separate discipline actually seem to work against this goal, as it marginalizes these issues or makes them afterthoughts to the core ideas of theory and practice. At the same time, couple therapy, with context as a central feature of its approach, seems poised to effectively integrate understanding diversity and culture with effective therapy. However, a concerted and conscious effort must be made to bring this about.

7 *Disseminate effective models into the world.* This challenge requires the couple therapist to accept a role as a scholar and researcher as well as a practitioner. In previous eras, practitioners were functionally separate from scholars and researchers. Some practitioners took on training roles but (with some notable exceptions) had a limited impact on the field as a whole. At the same time, researchers generally published their results in journals aimed at a scientific audience, which did not appeal to the majority of practitioners. As a result, knowledge created by one group was not well transferred to the other, regardless of the utility of the information. However, the real challenge is convincing current practitioners (and training new ones) of the importance of defining their practice as active, action-oriented research from which crucial data is produced. These practitioners must be encouraged to disseminate their findings in a forum where they can receive feedback and validation from other scholars and build on the empirical structure of previous research.

8 *Step beyond "archaeology" to the principles of effective practice in training and supervision.* The training of couple therapists needs to move away

from an exclusive focus on the historical and traditional theories of couple therapy, and include newer and more empirically sound approaches. This does not signal an abandonment of traditional schools of therapy (in fact, Sexton et al. encourage solid grounding in the history of couple therapy approaches) but rather a dynamic integration of the familiar and the foreign into training and practice.

Conclusion: The Undiscovered Country

We end this book, much as we began it, with the consideration that we are continuing to discover new details about the dynamic coupling process in humans. Despite its complexities, the coupling process has occurred, time and again, without the need for outside, professional intervention. However, an increasingly complex world has created serious and widespread breakdowns in the processes that once seemed automatic. This is not necessarily bad, as it signals societal changes that are leading all of us to reconsider long-held notions of power, equality, and assigned roles between the sexes, across cultures, and among people of differing sexual preferences. It also signals the opportunity to study and understand relationships better, as well as investigate the processes by which we attempt to intervene and help. Couple therapists find themselves entrusted with a legacy of answering these monumental challenges with revolutionary zeal. As a result, not only was a new type of therapy born, but also the entire field was impacted. The question remains as to whether or not couple therapy can answer the modern calls for boldness. Successfully guiding the field through another period of growth and definition will require a passion for difficult clinical work and exacting scientific rigor.

Shakespeare's *Hamlet* described the unknown aspects of the future as "the undiscovered country." In the end, we feel that this describes the plight that couple therapists face in the 21st century, as the field strives to gain further legitimization and claim a place as part of the human healing disciplines. Given its potency and potential for helping couples heal from or avoid pain and misery, it would seem that the undiscovered country of couple therapy is one worthy of continued discovery.

References

American Association of Marriage and Family Therapists (AAMFT). (2018). *About marriage and family therapists.* Retrieved from http://www.aamft.org/iMIS15/AAMFT/Content/About_AAMFT/About_Marriage_and_Family_Therapists.aspx

Baird, M. (2002). Comments on the commissioned report on health and behavior: The interplay of biological, behavioral, and societal influences. *Family Systems and Health, 20*(1), 1–6.

Bevcar, D. S. (2003). Eras of epistemology: A survey of family therapy thinking and theorizing. In T. L. Sexton, G. R. Weeks, & M. S. Robbins (Eds.), *Handbook of family therapy: The science and practice of working with families and couples* (pp. 3–20). New York, NY: Brunner-Routledge.

Blow, A. J., & Karam, E. A. (2017). The therapist's role in effective marriage and family therapy practice: The case for evidence based therapists. *Administrative Policy in Mental Health, 44*, 716–723. doi:10.1007/s10488-016-0768-8

Bureau of Labor Statistics, U.S. Department of Labor. (2018, April 21). *Occupational outlook handbook, marriage and family therapists.* Retrieved from https://www.bls.gov/ooh/community-and-social-service/marriage-and-family-therapists.htm.

Caldwell, B. (2017, July 10). *MFT license portability [Blog].* Retrieved from http://www.psychotherapynotes.com/mft-license-portability/

Civic Impulse. (2018). *S. 1879-115th Congress: Seniors mental health access improvement act of 2017.* Retrieved from https://www.govtrack.us/congress.bills/115/s1879

Cornille, T. A., McWey, L. M., Nelson, T. S., & West, S. H. (2003). How do master's level marriage and family therapists view their basic therapy skills? An examination of generic and theory specific clinical approaches to family therapy. *Contemporary Family Therapy, 25*(1), 41–61.

David, O. & Cobeanu, O. (2015). Evidence-based training in cognitive-behavioural coaching: Can personal development bring less distress and better performance?. *British Journal of Guidance and Counselling, 44.* doi:10.1080/03069885.2014.1002384

Doherty, W. J., McDaniel, S. H., & Baird, M. A. (1996). Five levels of primary care/behavioral healthcare collaboration. *Behavioral Healthcare Tomorrow, 5*, 25–28.

Doherty, W. J., McDaniel, S. H., & Hepworth, J. (2014). Contributions of medical family therapy to the changing health care system. *Family Process, 53*(3), 529–543. doi:10.1111/famp.12092

Falicov, C. J. (2003). Culture in family therapy: New variations on a fundamental theme. In T. L. Sexton, G. R. Weeks, & M. S. Robbins (Eds.), *Handbook of family therapy: The science and practice of working with families and couples* (pp. 37–55). New York, NY: Brunner-Routledge.

Fraenkel, P., & Pinsof, W. M. (2001). Teaching family therapy-centered integration: Assimilation and beyond. *Journal of Psychotherapy Integration, 11*(1), 59–85.

Halford, W. K., Peppping, C. A., & Oetch, J. (2016). The gap between couple therapy research efficacy and practice effectiveness. *Journal of Marital and Family Therapy, 42*(1), 32–44. doi:10.1111/jmft.12120

HRSA. (2018). *Behavioral health integration training needs in health care delivery system reform.* Retrieved from https://www.hrsa.gov/sites/default/files/hrsa/advisory-committees/primarycare-dentist/meetings/20160628/kepley-hrsa2.pdf

Johnson, S. M. (2003). Couple therapy research: Status and directions. In G. P. Sholevar (Ed.), *Textbook of family and couple therapy* (pp. 797–814). Alexandria, VA: American Psychiatric Publishing.

Jordan, K. (2016). *Couple, marriage and family therapy supervision.* New York, NY: Springer Publishing Co.

Kern, R. M., & Peluso, P. R. (1999). Using individual psychology concepts to compare family systems processes and organizational behavior. *The Family Journal: Counseling and Therapy for Couples and Families, 11*(3), 236–244.

Kovacs, K. C., & Corrie, S. (2017). Executive coaching in an era of complexity. Study 1. Does executive coaching work and if so how? A realist evaluation. *International Coaching Psychology Review, 12*(2), 74–89.

McDaniel, S. H., Grus, C. L., Cubic, B. A., Hunter, C. L., Kearney, L. K., Schuman, C. C., … Johnson, S. B. (2014). Competencies for psychology practice in primary care. *American Psychologist, 69*(4), 409–429. doi:10.1037/a0036072

Mozdzierz, G., Peluso, P. R., & Lisiecki, J. (2014). *Advanced principles of counseling and psychotherapy: Learning, integrating, and consolidating the nonlinear thinking of master practitioners.* New York, NY: Routledge.

Norcross, J. C., & Beutler, L. E. (2000). A prescriptive eclectic approach to psychotherapy training. *Journal of Psychotherapy Integration, 10*(3), 247–261.

Parker, E. O., Chang, J., & Thomas, V. (2016). A content analysis of quantitative research in *Journal of Marital and Family Therapy:* A 10 year review. *Journal of Marital and Family Therapy, 42*(1), 3–18. doi:10.1111/jmft.12138

Peluso, P. R., & Kern, R. M. (1998). The seven habits of highly effective people and individual psychology. *Canadian Journal of Individual Psychology, 28*(1), 9–16.

Peluso, P. R., & Stoltz, K. B. (2002). Using the Adlerian lifestyle construct as a strengths assessment tool for employee's success. In D. Sandhu (Ed.), *Counseling employees: A multifaceted approach* (pp. 83–103). Washington, DC: ACA Publishers.

Pinsof, W. M., & Wynne, L. C. (2000). Toward progress research: Closing the gap between family therapy practice and research. *Journal of Marital & Family Therapy, 26*(1), 1–8.

Ruddy, N. B., & McDaniel, S. H. (2003). Medical family therapy. In T. L. Sexton, G. R. Weeks, & M. S. Robbins (Eds.), *Handbook of family therapy: The science and practice of working with families and couples* (pp. 365–379). New York, NY: Brunner-Routledge.

Sexton, T. L., Ridley, C. R., & Kleiner, A. J. (2004). Beyond common factors: Multilevel-process models of therapeutic change in marriage and family therapy. *Journal of Marital & Family Therapy, 30*(2), 131–149.

Sexton, T. L., Weeks, G. R., & Robbins, M. S. (2003). The future of couple and family therapy. In T. L. Sexton, G. R. Weeks, & M. S. Robbins (Eds.), *Handbook of family therapy: The science and practice of working with families and couples* (pp. 449–466). New York, NY: Brunner-Routledge.

Shumway, S. T., Wampler, R. S., Dersch, C., & Arredondo, R. (2004). A place for marriage and family services in employee assistance programs (EAPs): A survey of EAP client problems and needs. *Journal of Marital and Family Therapy, 30*(1), 71–80.

Skovholt, T. M., & Ronnestad, M. H. (1992). Themes in therapist and counselor development. *Journal of Counseling and Development, 70*(4), 505–515.

Sperry, L. (1992). Recent developments in neuroscience, behavioral medicine, and psychoneuroimmunology: Implications for physical and psychological well-being. *Individual Psychology: Journal of Adlerian Theory, Research & Practice, 48*(4), 451–461.

Sperry, L. (2004). *Executive coaching.* New York, NY: Brunner-Routledge.

Sprenkle, D. H., & Blow, A. J. (2004). Common factors and our sacred models. *Journal of Marital & Family Therapy, 30*(2), 113–129.

Storm, C. L., McDowell, T., & Long, J. K. (2003). The metamorphosis of training and supervision. In T. L. Sexton, G. R. Weeks, & M. S. Robbins (Eds.), *Handbook of family therapy: The science and practice of working with families and couples* (pp. 431–446). New York, NY: Brunner-Routledge.

United States Department of Labor (US DOL). (2010, January 29). *Fact sheet: The mental health parity and addiction equity act of 2008 (MHPAEA).* Published by Employee Benefits Security Administration. Washington, DC.

Appendix

Codes of Professional Ethics Relevant to the Practice of Couple Therapy

International Association of Marriage and Family Counselors
IAMFC Code of Ethic
http://www.iamfconline.org/public/department3.cfm

American Association for Marriage & Family Therapy
AAMFT Code of Ethics
https://www.aamft.org/imis15/content/legal_ethics/code_of_ethics.aspx

American Counseling Association
ACA Code of Ethics
http://www.counseling.org/docs/ethics/2014-aca-code-of-ethics.pdf?sfvrsn=4

American Psychological Association
APA Ethical Principles of Psychologists and Code of Conduct
http://www.apa.org/ethics/code/index.aspx

National Association of Social Workers
NASW Code of Ethics
http://www.socialworkers.org/pubs/code/code.asp

Index

Note: Page numbers in **bold** denote tables, in *italic* denote figures